Guí

PHRASE BOOK
FOR TRAVELLERS

SPANISH

EVEREST
DICCIONARIOS

Idea and text: Rüdiger Gaertner

Editorial coordination: Yolanda Lobejón

Layout: Carmen García Rodríguez
            Nieves Canal Álvarez
            Ana Cristina López Viñuela

Revision: EURO:TEXT

All rights reserved. No part of this book may be reproduced, stored in a retrieval system, or transmitted, in any form or by any means, electronic, mechanical, photocopying, recording or otherwise, without the prior written permission of the holders of the Copyright.
This book is sold subject to the condition that it shall not, by way of trade or otherwise, be lent, re-sold, hired out, or otherwise circulate without the publisher's prior consent.

© EDITORIAL EVEREST, S. A.
Carretera León-La Coruña, km 5 - LEÓN
ISBN: 84-241-1289-X
Legal deposit: LE. 1092-2001
Printed in Spain

EDITORIAL EVERGRAFICAS, S. L.
Carretera León-La Coruña, km 5 - LEÓN (Spain)

Introduction

Our new **SPANISH PHRASE BOOK FOR TRAVELLERS** is probably one of the most complete language guides in the world.

A combination of **phrase examples**, a **dictionary** and a **gastronomy guide**, it includes a concise **grammar** for those users who would like to obtain some basic knowledge of the Spanish language.

In the first part we explain the Spanish alphabet by means of pronunciation examples and the symbols of the phonetic transcription used in this book. In the **phrase examples** and the **English-Spanish Dictionary** all Spanish words are accompanied by a simplified International Phonetic Transcription. In this way, even those people without any special linguistical knowledge will be able to understand the general rules of pronunciation.

In the second part we give the user of this phrase book the opportunity to learn some **basic rules** of Spanish grammar and to maintain a simple conversation. At the end of this part we explain how to use the phrase examples and to combine them with any other term from the dictionary.

The third section consists of two parts: a general part comprising the chapters «**About myself**», «**The weather**», «**Quantities, weights, measures**», «**Colours**», «**What time is it?**» and a special part featuring chapters on «**First contacts**» (*Arrival, Coming by car, Accommodation* and *Sightseeing*), «**Shopping**» (covering a wide variety of different shops and the most frequently used terms in each) and «**Services**» (with the chapters entitled *Bank, Gastronomy, Public Transport,* etc). At the end of this section there is part on «**Emergencies**» (with the chapters called *Medical Assistance* and *Police*).

A complete **Dictionary** with about 7.500 entries enables the user to combine a considerable number of terms with the phrase examples. This dictionary contains the most usual terms of gastronomy with their most frequent variations and practical examples.

It is followed by a **Spanish-English Gastronomy Dictionary** which allows the English-speaking user to understand the "cartas" and "menús" of Spanish restaurants. At the same time it may be used as a «**Cooking Guide**» because an explanation is given regarding the ingredients and the preparation of a large number of typical Spanish dishes. This will help you to understand the peculiarities of each particular dish. The dictionary will also encourage you to try and to get to know a range of new gastronomic specialities.

We hope that this **Phrase Book** will be useful to you during your stay in Spain or any other Spanish-speaking country. Finally, we would like to wish you a very nice journey and a pleasant stay.

Abbreviations

A		math.	mathematics
a.	adjective	Mech.	mechanics
a. dem.	demonstrative adjective	Med.	medicine
a. pos.	possesive adjective	mod. verb.	modal verb
ac.	direct object		
adv.	adverb	**N**	
Anat.	anatomy	n.	noun
Arch.	architecture	nomin.	nominative (subject)
art. def.	definite article		
art. indef.	indefinite article	**P**	
Auto.	automobile	part.	participle
aux.	auxiliary	P.C.	personal computer
		pers.	person
B		pl.	plural
Bot.	botany	Pol.	politics
		prep.	preposition
C		pron.	pronoun
C.D.	compact disc	pron. pers.	personal pronoun
conj.	conjunction	pron. pos.	possesive pronoun
Com.	commerce		
comp.	comparative	**R**	
		r.	regular verb
D			
dat.	indirect object	**S**	
		so.	someone
E		sth.	something
elect.	electricity	superl.	superlative
etc.	and so on		
		T	
F		Tel.	telephony
f.	feminine	temp.	temporal
		Theat.	theatre
G			
Gast.	gastronomy	**U**	
		u.c.	una cosa (something)
I		u.p.	una persona (somebody)
irr.	irregular verb		
		V	
M		vb.	verb
m.	masculine	vb. aux.	auxiliar verb

Contents

I.
PRONUNCIATION

■ VOWELS

a, e, i, o, u

Vowel	Example	Pronunciation similar to the:
a	ca**s**a *(kása)*	*"a" in cat*
e	c**e**lda *(θélda)*	*"e" in bed*
i	v**i**sta *(bísta)*	*"i" in thin*
o	c**o**sa *(kósa)*	*"o" in lot*
u	c**u**lto *(kúlto)*	*"u" in put*

■ DIPHTHONGS

Diphthong	Example	Pronunciation similar to the:
ai, ay	aire, rayo	*"ai" in aisle*
au	fauna	*"ow" in cow*
ei, ey	reina, rey	*"ai" in failure*
eu	Europa	*"e" in bed combined with the "u" in put*
oi, oy	oiga, soy	*"oi" in noise*
ia	academia	*"ya" in yard*
ie	sien	*"ye" in yet*
io	violeta	*"yo" in yonder*
iu	viuda	*"yu" in Yukon*
ua	agua	*"wa" in wag*
ue	vuelta	*"we" in well*
uo	antiguo	*"wo" in swot*
ui, uy	ruido, muy	*"we" in we*

■ CONSONANTS

Consonant	Symbol	Examples	Pronunciation similar to the:
b	b	*beber, Barcelona*	"*b*" in *baron*
c before *a, o, u*	k	*casa, cosa, culto*	"*c*" in *cartridge*
before *e, i*	θ	*celda, cita*	"*th*" in *thin*
ch	tch	*lucha, coche*	"*ch*" in *chocolate*
d	d	*desde, donde*	"*d*" in *dozen*
g before *a, o, u*	g	*gasto, gota, gusto*	"*g*" in *gate*
before *e, i*	x	*gesto, ginebra*	Scottish "*ch*" in *loch*
h	-	*hacha, historia*	the Spanish "*h*" is silent
j	x	*Jabugo, jota*	Scottish "*ch*" in *loch*
l	l	*libro, elegante*	"*l*" in *life*
ll	lj	*fallo, lleno*	"*ll*" in *William*
m	m	*Madrid, rama*	"*m*" in *Monday*
n	n	*nido, cena*	"*n*" in *never*
ñ	nj	*España, señal*	"*ni*" in *opinion*

Consonant	Symbol	Examples	Pronunciation similar to the:
p	p	*Pedro, copa*	*"p"* in *park*
q(u)	k	*qué, quiso*	*"k"* in *kettle*
r	r	*paro, comer*	Certain Scottish or Welsh pronuntiations of *"r"* in *roll*
rr or **r** at the beginning of a word	rr	*carro, rústico*	the multiple vibrant *"r"* does not exist in English
s	s	*sábado, vaso*	*"s"* in *symbol*
t	t	*tocar, roto*	*"t"* in *time*
v	b	*Valencia, enviar*	*"b"* in *baron*
w	w	*wáter*	*"w"* en *whisky* or *"b"* in *baron*
x	ks	*extranjero*	*"x"* in *exchange*
y	j	*ya, playa*	*"y"* in *yard*
	i	*y (and)*	*"i"* in *skin*
z	θ	*zapato, zorro*	*"th"* in *thin*

We have made use of the International Phonetic Alphabet, which has been simplified and adapted to this book. This transcription is indicated in the dictionary and the phrase book in brackets.

■ STRESS

The Spanish language follows the general rule of putting the stress on the penultimate syllable, unless there is an indication to the contrary.

> escapa**ra**te *(eskaparáte)*, **zo**rro *(θórro)*,
> ameri**ca**no *(amerikáno)*

Words which end in **d**, **l**, **r** and **z** are stressed on the last syllable.

> par**ed** *(paréd)*, mant**el** *(mantél)*, llam**ar** *(ljamár)*,
> vali**dez** *(balidéθ)*

Words which do not follow these general rules require a written accent on the stressed syllable.

> **lá**piz *(lápiθ)*, esta**ción** *(estaθjón)*, **tí**pico *(típiko)*

In order to make this phrase book easy to use, in our simplified phonetic transcription all stressed syllables are shown by an "accent mark".

Of course, in this phrase book it is not possible to deal thoroughly with all the special rules of pronunciation, so we have limited ourselves to the most important general rules, in order that you may pronounce the Spanish language in a more or less correct way.

II.
GRAMMAR

■ THE ARTICLE

In Spanish there are masculine and feminine nouns. The gender of these nouns is determined by the article.

Definite Article	el (los) m. *the*	la (las) f. *the*
Indefinite Article	un (unos) m. *a (some)*	una (unas) f. *a (some)*

The gender of Spanish nouns is marked by the letters **m.** (masculine), **f.** (feminine) and the plural forms are indicated in brackets.

The Spanish masculine definite article combines with the prepositions **"a"** (to) and **"de"** (from, of) to form a single word:

$$a + el = \quad al$$
$$de + el = \quad del$$

The neuter article is **"lo"**, but as there are not any neuter nouns it is only used for adjectives with the meaning of a noun.

bueno	**lo** bueno
good	*a good thing*
caro	**lo** caro
expensive	*an expensive thing*

Feminine nouns which begin with a stressed **"a"** take the masculine definite article.

el **a**gua f. *(el água)*
el **a**rte f.*(el árte)*
el **ha**mbre f. *(el ámbre)*

■ THE NOUN

As a general rule nouns ending in **"o"** are masculine and those ending in **"a"** are feminine.

el libr**o**   la mes**a**

But there are some exeptions.

la man**o** f.
el problem**a** m., el sistem**a** m., etc.

All nouns of Greek origin ending in "a", as **sistema, problema, esquema**, etc. are masculine.

All other nouns ending in a vowel or in a consonant, are generally masculine. But there are some exeptions:

-ción	la na**ción**
-sión	la televi**sión**
-dad	la e**dad**
-dez	la vali**dez**
-ed	la par**ed**
-iz	la perd**iz**
-sis	la sico**sis**

As you can see, these nouns are normally feminine.

THE PLURAL

Nouns ending in a vowel add the letter "**s**" to form the plural.

el libro	los libro**s**
the book	*the books*
la mesa	las mesa**s**
the table	*the tables*
el hombre	los hombre**s**
the man	*the men*

Those which end in a consonant add "**es**".

la nación	las nacion**es***
the nation	*the nations*
la pared	las pared**es**
the wall	*the walls*
la mujer	las mujer**es**
the woman	*the women*
el tren	los tren**es**
the train	*the trains*
el hotel	los hotel**es**
the hotel	*the hotels*

* Nouns ending in **-ión** lose the accent, because it becomes the penultimate syllable which is generally stressed.

▶ THE DECLENSION OF NOUNS

The subject and the direct object are formed by the article + noun.

| el hotel
the hotel | los hoteles
the hotels |
| la maleta
the suitcase | las maletas
the suitcases |

That means that there is no difference between the forms of the subject and the direct object. (See exeption of personal direct objects).

The genitive is formed by means of the preposition "**de**".

| del hotel*
of the hotel | de los hoteles
of the hotels |
| de la mesa
of the table | de las mesas
of the tables |

* **De** is combined with *el* to "**del**".

The indirect object is formed by means of the preposition "**a**".

| **al** hotel*
(to) the hotel | **a los** hoteles
(to) the hotels |
| **a la** mesa
(to) the table | **a las** mesas
(to) the tables |

* **A** is combined with *el* to "**al**".

▶ PERSONAL DIRECT OBJECT

The direct object of persons and animals is also formed by the preposition "**a**":

Veo **al** director en la calle
I see the manager in the street

Convierte **a los** indios
He converts the Indians

Saludo **a tu** hermano
I say hello to your brother

Llamamos **al** perro
We are calling the dog

when the noun is accompanied by the definite article or by a determining adjective (demonstrative, possessive, etc).

The preposition **"a"** is not used in the case of nouns without any article, with an indefinite article, an indefinite adjective or a numeral adjective.

Tenemos **un** inglés en casa
We have an Englishman at home (on a visit)

Conoce **personas** influyentes
He knows (some) important persons

Conozco **pocas** mujeres como ella
I know few women like her

Tenemos **muchos** empleados
We have many workers

■ THE ADJECTIVE

▶ QUALIFYING ADJECTIVES

The adjectives normally agree with the noun in gender and number. In most cases the masculine ending is **"o"** and the feminine **"a"**.

car**o**   car**a**
expensive

alem**án**   alem**ana**
German

Some adjectives have the same form in masculine and feminine.

dulc**e**   dulc**e**
sweet

verd**e**   verd**e**
green

The plural of adjectives is formed in the same way as the plural of nouns.

caro (a)   caro**s**(a**s**)
alemán (alemana)   aleman**es** (alemana**s**)
dulce   dulc**es**

In the dictionary the feminine form of adjectives are indicated in brackets. If there is not any indication in brackets the adjetive is invariable.

◆ **Position**

The qualifying adjectives are usually placed after the noun.

> el hombre **bueno**
> *the good man*

> la bebida **caliente**
> *the warm drink*

but the word order may be changed for special emphasis of an inherent quality or in fixed constructions.

> la **blanca** nieve
> *the white snow*

> el **frío** invierno
> *the cold winter*

> una **gran** persona
> *a great person*

This position is especially used for several adjectives.

> bueno *(good)*, malo (*bad*), mejor (*better*)
> peor (*worse*), etc.

Some of these adjectives placed before the noun lose their final vowel in the masculine form.

> un **buen** asunto
> *a good thing*

> un **mal** invento
> *a bad solution*

The adjective "grande" changes to "gran" placed before masculine or feminine nouns:

> un **gran** hombre
> *a great man*

> una **gran** mujer
> *a great woman*

▶ POSSESSIVE ADJECTIVES

They are always placed before the noun and agree with it in gender and number.

mi mesa **f.*** *my table*	mi**s** mesas *my tables*
mi coche **m.*** *my car*	mi**s** coches *my cars*

but

nuestr**a** mesa **f.*** *our table*	nuestr**as** mesas *our tables*
nuestr**o** coche **m.*** *our car*	nuestr**os** coches *our cars*

* **m.** means masculine and **f.** feminine.

Singular	*one thing*	*several things*
1st. person *2nd. person* *3rd. person*	mi tu* su*	mis tus* sus*
Plural	*one thing*	*several things*
1st. person *2nd. person* *3rd. person*	nuestro(a) vuestro(a)* su*	nuestros(as) vuestros(as)* sus*

* If you speak to a person in a formal situation, you have to use **"su, sus"**: su coche (*your car*), sus coches (*your cars*).

▶ DEMONSTRATIVE ADJECTIVES

They indicate a thing or a person in relation to a certain place or moment.

	Singular	**Plural**
near me	este/esta *this*	estos/estas *these*
near you	ese/esa *this*	esos/esas *these*
away from both	aquel/aquella *that*	aquellos/aquellas *those*

Note that the demonstrative adjectives do not have any written accent, unlike the demonstrative pronouns (**éste, ésta, ésto**).

> **este** coche es caro   *this car is expensive*
>
> **éste** es un coche caro   *this is an expensive car*

■ THE ADVERB

The adverbs qualify verbs, adjectives or other adverbs.

In the Spanish language there are two classes of adverbs:

▶ SIMPLE ADVERBS

These consist of one word, referring to a place, time, manner, etc:

> aquí (*place*)   hoy (*time*)   bien (*manner*)
> *here*   *today*   *well*
>
> mucho (*number*), etc.
> (*much, a lot*)

▶ COMBINED ADVERBS

These are formed from an adjective to which the ending **-mente** is added.

> fácil   fácilmente *(easily)*
> normal   normalmente *(normally)*

If the adjective has masculine and feminine forms, the adverb is formed from the feminine:

> rápido**(a)**   rápid**a**mente

When the word to be qualified is a verb, the qualifying adverb is placed after it.

> Mónica conduce **rápidamente**
> *Mónica drives fast*

When the word to be qualified is an adjective or adverb, the adverb is placed immediately before it.

> Tengo un coche **muy** grande
> *I have a very big car*
>
> Carmen conduce **muy** deprisa
> *Carmen drives very fast*

■ PERSONAL PRONOUNS

The Spanish personal pronouns are only used as subjects in very particular cases:

como	*I am eating*
beb**emos**	*we are drinking*

The subject is usually expressed by the ending of the conjugated verb. The personal pronoun is only used for emphasis or to prevent doubts.

yo pago	*I shall pay (nobody else)*

Usted (Vd.) sing. and **ustedes** (Vds.) pl. are the second person pronouns used for courtesy, but the accompanying verb is in the 3rd person.

¿Qué desea (Vd.)?	*What do you want? (one person)*
¿Qué desean (Vds.)?	*What do you want? (several persons)*

	Subject		Indirect object	Direct object
Singular				
1st. person	yo	*I*	me	me
2nd. person	tú	*you*	te	te
	usted	*you*	le	le, la
3rd. person	él	*he*	le	lo, le
	ella	*she*	le	la
Plural				
1st. person	nosotros(as)	*we*	nos	nos
2nd. person	vosotros(as)	*you*	os	os
	ustedes	*you*	les	les, las
3rd. person	ellos	*they*	les	los
	ellas	*they*	les	las

■ THE VERB

In this phrase book we will only show the present forms of the regular verbs and of the most frequent irregular verbs.

▶ REGULAR VERBS

As we have seen before, the subject of a sentence is expressed by the ending of the conjugated verb. There are three groups of regular verbs. The verb "tomar" (ending -ar) belongs to the 1st. conjugation, "comer" (-er) to the 2nd. and "vivir" (-ir) to the 3rd.

tom**ar**	tom**o**	**(o, as, a / amos, áis, an)**
take	*I take*	
com**er**	com**o**	**(o, es, e / emos, éis, en)**
eat	*I eat*	
viv**ir**	viv**o**	**(o, es, e / imos, ís, en)**
live	*I live*	

Regular verbs, when conjugated, keep the root of the infinitive unchanged and take the endings given in the following table of models of regular conjugations.

◆ **The present of regular verbs**

	-AR *1st. conjugation*	**-ER** *2nd. conjugation*	**-IR** *3rd. conjugation*
INFINITIVE	tom-**ar**	com-**er**	viv-**ir**
Singular			
1st. person	tom-**o**	com-**o**	viv-**o**
2nd. person	tom-**as**	com-**es**	viv-**es**
3rd. person	tom-**a**	com-**e**	viv-**e**
Plural			
1st. person	tom-**amos**	com-**emos**	viv-**imos**
2nd. person	tom-**áis**	com-**éis**	viv-**ís**
3rd. person	tom-**an**	com-**en**	viv-**en**
IMPERATIVE **Singular**			
2nd. person	tom-**a** *(take)*	com-**e** *(eat)*	viv-**e** *(live)*
3rd. person	tom-**e** *(take)*	com-**a** *(eat)*	viv-**a** *(live)*
Plural			
*1st. person**	tom-**emos** *(let us take)*	com-**amos** *(let us eat)*	viv-**amos** *(let us live)*
2nd. person	tom-**ad** *(take)*	com-**ed** *(eat)*	viv-**id** *(live)*
3rd. person	tom-**en** *(take)*	com-**an** *(eat)*	viv-**an** *(live)*
GERUND**	tom-**ando**	com-**iendo**	viv-**iendo**
PAST PARTICIPLE***	tom-**ado**	com-**ido**	viv-**ido**

Notes:

*   This form can be translated as "let us": "let us take (eat, live)".

**   The gerund is an invariable form.

*** If the participle is used as an adjective it agrees with the noun in gender and number: ***tomado(a), tomados(as)/comido(a), comidos(as)/vivido(a), vividos(as)***.

In the dictionary the regular verbs are marked by the letter "**r**". All regular verbs are conjugated in the way indicated above.

▶ **IRREGULAR VERBS**

Irregular verbs normally have two causes: changes of the stressed root vowel and alterations to the ending.

I. The following verbs change from "**e**" to "**ie**".

INFINITIVE	empez-**ar** (begin)	entend-**er** (understand)	sent-**ir** (feel)
Singular			
1st. person	emp**ie**z-**o**	ent**ie**nd-**o**	s**ie**nt-**o**
2nd. person	emp**ie**z-**as**	ent**ie**nd-**es**	s**ie**nt-**es**
3rd. person	emp**ie**z-**a**	ent**ie**nd-**e**	s**ie**nt-**e**
Plural			
1st. person	empez-**amos**	entend-**emos**	sent-**imos**
2nd. person	empez-**áis**	entend-**éis**	sent-**ís**
3rd. person	emp**ie**z-**an**	ent**ie**nd-**en**	s**ie**nt-**en**
IMPERATIVE			
Singular			
2nd. person	emp**ie**z-**a**	ent**ie**nd-**e**	s**ie**nt-**e**
3rd. person	emp**ie**c-**e**	ent**ie**nd-**a**	sient-**a**
Plural			
1st. person	empec-**emos**	entend-**amos**	sent-**amos**
2nd. person	empez-**ad**	entend-**ed**	sent-**id**
3rd. person	emp**ie**c-**en**	ent**ie**nd-**an**	s**ie**nt-**an**
GERUND	empez-**ando**	entend-**iendo**	s**i**nt-**iendo**
PAST PARTICIPLE	empez-**ado**	entend-**ido**	sent-**ido**

The following verbs belong to the same conjugation: **apretar, atender, calentar, cerrar, confesar, despertar, hervir, perder, preferir, querer, recomendar**, etc. In the dictionary all verbs which belong to this group are marked by **(ie)**.

II. Change of the stressed root vowel from "**o**" to "**ue**".

INFINITIVE	cont-**ar**	volv-**er**	dorm-**ir**
Singular			
1st. person	c**ue**nt-**o**	v**ue**lv-**o**	d**ue**rm-**o**
2nd. person	c**ue**nt-**as**	v**ue**lv-**es**	d**ue**rm-**es**
3rd. person	c**ue**nt-**a**	v**ue**lv-**e**	d**ue**rm-**e**
Plural			
1st. person	cont-**amos**	volv-**emos**	dorm-**imos**
2nd. person	cont-**áis**	volv-**éis**	dorm-**ís**
3rd. person	c**ue**nt-**an**	v**ue**lv-**en**	d**ue**rm-**en**
IMPERATIVE			
Singular			
2nd. person	c**ue**nt-**a**	v**ue**lv-**e**	d**ue**rm-**e**
3rd. person	c**ue**nt-**e**	v**ue**lv-**a**	d**ue**rm-**a**
Plural			
1st. person	cont-**emos**	volv-**amos**	durm-**amos**
2nd. person	cont-**ad**	volv-**ed**	dorm-**id**
3rd. person	c**ue**n-**ten**	v**ue**lv-**an**	d**ue**rm-**an**
GERUND	cont-**ando**	volv-**iendo**	d**u**rm-**iendo**
PAST PARTICIPLE	cont-**ado**	**vuelto** (irr.)	dorm-**ido**

The following verbs are conjugated in the same way: **almorzar, apostar, colgar, comprobar, costar, devolver, doler, dormir, encontrar, envolver, prober, torcer, volver**, etc. In the dictionary all verbs of this group are marked by the letters **(ue)**.

III. Change of the stressed root vowel from "**e**" to "**i**".

INFINITIVE	ped-**ir**	IMPERATIVE	
Singular		**Singular**	
1st. person	p**i**d-**o**		
2nd. person	p**i**d-**es**	*2nd. person*	p**i**d-**e**
3rd. person	p**i**d-**e**	*3rd. person*	p**i**d-**a**
Plural		**Plural**	
1st. person	ped-**imos**	*1st. person*	p**i**d-**amos**
2nd. person	ped-**is**	*2nd. person*	ped-**id**
3rd. person	p**i**d-**en**	*3rd. person*	p**i**d-**an**
GERUND	p**i**d-**iendo**	**PAST PARTICIPLE**	ped-**ido**

The following verbs are conjugated in the same way: **desteñir, expedir, medir, servir, teñir, vestir, etc.** In the dictionary they are marked by the letter **(i)**.

IV. All other irregular verbs are marked in the dictionary by **"irr."** or **"zc"**. Some of these verbs have only minor irregularities in the present tense.

caer	caigo, caes, cae / caemos, caéis, caen *(fall)*
dar	doy, das, da / damos, dáis, dan *(give)*
estar	estoy, estás, está / estamos, estáis, están *(be)*
haber	he, has, ha / hemos, habéis, han *(have)*
hacer	hago, haces, hace / hacemos, hacéis, hacen (*make, do*)
ir	voy, vas, va / vamos, váis, van *(go)*
oír	oigo, oyes, oye / oímos, oís, oyen *(hear)*
poder	puedo, puedes, puede / podemos, podéis, pueden *(can)*
poner	pongo, pones, pone / ponemos, ponéis, ponen *(put)*
saber	sé, sabes, sabe / sabemos, sabéis, saben *(know; can)*
salir	salgo, sales, sale / salimos, salís, salen *(go out)*
ser	soy, eres, es / somos, sois, son *(be)*
tener	tengo, tienes, tiene / tenemos, tenéis, tienen *(have got)*
traer	traigo, traes, trae / traemos, traéis, traen *(bring)*
venir	vengo, vienes, viene / venimos, venís, vienen *(come)*

▶ **SER AND ESTAR**

The English verb **"to be"** may be expressed by two different verbs: **"ser"** or **"estar"**. As the difference is not very easy to understand for English speaking persons, we shall give you the following rules.

◆ General rule

SER always expresses an inherent or permanent quality of a person or a thing.

ESTAR expresses a quality (or better a state or situation) which is neither permanent nor inherent.

◆ Ser + noun

Ser is normally used with nouns which express profession, nationality, confession, originy, materials, etc.

Pedro **es** camarero	*Pedro is a waiter*
Denise **es** francesa	*Denise is a Frenchwoman*
Ellos **son** católicos	*They are Catholics*
Soy de Frankfurt	*I am from Frankfurt*
La mesa **es** de madera	*The table is made of wood*

◆ Estar + noun

Estar is always used for local situations, as follows:

> **Estoy** en Barcelona
> *I am in Barcelona*
>
> La casa **está** en un bosque
> *The house is in a forest*

"There is" can never be expressed by "estar" if the Spanish noun is used without an article or with the indefinite article. In this case the following form must be used:

> **hay** *(there is, there are)*

> Aquí **hay** una farmacia
> *There is a chemist's (here)*
>
> ¿Dónde **hay** por aquí un restaurante típico?
> *Where is there a typical restaurant?*
>
> En la Costa Brava **hay** muchos hoteles
> *On the Costa Brava there are many hotels*

◆ Ser + adjective

Ser expresses a permanent or inherent quality.

> Este hotel **es** muy bueno
> *This hotel is very good*
>
> El metal **es** duro
> *Metal is hard*

◆ Estar + adjective

On the contrary, **estar** expresses a state or situation.

> La habitación **está** sucia
> *The room is dirty*
>
> El cielo **está** nublado
> *The sky is overcast*

Exceptions: although **rico** (rich) and **feliz** (happy) do not express any permanent quality, they are used with "ser". The same thing happens with **"pobre"** (poor) and **"infeliz"** (unhappy).

> Julia **es** feliz
> *Julia is happy*

> Este hombre **es** muy rico
> *This man is very rich*

In many cases **ser** or **estar** may be used, but the meaning is different:

> El cielo **es** azul
> *The sky is blue (you know that the colour of the sky is blue)*

> Hoy el cielo **está** azul
> *Today the sky is blue (there are not any clouds in the sky)*

> Esta mujer **es** muy guapa
> *This woman is very beautiful (as inherent quality)*

> **Estás** muy guapa
> *You are beautiful (today you are looking beautiful)*

> La verdura **es** buena para la salud
> *Vegetables are good for your health*

> La verdura **está** muy buena*
> *This vegetable is very good (it has a very good taste)*

* We can establish the additional rule that, in order to express a direct and spontaneous impression (principally referring to food and beverages) **"estar"** has to be used.

◆ Special forms

If the user wants to express the result of an action by means of a participle (as adjective) he has to use **"estar"**.

> Cierro la ventana   *I close the window (action)*
> La ventana **está** cerrada   *The window is closed (result)*

> Pedro vende los coches   *Pedro sells the car (action)*
> Los coches **están** vendidos   *The cars are sold (result)*

If the participle is used with **ser**, it does not express the result of an action but the action itself in the passive voice (in Spanish the use of the passive voice is not very frequent):

> Los coches **son** vendidos   *The cars are sold (action)*

The gerund is always used with **estar**

Estoy tomando una cerveza	*I am drinking a beer*
Pedro **está** escribiendo una carta	*Pedro is writing a letter*

when expressing a continuous action in the immediate present or an action which is interrupted by another one.

REFLEXIVE VERBS

Reflexive verbs are pronominal verbs which are conjugated together with a personal pronoun functioning as a complement and agreeing with the subject in person and number. Personal pronouns are put before the verb in all conjugated forms, but added onto the end of the infinitive or gerund.

lavarse	*to wash oneself*
me lavo	*I wash myself*
te lavas	*you wash yourself*
se lava	*he wash himself*
	she wash herself
nos lavamos	*we wash ourselves*
os laváis	*you wash yourselves*
se lavan	*they wash themselves*

MODAL VERBS

Modal verbs express, followed by the infinitive of any other verb, that something is "possible", "wanted", "necessary", "permitted", etc. The Spanish modal verbs are **poder** (can), **saber** (can/know how to), **deber** (must), **querer** (want), **desear** (wish).

PODER + INFINITIVE	can (*because something is permitted or the necessary condition is fulfilled*)
No **puedo comprar** el coche	I cannot buy the car (*because I have not got enough money*)
No **puede ir** al cine	He cannot go to the cinema (*because his parents do not allow to go*)

SABER + INFINITIVE	can *(because you have learnt how to do it)*
Mónica **sabe nadar**	Monika can swim
No **sé conducir**	I cannot drive a car
DEBER + INFINITIVE	must *(obligation)*
Debemos pagar la factura	We must pay the bill
Deben ir a casa	They must go home
QUERER + INFINITIVE	want *(wish)*
Quiero ir a comprar	I want to go shopping
Queremos descansar	We want to have a rest
DESEAR + INFINITIVE	wish, would like
Deseamos hacer vacaciones	We would like to go on holiday

The usual form to express a wish in an educated way is the subjuncti-ve of the verb **"querer"**.

quisiera	*I would like*
quisieras	*you would like*
quisiera	*he/she would like*
quisiéramos	*we would like*
quisierais	*you would like*
quisieran	*they would like*

Quisiera tomar una cerveza	I would like to drink a beer
Quisiéramos terminar el trabajo	We would like to finish this work

■ PHRASE BOOK

By means of the sentence examples the user of this book can make himself understood in many situations. It is possible to increase the number of these sentences replacing parts of them by other terms in the dictionary according to the situation he would like to resolve.

In the chapter **"shopping"**, for example, we use the structure

Quisiera	un kilo de patatas
I would like	*a kilo of potatoes*

If you want to buy something else you can replace a part of this sentence by another one.

| **Quisiera** | un kilo de manzanas |
| *I would like* | *a kilo of apples* |

or

| **Quisiera** | un litro de aceite |
| *I would like* | *a litre of oil* |

In this last structure we have replaced the whole direct object.

But it is also possible to replace the direct object –as explained in the "modal verbs" section– by an infinitive with its own object.

comprar un libro	*to buy a book*
tomar un café	*to have some coffee*
ir a bailar	*to go dancing*

| **Quisiera** | un litro de aceite |
| *I would like* | *a litre of oil* |

replaced by

| **Quisiera** | **comprar** un libro |
| *I would like* | *to buy a book* |

| **Quisiera** | **tomar** un café |
| *I would like* | *to have some coffee* |

| **Quisiera** | **ir** a bailar |
| *I would like* | *to go dancing* |

III.
NUMBERS

■ CARDINAL NUMBERS

0 **cero** *[θéro]*
1 **uno** *[úno]*
2 **dos** *[dos]*
3 **tres** *[tres]*
4 **cuatro** *[kwátro]*
5 **cinco** *[θínko]*
6 **seis** *[seis]*
7 **siete** *[sjéte]*
8 **ocho** *[ótcho]*
9 **nueve** *[nwébe]*

10 **diez** *[djeθ]*
11 **once** *[ónθe]*
12 **doce** *[dóθe]*
13 **trece** *[tréθe]*
14 **catorce** *[katórθe]*
15 **quince** *[kínθe]*
16 **dieciseis** *[djeθiséis]*
17 **diecisiete** *[djeθisjéte]*
18 **dieciocho** *[djeθiótcho]*
19 **diecinueve** *[djeθinwébe]*
20 **veinte** *[béinte]*
21 **veintiuno** *[beintiúno]*
22 **veintidos** *[beintidós]*
23 **veintitres** *[beintitrés]*
24 **veinticuatro** *[beintikwátro]*

30 **treinta** *[tréinta]*
32 **treinta y dos** *[tréinta i dos]*
33 **treinta y tres** *[tréinta i tres]*
34 **treinta y cuatro** *[tréinta i kwátro]*
35 **treinta y cinco** *[tréinta i θínko]*

40 **cuarenta** *[kwarénta]*
43 **cuarenta y tres** *[kwarénta i tres]*
44 **cuarenta y cuatro** *[kwarénta i kwátro]*
45 **cuarenta y cinco** *[kwarénta i θínko]*
46 **cuarenta y seis** *[kwarénta i seis]*

50 **cincuenta** *[θinkwénta]*
54 **cincuenta y cuatro**
    [θinkwénta i kwátro]
55 **cincuenta y cinco** *[θinkwénta i θínko]*
56 **cincuenta y seis** *[θinkwénta i seis]*
57 **cincuenta y siete** *[θinkwénta i sjéte]*

60 **sesenta** *[sesénta]*
65 **sesenta y cinco** *[sesénta i θínko]*

66 **sesenta y seis** *[sesénta i seis]*
67 **sesenta y siete** *[sesénta i sjéte]*
68 **sesenta y ocho** *[sesénta i ótcho]*

70 **setenta** *[seténta]*
76 **setenta y seis** *[seténta i seis]*
77 **setenta y siete** *[seténta i sjéte]*
78 **setenta y ocho** *[seténta i ótcho]*
79 **setenta y nueve** *[seténta i nwébe]*

80 **ochenta** *[otchénta]*
81 **ochenta y uno** *[otchénta i úno]*
82 **ochenta y dos** *[otchénta i dos]*
83 **ochenta y tres** *[otchénta i tres]*
84 **ochenta y cuatro** *[otchénta i kwátro]*

90 **noventa** *[nobénta]*
92 **noventa y dos** *[nobénta i dos]*
93 **noventa y tres** *[nobénta i tres]*
94 **noventa y cuatro** *[nobénta i kwátro]*
95 **noventa y cinco** *[nobénta i θínko]*

100 **cien(to)** *[θjénto]*
101 **ciento uno** *[θjénto úno]*
112 **ciento doce** *[θjénto dóθe]*
123 **ciento veintitres** *[θjénto beintitrés]*
134 **ciento treinta y cuatro**
    [θjénto tréinta i kwátro]

200 **doscientos(as)** *[dosθjéntos]*
202 **doscientos(as) dos** *[dosθjéntos dos]*
213 **doscientos(as) trece**
    [dosθjéntos tréθe]
224 **doscientos(as) veinticuatro**
    [dosθjéntos beintikwátro]
235 **doscientos(as) treinta y cinco**
    [dosθjéntos tréinta i θínko]

300 **trescientos(as)** *[tresθjéntos]*
303 **trescientos tres** *[tresθjéntos tres]*
330 **trescientos treinta**
    [tresθjéntos tréinta]

400 **cuatrocientos(as)** *[kwatroθjéntos]*
424 **cuatrocientos(as) veinticuatro**
    [kwatroθjéntos veintikwátro]
440 **cuatrocientos(as) cuarenta**
    [kwatroθjéntos kwarénta]

500 **quinientos(as)** *[kinjéntos]*

504 **quinientos(as) cuatro**
[kinjéntos kwátro]
550 **quinientos(as) cincuenta**
[kinjéntos θinkwénta]

600 **seiscientos(as)** *[seisθjéntos]*
605 **seiscientos(as) cinco**
[seisθjéntos θínko]
660 **seiscientos(as) sesenta**
[seis θjéntos sesénta]

700 **setecientos(as)** *[seteθjéntos]*
706 **setecientos(as) seis** *[seteθjéntos seis]*
770 **setecientos(as) setenta**
[seteθjéntos seténta]

800 **ochocientos(as)** *[otchoθjéntos]*
807 **ochocientos(as) siete**
[otchoθjéntos sjéte]
880 **ochocientos(as) ochenta**
[otchoθjéntos otchénta]
900 **novecientos(as)** *[nobeθjéntos]*
908 **novecientos(as) ocho**
[nobeθjéntos ótcho]

990 **novecientos(as) noventa**
[nobeθjéntos nobénta]

1 000 **mil** *[mil]*
1 010 **mil diez** *[mil djeθ]*
1 100 **mil cien** *[mil θjen]*

2 000 **dos mil** *[dos mil]*
3 000 **tres mil** *[tres mil]*
4 000 **cuatro mil** *[kwátro mil]*

10 000 **diez mil** *[djeθ mil]*
11 000 **once mil** *[ónθe mil]*
12 000 **doce mil** *[dóθe mil]*

100 000 **cien mil** *[θjen mil]*
200.000 **doscientos(as) mil**
[dosθjéntos mil]
500 000 **quinientos(as) mil**
[kinjéntos mil]

1 000 000 **un millón** *[un miljón]*
2 000 000 **dos millones** *[dos miljónes]*
3 000 000 **tres millones**
[tres miljónes]

■ ORDINAL NUMBERS

the **el (la)**	first	**primero(a)** *[priméro]*
	second	**segundo(a)** *[segúndo]*
	third	**tercero(a)** *[terθéro]*
	fourth	**cuarto(a)** *[kwárto]*
	fifth	**quinto(a)** *[kinto]*
	sixth	**sexto(a)** *[séksto]*
	seventh	**séptimo(a)** *[sétimo]*
	eighth	**octavo(a)** *[oktábo]*
	ninth	**noveno(a)** *[nobéno]*
	tenth	**décimo(a)** *[déθimo]*
	eleventh	**décimo(a) primero(a)** *[déθimo priméro]*
	twelfth	**décimo(a) segundo(a)** *[déθimo segúndo]*
	twentieth	**vigésimo(a)** *[bixésimo]*

IV.

PHRASE BOOK

GENERAL ASPECTS

■ ABOUT MYSELF

I am **Soy** *[sój]*	a foreigner **extranjero(a)** *[ekstranxéro]*
	English **inglés (inglesa)** *[inglés, inglésa]*
	American **americano(a)** *[amerikáno]*
	Irish **irlandés (irlandesa)** *[irlandés, irlandésa]*
	from England **de Inglaterra** *[de inglatérra]*
	from Australia **de Australia** *[de austrálja]*
	from Scotland **de Escocia** *[de eskóθja]*
	from London **de Londres** *[de lóndres]*

I am not from here
No soy de aquí
[no sój de akí]

I am here **Estoy aquí** *[estój akí]*	on holidays **de vacaciones** *[de bakaθjónes]*
	for business **en viaje de negocios** *[en bjáxe de negóθjos]*
	at the International Fair of Barcelona **en la feria internacional de Barcelona** *[en la férja internaθjonál de barθelóna]*
	for a visit **de visita** *[de bisíta]*

I have been here **Estoy aquí** *[estój akí]*	for (two weeks) **desde hace (dos semanas)** *[désde áθe dos semánas]*
	since (yesterday) **desde ayer** *[désde ajér]*

I have been here | since (July 15th)
Estoy aquí | **desde (el quince de julio)**
[estói akí] | *[désde el kínθe de xúljo]*

I am staying | at the (Meliá) Hotel
Resido | **en el hotel (Meliá)** *[en el otél meljá]*
[rresído]

| at the (Sol) appartments
| **en los apartamentos (Sol)** *[en los apartaméntos sol]*

| at the beach
| **junto a la playa** *[xúnto a la plája]*

| in (Marina) Street
| **en la calle (Marina)** *[en la kálje marína]*

| with friends
| **en casa de unos amigos** *[en kása de únos amígos]*

| rather far from here
| **bastante lejos de aquí** *[bastánte léxos de akí]*

| very near here
| **cerca de aquí** *[θérka de akí]*

I live here
Vivo aquí *[bíbo akí]*

I don't live here
No vivo aquí *[no bíbo akí]*

I only speak | a little Spanish
Sólo hablo | **un poco de español** *[un póko de espanjól]*
[sólo áblo]

| English
| **inglés** *[inglés]*

| French
| **francés** *[franθés]*

| (some) Italian
| **(algo de) italiano** *[álgo de italjáno]*

| English and French
| **inglés y francés** *[inglés i franθés]*

I don't speak Spanish
No hablo español
[no áblo espanjól]

Do you speak | English?
¿Habla Vd. | **inglés?** *[inglés]*
[ábla ustéd]

| German?
| **alemán?** *[alemán]*

| French?
| **francés?** *[franθés]*

| Italian?
| **italiano?** *[italjáno]*

My name is (Monica)
Me llamo (Mónica) *[me ljámo mónika]*

His name is (Karl)
Se llama (Karl) *[se ljáma karl]*

Her name is (Mary)
Se llama (María) *[se ljáma maría]*

I am staying here | for only a few days
Me quedaré | **poco tiempo** *[póko tjémpo]*
[me kedaré]

| for (fifteen) days
| **(quince) días** *[kínθe días]*

| for one week (two weeks)
| **una (dos) semanas** *[úna (dos) semánas]*

| for one month (some months)
| **un mes (varios meses)**
| *[un mes (bárjos méses)]*

| until (the 31st of August)
| **hasta el (treinta y uno de agosto)**
| *[ásta el tréjnta i úno de agósto]*

| until tomorrow
| **hasta mañana** *[ásta manjána]*

| until next (Sunday)
| **hasta el próximo (domingo)**
| *[ásta el próksimo (domíngo)]*

I am married
Estoy casado(a) *[estói kasádo]*

I am single
Soy soltero(a) *[soi soltéro]*

I am (25) years old
Tengo veinticinco años *[téngo beintiθínko ánjos]*

I have got	(2) children
Tengo	**(dos) hijos** *[dos íxos]*
[téngo]	
	one son (one daughter)
	un hijo (una hija) *[un íxo (úna íxa)]*

I haven't got any children
No tengo hijos *[no téngo íxos]*

I don't drink	alcohol
No tomo	**alcohol** *[alkól]*
[no tómo]	
	coffee
	café *[kafé]*

I only drink water
Tomo solamente agua *[tómo solaménte ágwa]*

I like	wine
Me gusta	**el vino** *[el bíno]*
[me gústa]	
	beer
	la cerveza *[la θerbéθa]*
	milk
	la leche *[la létje]*
	tea
	el té *[el te]*
	coffee
	el café *[el kafé]*

I like	fish
Me gusta	**el pescado** *[el peskádo]*
[me gústa]	
	fruit
	la fruta *[la frúta]*
	meat
	la carne *[la kárne]*
	vegetables
	la verdura *[la berdúra]*
	sweets
	el dulce *[el dúlθe]*

I don't like
No me gusta(n)
[no me gusta(n)]

fish
el pescado *[el peskádo]*

fruit
la fruta *[la frúta]*

meat
la carne *[la kárne]*

sweets
los dulces *[los dúlθes]*

I can't eat
No puedo comer
[no puédo komêr]

pork
carne de cerdo
[kárne de θérdo]

eggs
huevos *[wébos]*

fat
grasa *[grása]*

sweets
dulces *[dúlθes]*

I am on a diet
Estoy a régimen *[estój a rréximen]*

I (don't) eat (much) a lot
Como mucho (poco) *[kómo mútcho (póko)]*

I (don't) drink (much) a lot
Bebo mucho (poco) *[bébo mútcho (póko)]*

I only smoke
Fumo sólo
[fúmo sólo]

en pipa
en pipa *[en pípa]*

black tobacco
tabaco negro *[tabáko négro]*

cigars
puros *[púros]*

I don't smoke
No fumo *[no fúmo]*

I don't smoke
No fumo
[no fúmo]

cigarettes
cigarrillos
[θigarríljos]

I don't smoke	cigars
No fumo	**puros** *[púros]*
[no fúmo]	
	black cigarettes
	tabaco negro *[tabáko négro]*

◼ SITUATIONS

I am	(very) hungry
Tengo	**(mucha) hambre** *[mútcha ámbre]*
[téngo]	
	(very) thirsty
	(mucha) sed *[mútcha sed]*

I have an appetite
Tengo apetito *[téngo apetíto]*

I don't feel	hungry
No tengo	**hambre** *[ámbre]*
[no téngo]	
	thirsty
	sed *[sed]*

I don't have an appetite
No tengo apetito *[no téngo apetíto]*

I feel sleepy
Tengo sueño *[téngo swénjo]*

I'm tired
Estoy cansado(a) *[estói kansádo]*

I'm	cold
Tengo	**frío** *[frío]*
[téngo]	
	hot
	calor *[kalór]*

I am (very) well
Estoy (muy) bien *[estói (mui) bien]*

We are (very) well
Estamos (muy) bien *[estámos (mui) bien]*

I'm not (very) well
No estoy (muy) bien *[no estói (mui) bien]*

We are not (very) well
No estamos (muy) bien *[no estámos (mui) bien]*

I feel bad
   Me encuentro mal *[me enkwéntro mal]*

I don't feel (very) well
   No me encuentro (muy) bien *[no me enkwéntro (mui) bien]*

How are you?
   ¿Qué tal? *[ké tal]*

How are you?
   ¿Cómo estás (estáis)? *Sing./Pl. [kómo estás (estájs)]*

How do you do?
   ¿Cómo está (están)? *Sing./Pl. [ustéd (ustédes)]*
   [Kómo está (están)]

How is	
¿Cómo está	your wife?
[Kómo está]	**su esposa?** *[su espósa]*
	your husband?
	su esposo? *[su espóso]*
	your family?
	su familia? *[su família]*

▦ GREETINGS

Hello!
   ¡Hola! *[óla]*

Good	morning (day)!
	¡Buenos días! *[buénos días]*
	afternoon!
	¡Buenas tardes! *[buénas tárdes]*
	evening!
	¡Buenas tardes! *[buénas tárdes]*
	evening!
	¡Buenas noches! *[buénas nótches]*
	(after dinner)
	night!
	¡Buenas noches! *[buénas nótches]*

Goodbye!
   ¡Adiós! *[adjós]*
   ¡Hasta la vista! *[ásta la bísta]*

See you soon / in a minute!
   Hasta ahora *[ásta aóra]*

See you later!
   Hasta luego *[ásta lwégo]*

See you | tomorrow
Hasta | **mañana** *[manjána]*
[ásta]

   | again!
   | **la próxima vez**
   | *[la próksima beθ]*

■ OTHER EXPRESSIONS

Speak (more) slowly, please
   Hable más despacio, por favor
   [áble mas despáθjo, por fabór]

I don't understand
   No comprendo
   [no kompréndo]

Can you repeat that?
   ¿Puede repetirlo?
   [pwéde rrepetírlo]

Yes!
¡Sí! *[si]*

No!
¡No! *[no]*

Of course
   Naturalmente *[naturalménte]*
   Desde luego *[désde lwégo]*

Yes, of course
   Claro que sí *[kláro ke si]*

Of course not
   Claro que no *[kláro ke no]*

Possibly
   Posiblemente *[posibleménte]*

Probably
   Probablemente *[probableménte]*

Are you sure?
¿Está (Vd.) seguro(a)?
[está (ustéd) segúro]

I am (completely) sure
Estoy (completamente) seguro(a)
[estói (kompletaménte) segúro]

I like it (very much)
Me gusta (mucho)
[me gústa (mútcho)]

I don't like it (very much)
No me gusta (mucho)
[no me gústa (mútcho)]

I know
Lo sé *[lo se]*

I don't know
No lo sé *[no lo se]*

I hope   so
Espero   **que sí** *[ke sí]*
[espéro]
                not
                que no *[ke no]*

I think   so
Creo   **que sí** *[ke si]*
[kréo]
                not
                que no *[ke no]*

Please!
¡Por favor! *[por fabór]*

Thank you!
¡Gracias! *[gráθjas]*

Thank you very much!
¡Muchas gracias! *[mútchas gráθjas]*

Don't mention it!
¡No hay de qué! *[no ai de ke]*
¡De nada! *[de náda]*

Excuse me, please!
¡Disculpe, por favor! *[diskúlpe, por fabór]*

Sorry!
¡Perdón! [perdón]

I wish you
Le (te) deseo
[le deséo]

a pleasant day
un día agradable [un día agradáble]

a good journey
un buen viaje [un bwen bjáxe]

good luck
mucha suerte [mútcha swérte]

Have fun
¡Que se divierta! [ke se dibjérta]

With pleasure!
¡Con mucho gusto [kon mútcho gústo]

I'm (very) sorry!
¡Lo siento (mucho)! [lo sjénto (mútcho)]

It's a pity!
¡Qué lástima! [ke lástima]

May I invite you
¿Puedo invitarlo(la)
[pwédo imbitárlo]

for dinner?
a cenar? [a θenár]

to dance?
a bailar? [a bailár]

for a drink?
a tomar algo?
[a tomár álgo]

Thank you for
¡Muchas gracias por
[mútchas gráθjas por]

such a wonderful day
este día tan agradable!
[éste día tan agradáble]

the invitation
la invitación! [la imbitaθjón]

your visit
su visita! [su bisíta]

I will hurry up
Me voy a dar prisa [me bój a dar prísa]

I will be back right away
Vuelvo en seguida
[bwélbo en segída]

I have no time
No tengo tiempo *[no téngo tjémpo]*

I am not in a hurry
No tengo prisa *[no téngo prísa]*

I have (a lot of) time
Tengo (mucho) tiempo *[téngo (mútcho) tjémpo]*

I am in a (great) hurry
Tengo (mucha) prisa *[téngo (mútcha) prísa]*

One moment, please!
¡Un momento, por favor! *[un moménto por fabór]*

Excuse me (please)!
¡Oiga (por favor)! *[ójga (por fabór)]*

Come here (please)!
¡Venga (por favor)! *[bénga (por fabór)]*

Go away (please)!
¡Váyase (por favor)! *[bájase (por fabór)]*

Look here!
¡Mire Vd.! *[míre ustéd]*

It is not hard for me
No me cuesta nada *[no me kwésta náda]*

It doesn't matter
Me da igual *[me da igwál]*
No me importa *[no me impórta]*

Never mind
No pasa nada *[no pása náda]*

I don't mind
No tengo inconveniente *[no téngo inkombenjénte]*

You are very kind
Es Vd. muy amable *[es ustéd mui amáble]*

That's all
 Es todo *[es tódo]*

Nothing else
 Nada más *[náda mas]*

Please, can you repeat that?
 Otra vez, por favor *[ótra beθ por fabór]*

Another one, please
 Otro(a), por favor *[ótro por fabór]*

■ THE WEATHER

What's the weather like?
 ¿Qué tiempo hace?
 [ke tjémpo áθe]

The weather is	fine
Hace	**buen tiempo** *[bwen tjémpo]*
[áθe]	
	bad
	mal tiempo *[mal tjémpo]*

It's raining (snowing)	a little
Está lloviendo (nevando)	**un poco** *[un póko]*
[está ljobjéndo (nebándo)]	
	hard
	mucho *[mútcho]*

The sun is shining
 Hace sol *[áθe sol]*

The sun is not shining
 No hace sol *[no áθe sol]*

The sky is	overcast
(El cielo) está	**nublado** *[nubládo]*
[(el θjélo) está]	
	cloudless
	despejado *[despexádo]*

It's	(very) hot
Hace	**(mucho) calor**
[áθe]	*[(mútcho) kalór]*

It's	(very) cold
Hace	**(mucho) frío** *[(mútcho) frío]*
[áθe]	
	cool
	fresquito *[freskíto]*
	close
	bochorno *[botchórno]*

It's	(very) windy
Hay	**(mucho) viento** *[(mútcho) bjénto]*
[ai]	
	(very) humid
	(mucha) humedad *[(mútcha) umedád]*
	stormy
	tormenta *[torménta]*

What's the temperature?
¿Qué temperatura hay? *[ke temperatúra ai]*

The temperature is very pleasant
Hay una temperatura agradable
[ai úna temperatúra agradáble]

The temperature is 30ºC (in the shade)
Estamos a treinta grados a la sombra
[estámos a tréinta grádos a la sómbra]

The water is	(very) cold
El agua está	**(muy) fría** *[(mui) fría]*
[el ágwa está]	
	warm
	templada *[templáda]*
	hot
	caliente *[kaljénte]*

There is a lot of snow here
Aquí hay mucha nieve *[akí ai mútcha njébe]*

Here there is ice everywhere
Aquí está todo helado *[akí está tódo eládo]*

The roads are icy
Hay hielo en las carreteras *[ai jélo en las karretéras]*

■ QUANTITIES, WEIGHTS, MEASURES

How much does it weigh?
¿Cuánto pesa? *[kwánto pésa]*
¿Qué peso tiene? *[ke péso tjéne]*

It weighs (900) g
Pesa (novecientos) gramos
[pésa (nobeθjéntos) grámos]

Give me	(1) Kg
Déme	**(un) kilo** *[(un) kílo]*
[déme]	
Póngame	(100) g
[póngame]	**(cien) gramos** *[(θjen) grámos]*
	(half) a kilo
	(medio) kilo *[(médjo) kílo]*
	a dozen
	una docena *[úna doθéna]*
	(three) units (pieces)
	(tres) unidades *[(tres) unidádes]*
	(2) litres
	(dos) litros *[(dos) lítros]*

How much is	each piece?
¿Cuánto vale	**la pieza?** *[la pjéθa]*
[kwánto bále]	
	one litre?
	el litro? *[el lítro]*
	one bottle?
	la botella? *[la botélja]*
	one kilo?
	el kilo? *[el kílo]*

How much are	100 g
¿Cuánto valen	**los cien gramos?**
[kwánto bálen]	*[los θjen grámos]*
	(2) dozen
	(dos) docenas? *[(dos) doθénas]*

How much are	these(those)?
¿Cuánto valen	**éstos (éstas)?**
[kwánto bálen]	*[éstos]*

How	long ...	
¿Qué	**longitud ...** *[lonxitúd]*	
[ke]		
	high ...	
	altura ... *[altúra]*	
	wide ...	... is it?
	anchura ... *[antchúra]*	**... tiene?** *[tjéne]*
	deep ...	... are they?
	profundidad ... *[profundidád]*	**... tienen?** *[tjénen]*

It is	(1) km long
Tiene	**(un) km de largo** *[(un) kilómetro de lárgo]*
[tjéne]	
They are	(3) m high
Tienen	**una altura de (tres) metros**
[tjénen]	*[úna altúra de (tres) métros]*
	(50) cm wide
	(cincuenta) centímetros de ancho
	[(θinkwénta) θentímetros de ántcho]
	(2) m deep
	una profundidad de (dos) metros
	[úna profundidád de (dos) métros]

How many square meters is	this flat?
¿Cuántos metros (cuadrados) tiene	**este piso?** *[éste piso]*
[kwántos métros (kwadrádos) tjéne]	
	this plot?
	este terreno?
	[éste terréno]
	this terrace?
	esta terraza?
	[ésta terráθa]

It is (60) meters
Tiene (sesenta) metros cuadrados
[tjéne (sesénta) métros kwadrádos]

How far is it from Barcelona?
¿A qué distancia de Barcelona está?
[a ke distánθja de barθelóna está]

How far is it to Madrid?
¿Qué distancia hay a Madrid?
[ke distánθja ai a madríd]

We are	still far from Málaga
Estamos	**lejos de Málaga** *[léxos de málaga]*
[estámos]	
	near Gerona
	cerca de Gerona *[θérka de xeróna]*
	on the A 17 at km (184)
	en la A diecisiete, en el km (ciento ochenta y cuatro) *[en la a djeθisjéte en el kilómetro cjénto otchénta i kwátro]*
	on the road from León to La Coruña
	en la carretera de León a La Coruña *[en la karretéra de león a la korúnja]*

I only want	half of it (them)
Solo quisiera	**la mitad** *[la mitád]*
[sólo quisjéra]	
	a dozen
	una docena *[úna doθéna]*
	half a litre
	medio litro *[médjo lítro]*
	one
	uno (una) *[úno]*
	a few
	algunos(as) *[algúnos]*

Give me	a lot
Póngame	**mucho** *[mútcho]*
[póngame]	
	a little
	poco *[póko]*
	a little more
	algo más *[álgo mas]*

Give me	a little
Póngame	**algo menos**
[póngame]	*[álgo ménos]*

◼ COLOURS

What colours have you got?
¿De qué color lo (la) tiene? *[de ke kolór lo tjéne]*

I like this colour (a lot)
Este color me gusta (mucho) *[éste kolór me gústa (mútcho)]*

I don't like this colour
Este color no me gusta *[éste kolór no me gústa]*

Haven't you got any other colour?
¿Lo (la) tiene de otro color? *[lo tjéne de ótro kolór]*

I would like it in	red
Lo (la) quisiera	**rojo(a)** *[rróxo]*
[lo kisjéra]	
	blue
	azul *[aθúl]*
	green
	verde *[bérde]*
	yellow
	amarillo(a) *[amaríljo]*

I would like it	a little lighter
Lo (la) quiero	**algo más claro(a)**
[lo kjéro]	*[álgo mas kláro]*
	a little darker
	algo más oscuro(a)
	[álgo mas oskúro]
	not so colourful
	algo menos colorido(a)
	[álgo ménos kolorído]
	in light blue
	en azul claro
	[en aθúl kláro]

I would like it	in dark green
Lo (la) quiero	**en verde oscuro**
[lo kjéro]	*[en bérde oskúro]*

■ WHAT TIME IS IT?

▶ TELLING THE TIME

What time is it?
  ¿Qué hora es? *[ke óra es]*

It is	1.00 o'clock
Es	**la una**
[es]	*[la úna]*

It is	6.00 o'clock
Son	**las seis** *[las seis]*
[son]	

	a quarter past six
	las seis y cuarto *[las seis i kwárto]*
	half past six
	las seis y media *[las seis i médja]*
	a quarter to seven
	las siete menos cuarto *[las sjéte ménos kwárto]*
	twenty minutes past nine
	las nueve y veinte *[las nwébe i béinte]*
	twenty five minutes to two
	las dos menos veinticinco
	[las dos ménos beintiθínko]
	ten o'clock sharp
	las diez en punto *[las djéθ en púnto]*

▶ OFFICIAL TIME

At	13.00
A	**las trece (horas)** *[las tréθe (óras)]*
[a]	
	14.05
	las catorce cero cinco *[las katórθe θéro θínko]*

At **A** *[a]*	15.10 **las quince diez** *[las kínθe djeθ]*
	16.15 **las dieciséis quince** *[las djeθiséis kínθe]*
	17.30 **las diecisiete treinta** *[las djeθisjéte tréinta]*
	18.40 **las dieciocho cuarenta** *[las djeθiótcho kwarénta]*
	19.45 **las diecinueve cuarenta y cinco** *[las djeθinwébe kwarénta i θínko]*

It is **Son** *[son]*	nine o'clock (in the morning) **las nueve de la mañana** *[las nwébe de la manjána]*
	twelve o'clock (noon) **las doce del mediodía** *[las dóθe del medjodía]*
	three o'clock (in the afternoon) **las tres de la tarde** *[las tres de la tárde]*
	eleven o'clock (in the evening) **las once de la noche** *[las ónθe de la nótche]*
	twelve o'clock (midnight) **las doce de la noche** *[las dóθe de la nótche]*

At **A** *[a]*	one o'clock sharp **la una en punto** *[la úna en púnto]*
	two o'clock sharp **las dos en punto** *[las dos en púnto]*

Around ten o'clock
    Alrededor de las diez *[alrrededór de las djeθ]*

At about eleven o'clock
    Hacia las once *[áθja las ónθe]*

	What time?
¿A	**qué hora?**
[a]	*[ke óra]*

Until	what time?
Hasta	**qué hora?**
[ásta]	*[ke óra]*

Since
Desde
[désde]

From
A partir de
[a partír de]

In	one hour
Dentro de	**una hora**
[déntro de]	*[úna óra]*

	Half an hour …	
Hace	**… media hora**	
[áθe]	*[médja óra]*	
	A quarter of an hour …	
	… un cuarto de hora	
	[un kwárto de óra]	
	Three quarters of an hour …	
	… tres cuartos de hora	
	[tres kwártos de óra]	
	Two hours …	
	… dos horas	
	[dos óras]	
	Five minutes …	
	… cinco minutos	
	[θínko minútos]	
	A few minutes …	… ago
	… unos minutos	
	[únos minútos]	

▶ Days

Today   **hoy** *[oi]*

This **Esta** *[ésta]*	morning **mañana** *[manjána]*
	afternoon **tarde** *[tárde]*
	evening **noche** *[nótche]*

Yesterday   **ayer** *[ajér]*

Yesterday **Ayer** *[ajér]*	morning **por la mañana** *[por la manjána]*
	evening **por la tarde** *[por la tárde]*

Last night
   Ayer por la noche *[ajér por la nótche]*
   Anoche *[anótche]*

Tomorrow   **mañana** *[manjána]*

Tomorrow **Mañana** *[manjána]*	morning **por la mañana** *[por la manjána]*
	afternoon **por la tarde** *[por la tárde]*
	evening (night) **por la noche** *[por la nótche]*

What day is it today?
   ¿Qué día es (hoy)? *[ke día es (oi)]*

Today is **Hoy es** *[oi es]*	Monday **lunes** *[lúnes]*
	Tuesday **martes** *[mártes]*

Today is **Hoy es** *[oi es]*	Wednesday **miércoles** *[mjérkoles]*
	Thursday **jueves** *[xwébes]*
	Friday **viernes** *[bjérnes]*
	Saturday **sábado** *[sábado]*
	Sunday **domingo** *[domíngo]*

He is coming **Vendrá** *[bendrá]*	on Monday **el lunes** *[el lúnes]*
	next Monday **el próximo lunes** *[el próksimo lúnes]*

She arrived last Monday
    Llegó el lunes pasado *[ljegó el lúnes pasádo]*

Every day
    Cada día *[káda día]*

All day
    Todo el día *[tódo el día]*

Every day
    Todos los días *[tódos los días]*

▶ **DATES**

The date	**la fecha** *[la fétcha]*

What date is it today?
    ¿Qué fecha es hoy? *[ke fétcha es oi]*

Today is the 15th of July
    Hoy es el quince de julio *[oi es el kínθe de xúljo]*

The **El** *[el]*	20th of August **veinte de agosto** *[béinte de agósto]*

Until **Hasta el** *[ásta el]*	the 8th of October **ocho de octubre** *[ótcho de oktúbre]*

Since | the 18th of February
Desde el | **dieciocho de febrero**
[désde el] | *[djeθiótcho de febréro]*

▶ WEEKS

The week   **la semana** *[la semána]*

Next week
    La próxima semana *[la próksima semána]*

Last week
    La semana pasada *[la semána pasáda]*

This week
    Esta semana *[ésta semána]*

Within | (two) weeks
Dentro de | **dos semanas**
[déntro de] | *[dos semánas]*

One week ago
    Hace una semana
    [áθe úna semána]

Every week
    Cada semana *[káda semána]*

For the whole week
    (Durante) toda la semana
    [duránte tóda la semána]

▶ MONTHS

The month   **el mes** *[el mes]*

In | January
En | **enero** *[enéro]*
[en] |
| February
| **febrero** *[febréro]*
|
| March
| **marzo** *[márθo]*

Until **Hasta** *[ásta]*	April **abril** *[abríl]*
	May **mayo** *[májo]*
	June **junio** *[xúnjo]*
Since **Desde** *[désde]*	July **julio** *[xúljo]*
	August **agosto** *[agósto]*
	September **septiembre** *[setjémbre]*
As from **A partir de** *[a partír de]*	October **octubre** *[oktúbre]*
	November **noviembre** *[nobjémbre]*
	December **diciembre** *[diθjémbre]*
During **Durante** *[duránte]*	this month **este mes** *[éste mes]*
	the next month **el próximo mes** *[el próksimo mes]* **el mes que viene** *[el mes ke bjéne]*
	the last month **el mes pasado** *[el mes pasádo]*

For the whole month
(Durante) todo el mes
[(duránte) tódo el mes]

Every month
Todos los meses *[tódos los méses]*

In May
En mayo *[en májo]*

Until July
Hasta julio *[ásta xúljo]*

Since August
Desde agosto *[désde agósto]*

▶ **SEASONS**

Spring
La primavera *[la primabéra]*

Summer
El verano *[el beráno]*

Autumn
El otoño *[el otónjo]*

Winter
El invierno *[el imbjérno]*

In Spring
En primavera *[en primabéra]*

Until Spring
Hasta la primavera *[ásta la primabéra]*

Since Summer
Desde el verano *[désde el beráno]*

Last Autumn
El otoño pasado *[el otónjo pasádo]*

Next Winter
El próximo invierno *[el próksimo imbjérno]*

▶ **YEARS**

The year
El año
[el ánjo]

Next year
El próximo año
[el próksimo ánjo]

Last year
> **El año pasado**
> *[el ánjo pasádo]*

One year ago
> **Hace un año**
> *[áθe un ánjo]*

Within	a year
Dentro de	**un año**
[déntro de]	*[un ánjo]*

For (two) years
> **Durante (dos) años** *[duránte dos ánjos]*

Until next year
> **Hasta el año que viene** *[ásta el ánjo ke bjéne]*

For the whole year
> **(Durante) todo el año** *[duránte tódo el ánjo]*

Each year
> **Cada año** *[káda ánjo]*

Every year
> **Todos los años** *[tódos los ánjos]*

FIRST CONTACTS

■ **ARRIVAL**

What time	shall we arrive in (Madrid)?
¿A qué hora	**llegaremos a (Madrid)?** *[ljegarémos a madríd]*
[a ke óra]	

can I take a connecting flight to (Palma)?
hay un vuelo de enlace a (Palma)?
[ai un bwélo de enláθe a (pálma)]

is there a train to (Bilbao)?
sale un tren para (Bilbao)?
[sále un tren pára (bilbáo)]

My luggage is coming from (Manchester)
Mi equipaje viene de (Manchester)
[mi ekipáxe bjéne de (mántchester)]

On which conveyor belt does the luggage from (London) arrive?
¿En qué cinta llega el equipaje de (Londres)?
[en ke θínta ljéga el ekipáxe de (lóndres)]

I have come on flight BA 170 from (Glasgow)
He venido en el vuelo BA 170 de (Glasgow)
[e benído en el bwélo éle átche θjénto seténta de (glásgou)]

Where can I find	a porter?
¿Dónde encuentro	**un mozo?** *[un móθo]*
[dónde enkwéntro]	

a luggage trolley
un carro para el equipaje?
[un kárro pára el ekipáxe]

a public telephone?
un teléfono público?
[un teléfono públiko]

These are my cases
Éstas son mis maletas *[éstas son mis malétas]*

Take the cases	to the train for (Tarragona)
Lleve el equipaje	**al tren de Tarragona**
[ljébe el ekipáxe]	*[al tren de (tarragóna)]*

to the exit
a la salida *[a la salída]*

to the taxi rank
a la parada de taxis
[a la paráda de táksis]

Take the cases **Lleve el equipaje** *[ljébe el ekipáxe]*	to the bus stop **a la parada del autobús** *[a la paráda del autobús]*

Where is **¿Dónde está** *[dónde está]*	the passport control? **el control de pasaportes?** *[el kontról de pasapórtes]*
	the left-luggage office? **la consigna?** *[la konsígna]*

Where are the left-luggage lockers?
¿Dónde están las consignas automáticas?
[dónde están las konsígnas automátikas]

Where is (are) **¿Dónde está** *[dónde está]*	the (Iberia) counter? **el mostrador de (Iberia)?** *[el mostradór de ibérja]*
	the Tourist Information Office? **la información turística?** *[la informaθjón turístika]*
	the gates for transit passengers? **la salida para pasajeros de tránsito?** *[la salída pára pasaxéros de tránsito]*

I want to find **Estoy buscando** *[estói buskándo]*	a luxury hotel **un hotel de lujo** *[un otél de lúxo]*
	a three-star hotel **un hotel de tres estrellas** *[un otél de tres estréljas]*
	a boarding house **una pensión** *[úna pensjón]*
	a hotel in (Torremolinos) **un hotel en (Torremolinos)** *[un otél en (torremolínos)]*

Where can I **¿Dónde puedo** *[dónde puédo]*	get my (transit) boarding card? **recoger mi tarjeta de embarque (de tránsito)?** *[rrekoxér mi tarxéta de embárke (de tránsito)]*
	rent a car? **alquilar un coche?** *[alkilár un kótche]*
	change money? **cambiar dinero?** *[kambjár dinéro]*

Where can I	find a taxi?
¿Dónde puedo	**encontrar un taxi?**
[dónde pwédo]	*[enkontrár un táksi]*

Where do the the buses leave from for the city?
¿De dónde salen los autobuses al centro de la ciudad?
[de dónde sálen los autobúses al θéntro de la θjudád]

When does the next bus go to (Barcelona)?
¿A qué hora sale el próximo autobús para (Barcelona)?
[a ke óra sále el próksimo autobús pára (barθelóna)]

Taxi!
¡Taxi! *[táksi]*

Are you free?
¿Está libre? *[está líbre]*

Take me to	the centre of (Valencia)
Lléveme	**al centro de (Valencia)** *[al θéntro de (balénθja)]*
[ljébeme]	
	(Menéndez Pelayo) Street
	a la calle (Menéndez Pelayo)
	[a la kálje (menéndeθ pelájo)]
	to the (Plaza) Hotel
	al hotel (Plaza) *[al otél (pláθa)]*
	to (Marbella)
	a (Marbella) *[a (marbélja)]*

▮ COMING BY CAR

Can you tell me the way to (Tarragona)?
¿Puede indicarme el camino para (Tarragona)?
[pwéde indikárme el kamíno pára (tarragóna)]

Which is	the shortest way to (Lloret de Mar)?
¿Cuál es	**el camino más corto para (Lloret de Mar)?**
[kwál es]	*[el kamíno más kórto pára (ljorét de mar)]*
	the best way to (Vigo)?
	el mejor camino para (Vigo)?
	[el mexór kamíno pára (bígo)]
	the fastest way to (Marbella)?
	el camino más rápido para (Marbella)?
	[el kamíno más rrápido pára (marbélja)]

How far is it to (Madrid)?
¿Qué distancia hay para (Madrid)?
[ke distánθja ai pára (madríd)]

How can I get onto **¿Cómo llego** *[kómo ljégo]*	the motorway to (France)? **a la autopista de (Francia)?** *[a la autopísta de (fránθja)]*
	the road to (Torrevieja)? **a la carretera de (Torrevieja)?** *[a la karretéra de (torrebjéxa)]*
	the dual-carriageway to (Castelldefels)? **a la autovía de (Castelldefels)?** *[a la autobía de (kasteljdeféls)]*

Can you show me on the map?
¿Puede indicármelo en el mapa?
[pwéde indikármelo en el mápa]

Where is **¿Dónde está** *[dónde está]*	the nearest petrol station? **la gasolinera más próxima?** *[la gasolinéra más próksima]*
	the nearest garage? **el taller (de reparaciones) más cercano?** *[el taljér (de rreparaθjónes) más θerkáno]*

Where is there an Opel garage?
¿Dónde hay (por aquí) un taller de Opel?
[dónde ai (por akí) un tallér de ópel]

▶ **PETROL STATION**

I want **Quisiera** *[kisjéra]*	(20) litres of unleaded petrol **(veinte) litros de gasolina sin plomo** *[(béinte) lítros de gasolína sin plómo]*
	(15) litres of leaded petrol **(quince) litros de gasolina con plomo** *[(kínθe) lítros de gasolína kon plómo]*
	(30) Euros of four-star petrol **(30) euros de gasolina súper** *[(tréinta) éuros de gasolína súper]*

I want
Quisiera
[kisjéra]

(25) litres of Diesel
(veinticinco) litros de diesel
[(beintiθínko) lítros de djésel]

Please fill the tank
Llene el depósito, por favor
[ljéne el depósito por fabór]

Can you check
Puede comprobar
[pwéde komprobár]

the brake fluid?
el líquido de los frenos?
[el líkido de los frénos]

the oil level?
el nivel del aceite?
[el nibél del aθéjte]

the tyre pressure?
la presión de los neumáticos?
[la presjón de los neumátikos]

the water in the battery?
el agua de la batería?
[el ágwa de la batería]

the water in the radiator?
el agua del radiador?
[el ágwa del rradjadór]

Can you
¿Pueden
[pwéden]

charge the battery?
cargar la batería?
[kargár la batería]

clean the windows?
limpiar los cristales?
[limpjár los kristáles]

inflate the tyres (to the correct pressure)?
subir la presión en los neumáticos?
[subír la presijón en los neumátikos]

put in some oil?
poner aceite? *[ponér aθéjte]*

change the oil?
cambiar el aceite?
[kambjár el aθéjte]

▶ **SERVICE STATION**

Could you
  ¿Podrían
  [podrían]

wash my car?
lavar el coche? *[labár el kótche]*

oil the door locks?
engrasar las cerraduras?
[engrasár las θerradúras]

clean the air filter?
limpiar el filtro de aire?
[limpjár el fíltro de áire]

clean the plugs?
limpiar las bujías?
[limpjár las buxías]

change the air filter?
cambiar el filtro de aceite?
[kambjár el fíltro de aθéite]

▶ **WORKSHOP**

Where is there
  ¿Dónde hay (por aquí)
  [dónde ai por akí]

a garage near here?
un taller de reparaciones?
[un taljér de rreparaθjónes]

a towing service?
un servicio de remolque?
[un serbíθjo de rremólke]

My car has broken down
Mi coche está averiado *[mi kótche está aberjádo]*

Can you
  ¿Pueden
  [pwéden]

get it to a workshop?
llevarlo a un taller?
[ljebárlo a un taljér]

repair it here?
repararlo aquí? *[rreparárlo akí]*

I am
  Estoy
  [estói]

on the dual-carriageway to (Castelldefels)
en la autovía de (Castelldefels)
[en la autobía de (kasteljdeféls)]

at km 17 on the way to Sitges
en el kilómetro diecisiete dirección a Sitges
[en el kilómetro djeθisjéte direkθjón a (sítches)]

I am	between Gavá and La Pineda
Estoy	**entre (Gavá) y (La Pineda)**
[estói]	*[éntre (gabá) i (la pinéda)]*

on the A-17 at km 214
en la A diecisiete, km 214
[en la a djeθisjéte kilómetro dosθjéntos katórθe]

on the road from Sitges to Villanueva
en la carretera de Sitges a Villanueva
[en la karretéra de sítches a biljanwéba]

I have a dark red Renault "Mégane" with an English numberplate
Tengo un Renault "Megane" rojo oscuro con matrícula inglesa
[téngo un rrenól megáne rróxo oskúro kon matríkula inglésa]

The registration number is: F 47813 BE
La matrícula es: efe cuatro, siete, ocho, uno, tres, be, e
[la matríkula es éfe kwátro sjéte ótcho úno tres be e]

SYMPTOMS OF BREAK DOWN

The lights won't dip
No funcionan las luces de cruce
[no funθjónan las lúθes de krúθe]

The starter motor doesn't work
No funciona el motor de arranque
[no funθjóna el motór de arránke]

The indicators don't work
Los intermitentes no funcionan *[los intermiténtes no funθjónan]*

The brake is weak
El freno está flojo *[el fréno está flóxo]*

The brake-lights don't work
No funcionan las luces de freno
[no funθjónan las lúθes de fréno]

It jumps out of gear
El cambio de marchas salta *[el kámbjo de mártchas sálta]*

The bodywork is rattling
La carrocería hace ruido *[la karroθería áθe rrwído]*

The radiator is losing water
El radiador pierde agua *[el rradjadór pjérde ágwa]*

The engine	is backfiring
El motor	**hace falsas explosiones** *[áθe fálsas eksplosjónes]*
[el motór]	

hasn't any power
no tiene potencia *[no tjéne poténθja]*

is overheating
se calienta mucho *[se kaljénta mútcho]*

is losing oil
pierde aceite *[pjérde aθéjte]*

is making a strange noise
hace un ruido raro *[áθe un rrwído rráro]*

There is smoke coming out of the engine
El motor despide humo *[el motór despíde úmo]*

The lock is broken
La cerradura está estropeada *[la θerradúra está estropeáda]*

The steering is vibrating
La dirección vibra *[la direkθjón bíbra]*

The door makes a noise
La puerta hace ruido *[la puérta áθe rrwído]*

It smells of petrol inside the car
Dentro del coche huele a gasolina
[déntro del kótche wéle a gasolína]

The car won't start up
El coche no se pone en marcha
[el kótche no se póne en mártcha)

The water in the radiator is boiling
Hierve el agua del radiador *[jérbe el ágwa del rradjadór]*

I have a puncture
Tengo una rueda pinchada *[téngo una rrwéda pintcháda]*

Please, check	the battery
Revise	**la batería** *[la batería]*
[rrebíse]	

the brakes
los frenos *[los frénos]*

the points
los platinos *[los platínos]*

Please, check
Revise
[rrebíse]

the steering
la dirección *[la direkθjón]*

the dynamo
la dinamo *[la dinámo]*

the engine
el motor *[el motór]*

the electrical system
el circuito eléctrico *[el θirkwíto eléktriko]*

gear box
el cambio *[el kámbjo]*

the shock absorbers
los amortiguadores *[los amortigwadóres]*

the carburettor
el carburador *[el karburadór]*

the distributor cap
la tapa del delco *[la tápa del délko]*

the plugs
las bujías *[las buxías]*

the ignition coil
la bobina de encendido
[la bobína de enθendído]

Can you
¿Pueden
[pwéden]

adjust the carburettor?
ajustar el carburador?
[áθér rregláxe del karburadór]

change the plugs?
cambiar las bujías? *[kambjár las buxías]*

change the fan-belt?
cambiar la correa del ventilador?
[kambjár la korréa del bentiladór]

change this tyre?
cambiar este neumático?
[kambjár éste neumátiko]

repair this tyre?
reparar este neumático?
[rreparár éste neumátiko]

Can you **¿Pueden** *[pwéden]*	repair the exhaust pipe? **reparar el tubo de escape?** *[rreparár el túbo de eskápe]* fit a new exhaust pipe? **poner un nuevo tubo de escape?** *[ponér un nwébo túbo de eskápe]*

Can you order this (these) spare part(s)?
¿Puede pedir esta(s) pieza(s)? *[pwéde pedír ésta pjéθa]*

When will you receive this (these) part(s)?
¿Cuándo tendrá la(s) pieza(s)? *[kwándo tendrá la pjéθa]*

How long will the repair take?
¿Cuánto tiempo tarda en reparar el coche?
[kwánto tjémpo tárda en rreparár el kótche]

How much will the spare part(s) cost?
¿Cuánto vale(n) la(s) pieza(s)? *[kwánto bále la pjéθa]*

Is the car ready?
¿Está el coche listo? *[está el kótche lísto]*

Make me out a detailed bill.
Prepárenme una factura detallada
[prepárenme úna faktúra detaljada]

■ ACCOMMODATION

▶ HOTEL

I am looking for **Estoy buscando** *[estói buskándo]*	a three (four)-star hotel **algún hotel de tres (cuatro) estrellas** *[algún otél de tres (kwátro) estréljas]* a luxury hotel **algún hotel de lujo** *[algún otél de lúxo]* a cheap hotel **algún hotel sencillo** *[algún otél senθíljo]* a "parador nacional" **un parador nacional** *[un paradór naθjonál]* a boarding house **una pensión** *[úna pensjón]*

How can I get | there?
¿Cómo llego | **allí?** *[aljí]*
[kómo ljégo]

to the (Plaza) hotel?
al hotel (Plaza)? *[al otél (pláθa)]*

to this boarding house?
a esta pensión? *[a ésta pensjón]*

Where is the reception, please?
¿Dónde está la recepción, por favor?
[dónde está la rreθepθjón por fabór]

Do you speak English?
¿Habla Vd. inglés? *[ábla ustéd inglés]*

My name is...
Me llamo... *[me ljámo]*

I have reserved one (two) room(s)
Tengo una (dos) habitación (habitaciones) reservada(s)
[téngo úna abitaθjón rreserbáda]

I made the reservation | ...by phone
Hice una reserva | **... por teléfono**
[íθe úna rresérba] | *[por teléfono]*

... by fax
... por fax *[por faks]*

... by mail
... por carta *[por kárta]*

... at the "Touropa"
travel agency
**... por la agencia de viajes
"Touropa"**
[por la axénθja de bjáxes turópa]

Here is | the confirmation
Aquí está | **la confirmación** *[la confirmaθjón]*
[akí está]
the voucher
el cupón de hotel *[el kupón de otél]*

Do you have any rooms free?
¿Tienen alguna habitación libre?
[tjénen algúna abitaθjón líbre]

I want	a room
Deseo	**una habitación** *[úna abitaθjón]*
[deséo]	

(two) rooms
(dos) habitaciones *[(dos) abitaθjónes]*

a single room
una habitación individual *[úna abitaθjón indibidwál]*

a double room
una habitación doble *[úna abitaθjón dóble]*

a suite
una suite *[úna swít]*

a room with a bathroom
una habitación con baño *[úna abitaθjón kon bánjo]*

a room with a balcony
una habitación con terraza
[úna abitaθjón kon terráθa]

a room with a sea view
una habitación con vista al mar
[úna abitaθjón kon bísta al mar]

I want	the room only
Quisiera	**sólo la habitación** *[sólo la abitaθjón]*
[kisjéra]	

bed and breakfast
la habitación con desayuno
[la abitaθjón kon desajúno]

half board
media pensión *[médja pensjón]*

full board
pensión completa *[pensjón kompléta]*

How much is	the room	
¿Cuánto vale	**la habitación** *[la abitaθjón]*	
[kwánto bále]		

bed and breakfast
la habitación con desayuno
[la abitaθjón kon desajúno]

half board per person and	per day?
la media pensión por persona y	**por día?**
[la médja pensjón por persóna i]	*[por día]*

How much is | full board per person and |
¿Cuánto vale | **la pensión completa** | per day?
[kwánto bále] | **por persona y** | **por día?**
 | *[la pensjón kompléta por persóna i]* | *[por día]*

Can you show me the room(s)?
¿Puede enseñarme la(s) habitación (habitaciones)?
[pwéde ensenjárme la abitaθjón]

It is very | small
Es muy | **pequeña** *[pekénja]*
[es mui] |
 | dark
 | **oscura** *[oskúra]*

Haven't you | a bigger one?
¿Tienen alguna | **más grande?** *[mas gránde]*
[tjénen algúna] |
 | a cheaper one?
 | **más barata?** *[mas baráta]*
 |
 | a quieter one?
 | **más tranquila?** *[mas trankíla]*
 |
 | one with more light?
 | **más luminosa?** *[mas luminósa]*

I like this room
La habitación me gusta *[la abitaθjón me gústa]*

I don't like this room
La habitación no me gusta *[la abitaθjón no me gústa]*

I will take it
Me la quedo *[me la kédo]*

I won't take it
No me la quedo *[no me la kédo]*

I will stay | one night
Me quedaré | **una noche**
[me kedaré] | *[úna nótche]*
 | a few days
 | **unos días** *[únos días]*
 |
 | (3) weeks
 | **(tres) semanas**
 | *[(tres) semánas]*

I will stay	until next Sunday
Me quedaré	**hasta el próximo (domingo)**
[me kedaré]	*[ásta el próksimo (domíngo)]*

	until the (20th of July)
	hasta el (veinte de julio)
	[ásta el (béinte de xúljo)]

Can you send up my cases?
¿Pueden llevarme el equipaje a la habitación?
[pwéden ljebárme el ekipáxe a la abitaθjón]

Do you have any parking facilities?
¿Tienen parking?
[tjénen párking]

What is the number of my room?
¿Qué número de habitación tengo?
[ke número de abitaθjón téngo]

Can you give me the key to the room?
¿Puede darme la llave de la habitación?
[pwéde dárme la ljábe de la abitaθjón]

Can you return my passport?
¿Puede devolverme el pasaporte?
[pwéde debolbérme el pasapórte]

Where is there	a tobacconist's?
¿Dónde hay	**un estanco?** *[un estánko]*
[dónde ai]	

	a letter box?
	un buzón? *[un buθón]*

	a hairdresser's?
	una peluquería? *[úna pelukería]*

Where is (are)	the dining room?
¿Dónde está	**el comedor?** *[el komedór]*
[dónde está]	

	the swimming pool?
	la piscina? *[la pisθína]*

	the restaurant?
	el restaurante?
	[el rrestawránte]

	the toilets?
	el lavabo? *[el labábo]*

Where is | the bar?
¿Dónde está | **el bar?**
[dónde está] | *[el bar]*

What time do you serve | breakfast?
¿A qué hora sirven | **el desayuno?** *[el desajúno]*
[a ke óra sírben] |
| lunch?
| **la comida del mediodía?**
| *[la komída del medjodía]*
|
| dinner?
| **la cena?** *[la θéna]*

Can you connect me with | room number (208)?
¿Puede ponerme con | **la habitación (doscientos ocho)?**
[pwéde ponérme kon] | *[la abitaθjón dosθjéntos ótcho]*
|
| number (...)
| of Barcelona ...
| **el (...) de Barcelona?**
| *[el (...) de barθelóna]*
|
| England?
| **Inglaterra?**
| *[inglatérra]*

Can you | clean my shoes?
¿Pueden | **limpiarme los zapatos?**
[pwéden] | *[limpjárme los θapátos]*
|
| wash some shirts for me?
| **lavarme algunas camisas?**
| *[labárme algúnas kamísas]*
|
| clean a suit for me?
| **limpiarme un traje?**
| *[limpjárme un tráxe]*
|
| iron these clothes?
| **plancharme esta ropa?**
| *[plantchárme ésta rrópa]*
|
| serve breakfast
| in my room?
| **servirme el desayuno**
| **en la habitación?**
| *[serbírme el desajúno*
| *en la abitaθjón]*

Can you	wake me tomorrow morning at seven o'clock?
¿Pueden	**despertarme a las siete**
[puéden]	**de la mañana?**
	[despertárme a las sjéte
	de la manjána]

I have to leave at once.
Debo marcharme en seguida
[débo martchárme en segída]

I shall be leaving tomorrow morning
Voy a marcharme mañana por la mañana
[boi a martchárme manjána por la manjána]

Get my bill ready, please
Prepárenme la factura, por favor
[prepárenme la faktúra por fabór]

Call a taxi for me
Llámenme un taxi *[ljámenme un táksi]*

I want a taxi for (three) o'clock
Quisiera un taxi para las (tres) *[kisjéra un táksi pára las (tres)]*

Can you bring my cases down?
¿Pueden bajar las maletas? *[puéden baxár las malétas]*

▶ **APARTMENTS**

Do you have any apartments free?
¿Tienen algún apartamento libre?
[tjénen algún apartaménto líbre]

I want an apartment	for (4) persons
Quisiera un apartamento	**para (cuatro) personas**
[kisjéra un apartaménto]	*[pára (kwátro) persónas]*
	with (3) bedrooms
	con (tres) dormitorios
	[kon (tres) dormitórjos]
	with a separate kitchen
	con cocina por separado
	[kon koθína por separádo]
	with a large balcony
	con una terraza grande
	[kon úna terráθa gránde]

I want an apartment
    Quisiera un apartamento
    [kisjéra un apartaménto]

near the beach
en la playa *[en la plája]*

near the sea
en primera línea del mar
[en priméra línea del mar]

How much is it?
    ¿Qué precio tiene?
    [ke préθjo tjéne]

How much is the deposit?
    ¿Cuánto tengo que dejar como depósito?
    [kwánto téngo ke dexár kómo depósito]

I want it
    Lo quiero
    [lo kjéro]

for one week
para una semana *[pára úna semána]*

for two (three) weeks
para dos (tres) semanas *[pára dos semánas]*

for one month
para un mes *[pára un mes]*

until the (15th of August)
hasta el (quince de agosto)
[ásta el (kínθe de agósto)]

Do you have
    ¿Tienen
    [tjénen]

a restaurant?
restaurante? *[un rrestauránte]*

a bar?
bar? *[un bar]*

a coffee bar?
cafetería? *[kafetería]*

a swimming pool?
piscina? *[pisθína]*

Where can I
    ¿Dónde se puede
    [dónde se pwéde]

have breakfast?
desayunar? *[desajunár]*

eat well?
comer bien? *[komér bien]*

eat for a reasonable price?
comer a un precio razonable?
[komér a un préθjo rraθonáble]

Where is there
¿Dónde hay por aquí
[dónde ai por akí]

a supermarket?
un supermercado? [un supermerkádo]

a butcher's?
una carnicería? [úna karniθería]

a baker's?
una panadería? [una panadería]

■ SIGHTSEEING

How can I get
¿Por dónde se va
[por dónde se ba]

to the centre of the city?
al centro de la ciudad?
[al θéntro de la θjudád]

to...?
a ...? [a]

I want to go
Deseo ir
[deséo ir]

to the Town Hall
al ayuntamiento
[al ajuntamjénto]

to the cathedral
a la catedral [a la katedrál]

to the (Prado) Museum
al museo del Prado
[al muséo del prádo]

to the harbour
al puerto [al pwérto]

to the central station
a la estación central
[a la estaθjón θentrál]

What
¿Qué
[ke]

bus ...
autobús ... [autobús]

underground line...
metro ... [métro]

tram ...
tranvía ... [trambía]

train ....
tren ...
[tren]

... must I take?
... he de tomár?
[e de tomár]

Where is the
¿Dónde está el
[dónde está el]

monument to...?
monumento a ...? *[monuménto a]*

... building?
edificio de ...? *[edifíθjo de]*

(Picasso) museum?
museo de (Picasso)? *[muséo de (pikáso)]*

(Goya) theatre?
teatro (Goya)? *[teátro (gója)]*

Where are
¿Dónde están
[dónde están]

the department stores?
los grandes almacenes?
[los grándes almaθénes]

the typical restaurants?
los restaurantes típicos?
[los rrestaurántes típikos]

Can you show me on the map?
¿Puede enseñármelo en el plano?
[pwéde ensenjármelo en el pláno]

How far is it?
¿A qué distancia está de aquí?
[a ke distánθja está de akí]

What time do
**¿A qué hora abren
(cierran)**
[a ke óra ábren (θjérran)]

the museums ...
los museos?
[los muséos]

the shops ...
los comercios?
[los komérθjos]

the banks ...
los bancos?
[los bánkos]

... open (close)?

I have got lost
Me he perdido
[me e perdído]

Where are we?
¿Dónde estámos aquí?
[dónde estámos akí]

SHOPPING

■ GENERAL EXPRESSIONS

Where is there
¿Dónde hay (por aquí)
[dónde ai (por akí)]

Is there
¿Hay por aquí
[ai por akí]

an antique shop?
una tienda de antigüedades?
[úna tjénda de antigwedádes]

a bookshop?
una librería?
[úna librería]

a baker's?
una panadería? [úna panadería]

a butcher's?
una carnicería? [úna karniθería]

a cake shop?
una pastelería?
[úna pastelería]

a chemist's?
una farmacia? [úna farmáθja]

a childrens-wear shop?
una tienda de ropa infantil?
[úna tjénda de rrópa infantíl]

a delicatessen shop?
una charcutería?
[úna tcharkutería]

a department store?
unos grandes almacenes?
[únòs grándes almaθénes]

a draper's?
una tienda de lencería?
[úna tjénda de lenθería]

a boutique?
una tienda de modas?
[úna tjénda de módas]

a fishmonger's?
una pescadería?
[úna peskadería]

Where is there
¿Dónde hay (por aquí)
[dónde ai (por akí)]

Is there
¿Hay por aquí
[ai por akí]

a florist's?
una floristería?
[úna floristería]

a grocer's?
un colmado? [un kolmádo]
una tienda de ultramarinos?
[úna tjénda de ultramarínos]

a footwear shop?
una zapatería? [úna θapatería]

a fruit shop?
una frutería? [úna frutería]

a furrier's?
una peletería?
[úna peletería]

a greengrocer's
una verdulería? [úna berdulería]

a hardware and kitchen shop?
una tienda de menaje?
[úna tjénda de menáxe]

a hardware store?
una ferretería? [úna ferretería]

a hat shop?
una sombrerería?
[úna sombrerería]

a home textiles' shop?
una tienda de artículos del hogar?
[úna tjénda de artíkulos del ogár]

a household goods shop?
una droguería?
[úna drogería]

an imitation jewellery shop?
una bisutería? [úna bisutería]

a jeweller's?
una joyería? [úna xojería]

Where is there
¿Dónde hay (por aquí)
[dónde ai (por akí)]

Is there
¿Hay por aquí
[ai por akí]

a leather goods shop?
una tienda de artículos de piel?
[úna tjénda de artíkulos de pjél]

a market?
un mercado?
[un merkádo]

a music shop?
una tienda de música?
[úna tjénda de músika]

a haberdashery?
una mercería? *[úna merθería]*

a newspaper kiosk?
un quiosco de periódicos?
[un kjósko de perjódikos]

a gentlemen's outfitter's?
una tienda de confección para caballeros?
[úna tjénda de konfekθjón pára kabaljéros]

a perfume shop?
una perfumería?
[úna perfumería]

a photografic equipment shop?
una tienda de material fotográfico?
[úna tjénda de materjál fotográfiko]

a pork butcher's?
una tocinería? *[úna toθinería]*

a poultry shop?
una pollería? *[úna poljería]*

a gift shop?
una tienda de objetos de regalo?
[úna tjénda de obxétos de rregálo]

a ready-to-wear clothes shop for ladies
una tienda de confección para señoras?
[úna tjénda de konfekθjón pára senjóras]

Where is there
¿Dónde hay (por aquí)
[dónde ai (por akí)]

Is there
¿Hay por aquí
[ai por akí]

a record shop?
una tienda de discos?
[úna tjénda de dískos]

a shirt shop?
una camisería?
[úna kamisería]

a souvenir shop?
una tienda de recuerdos?
[úna tjénda de rrekwérdos]

a sports shop?
una tienda de deportes?
[úna tjénda de depórtes]

a stationer's?
una papelería? *[úna papelería]*

a supermarket?
un supermercado?
[un supermerkádo]

a tobacconist's?
un estanco? *[un estánko]*

a watchmaker's?
una relojería? *[úna rreloxería]*

a wine and spirits shop?
una bodega? *[úna bodéga]*
una tienda de vinos y licores?
[úna tjénda de bínos i likóres]

Where is there a good shop for...?
¿Dónde hay (por aquí) una buena tienda de ... ?
[dónde ai (por akí) úna bwéna tjénda de]

Where can I find... ?
¿Dónde encuentro ... ? *[dónde enkwéntro]*

Have you got... ?
¿Tienen (Vds.) ... ? *[tjénen (ustédes)]*

I want...
Quisiera ... *[kisjéra]*

Give me...
   Déme ... *[déme]*
   Póngame ... *[póngame]*

Could you show it to me, please?
   ¿Puede enseñármelo(la), por favor?
   [puéde ensenjármelo por fabór]

I want	to change this
Quisiera	**cambiarlo(la)** *[kambjárlo]*
[kisjéra]	
	to return this
	devolverlo(la) *[debolbérlo]*
	you to alter it
	hacerlo(la) arreglar *[aθérlo arreglár]*

When can I pick it up?
   ¿Cuándo puedo recogerlo(a)? *[kuándo puédo rrekoxérlo]*

■ AT THE CHEMIST'S

Where is there a duty chemist's?
   ¿Dónde hay una farmacia de guardia?
   [dónde ai úna farmáθja de guárdja]

I want some medicine for	hay fever
Quisiera algo contra	**la alergia?** *[la alérxja]*
[kisjéra álgo kóntra]	
	diarrhoeal
Have you got something for	**la diarrea?** *[la djarréa]*
¿Tienen algo contra	
[tjénen álgo kóntra]	influenza?
	la gripe? *[la grípe]*
	a sore throat?
	el dolor de garganta?
	[el dolór de gargánta]
	a cough?
	la tos? *[la tos]*
	a headache?
	el dolor de cabeza? *[el dolór de kabéθa]*
	stomachache?
	el dolor de estómago?
	[el dolór de estómago]

Have you got something for
   ¿Tienen algo contra
   [tjénen álgo kóntra]

nettle-rash?
   la urticaria?
   [la urtikárja]

Give me
   Déme
   [déme]

a tranquilizer
un calmante *[un kalmánte]*

some aspirins
aspirinas *[aspirínas]*

some contraceptive pills
píldoras anticonceptivas
[píldoras antikonθeptíbas]

an antacid
un antiácido *[un antiáθido]*

some sleeping tablets
algo contra el insomnio
[álgo kóntra el insómnjo]

something for a toothache
algo contra el dolor de muelas
[álgo kóntra el dolór de mwélas]

Can you give me an injection?
   ¿Pueden ponerme una inyección?
   [pwéden ponérme úna injekθjón]

I am allergic to
   Soy alérgico(a)
   [soi alérxiko]

penicillin
a la penicilina *[a la péniθilína]*

antibiotics
a los antibióticos *[a los antibjótikos]*

sulphamides
a las sulfamidas *[a las sulfamídas]*

I suffer from diabetes
   Soy diabético(a)
   [soi djabétiko]

I have heart trouble
   Tengo problemas cardíacos
   [téngo problémas kardíakos]

I have circulatory trouble
   Tengo problemas de circulación
   [téngo problémas de θirkulaθjón]

Could you take my blood pressure?
¿Puede tomarme la tensión?
[pwéde tomárme la tensjón]

I have no prescription
No tengo receta
[no téngo rreθéta]

How must I take this medicine?
¿Cómo he de tomar este medicamento?
[kómo e de tomár éste medikaménto]

How many times a day?
¿Cuántas veces al día?
[kwántas béθes al día]

How many	tablets...	
¿Cuántas	**pastillas ...**	
[kwántas]	*[pastíljas]*	
	drops...	
	gotas ...	
	[gótas]	
	injections...	... must I take?
	inyecciones ...	**... he de tomar?**
	[injekθjónes]	*[e de tomár]*

AT THE BREAD SHOP

I want	half a kilo loaf
Quisiera	**una barra de (medio) kilo**
[kisjéra]	*[úna bárra de (médjo) kílo]*
Give me	(2) quarter-kilo loaves
Déme	**(dos) barras de cuarto**
[déme]	*[(dos) bárras de kwárto]*
	a round loaf
	un pan redondo
	[un pan rredóndo]
	a packet of English bread
	un paquete de pan inglés
	[un pakéte de pan inglés]
	a sliced loaf
	un pan de molde *[un pan de mólde]*

I want	(5) bread rolls
Deseo	**(cinco) panecillos**
[deséo]	*[(θínko) paneθíljos]*

(2) brioches
(dos) brioches
[(dos) brjóches]

(3) croissants
(tres) croissants
[(tres) krwasánts]

(4) spiral pastries (from Majorca)
(cuatro) ensaimadas
[(kwátro) ensaimádas]

Have you got	any wholemeal bread?
¿Tienen Vds.	**pan integral?** *[pan integrál]*
[tjénen ustédes]	

any toasted bread?
pan tostado? *[pan tostádo]*

any melba toast?
biscotes? *[biskótes]*

any flour?
harina? *[arína]*

any breadcrumbs?
pan rallado? *[pan rraljádo]*

I don't want it baked too much
No lo quisiera muy cocido
[no lo kisjéra mui koθído]

I want it	well baked.
Lo quisiera	**bien cocido** *[bien koθído]*
[lo kisjéra]	

sliced
cortado *[kortádo]*

Give me	one
Déme	**uno(a)** *[úno]*
[déme]	

one bag
una bolsa *[úna bólsa]*

one portion
una ración *[úna rraθjón]*

CLOTHING FOR LADIES AND GENTLEMEN

Can you show me	a dress ...	
¿Puede enseñarme	**un vestido ...**	
[pwéde ensenjárme]	*[un bestído]*	
	a skirt ...	
	una falda ...	
	[úna fálda]	
	a blouse ...	
	una blusa ...	
	[úna blúsa]	
	a suit ...	... in the window?
	un traje ...	**... del escaparate?**
	[un tráxe]	*[del eskaparáte]*

I want   a suit
Quisiera   **un traje** *[un tráxe]*
[kisjéra]

a jacket suit
un traje chaqueta *[un tráxe tchakéta]*

a trouser suit
un traje pantalón *[un tráxe pantalón]*

a jacket
una americana *[úna amerikána]*

a pair of trousers
un pantalón *[un pantalón]*

some shirts
algunas camisas *[algúnas kamísas]*

I am size (48)
Uso la talla (cuarenta y ocho)
[úso la tálja (kwarénta i ótcho)]

Can you take my measurements?
¿Puede tomarme las medidas? *[pwéde tomárme las medídas]*

I want to try it on
Deseo probármelo *[deséo probármelo]*

Where is there a fitting room?
¿Dónde hay un probador? *[dónde ai un probadór]*

I (don't) like it
(No) me gusta
[(no) me gústa]

I (don't) like | this colour
(No) me gusta | **este color**
[(no) me gústa] | *[éste kolór]*

| this material
| **esta tela**
| *[ésta téla]*

| this cut
| **este corte**
| *[éste kórte]*

Do you have | it in another colour?
¿No tienen | **otro color?** *[ótro kolór]*
[no tjénen] |

| another model?
| **otro modelo?** *[ótro modélo]*

| it in another material?
| **otro tipo de tela?** *[ótro típo de téla]*

I want it in | cotton
Lo (la) quiero de | **algodón** *[algodón]*
[lo (la) kjéro de] |

| pure wool
| **pura lana** *[púra lána]*

| silk
| **seda** *[séda]*

| linen
| **lino** *[líno]*

I don't want any artificial fibre
No quiero fibra sintética
[no kjéro fíbra sintétika]

It is very | big
Es muy | **grande** *[gránde]*
[es mui] |

| short
| **corto(a)** *[kórto]*

| tight (here)
| **estrecho(a) (aquí)** *[estrétcho (akí)]*

It is very
Es muy
[es mui]

wide (here)
ancho(a) (aquí) *[ántcho (akí)]*

long
largo(a) *[lárgo]*

The sleeves (legs) are too
Las mangas (piernas) son demasiado
[las mángas (pjérnas) son demasjádo]

short
cortas *[kórtas]*

long
largas *[lárgas]*

narrow
estrechas
[estrétchas]

wide
anchas *[ántchas]*

Can you
¿Pueden
[pwéden]

alter it for me ...
arreglármelo ...
[arreglármelo]

take it in ...
estrecharlo ...
[estretchárlo]

let it out ...
ensancharlo ...
[ensantchárlo]

shorten it ...
acortarlo ...
[akortárlo]

... here?
... aquí?
[akí]

How long will it take?
¿Cuánto tiempo tardarán?
[kwánto tjémpo tardarán]

Can I
Puedo
[pwédo]

wash it?
lavarlo (la)?
[labárlo]

iron it?
plancharlo (la)? *[plantchárlo]*

Do I have to take it to the dry cleaner's?
¿Hay que llevarlo (la) a la tintorería?
[ai ke ljebárlo a la tintorería]

▶ **MADE TO MEASURE**

I want	a suit ...	
Deseo	**un traje ...**	
[deséo]	*[un tráxe]*	

a pair of trousers ...
unos pantalones ...
[únos pantalónes]

a jacket ...
una americana ...
[úna amerikána]

a trouser suit ...
un traje pantalón ...
[un tráxe pantalón]

a jacket suit ...	... made to measure
un traje chaqueta ...	**... a medida**
[un tráxe tchakéta]	*[a medída]*

Can you show me samples of material?
¿Puede enseñarme muestras de tela?
[pwéde ensenjárme mwéstras de téla]

I want	cotton
Quisiera	**algodón** *[algodón]*
[kisjéra]	

silk
seda natural *[séda naturál]*

pure wool
pura lana *[púra lána]*

linen
lino *[líno]*

It doesn't matter if it contains artificial fibres
No importa que tenga fibra sintética
[no impórta ke ténga fíbra sintétika]

I would like to show you a fabric in the shop window.
Quisiera enseñarle una tela del escaparate
[kisjéra ensenjárle úna téla del eskaparáte]

Can you take my measurements?
¿Puede tomarme las medidas? *[pwéde tomárme las medídas]*

When is the first fitting?
¿Cuándo será la primera prueba?
[kwándo será la priméra prwéba]

When will it be ready?
¿Cuándo estará listo(a)? *[kwándo estará lísto]*

Should I leave a deposit?
¿Qué señal he de dejar? *[ke pága y senjál e de dexár]*

AT THE FISHMONGER'S

I want **Quisiera** *[kisjéra]*	(one) kilo of sardines **(un) kilo de sardinas** *[(un) kílo de sardínas]*
Give me **Póngame** *[póngame]*	(half) a kilo of prawns **(medio) kilo de gambas** *[(médjo) kílo de gámbas]*
	a gilthead bream **una dorada** *[úna doráda]*
	(8) fillets of sole **(ocho) filetes de lenguado** *[(ótcho) filétes de lengwádo]*
	one (two) dozen oysters **una (dos) docena(s) de ostras** *[úna doθéna de óstras]*
Have you got **¿Tienen** *[tjénen]*	any fresh fish? **pescado fresco?** *[peskádo frésko]*
	any fresh seafood? **mariscos frescos?** *[marískos fréskos]*
	any frozen fish? **pescado congelado?** *[peskádo konxeládo]*
	any frozen seafood? **mariscos congelados?** *[marískos konxeládos]*
I want it **Lo (la) quisiera** *[lo kisjéra]*	fresh **fresco(a)** *[frésko]*
	sliced **en rodajas** *[en rrodáxas]*

I want it
Lo (la) quisiera
[lo kisjéra]

in one piece
entero(a) [entéro]

as fillets
en filetes [en filétes]

for frying
para freír [pára freír]

for baking (in the oven)
para el horno [pára el órno]

for the grill
para la plancha [pára la plántcha]

for frying in breadcrumbs
para rebozar [pára rreboθár]

fresh today
de hoy [de oi]

Can you
¿Puede
[pwéde]

clean it for me?
limpiarlo(la)?
[limpjárlo]

take the scales off?
quitar las escamas?
[kitár las eskámas]

cut it into slices?
cortarlo(la) en rodajas?
[kortárlo en rrodáxas]

cut it into fillets?
cortarlo(la) en filetes?
[kortárlo en filétes]

■ AT THE POULTRY SHOP

Give me
Póngame
[póngame]

a whole chicken
un pollo (entero) [un póljo (entéro)]

I want
Quisiera
[kisjéra]

a quartered chicken
un pollo (cortado) en cuartos
(un póljo (kortádo) en kwártos]

half a chicken
medio pollo [médjo póljo]

I want **Quisiera** *[kisjéra]*	(two) legs of chicken (turkey) **(dos) muslos de pollo (pavo)** *[(dos) múslos de póljo (pábo)]*
	(three) breasts **(tres) pechugas** *[(tres) petchúgas]*
	a chicken for stewing **un pollo para estofar** *[un póljo pára estofár]*
	(one) kilo of turkey fillets **(un) kilo de filetes de pavo** *[(un) kílo de filétes de pábo]*
Have you **Tienen** *[tjénen]*	any fresh eggs? **huevos frescos?** *[wébos fréskos]*
	any partridges? **codornices?** *[kodorníθes]*
I want to order **Quisiera encargar** *[kisjéra enkargár]*	a rabbit **un conejo** *[un konéxo]*
	a pheasant **un faisán** *[un faisán]*
	a duck **un pato** *[un páto]*
Can you **¿Puede** *[pwéde]*	clean it? **limpiarlo(a)?** *[limpjárlo]*
	take the bones out? **quitar los huesos?** *[kitár los wésos]*

■ AT THE DEPARTMENT STORES

Where is there **¿Hay (por) aquí** *[ai (por) akí]*	a department store? **unos grandes almacenes?** *[únos grándes almaθénes]*
	a hypermarket? **un hipermercado?** *[un ipermerkádo]*
	a shopping centre? **un centro comercial?** *[un θéntro komerθjál]*

Where is
¿Dónde está
[dónde está]

On which floor is
¿En qué planta está
[en ke plánta está]

the department for ...
el departamento de ...
[el departaménto de]

... baby articles?

... artículos para bebés?
[artíkulos pára bebés]

... beach goods?

... artículos de playa?
[artíkulos de plája]

... camping goods?

... artículos de camping?
[artíkulos de kámping]

... car accessories?

... accesorios de coche?
[akθesórjos de kótche]

... carpets?

... alfombras? [alfómbras]

... children's wear?

... ropa infantil [rrópa infantíl]

... cleaning materials?

... artículos de limpieza?
[artíkulos de limpjéθa]

... clocks?

... relojería? [rreloxería]

... cosmetics?

... cosméticos? [kosmétikos]

... household linen?

... ropa del hogar? [rrópa del ogár]

... electric cookers?

... cocinas eléctricas? [koθínas eléktrikas]

... electrical goods?

... material eléctrico?
[materjál eléktriko]

... electrical appliances?

... electrodomésticos?
[elektrodoméstikos]

... fabrics?

... tejidos? [texídos]

... foot-wear?

... calzado? [kalθádo]

... furniture?

...muebles? [mwébles]

... garden furniture?

... muebles de jardín?
[mwébles de xardín]

Where is
¿Dónde está
[dónde está]

On which floor is
¿En qué planta está
[en ke plánta está]

the department for ...
el departamento de ...
[el departaménto de]

... gardening materials? | **... jardinería?** [xardinería]

... gas cookers? | **... cocinas de gas?** [koθínas de gas]

... glassware? | **... cristalería?** [kristalería]

... hardware? | **... ferretería?** [ferretería]

... household goods? | **... menaje?** [menáxe]

... imitation jewellery? | **... bisutería?** [bisutería]

... jewellery? | **... joyería?** [xojería]

... kitchen furniture? | **... muebles de cocina?**
[mwébles de koθína]

... ladies wear? | **... confección para señoras?**
[konfekθjón pára senjóras]

... lamps? | **... lámparas?** [lámparas]

... leather clothing? | **... ropa de piel?** [rrópa de pjél]

... leatherware? | **... marroquinería?** [marrokinería]

... linen goods? | **... lencería?** [lenθería]

... mens' wear? | **... confección para caballeros?**
[konfekθjón pára kabaljéros]

... musical instruments? | **... instrumentos musicales?**
[instruméntos musikáles]

... perfumes? | **... perfumería?** [perfumería]

... photographic goods? | **... fotografía?** [fotografía]

... gifts? | **... objetos de regalo?** [obxétos de rregálo]

... records? | **... discos?** [dískos]

Where is
¿Dónde está
[dónde está]

On which floor is
¿En qué planta está
[en ke plánta está]

the department for ...
el departamento de ...
[el departaménto de]

... smoker's requisites?

... artículos de fumador?
[artíkulos de fumadór]

... souvenirs?

... recuerdos? *[rrekwérdos]*

... sports goods?

... artículos de deporte?
[artíkulos de depórte]

... toys?

... juguetería? *[xugetería]*

... travel goods?

... artículos de viaje? *[artíkulos de bjáxe]*

... underwear?

... ropa interior? *[rrópa interjór]*

... wall paper?

... papeles pintados? *[papéles pintádos]*

... stationery?

... papelería? *[papelería]*

Where is
¿Dónde está
[dónde está]

On which floor is
¿En qué planta está
[en ke plánta está]

the information desk?
el mostrador de información?
[el mostradór de informaθjón]

the coffee bar?
la cafetería?
[la kafetería]

the hairdresser's?
la peluquería de señoras?
[la pelukería de senjóras]

the barber's?
la peluquería de caballeros?
[la pelukería de kabaljéros]

the cash desk?
la caja?
[la káxa]

the customer services department?
el servicio de atención al cliente?
[el serbíθjo de atenθjón al kljénte]

On which floor is | the travel agency?
¿En qué planta está | **la agencia de viajes?**
[en ke plánta está] | *[la axénθja de bjáxes]*

Where is | the supermarket?
¿Dónde está | **el supermercado?** *[el supermerkádo]*
[dónde está] |

| there a telephone?
| **el teléfono?** *[el teléfono]*

| the toilet?
| **el lavabo?** *[el labábo]*

| the bureau de change?
| **el cambio de divisas?**
| *[el kambjo de dibísas]*

■ AT THE CAKE AND PASTRY SHOP

I want | something typical of these parts
Quisiera | **algo típico de aquí** *[álgo típiko de akí]*
[kisjéra] |

| a (quarter) of a kilo of tea biscuits
| **un (cuarto de) kilo de pastas de té**
| *[un (kwárto de) kílo de pástas de te]*

| (half) a kilo of assorted cakes
| **(medio) kilo de pasteles**
| *[(médjo) kílo de pastéles]*

| (one) kilo of buns
| **un kilo de lionesas** *[un kílo de ljonésas]*

Give me | (3) portions of this tart
Póngame | **(tres) raciones de esta tarta**
[póngame] | *[(tres) rraθjónes de ésta tárta]*

| (2) portions of apple tart
| **(dos) raciones de tarta de manzana**
| *[(dos) rraθjónes de tárta de manθána]*

| a portion of cheesecake
| **una ración de tarta de queso**
| *[úna rraθjón de tárta de késo]*

| a Swiss roll filled with cream
| **un brazo de gitano de nata**
| *[un bráθo de xitáno de náta]*

Give me	a Swiss roll filled with custard
Póngame	**un brazo de gitano de crema**
[póngame]	*[un bráθo de xitáno de kréma]*

I want	(2) portions of this cake
Deseo	**(dos) raciones de este pastel**
[deséo]	*[(dos) rraθjónes de éste pastél]*

(3) of these pastries
(tres) de estas pastas
[(tres) de éstas pástas]

Have you got	any croissants?
¿Tienen	**croissants?** *[krwasánts]*
[tjénen]	

any croissants with ham?
croissants con jamón? *[krwasánts con xamón]*

any croissants with cheese?
croissants con queso? *[krwasánts kon késo]*

any custard pastries?
alguna pasta de crema?
[algúna pásta de kréma]

■ AT THE FOOD SHOP

Have you got	any fresh eggs?
¿Tienen	**huevos frescos?** *[wébos fréskos]*
[tjénen]	

any cured ham?
jamón serrano? *[xamón serráno]*
jamón del país? *[xamón del país]*

any fruit?
fruta? *[frúta]*

any vegetables?
verdura? *[berdúra]*

any loaves of bread?
pan de molde? *[pan de mólde]*

any sunflower oil?
aceite de girasol? *[aθéite de xirasól]*

any cold meats?
embutidos? *[embutídos]*

I want
Quisiera
[kisjéra]

one litre of milk
un litro de leche
[un lítro de létche]

a bottle of vinegar
una botella de vinagre [úna botélja de binágre]

one litre of olive oil
un litro de aceite de oliva
[un lítro de aθéite de olíba]

(200) grams of dry (semi-dry, soft) Manchego
cheese
**(doscientos) gramos de queso manchego seco
(semiseco, tierno)** [(dosθjéntos) grámos de késo
mantchégo séko (semiséko, tjérno)]

a tin of lentils (beans, chickpeas)
un bote de lentejas (judías blancas, garbanzos)
[un bóte de lentéxas (xudías blánkas, garbánθos)]

a packet of rice (vermicelli, sugar, salt)
un paquete de arroz (fideos, azúcar, sal)
[un pakéte de arróθ (fidéos, aθúkar, sal)]

Give me
Déme
[déme]

one tin (two tins)
un bote (dos botes) [un bóte (dos bótes)]

one litre (two litres)
un litro (dos litros)
[un lítro (dos lítros)]

a dozen (two dozens)
una docena (dos docenas)
[úna doθéna (dos doθénas)]

half a dozen
media docena [médja doθéna]

one bottle (two bottles)
una botella (dos botellas)
[úna botélja (dos botéljas)]

one kilo (two kilos)
un kilo (dos kilos) [un kílo (dos kílos)]

about 250 grams
doscientos cincuenta gramos aproximadamente
[dosθjéntos θinkwénta grámos aproksimadaménte]

How much is it?
¿Cuánto le debo? *[kwánto le débo]*

Can you give me a plastic bag, please?
Déme una bolsa de plástico, por favor
[déme úna bólsa de plástiko, por fabór]

■ **BUTCHER'S**

Have you got any **¿Tienen** *[tjénen]*	veal? **carne de ternera?** *[kárne de ternéra]*
	mutton? **carne de cordero?** *[kárne de kordéro]*
	beef? **carne de buey?** *[kárne de bwei]*

| I want it **La quiero** *[la kjéro]* | for stewing
para estofar *[pára estofár]* |
| | for roasting
para asar *[pára asár]* |

How much is it a kilo?
¿Cuánto vale el kilo? *[kwánto bále el kílo]*

I want **Quisiera** *[kisjéra]*	(4) beefsteaks **(cuatro) bistecs** *[(kwátro) bistéks]*
	(2) pork loins **(dos) trozos de lomo** *[(dos) tróθos de lómo]*
	(3) sirloins (beef) **(tres) solomillos de buey** *[(tres) solomíljos de bwei]*
	(5) pieces of lean meat **(cinco) trozos de carne magra** *[(θínko) tróθos de kárne mágra]*
	(6) veal escalopes **(seis) escalopes de ternera** *[(séis) eskalópes de ternéra]*

| Give me **Déme** *[déme]* | one hamburger (of veal)
una hamburguesa (de ternera)
[úna amburgésa (de ternéra)] |

Give me **Déme** *[déme]*	(250) grams of minced veal **(doscientos cincuenta) gramos de carne** **picada de ternera** *[(dosθjéntos θinkwénta)* *grámos de kárne pikáda de ternéra]* a kilo of mutton chops **un kilo de chuletas de cordero** *[un kílo de tchulétas de kordéro]* a leg of mutton **una pierna de cordero** *[úna pjérna de kordéro]*
I want **Los (las) quiero** *[los kjéro]*	thick slices **gruesos(as)** *[grwésos]* thin slices **delgados(as)** *[delgádos]* it without fat **sin grasa** *[sin grása]* it without bones **sin huesos** *[sin wésos]*
I want **Quiero** *[kjéro]*	(500) grams of little sausages (for roasting) **(quinientos) gramos de salchichas del país** *[kinjéntos grámos de saltchítchas del país]* (200) grams of cured ham **(doscientos) gramos de jamón del país** *[(dosθjéntos) grámos de xamón del país]* (2) sausages for roasting **(dos) butifarras (crudas)** *[(dos) butifárras (krúdas)]* (300) grams of cooked ham **(trescientos) gramos de jamón en dulce** *[(tresθjéntos) grámos de xamón en dúlθe]* (150) grams of Salami (Spanish style) **(ciento cincuenta) gramos de salchichón** *[(θjénto θinkwénta) grámos de saltchitchón]*

■ **FRUIT AND VEGETABLES**

Give me **Póngame** *[póngame]*	a kilo of pears **un kilo de peras** *[un kílo de péras]*

Give me **Póngame** *[póngame]*	(2) kilos of green apples **(dos) kilos de manzanas verdes** *[(dos) kílos de manθánas bérdes]* one kilo of these oranges (tangerines) **un kilo de estas naranjas (mandarinas)** *[un kílo de éstas naránxas (mandarínas)]*
I want **Quisiera** *[kisjéra]*	some onions (potatoes) **cebollas (patatas)** *[θebóljas (patátas)]* a lettuce **una lechuga** *[úna letchúga]* (a kilo) of green tomatoes **un kilo de tomates verdes** *[un kílo de tomátes bérdes]* (half a kilo) of ripe tomatoes (for cooking) **(medio kilo de) tomates maduros** *[(médjo kílo de) tomátes madúros]*
I want **Quiero** *[kjéro]*	(3) medium sized cucumbers **(tres) pepinos medianos** *[(tres) pepínos medjános]* some haricot beans **judías verdes** *[xudías bérdes]* some fresh spinach **espinacas frescas** *[espinákas fréskas]* a cauliflower (cabbage) **una coliflor (col valenciana)** *[koliflór (kol balenθjána)]* some mixed herbs for the soup **un paquete de hierbas para la sopa** *[un pakéte de jérbas pára la sópa]*
I want it **Lo(la) quiero** *[lo kjéro]*	quite ripe **bastante maduro(a)** *[bastánte madúro]* not very ripe **no muy maduro(a)** *[no mui madúro]* a little green **algo verde** *[álgo bérde]*

I want them	quite ripe
Los(las) quiero	**bastante maduros(as)** *[bastánte madúros]*
[los kjéro]	

■ BOOKSHOP, STATIONER'S, KIOSK

I want	an English newspaper
Quisiera	**un periódico inglés** *[un perjódiko inglés]*
[kisjéra]	
	an American magazine
	una revista americana *[úna rrebísta amerikána]*
	a novel in English
	una novela en inglés *[úna nobéla en inglés]*

Do you have	any English newspapers?
¿Tienen	**periódicos ingleses?** *[perjódikos ingléses]*
[tjénen]	
	any American magazines?
	revistas americanas? *[rrebístas amerikánas]*
	the Washington Post?
	el diario The Washington Post? *[el djárjo]*
	the Time Magazine?
	la revista "Time"? *[la rrebísta]*
	any books in English?
	libros en inglés? *[líbros en inglés]*

Give me	this book
Déme	**este libro** *[éste líbro]*
[déme]	
	a Spanish grammar
	una gramática española
	[úna gramátika espanjóla]
	an English-Spanish dictionary
	un diccionario inglés-español
	[un dikθjonárjo inglés-espanjól]
	a Spanish course with tapes
	un curso de español con casetes
	[un kúrso de espanjól kon kasétes]
	a tourist guide in English
	una guía en inglés
	[úna gía en inglés]

Give me | a map of (Madrid)
Déme | **un plano de (Madrid)** *[un pláno de madríd]*
[déme] |

| a road map of Catalonia
| **un mapa de carreteras de Cataluña**
| *[un mápa de carretéras de katalúnja]*

| a road atlas (map) of Spain
| **un mapa de carreteras de España**
| *[un mápa de karretéras de espánja]*

I want some postcards | of this town
Quisiera postales | **de esta ciudad** *[de ésta θjudád]*
[kisjéra postáles] |

| with works of Gaudi (Picasso)
| **con temas de Gaudí (Picasso)**
| *[kon témas de gaudí (pikáso)]*

| of the old part of the town
| **del casco antíguo**
| *[del kásko antígwo]*

| of the cathedral
| **de la catedral** *[de la katedrál]*

Do you have stamps too?
¿Tienen sellos también?
[tjénen séljos tambjén]

Give me | a block of writing paper
Déme | **un bloc de papel de cartas**
[déme] | *[un blok de papél de kártas]*

| a notebook
| **un bloc de notas** *[un blok de nótas]*

| 100 sheets of typewriting paper
| **cien hojas de papel de máquina**
| *[θjén óxas de papél de mákina]*

| (10) envelopes
| **(diez) sobres** *[(djeθ) sóbres]*

| some adhesive tape
| **un rollo de cinta adhesiva**
| *[un rróljo de θínta adesíba]*

| a ball point pen
| **un bolígrafo** *[un bolígrafo]*

■ SUPERMARKET

As you can choose the goods yourself, it is not necessary to ask many questions.

Where is (are) **¿Dónde tienen** [dónde tjénen]	the coffee? **el café?** [el kafé]
	the sugar? **el azúcar?** [el aθúkar]
	the frozen food? **los congelados?** [los konxeládos]
	the bread? **el pan?** [el pan]
	the detergents (the cleaning products)? **los detergentes (los productos de limpieza)?** [los deterxéntes (los prodúktos de limpjéθa)]

Where is (are) **¿Dónde está** [dónde está]	the fruit? **la fruta?** [la frúta]
	the vegetables? **la verdura?** [la berdúra]
	the butcher's? **la carnicería?** [la karniθería]
	the milk? **la leche?** [la létche]

Have you got any **¿Tienen** [tjénen]	fresh fish? **pescado fresco?** [peskádo frésko]
	frozen fish? **pescado congelado?** [peskádo konxeládo]
	frozen fruit (vegetables)? **fruta (verdura) congelada?** [frúta (berdúra) konxeláda]
	quality wines? **vinos de marca?** [bínos de márka]
	cakes and pastries? **productos de pastelería?** [prodúktos de pastelería]

■ THE TOBACCONIST'S

At the tobacconist's (estancos) they sell tobacco, smokers' requisites, writing paper, postcards and stamps.

Where is there a tobacconist's ?
¿Dónde hay un estanco? *[dónde ai un estánko]*

I want a packet of **Quisiera un paquete de** *[kisjéra un pakéte de]*	(Winston) **(Winston)** (American) cigarettes **tabaco (americano)** *[tabáko (amerikáno)]* (black) cigarettes **tabaco (negro)** *[tabáko (négro)]*
Give me **Déme** *[déme]*	a carton of (Marlboro) **un cartón de (Marlboro)** *[un kartón de (Marlbóro)]* a box of (Havanna) cigars **una caja de puros habanos** *[úna káxa de púros abános]* a tin of pipe tobacco **una lata de tabaco de pipa** *[úna láta de tabáko de pípa]* a box of matches **una caja de cerillas** *[úna káxa de θeríljas]*
I want **Quisiera** *[kisjéra]*	a lighter **un encendedor** *[un enθendedór]* a refill for this lighter **una carga para este encendedor** *[úna kárga pára éste enθendedór]* a pipe **una pipa** *[úna pípa]*
Have you any postcards of **¿Tienen postales de** *[tjénen postáles de]*	the town? **la ciudad?** *[la θjudád]* the coast (seaside)? **la costa?** *[la kósta]*

Have you any postcards of
    ¿Tienen postales de
    [tjénen postáles de]

the monuments?
los monumentos artísticos?
[los muménntos artístikos]

the cathedral
la catedral? *[la katedrál]*

I need
    Necesito
    [neθesíto]

some writing paper
papel de cartas *[papél de kártas]*

some envelopes
sobres *[sóbres]*

some airmail paper
papel para correo aéreo *[papél para korréo aéreo]*

some airmail envelopes
sobres para correo aéreo *[sóbres para korréo aéreo]*

a ball point pen (fountain pen)
un bolígrafo (una pluma estilográfica)
[un bolígrafo (úna plúma estilográfika)]

Give me (6) stamps
    Déme (seis) sellos para
    [déme (seis) séljos pára]

for local mail
la ciudad *[la θjudád]*

for mail to national addresses
las provincias *[las probínθjas]*

for mail to the EU
cartas a países de la UE
[kártas a países de la unjón européa]

for an express letter to ...
una carta urgente a ...
[úna kárta urxénte a]

What postage do I need for
    ¿Qué franqueo necesito para
    [ke frankéo neθesíto pára]

this letter?
esta carta? *[ésta kárta]*

a letter to ...?
una carta a ...? *[úna kárta a]*

a packet to ...?
un paquete a ...? *[un pakéte a]*

an airmail packet to ...?
un paquete aéreo a ...?
[un pakéte aéreo a]

How much does this letter weigh?
¿Qué peso tiene esta carta? *[ke péso tjéne ésta kárta]*

It weighs 20 (200) grams
Pesa veinte (doscientos) gramos
[pésa béinte (dosθjéntos) grámos]

Can you fill this lighter, please?
¡Cárgueme este encendedor, por favor!
[kárgeme éste enθendedór por fabór]

I would like **Quisiera** *[kisjéra]*	a 6 (12) Euros phonecard **una tarjeta de teléfono de 6 (12)** **euros** *[úna tarxéta de teléfono de séis (dóθe)* *éuros]*
	a bus-pass **una tarjeta de autobús** *[úna tarxéta de autobús]*

■ THE WINE AND SPIRITS SHOP

Where is there a **¿Dónde hay una** *[dónde ai úna]*	wine cellar? **bodega?** *[bodéga]*
	wine and spirits shop **tienda de vinos y licores?** *[tjénda de bínos y likóres]*
Do you have **¿Tienen** *[tjénen]*	any good quality wines (table wines)? **vinos de marca (vinos de mesa)?** *[bínos de márka (bínos de mésa)]*
	any draught wines? **vino a granel?** *[bíno a granél]*
	one litre bottles of beer? **cervezas de litro?** *[θerbéθas de lítro]*
I want **Quisiera** *[kisjéra]*	one litre of draught red wine (white wine) **un litro de vino tinto (vino blanco) a granel** *[un lítro de bíno tínto (bíno blánko) a granél]*
	a bottle of red wine (white wine, rosy wine) **una botella de vino tinto (vino blanco,** **vino rosado)** *[úna botélja de bíno tínto* *(bíno blánko, bíno rrosádo)]*

I want **Quisiera** *[kisjéra]*	a carafe of red wine **una garrafa de vino tinto** *[úna garráfa de bíno tínto]*
	a bottle of wine for dessert **un vino de postre** *[un bíno de póstre]*
	a big bottle of beer **una botella grande de cerveza** *[úna botélja gránde de θerbéθa]*
Give me **Déme** *[déme]*	a white wine from Tarragona **un vino blanco de Priorato** *[un bíno blánko de prjoráto]*
	a red wine from La Rioja **un vino tinto de Rioja** *[un bíno tínto de rrjóxa]*
How much is it **¿Cuánto vale** *[kwánto bále]*	a litre? **el litro?** *[el lítro]*
	a bottle? **la botella?** *[la botélja]*
	a carafe? **la garrafa?** *[la garráfa]*
I want **Deseo** *[deséo]*	one litre of orange juice **un litro de zumo de naranja** *[un lítro de θúmo de naránxa]*
	(2) bottles of sparkling (still) mineral water **(dos) botellas de agua mineral con (sin) gas** *[(dos) botéljas de ágwa minerál kon (sin) gas]*
	(1) bottle of white rum **(una) botella de ron blanco** *[(úna) botélja de rron blánko]*
	(3) bottles of champagne brut **(tres) botellas de cava brut** *[(tres) botéljas de kába brut]*
Give me **Déme** *[déme]*	one litre of milk **un litro de leche** *[un lítro de létche]*

Give me
Déme
[déme]

| a bottle of olive oil
| **una botella de aceite de oliva**
| *[úna botélja de aθéite de olíba]*

a big bottle of orangeade
una naranjada grande
[úna naranxáda gránde]

SERVICES

BANK

Where is there	a bank?
¿Dónde hay (por aquí)	**un banco?**
[dónde ai (por akí)]	*[un bánko]*

a savings bank?
una caja de ahorros?
[úna káxa de aórros]

a post office savings bank?
una caja postal?
[úna káxa postál]

a bureau de change?
una oficina de cambio?
[úna ofiθína de kámbjo]

What time do the banks open (shut)?
¿A qué hora abren (cierran) los bancos?
[a ke óra ábren (θjérran) los bánkos]

I want	to deposit some money here
Quisiera	**depositar una cantidad aquí**
[kisjéra]	*[depositár úna kantidád akí]*

to open a current account
abrir una cuenta corriente
[abrír úna kwénta korrjénte]

to withdraw money from my account
retirar dinero de mi cuenta
[rretirár dinéro de mi kwénta]

to pay some money into my account
hacer un ingreso en mi cuenta
[aθér un ingréso en mi kwénta]

to cash these traveller's cheques
cobrar estos cheques de viaje
[kobrár éstos tchékes de bjáxe]

to collect a transfer from (England)
recoger una transferencia de (Inglaterra)
[rrekoxér una transferénθja de (inglatérra)]

to send a SWIFT transfer
realizar una transferencia SWIFT
[rrealiθár úna transferénθja swift]

Can you change

¿Pueden cambiarme
[pwéden kambjárme]

those pounds...	
estas libras...	
[éstas líbras]	

those traveler's checks...
estos cheques de viaje...
[éstos tchékes de bjáxe]

those dollars...	...into Euros?
estos dólares...	**...en euros?**
[éstos dólares]	[en éuros]

■ **HAIRDRESSER'S**

▶ **HAIRDRESSER'S**

Can you fit me in for tomorrow?
¿Pueden darme hora para (mañana)?
[pwéden dárme óra pára (manjána)]

I want

Por favor
[por fabór]

a wash and set
lavar y marcar
[labár i markár]

my hair cut
cortar (el pelo) [kortár (el pélo)]

a permanent wave
la permanente [la permanénte]

it dyed
teñir (el cabello) [tenjír (el kabéljo)]

Can you dye it

¿Pueden teñirlo
[pwéden tenjírlo]

the same colour?
del mismo color?
[del mísmo kolór]

a darker colour?
algo más oscuro?
[álgo mas oskúro]

a lighter colour?
algo más claro?
[álgo mas kláro]

blonde (brown, black)?
de color rubio (castaño, negro)?
[de kolór rrúbjo, (kastánjo, négro)]

Do you have a shade-card?
¿Tienen muestras de color? *[tjénen mwéstras de kolór]*

I want this colour
Deseo este color *[deséo éste kolór]*

Do me **Hágame** *[ágame]*	a bun **un moño** *[un mónjo]* a pony tail **una coleta** *[úna koléta]* curls **el pelo rizado** *[el pélo rriθádo]* a fringe **flequillo** *[flekíljo]*
Cut my hair **Córtemelo** *[kórtemelo]*	(very) short **(muy) corto** *[(mui) kórto]* a little shorter at the front **algo más corto por delante** *[álgo mas kórto por delánte]* a little shorter at the back **algo más corto por detrás** *[álgo mas kórto por detrás]*

Just touch it up
Sólo un retoque *[sólo un rretóke]*

Don't cut it too short
No me lo corte demasiado *[no me lo kórte demasjádo]*

Leave it as long as it is
No me corte nada *[no me kórte náda]*

Wash it with shampoo **Lávemelo con champú** *[lábemelo kon tchampú]*	for greasy hair **para cabello graso** *[pára kabéljo gráso]* for dry hair **para cabello seco** *[pára kabéljo séko]* for normal hair **para cabello normal** *[pára kabéljo normál]*

Wash my hair with anti-dandruff shampoo
Lávemelo con champú anticaspa
[lábemelo kon tchampú antikáspa]

▶ **BEAUTY TREATMENT**

Give me please	a facial massage
Hágame, por favor	**un masaje facial** *[un masáxe faθjál]*
[ágame por fabór]	
	a body massage
	un masaje corporal
	[un masáxe korporál]
	a manicure
	la manicura *[la manikúra]*
	a pedicure
	la pedicura *[la pedikúra]*
	a skin cleaning
	una limpieza de cutis
	[úna limpjéθa de kútis]

Remove	these hairs
Hágame	**un depilado aquí** *[un depiládo akí]*
[ágame]	
	the hairs on my face
	un depilado de cara *[un depiládo de kára]*
	the hairs on my legs
	un depilado de piernas *[un depiládo de pjérnas]*

▶ **AT THE BARBER'S**

I want a wash and cut, please
Por favor, lavar y cortar (el pelo)
[por fabór labár i kortár (el pélo)]

Cut my hair	with scissors
Deseo	**un corte a tijera** *[un kórte a tixéra]*
[deséo]	
	with a razor
	un corte a navaja *[un kórte a nabáxa]*

Leave my hair	short
Déjeme el pelo	**corto**
[déxeme el pélo]	*[kórto]*

Leave my hair
  Déjeme el pelo
  [déxeme el pélo]

  long
  largo *[lárgo]*

  (short) at the front
  (corto) por delante
  [(kórto) por delánte]

  (long) at the back
  (largo) por detrás
  [(lárgo) por detrás]

Thin my hair out
  Vacíeme el pelo *[baθíeme el pélo]*

I (don't) want
  (No) deseo
  [(no) deséo]

  (any) side-whiskers
  patillas *[patíljas]*

  a (any) parting
  raya *[rrája]*

I want the parting
  Quisiera la raya
  [kisjéra la rrája]

  on the right
  a la derecha *[a la derétcha]*

  on the left
  a la izquierda *[a la iθkjérda]*

  in the middle
  en el centro *[en el θéntro]*

Comb it dry
  Péineme en seco *[péineme en séko]*

Give me
  Quisiera
  [kisjéra]

  some hair lotion
  una loción
  [úna loθjón]

  some eau-de cologne
  agua de colonia
  [ágwa de kolónja]

Give me a shave, please
  Aféiteme, por favor *[aféiteme por fabór]*

Trim
  Arrégleme
  [arrégleme]

  my moustache
  el bigote
  [el bigóte]

  my beard
  la barba *[la bárba]*

Shave off	my moustache
Aféiteme	**el bigote** *[el bigóte]*
[aféiteme]	
	my beard
	la barba *[la bárba]*

Give me a facial massage
Deseo un masaje facial *[deséo un masáxe faθjál]*

■ GASTRONOMY

▶ RESTAURANT

Where is there	a good restaurant?
¿Hay por aquí	**un restaurante bueno?**
[ai por akí]	*[un rrestauránte bwéno]*
	a typical restaurant?
	un restaurante típico? *[un rrestauránte típiko]*
	a sea-food restaurant?
	una marisquería? *[úna mariskería]*
	a cheap restaurant?
	un restaurante económico?
	[un rrestauránte ekonómiko]
	a luxury restaurant?
	un restaurante de lujo?
	[un rrestauránte de lúxo]

Where is this restaurant?
¿Dónde está este restaurante?
[dónde está éste rrestauránte]

Is it	far from here?
¿Está	**lejos de aquí?** *[léxos de akí]*
[está]	
	near?
	cerca de aquí? *[θérka de akí]*

Can you reserve me a table for	(4) persons?
Quisiera reservar	**(cuatro) personas**
una mesa para	*[(kwátro) persónas]*
[kisjéra rreserbár	
úna mésa pára]	noon today?
	este mediodía
	[éste medjodía]

Can you reserve me a table for
   **Quisiera reservar
   una mesa para**
   *[kisjéra rreserbár
   úna mésa pára]*

tonight?
esta noche *[ésta nótche]*

tomorrow night?
mañana por la noche
[manjána por la nótche]

Have you a table free?
   ¿Tienen alguna mesa libre? *[tjénen algúna mésa líbre]*

There are three of us
   Somos tres personas *[sómos tres persónas]*

We have a table reserved for (5) persons
   Tenemos una mesa reservada para (cinco) personas
   [tenémos úna mésa rreserbáda pára (θínko) persónas]

In the name of Mr. Walker
   A nombre de (Walker) *[a nómbre de]*

Please bring me the menu
   Tráiga la carta, por favor *[tráiga la kárta por fabór]*

I want
   Deseo
   [deséo]

something typical of the house
una especialidad de la casa
[úna espeθjalidád de la kása]

something typical of this part of the country
algo típico de esta región
[algo típiko de ésta rrexjón]

a typical Spanish dish
un plato típico español *[un pláto típiko espanjól]*

some fish
un plato de pescado *[un pláto de peskádo]*

some meat
un plato de carne *[un pláto de kárne]*

some sea-food
mariscos *[maaliment:ískos]*

What can you recommend me?
   ¿Qué me recomienda? *[ke me rrekomjénda]*

I'll have
   Tomaré
   [tomaré]

(olives and ham) as an aperitive
(aceitunas y tacos de jamón) como aperitivo
[(aθeitúnas i tákos de xamón) kómo aperitíbo]

I'll have | (mixed hors d'oeuvres) for the first course
Tomaré | **(entremeses variados) como primer plato**
[tomaré] | *[(entreméses barjádos) kómo primér pláto]*

| (a paella) for the second course
| **(una paella) de segundo plato**
| *[(úna paélja) de segúndo pláto]*

| (a crème brûlée) for dessert
| **(una crema catalana) de postre**
| *[(úna kréma katalána) de póstre]*

Please bring me | a dry (sweet) sherry
Tráigame por favor | **un jerez seco (dulce)**
[trájgame por fabór] | *[un xeréθ séko (dúlθe)]*

| the wine list
| **la carta de vinos** *[la kárta de bínos]*

| the salt
| **la sal** *[la sal]*

| the pepper
| **pimienta** *[pimjénta]*

| some vinegar
| **vinagre** *[binágre]*

| some oil
| **aceite** *[aθéite]*

I want | a cup of coffee
Quisiera | **un café** *[un kafé]*
[kisjéra] |

| a liqueur
| **algún licor** *[algún likor]*

| a Havana-cigar
| **un puro habano** *[un púro abáno]*

Please bring me the bill
Tráiga la factura, por favor
[tráiga la faktúra, por fabór]

Put it all on one bill
Cóbrelo todo junto *[kóbrelo tódo xúnto]*

Make out separate bills
Cóbrelo por separado *[kóbrelo por separádo]*

How much is it?
¿Cuánto es? *[kuánto es]*

Thank you, keep the change
Gracias, quédese con el cambio *[gráθjas, kédese kon el kámbjo]*

▶ **CAFE, SNACK BAR, ETC.**

Please give me **Póngame** *[póngame]*	a beer **una cerveza** *[úna θerbéθa]*
	a carafe of sangría **una jarra de sangría** *[úna xárra de sangría]*
	a glass of red wine **un vaso de vino tinto** *[un báso de bíno tínto]*
	a bottle of sparkling mineral water **una botella de agua mineral con gas** *[úna botélja de água minerál kon gas]*

I'll have **Quisiera** *[kisjéra]*	a cup of coffee **una taza de café** *[úna táθa de kafé]*
	a coffee with a dash of milk **un cortado** *[un kortádo]*
	a white coffee **un café con leche** *[un kafé kon létche]*
	a cup of lemon tea **un té con limón** *[un te kon limón]*
	a glass of brandy **una copa de brandy** *[úna kópa de brándi]*

Bring me **Tráigame una ración de** *[tráigame úna rraθjón de]*	some mussels **mejillones** *[mexiljónes]*
	some olives **aceitunas** *[aθejtúnas]*
	some fried squid rings **calamares a la romana** *[kalamáres a la rromána]*

Bring me
Tráigame una ración de
[tráigame úna rraθjón de]

some prawns with garlic
gambas al ajillo
[gámbas al axíljo]

a piece of potato omelette
tortilla de patatas
[tortílja de patátas]

some pieces of cheese
tacos de queso
[tákos de késo]

Do you serve
¿Sirven
[sírben]

toasted sandwiches?
bocadillos calientes?
[bokadíljos kaljéntes]

ham and cheese sandwiches?
sandwiches de jamón y queso?
[sandwítches de xamón i késo]

I want
Quisiera
[kisjéra]

a croissant
un croissant
[un crwasánt]

an "ensaimada"
una ensaimada
[úna ensaimáda]

a piece of apple tart
una ración de tarta de manzana
[úna rraθjón de tárta de manθána]

What kind of "tapas" do you have?
¿Qué tapas tienen?
[ke tápas tjénen]

Do you have
¿Tienen
[tjénen]

any aspirins?
aspirinas?
[aspirínas]

any bicarbonate?
bicarbonato?
[bikarbonáto]

I want to pay
¿Quiere cobrar? [kjére kobrár]

How much is it?
¿Cuánto le debo? [kwánto le débo]

■ SELF-DRIVE CARS

Where can I hire a car?
¿Dónde encuentro un coche de alquiler?
[dónde enkwéntro un kótche de alkilér]

I want **Deseo** *[deséo]*	a small car **un coche pequeño** *[un kótche pekénjo]*
	a medium sized car **un coche mediano** *[un kótche medjáno]*
	a big car **un coche grande** *[un kótche gránde]*

Do you have any (Mercedes)?
¿Tienen algún (Mercedes)? *[tjénen algún (merθédes)]*

I want it **Lo quiero** *[lo kjéro]*	for today only **solamente para hoy** *[sólaménte pára oi]*
	for one day **para un día** *[pára un día]*
	for several days **para varios días** *[pára bárjos días]*
	for one week **para una semana** *[pára úna semána]*
	until next (Friday) **hasta el próximo (viernes)** *[ásta el próksimo (bjérnes)]*

| How much do you charge
¿Cuánto cuesta
[kwánto kwésta] | per day?
por día? *[por día]* |
| | per kilometre?
por kilómetro? *[por kilómetro]* |

How much do I have to pay now?
¿Cuánto he de pagar ahora? *[kwánto e de pagár aóra]*

Can you bring the car to my hotel?
Lléveme el coche al hotel *[ljébeme el kótche al otél]*

Where is the car parked?
¿Dónde tienen el coche aparcado?
[dónde tjénen el kótche aparkádo]

I'll go to (Madrid)
Voy a viajar a (Madrid) *[boi a bjaxár a (madríd)]*

Where can I return the car there?
¿Dónde puedo entregar el coche allí?
[dónde pwédo entregár el kótche aljí]

I have come to return a car
Quisiera entregarles un coche
[kisjéra entregárles un kótche]

Here are the documents of the car
Aquí tengo la documentación del coche
[akí téngo la dokumentaθjón del kótche]

How much is it all together?
¿Cuánto es en total? *[kwánto es en totál]*

■ PUBLIC TRANSPORT

Which **¿En qué** *[en ke]*	bus ... **autobús ...** *[autobús]*	
	underground line ... **metro ...** *[métro]*	
	tram ... **tranvía ...** *[trambía]*	
	train ... **tren ...** *[tren]*	... can I take to go to...? **... puedo ir a ...?** *[pwédo ir a]*

How can I go to ...?
¿Cómo puedo ir a ...?
[kómo pwédo ir a]

Where is **¿Dónde está** *[dónde está]*	the nearest (bus) stop? **la parada más próxima?** *[la paráda mas próksima]*
	the nearest station? **la estación más cercana?** *[la estaθjón más θerkána]*

What route does
¿Por dónde pasa
[por dónde pása]

this bus ...
este autobús? *[éste autobús]*

this underground line ...
este metro? *[éste métro]*

this tram ...
este tranvía? *[éste trambía]*

this train ..
este tren? *[éste tren]*

... take?

Where is the ticket office?
¿Dónde está la taquilla de billetes?
[dónde está la takílja de biljétes]

Where is there a ticket machine?
¿Dónde hay una expendedora de billetes?
[dónde ai úna ekspendedóra de biljétes]

Where do I
¿Dónde he de
[dónde e de]

get off?
bajar? *[baxár]*

change?
hacer trasbordo? *[aθér trasbórdo]*

How far is it from...?
¿A qué distancia está de ...? *[a ke distánθja está de]*

I am going to ...
Quiero ir a ... *[kjéro ir a]*

Where can I find a taxi?
¿Dónde encuentro un taxi (por aquí)?
[dónde enkwéntro un táksi (por akí)]

Where is there a taxi rank?
¿Dónde hay alguna parada de taxis?
[dónde ai algúna paráda de táksis]

Can you call me a taxi?
¿Puede llamarme un taxi?
[pwéde ljamárme un táksi]

Are you free?
¿Está libre? *[está líbre]*

Can you take me to ...?
¿Puede llevarme a ...? *[pwéde ljebárme a]*

Pass through (over) ...
Vaya por ... *[bája por]*

Which way are you going to take?
¿Por dónde piensa pasar? *[por dónde pjénsa pasár]*

Stop	here
Por favor, pare	**aquí** *[akí]*
[por fabór páre]	
	at the next corner
	en la próxima esquina
	[en la próksima eskína]
	on the right (left) side
	en el lado derecho (izquierdo)
	[en el ládo derétcho (iθkjérdo)]
	before crossing Gran Vía
	antes de cruzar la Gran Vía
	[ántes de kruθár la gran bía]
	after crossing Gran Vía
	después de la Gran Vía
	[despwés de la gran bía]

Wait here, please
Espéreme aquí, por favor
[espéreme akí por fabór]

How much is it?
¿Cuánto es?
[kwánto es]

POST OFFICE, TELEGRAMS, TELEPHONES

▶ **Post**

Where is there a post office?
¿Dónde hay (por aquí) una oficina de correos?
[dónde ai (por akí) úna ofiθína de korréos]

Where is the central post office?
¿Dónde está la central de correos?
[dónde está la θentrál de korréos]

I want to send this letter	to (London)
Quiero enviar esta carta	**a (Londres)**
[kjéro embjár ésta kárta]	*[a (lóndres)]*

I want to send this letter
Quiero enviar esta carta
[kjéro embjár éste kárta]

by express mail
urgente *[urxénte]*

by registered mail
certificada
[θertifikáda]

I want to send this parcel
Quisiera enviar este paquete *[kisjéra embjár éste pakéte]*

How much does it cost?
¿Cuánto me va a costar? *[kwánto me ba a kostár]*

Give me 2 (5) stamps of 21 (90) cents
Déme 2 (5) sellos de 21 (90) céntimos de euro
[déme dós (θínko) séljos de beintiún (nobénta) θéntimos de éuro]

How much does a letter cost
¿Cuánto vale una carta
[kwánto bále úna kárta]

to a local address?
aquí en la ciudad?
[akí en la θjudád]

to an address in this province?
a la provincia? *[a la probínθja]*

to a country in the European Union?
a un país de la Unión Europea?
[a un país de la unjón européa]

to America?
a América? *[a américa]*

How much is
¿Cuánto vale
[kwánto bále]

a letter by air mail?
una carta aérea? *[úna karta aérea]*

a parcel by air mail?
un paquete aéreo? *[un pakéte aéreo]*

an express letter?
una carta urgente? *[úna kárta urxénte]*

a letter by registered post?
una carta certificada? *[úna kárta θertifikáda]*

It weighs 200 grams
Pesa (doscientos) gramos *[pésa (dosθjéntos) grámos]*

I want
Quisiera
[kisjéra]

to send a money order
poner un giro (telegráfico)
[ponér un xíro (telegráfiko)]

I want	to collect a money order
Quisiera	**recoger un giro (telegráfico)**
[kisjéra]	*[rrekoxér un xíro (telegráfiko)]*

It is	coming from (England)
Viene	**de Inglaterra** *[de inglatérra]*
[bjéne]	
	addressed to (Mr. Miller)
	a nombre del (Sr. Miller) *[a nómbre del senjiór]*

The amount is (500) pounds
Son (quinientas) libras *[son (kinjéntas) líbras]*

Where is the window for	stamps?
¿Dónde está la taquilla para	**sellos?** *[séljos]*
[dónde está la takílja pára]	
	money orders?
	giros (telegráficos)?
	[xíros (telegráfikos)]
	international money orders?
	giros internacionales?
	[xíros internaθjonáles]
	parcels?
	el envío de paquetes postales?
	[el embío de pakétes postáles]

Where is	the information counter?
¿Dónde está	**la información?**
[dónde está]	*[la informaθjón]*
	the Poste Restante?
	la lista de correos? *[la lísta de korréos]*

▶ **TELEGRAMS**

Where is there a telegraph office?
¿Dónde hay (por aquí) una oficina de telégrafos?
[dónde ai (por akí) úna ofiθína de telégrafos]

I want	to send a telegram
Quisiera	**poner un telegrama**
[kisjéra]	*[ponér un telegráma]*
	to send a money order
	enviar un giro telegráfico
	[embjár un xíro telegráfiko]

Give me a form, please
  Déme el correspondiente impreso
  [déme el korrespondjénte impréso]

What is the rate for	a telegram?
¿Cuánto vale	**el telegrama?** *[el telegráma]*
[kwánto bále]	
	a money order?
	el giro? *[el xíro]*

I want to send it to (London)
  Quiero enviarlo(la) a (Londres) *[kjéro embjárlo a] (lóndres)*

It is consists of (20) words
  Son (veinte) palabras *[son (béinte) palábras]*

It is for (1.500) pounds
  Son (mil quinientas) libras *[son (mil kinjéntas) líbras]*

I want to send a fax to (Manchester)
  Quisiera enviár un fax a (Manchester)
  [kisjéra embjár un faks a]

The number is ....
  El número es el ... *[el número es el]*

▶ **TELEPHONE**

Where is there a telephone exchange?
  ¿Dónde está la central de teléfonos?
  [dónde está la θentrál de teléfonos]

Where is there	a telephone booth?
¿Dónde hay	**un locutorio telefónico?** *[un lokutórjo telefóniko]*
[dónde ai]	
	a telephone box?
	una cabina de teléfono? *[úna kabína de teléfono]*

I want a call to number ...in France
  Póngame con el número ... de Francia
  [póngame kon el número ... de fránθja]

The code is....
  El prefijo es el ... *[el prefíxo es el]*

I want to make a reversed charge call to Switzerland
  Deseo una conferencia a cobro revertido con Suiza
  [deséo una konferénθja a kóbro rrebertído kon swíθa]

Do you have telephone cards?
¿Tienen tarjetas telefónicas? *[tjénen tarxétas telefónikas]*

I would like a 6 (12) Euros card
Quisiera una tarjeta de 6 (12) euros
[kisjéra úna tarxéta de séis (dóθe) éuros]

■ AT THE TRAVEL AGENT'S

▶ RESERVATIONS

I want to go
Quisiera viajar
[kisjéra bjaxár]

| to (Madrid)
a (Madrid) *[a (madríd)]*

to (Portugal)
a (Portugal)
[a (portugál)]

to the Canary Islands
a las Islas Canarias
[a las íslas kanárjas]

Can I go
¿Puedo ir en
[pwédo ir en]

| by train?
tren? *[tren]*

by sea?
barco? *[bárko]*

by air?
avión? *[abjón]*

How much is the journey
¿Cuánto vale el viaje
[kwánto bále el bjáxe]

| by air?
en avión? *[en abjón]*

by sea?
en barco? *[en bárko]*

by train?
en tren? *[en tren]*

in first class?
en primera clase? *[en priméra kláse]*

in second class?
en segunda clase? *[en segúnda kláse]*

in a sleeping car?
en coche-cama? *[en kótche-káma]*

How much is the journey | in a cabin?
¿Cuánto vale el viaje | **en camarote?**
[kwánto bále el bjáxe] | *[en kamaróte]*

What time does | ... the train ...
¿A qué hora sale | **el tren?** *[el tren]*
[a ke óra sále] |
| ... the ship ...
| **el barco?** *[el bárko]* | ... leave?

What time does the plane leave?
¿A qué hora sale el avión? *[a ke óra sále el abjón]*

How long does the journey last | by train?
¿Cuánto tarda el viaje en | **tren?** *[tren]*
[kwánto tárda el bjáxe en] |
| by sea?
| **barco?** *[bárko]*
|
| by air?
| **avión?** *[abjón]*

What time does | the train ...
¿A qué hora llega | **el tren?** *[el tren]*
[a ke óra ljéga] |
| the ship ...
| **el barco?** *[el bárko]*
|
| the plane ...
| **el avión?** *[el abjón]* | ... arrive?

Give me a one-way ticket
Déme un billete de ida *[déme un biljéte de ída]*

I want a return ticket
Quisiera un billete de ida y vuelta
[kisjéra un biljéte de ída i bwélta]

I want to leave on (Monday) and to return on (Friday)
La ida para el (lunes) y la vuelta para el (viernes)
[la ída pára el (lúnes) i la bwélta pára el (bjérnes)]

Reserve me a seat | to (Madrid)
Quisiera reservar | **a (Madrid)**
una plaza | *[a (madríd)]*
[kisjéra rreserbár |
úna pláθa] | for (Thursday)
| **para el (jueves)**
| *[pára el (xwébes)]*

Reserve me a seat | for this afternoon
Quisiera reservar | **para esta tarde**
una plaza | *[pára ésta tárde]*
[kisjéra rreserbár
úna pláθa] | for tomorrow morning
| **para mañana**
| **por la mañana**
| *[pára manjána*
| *por la manjána]*

I already have the ticket
Ya tengo el billete *[ja téngo el biljéte]*

I'd like to travel | first class
Quisiera | **primera clase** *[priméra kláse]*
[kisjéra]
| second class
| **segunda clase** *[segúnda kláse]*

| economy class
| **clase turista** *[kláse turísta]*

| in a cabin
| **un camarote** *[un kamaróte]*

Can you make a hotel reservation?
¿Puede hacerme una reserva de hotel?
[púede aθérme úna rresérba de otél]

I want a room in | a boarding house
Deseo | **una pensión** *[úna pensjón]*
[deséo]
| a 3-star hotel
| **un hotel de tres estrellas**
| *[un otél de tres estréljas]*

| a luxury hotel
| **un hotel de lujo** *[un otél de lúxo]*

I want | bed and breakfast
Deseo | **la habitación con desayuno**
[deséo] | *[la abitaθjón kon desajúno]*

| half board
| **media pensión** *[médja pensjón]*

| full board
| **pensión completa**
| *[pensjón kompléta]*

I'll stay
Pienso quedarme
[pjénso kedárme]

until (Monday)
hasta (el lunes)
[ásta el lúnes]

for (3) days
(tres) días
[tres días]

for (one) week
(una) semana
[úna semána]

EXCURSIONS

I want to go on an excursion
**Quisiera hacer
una excursión**
[kisjéra aθér
úna ekskursjón]

to (Barcelona)
a (Barcelona)
[a barθelóna]

to the Costa Brava
a la Costa Brava
[a la kósta brába]

to the Escorial
al Escorial
[al eskorjál]

I want to go (on an excursion)
Deseo la excursión
[deséo la ekskursjón]

tomorrow
para mañana
[pára manjána]

at the weekend
para el fin de semana
[pára el fin de semána]

next week
para la próxima semana
[pára la próksima semána]

How much does it cost per person?
¿Cuánto cuesta la excursión por persona?
[kwánto kwésta la ekskursjón por persóna]

What services does this price include?
¿Qué servicios están comprendidos en el precio?
[ke serbíθjos están komprendídos en el préθjo]

Where does the coach leave from?
¿De dónde sale el autocar? [de dónde sále el autokár]

What time | does the coach leave?
¿A qué hora | **sale el autocar?** *[sále el autokár]*
[a ke óra]

| shall we be back?
| **estaremos de vuelta?** *[estarémos de bwélta]*

I would like to go on a trip round the city
Quisiera participar en un recorrido por la ciudad
[kisjéra partiθipár en un rrekorrído por la θjudád]

How long does it last?
¿Cuánto tiempo dura?
[kwánto tjèmpo dúra]

What museums
¿Qué museos
[ke muséos]

What churches
¿Qué iglesias
[ke iglésjas]

What historical buildings | are we going to see?
¿Qué monumentos | **vamos a ver?**
[ke monuméntos] | *[bámos a ber]*

What time does the sightseeing tour begin?
¿A qué hora comienza el recorrido (por la ciudad)?
[a ke óra komjénθa el rrekorrído (por la θjudád)]

▶ **RETURN JOURNEY**

Can you | confirm this reservation?
¿Pueden | **confirmarme esta reserva?**
[pwéden] | *[konfirmárme ésta rresérba]*

| change this reservation for (Monday)?
| **cambiar esta reserva para el lunes?**
| *[kambjár ésta rresérba pára el lúnes]*

| reserve me a seat for (Saturday)?
| **reservarme una plaza para el (sábado)?**
| *[rreserbárme úna pláθa pára el (sábado)]*

I want to leave (tomorrow)
Quisiera partir mañana
[kisjéra partír manjána]

I have to leave
Debo partir
[débo partír]

earlier
antes [ántes]

today
hoy mismo [oi mísmo]

as soon as possible
cuanto antes
[kwánto ántes]

LAUNDRY AND DRY CLEANING

Where is there
¿Dónde hay
[dónde ai]

a laundry?
una lavandería? [una lavandería]

a dry-cleaner's
una tintorería? [úna tintorería]

I want these clothes washed and cleaned, please
¿Pueden lavar y planchar esta ropa?
[pwéden labár i planchár ésta rrópa]

Can you clean
¿Pueden limpiarme
[pwéden limpjárme]

this suit?
este traje? [éste tráxe]

these trousers?
este pantalón?
[éste pantalón]

this jacket?
esta americana?
[ésta amerikána]

this skirt?
esta falda?
[ésta fálda]

these shirts?
estas camisas
[éstas kamísas]

When will it be ready?
¿Cuándo estará listo(a)?
[kwándo estará lísto]

When will they be ready?
¿Cuándo estarán listos(as)?
[kwándo estarán lístos]

I need it
Lo(la) voy a necesitar
[lo boi a neθesitár]

today
hoy *[oi]*

for tomorrow morning
mañana por la mañana
[manjána por la manjána]

before (Friday)
antes del viernes
[ántes del bjérnes]

during this week
durante esta semana
[duránte ésta semána]

as soon as possible
cuánto antes *[kwánto ántes]*

How much does it cost?
¿Cuánto va a costar? *[kwánto ba a kostár]*

EMERGENCIES

■ **MEDICAL ASSISTANCE**

Where is there	a doctor?
¿Dónde hay	**un médico?** *[un médiko]*
[dónde ai]	
	a dispensary?
	un dispensario? *[un dispensárjo]*

Take me to	a doctor
Lléveme a	**un médico** *[un médiko]*
[ljébeme a]	
	a dispensary
	un dispensario *[un dispensárjo]*
	a hospital
	un hospital *[un ospitál]*

I want to go to	a private doctor
Quisiera ir a	**un médico privado** *[un médiko pribádo]*
[kisjéra ir a]	
	a private hospital
	una clínica *[úna klínika]*
	a dentist
	un dentista *[un dentísta]*
	an eye-specialist
	un oftalmólogo *[un oftalmólogo]*

Can you phone a doctor?
¿Puede llamar un médico? *[pwéde ljamár un médiko]*

What days and hours does he (she) visit?
¿Qué horas de visita tiene? *[ke óras de bisíta tjéne]*

I have a pain in	my eyes
Me duele(n)	**los ojos** *[los óxos]*
[me dwélen]	
	my intestines
	el vientre *[el bjéntre]*
	my chest
	el tórax *[el tóraks]*
	my throat
	la garganta *[la gargánta]*

I have a pain in
   Me duele(n)
   [me dwéle]

my head
la cabeza *[la kabéθa]*

my stomach
el estómago *[el estómago]*

my kidneys
los riñones *[los rrinjónes]*

my ears
los oídos *[los oídos]*

my back
la espalda *[la espálda]*

I have the pain here
   Me duele aquí *[me dwéle akí]*

I have a pain in
   Me duele(n)
   [me dwéle]

my arm
el brazo *[el bráθo]*

my leg(s)
la(s) pierna(s) *[la pjérna]*

my fingers
los dedos *[los dédos]*

my foot (my feet)
el pie (los pies) *[el pje (los pjes)]*

my ankle
el tobillo *[el tobíljo]*

my hand
la mano *[la máno]*

my hip
la cadera *[la kadéra]*

my thigh
el muslo *[el múslo]*

my shoulder
el hombro *[el ómbro]*

my forearm
el antebrazo *[el antebráθo]*

I have fallen
Me he caído *[me e kaído]*

I have had an accident
He tenido un accidente *[e tenído un akθidénte]*

I have got a splinter here
Me he clavado una astilla aquí *[me e klabádo una astílja akí]*

| I have been
Me ha
[me a] | stung by an insect
picado un insecto *[pikádo un insékto]* |
| | bitten by a dog
mordido un perro *[mordído un pérro]* |

I feel **Tengo** *[téngo]*	breathless **ahogo** *[aógo]*
	tired **cansancio** *[kansánθjo]*
	faint **desmayo** *[desmájo]*

I am **Tengo** *[téngo]*	shivering **escalofríos** *[eskalofríos]*
	sweating **sudoración** *[sudoraθjón]*
	constipated **estreñimiento** *[estrenjimjénto]*

I have **Tengo** *[téngo]*	some spots **una erupción** *[una erupθjón]*
	a fever **fiebre** *[fjébre]*
	a boil **un forúnculo** *[un forúnkulo]*
	a cough **tos** *[tos]*

I have
Tengo
[téngo]

cramp
un calambre *[un kalámbre]*

some bleeding
una hemorragia *[úna emoráxja]*

a lump
una contusión *[úna kontusjón]*

a cut
un corte *[un kórte]*

eczema
un eczema *[un ekθéma]*

an inflammation
una inflamación *[úna inflamaθjón]*

a swelling
una hinchazón *[úna intchaθón]*

sunstroke
una insolación *[úna insolaθjón]*

diarrhoea
diarrea *[djarréa]*

a burn
quemaduras *[kemadúras]*

an injury
una lesión *[úna lesjón]*

a wound
una herida *[úna erída]*

I am seasick
Estoy mareado(a) *[estói mareádo(a)]*

I feel dizzy
Tengo vértigos *[téngo bértigos]*

I feel
Estoy
[estói]

agitated
nervioso(a) *[nerbjóso]*

depressed
deprimido(a) *[deprimído]*

Can you give me a checkup?
  ¿Podría examinarme? *[podría eksaminárme]*

Do you suffer from | diabetes?
  ¿Tiene | **diabetes?** *[djabétes]*
  [tjéne] |
  | asthma?
  | **asma?** *[ásma]*

Do you have heart trouble?
  ¿Tiene una enfermedad cardíaca?
  [tjéne úna enfermedád kardíaka]

Are you allergic to | penicillin?
  ¿Tiene alergia a | **la penicilina?**
  [tjéne alérxja a] | *[la peniθilína]*
  | sulphonamides?
  | **las sulfamidas?**
  | *[las sulfamídas]*
  | antobiotics?
  | **los antibióticos?**
  | *[los antibjótikos]*

Are you pregnant?
  ¿Está embarazada? *[está embaraθáda]*

Cough, please!
  ¡Tosa, por favor! *[tósa por fabór]*

Does it hurt you here?
  ¿Le duele aquí? *[le dwéle akí]*

You have | a sore thoat
  Vd. tiene | **anginas**
  [ustéd tjéne] | *[anxínas]*
  | arthritis
  | **artritis** *[artrítis]*
  | appendicitis
  | **apendicitis** *[apendiθítis]*
  | bronchitis
  | **bronquitis** *[bronkítis]*

You have
Vd. tiene
[ustéd tjéne]

a fracture
una fractura *[úna fraktúra]*

colitis
colitis *[kolítis]*

an embolism
una embolia *[una embólja]*

an inflammation
una inflamación
[úna inflamaθjón]

epilepsy
epilepsia *[epilépsja]*

lumbago
lumbago *[lumbágo]*

a heart attack
un infarto *[un infárto]*

catarrh
un catarro *[un katárro]*

colic
un cólico *[un kóliko]*

bronchopneumonia
bronconeumonía *[bronkoneumónja]*

gastritis
gastritis *[gastrítis]*

neurosis
una neurosis *[úna neurósis]*

rheumatism
reúma *[rreúma]*

a fainting fit
un desmayo *[un desmájo]*

heat-stroke
una insolación
[úna insolaθjón]

You have **Vd. tiene** *[ustéd tjéne]*	indigestion **indigestión** *[indixestjón]*
	food poisoning **una intoxicación** *[úna intoxikaθjón]*
	a sprain **un esguince** *[un esgínθe]*

It is necessary **Tenemos que hacer** *[tenémos ke aθér]*	to take an X-ray **una radiografía** *[úna rradjografía]*
	to do an analysis **unos análisis** *[únos análisis]*
	to have an operation **una intervención quirúrgica** *[úna interbenθjón kirúrxika]*
	to put it in plaster **un enyesado** *[un enjesádo]*

You should have some injections
Debe ponerse unas inyecciones
[débe ponérse únas injekθjónes]

You should take **Debe tomar** *[débe tomár]*	this medicine **este medicamento** *[éste medikaménto]*
	these pills **estas pastillas** *[éstas pastíljas]*
	these tablets **estas grageas** *[éstas graxéas]*
	these capsules **estas cápsulas** *[éstas kápsulas]*
	these drops **estas gotas** *[éstas gótas]*

You should take it   (3) times a day after (before) meals
Debe tomarlo   **(tres) veces al día después (antes)**
[débe tomárlo]   **de comer**
                     [(tres) béθes al día despwés (ántes)
                     de komér]

You should take these suppositories
Debe ponerse estos supositorios
[débe ponérse éstos supositórjos]

Here is the prescription
Aquí está la receta [akí está la rreθéta]

■ POLICE

Where is there   a Police Station?
¿Dónde hay   **una comisaría?** [úna komisaría]
[dónde ai]
                     a headquarters of the Guardia Civil?
                     un cuartel de la guardia civil
                     [un kwartél de la gwárdja θibíl]

I want to report   a loss
Quisiera denunciar **una pérdida**
[kisjéra denunθjár]   [úna pérdida]

                     a theft
                     un robo [un rróbo]

                     a robbery
                     un atraco
                     [un atráko]

                     an accident
                     un accidente
                     [un akθidénte]

I have lost my   passport
He perdido   **el pasaporte** [el pasapórte]
[e perdído]
                     my luggage
                     el equipaje [el ekipáxe]

                     my wallet
                     la cartera [la kartéra]

Somebody has stolen | my passport
Me han robado | **el pasaporte** *[el pasapórte]*
[me an rrobádo] |

| my wallet
| **la cartera** *[la kartéra]*

| my car (motorbike)
| **el coche (la moto)**
| *[el kótche (la móto)]*

| my camera
| **la cámara de fotos**
| *[la kámara de fótos]*

It happened | today
Sucedió | **hoy** *[oi]*
[suθédjo] |

| at (6) o'clock
| **a las seis de la tarde**
| *[a las seis de la tárde]*

| a few minutes ago
| **hace pocos minutos**
| *[áθe pókos minútos]*

| this morning
| **esta mañana**
| *[ésta manjána]*

| yesterday
| **ayer** *[ajér]*

| yesterday evening
| **anoche** *[anótche]*

It happened | at the hotel
Ocurrió en | **el hotel** *[el otél]*
[okurrjó en] |

| in the car
| **el coche** *[kótche]*

| on the beach
| **la playa** *[la plája]*

| in the street
| **la calle** *[la kálje]*

It happened	on the road
Ocurrió en	**la carretera** *[la karretéra]*
[okurrjó en]	
	at the station
	la estación *[la estaθjón]*
	in the garage
	el garaje *[el garáxe]*
	at the airport
	el aeropuerto
	[el aeropwérto]

The value is about ... pounds
El valor es de ... libras aproximadamente
[el balór es de ... líbras aproximadaménte]

When shall I know something?
¿Cuándo voy a saber algo? *[kwándo boi a sabér álgo]*

I am staying	at the Plaza Hotel
Resido	**en el hotel Plaza** *[en el otél pláθa]*
[rresído]	
	in the "Miramar" apartments
	en los apartamentos Miramar
	[en los apartaméntos miramár]
	at Paseo Marítimo (19)
	en el paseo marítimo número (diecinueve)
	[en el paséo marítimo número djeθinwébe]

ENGLISH

SPANISH

DICTIONARY

a *art indef.* un *m.* [*un*], una *f.* [*úna*] (see grammar)

abdominal *a.* abdominal [*abdominál*]

abed *adv.* en cama [*en káma*], acostado(a) [*akostádo*]

able *a.* capaz [*kapáθ*]; **to be - to do**, poder *irr.* hacer [*podér aθér*], saber *irr.* hacer [*sabér*] (see grammar: modal verbs)

aboard *adv.* a bordo [*a bórdo*]; **to go -**, embarcarse *r.* [*embarkárse*]

abort (to) abortar *r.* [*abortár*]; **-ion** aborto *m.* [*abórto*]

about *prep.* cerca de [*θérka de*], alrededor de [*alrrededór de*]; **- ten o'clock,** alrededor de las diez [*de las djeθ*]

above *prep.* sobre [*sóbre*], por encima de [*por enθíma de*]

abroad *adv.* fuera [*fwéra*], en el extranjero [*en el ekstranxéro*]; **to be -,** estar *irr.* en el extranjero [*estár en el*] ‖ **2.** (a)fuera [*afwéra*], al extranjero [*al ekstranxéro*]; **to go -,** ir(se) *irr.* al extranjero [*írse al*]

abscess absceso *m.* [*abθéso*]

absen/ce ausencia *f.* [*ausénθja*]; **-t** *a.* ausente [*ausénte*]

absinthe ajenjo *m.* [*axénxo*]

absolute *a.* absoluto(a) [*absolúto*], completo(a) [*kompléto*]; **-ly** *adv.* absolutamente [*absolutaménte*], completamente [*kompletaménte*]; **- not**, en absoluto [*en absolúto*]

abstemious *a.* abstemio(a) [*abstémjo*]

abstain (to) abstenerse *irr.* [*abstenérse*] (from/de)

abstinence abstinencia *f.* [*abstinénθja*]

absurd *a.* absurdo(a) [*absúrdo*]

accelerat/e (to) acelerar *r.* [*aθelerár*]; **-ion** aceleración *f.* [*aθeleraθjón*]; **-or** acelerador *m.* [*aθeleradór*]

accent acento *m.* [*aθénto*]

accept (to) aceptar *r.* [*aθeptár*]; admitir *r.* [*admitír*]; **-able** *a.* aceptable [*aθeptáble*]

access acceso *m.* [*akθéso*]

accessories accesorios *m. pl.* [*akθesórjos*]; **- case** estuche *m.* para accesorios [*estútche pára*]

accident accidente *m.* [*akθidénte*]; **by -,** por casualidad [*por kaswalidád*]; **-al** *a.* accidental [*akθidentál*], casual [*kaswál*]; **-ally** *adv.* accidentalmente [*akθidentalménte*], casualmente [*kaswalménte*]

acclaim (to) aclamar *r.* [*aklamár*]

acclamation aplauso *m.* [*apláuso*]

accomodation alojamiento *m.* [*aloxamjénto*]

accompany (to) acompañar *r.* [*akompanjár*]

accord acuerdo *m.* [*akwérdo*]; **-ance** conformidad *f.* [*konformidád*]; **in - with**, de acuerdo con [*de akwérdo kon*]; **-ing: - to,** según (según)

account cuenta *f.* [*kwénta*]; **bank -,** cuenta bancaria [*bankárja*]; **current -,** cuenta corriente [*korrjénte*]; **to open an -,** abrir *r.* una cuenta [*abrír úna kwénta*]

ache dolor *m.* [*dolór*]

acid *a.* ácido(a) [*áθido*] ‖ **2.** *n.* ácido *m.*

acknowledgement: - of receipt, acuse *m.* de recibo [*akúse de rreθíbo*]

acne acné *m.* [*akné*]

acquire (to) adquirir (ie) [*adkirír*]

acrobat acróbata *m.-f.* [*akróbata*]; **-ic** *a.* acrobático(a) [*akrobátiko*]

across *prep.* a través de [*a trabés de*]; **to go -,** atravesar (ie) [*atrabesár*], cruzar *r.* [*kruθár*] ‖ **2.** al otro lado de [*al ótro ládo de*]; **the restaurant is - the road**, el restaurante está al otro lado de la carretera [*el rrestauránte está al ótro ládo de la karretéra*]

act (to) actuar *r.* [*aktuár*] ‖ **2.** *n.* acto *m.* [*ákto*]

active *a.* activo(a) [*aktíbo*]; **-ly** *adv.* activamente [*aktibaménte*]

activities actividades *f.pl.* [*aktibidádes*]

actor actor *m.* [*aktór*]

actress actriz *f.* [*aktríθ*]

actual *a.* verdader(o) [*berdadéro*], real [*rreál*]; **-ly** *adv.* realmente [*rrealménte*], en efecto [*en efékto*]

acute *a.* agudo(a) [*agúdo*]

add (to) sumar *r.* [*sumár*] ‖ **2.** añadir *r.* [*anjadír*] (to/a)

addict adicto(a) *m.-f.* [*adíkto*]; **drug -,** drogadicto(a) *m.-f.* [*drogadíkto*]

addition adición *f.* [*adiθjón*]; suma *f.* [*súma*]; **in - to,** además de [*además de*]; **-al** *a.* adicional [*adiθjonál*], suplementario(a) [*suplementárjo*]; **-ally** *adv.* adicionalmente [*adiθjonalménte*]

address (to) dirigir *r.* [*dirixír*], enviar *r.* [*embjár*] (letter, etc) (to/a) ‖ **2.** señas *f. pl.* [*sénjas*], dirección *f.* [*direkθjón*]; **home -,** domicilio *m.* [*domiθíljo*]; **-ee** destinatario(a) *m.-f.* [*destinatárjo*]

adequate *a.* adecuado(a) [*adekwádo*], suficiente [*sufiθjénte*]; **-ly** *adv.* suficientemente [*sufiθjenteménte*], adecuadamente [*adekwadaménte*]

adherent *a.* adherente [*aderénte*]

adhesive *a.* adhesivo(a) [*adesíbo*]; **- tape**, cinta *f.* adhesiva [*θínta*] ‖ **2.** *n.* adhesivo *m.* [*adesíbo*], pegamento *m.* [*pegaménto*]

admission entrada *f.* [*entráda*]; *free -*, entrada libre [*líbre*]

admit (to) admitir *r.* [*admitír*], dejar *r.* entrar [*dexár entrár*]; **-tance** entrada *f.* [*entráda*]; **no -**, se prohibe la entrada [*se proíbe la*]

adrenalin adrenalina *f.* [*adrenalína*]

adult adulto(a) *m.-f.* [*adúlto*]

advance (to) adelantar *r.* [*adelantár*], anticipar *r.* [*antiθipár*] (money, etc.) ‖ **2.** *a.* adelantado(a) [*adelantádo*], anticipado(a) [*antiθipádo*]; **- booking** venta anticipada [*bénta antiθipáda*] ‖ **3.** *n.* adelanto *m.* [*adelánto*], anticipo *m.* [*antíθipo*]; **to pay in -**, pagar *r.* por adelantado [*pagár por adelantádo*]

adventure aventura *f.* [*abentúra*]

advertise (to) anunciar *r.* [*anunθjár*]; **-ment** anuncio *m.* [*anúnθjo*]

advise (to) avisar *r.* [*abisár*]

advocate abogado(a) *m.-f.* [*abogádo*]

aerial antena *f.* [*anténa*]

aeroplane avión *m.* [*abjón*]

aesthetic *a.* estético(a) [*estétiko*]

affected *a.* afectado(a) [*afektádo*] (by/por)

after *prep.* después de [*despwés de*]; **- dinner**, de sobremesa [*de sobremésa*]; *the day - tomorrow,* pasado mañana [*pasádo manjána*] ‖ **2.** detrás de [*detrás de*]; **-noon** tarde *f.* [*tárde*]; *good -!* ¡buenas tardes! [*bwénas tárdes*]; *in the -*, por la tarde [*por la*]; **- shave lotion** loción *f.* para después del afeitado [*loθjón pára despwés del afeitádo*]; **-wards** *adv.* después [*despwés*], luego [*lwégo*]

again *adv.* de nuevo [*de nwébo*], otra vez [*ótra beθ*]; *to do -*, volver (ue) a hacer [*bolbér a aθér*]; **-st** *prep.* contra [*kóntra*], en contra de [*en kóntra de*]

age edad *f.* [*edád*]

agency agencia *f.* [*axénθja*]; *estate -*, agencia inmobilaria [*inmobiljárja*]; *travel -*, agencia de viajes [*de bjáxes*]

ago *adv.* (desde) hace: *one year -*, hace un año [*áθe un ánjo*]

agreeable *a.* agradable [*agradáble*]

agricultur/al *a.* agrícola [*agríkola*]; **-e** agricultura *f.* [*agrikultúra*]

aid auxilio *m.* [*auksíljo*], socorro *m.* [*sokórro*]

air aire *m.* [*áire*]; *by -*, por avión [*por abjón*]; *in the open -*, al aire libre [*al áire líbre*]; **- bed** colchón *m.* neumático [*koltchón neumátiko*]; **- brake** freno *m.* neumático [*fréno neumátiko*]; **- conditioned** aire *m.* con aire acondicionado [*kon áire akondiθjonádo*]; **- conditioning** aire *m.* acondicionado [*áire akondiθjonádo*]; **-craft** avión *m.* [*abjón*]; **- filter** filtro *m.* de aire [*filtro de áire*]; **- freight** carga *f.* aérea [*kárga aérea*]; **- freshener,** ambientador *m.* de hogar [*ambjentadór de ogár*]; **- hostess** azafata *f.* [*aθafáta*]; **- letter** carta *f.* aérea [*kárta aérea*]; **-line** línea *f.* aérea [*línea aérea*]; **- mail** correo *m.* aéreo [*korréo aéreo*]; **-port** aeropuerto *m* [*aeropwérto*]; **- pressure** presión *f.* atmosférica [*presjón atmosférika*]; **- terminal** terminal *f.* aérea [*terminál aérea*]

alabaster alabastro *m.* [*alabástro*]; *of -*, de alabastro [*de*]

alarm alarma *f.* [*alárma*]; **- clock** despertador *m.* [*despertadór*]

album álbum *m.* [*álbum*]

alcohol alcohol *m.* [*alkoól*]; **-ic** *a.* alcohólico(a) [*alkoóliko*]; **- drink,** bebida *f.* alcohólica [*bebída alkoólika*] ‖ **2.** *n.* alcohólico(a) *m.-f.* [*alkoóliko*]

alimentary *a.* alimenticio(a) [*alimentíθjo*]

alive *a.* vivo(a) [*bíbo*]; *to be -*, estar *irr.* vivo(a) [*estár*]

all *a.* todo(a) [*tódo*], todos(as) [*tódos*]; *- the country*, todo el país [*el país*]; *- day*, todo el día [*el día*] ‖ **2.** *pron.* *after -*, después de todo [*despwés de tódo*]; *not at -*, en absoluto [*en absolúto*]; *that's -!* ¡ya está! [*ja está*]

allerg/ic *a.* alérgico(a) [*alérxiko*]; **-y** alergia *f.* [*alérxja*]

allow (to) permitir *r.* [*permitír*]; **-ance** asignación *f.* [*asignaθjón*]

all right *a.* bien [*bjen*]; *it's -*, está bien [*está*]

almond almendra *f.* [*alméndra*]; *toasted -s,* almendras *pl.* tostadas [*tostádas*]; **- chocolate** chocolate *m.* de almendra [*de alméndra*]; **- tree** almendro *m.* [*aléndro*]

almost *adv.* casi [*kási*]

alone *adv.* solo(a) [*sólo*]

along *adv.* a lo largo [*a lo lárgo*], adelante [*adelánte*]: *come -!* ¡pasa! [*pása*], ¡ven! [*ben*], ¡adelante! [*adelánte*]

alpine *a.* alpino(a) [*alpíno*]

Alps, the los Alpes *m. pl.* [*los álpes*]

already *adv.* ya [*ja*]

also *adv.* también [*tambjén*]

altar altar *m.* [*altár*]

alter (to) arreglar *r.* [*arreglár*], retocar *r.* [*rretokár*]

although *conj.* aunque [*áwnke*]

aluminium aluminio *m.* [*aluminjo*]

always *adv.* siempre [*sjémpre*]

amber ámbar *m.* [*ámbar*]

ambulance ambulancia *f.* [*ambulánθja*]

American *a.* americano(a) [*amerikáno*] ‖ **2.** americano(a) *m.-f.*: **North-**, norteamericano(a) *m.-f.* [*norteamerikáno*], estadounidense *m.-f.* [*estadounidénse*] (USA)

amethyst amatista *f.* [*amatísta*]

among *prep.* entre [*éntre*]

amount importe *m.* [*impórte*] ‖ **2.** ración [*rraθjón*]: *small -*, pequeña ración [*pekénja*]

ampère amperio *m.* [*ampérjo*]

amphora ánfora *f.* [*ánfora*]

ample *a.* amplio(a) [*ámpljo*]

amplif/ier amplificador *m.* [*amplifikadór*]; **-y to** amplificar *r.* [*amplifikár*]

ampoule ampolla *f.* [*ampólja*]

amputat/e to amputar *r.* [*amputár*]; **-ion** amputación *f.* [*amputaθjón*]

amulet amuleto *m.* [*amuléto*]

amus/e (to): to - oneself, divertirse (ie) [*dibertírse*], **-ement** diversión *f.* [*dibersjón*], **-ing** *a.* divertido(a) [*dibertído*]

an *art. indef.* un, una [*un, úna*]

anaemia anemia *f.* [*anémja*]

anaesthesia anestesia *f.* [*anestésja*]

anagram anagrama *m.* [*anagráma*]

analgesic *a.* analgésico(a) [*analxésiko*] ‖ **2.** *n.* analgésico [*analxésiko*]

analysis análisis *m.* [*análisis*]

anchor ancla *f.* [*ánkla*]

anchovy anchoa *f.* [*antchóa*], boquerón *m.* [*bokerón*] (fresh)

ancient *a.* antiguo(a) [*antíguo*]

and *conj.* y [*i*], *you - me,* tú y yo [*tu i jo*] ‖ **2.** e [*e*] (before "i" and "hi"): *Spanish - English*, español e inglés [*espanjól e inglés*]

Andalusia Andalucía *f.* [*andaluθía*]; **-n** *a.* andaluz(a) [*andalúθ*] ‖ **2.** *n.* andaluz(a) *m.-f.*

anemone anémona *f.* [*anémona*]

angle ángulo *m.* [*ángulo*]: *- of sight,* ángulo *m.* de visión [*de bisjón*]

angler pescador *m.* de caña [*peskadór de kánja*], **-fish** rape *m.* [*rrápe*]; *fried -*, rape frito [*fríto*]; *- fried in batter*, rape a la romana [*a la romána*], *grilled -*, rape a la parrilla [*a la parrílja*]; *steamed -*, rape a la marinera [*a la marinéra*]

animal animal *m.* [*animál*]

animated *a.* animado(a) [*animádo*]: *- cartoons,* dibujos *m. pl.* animados [*dibúxos animádos*]

anis anís *m.* [*anís*]; **-eed:** *- liqueur,* licor *m.* de anís [*likór de*]

ankle tobillo *m.* [*tobíljo*]

annexe anexo *m.* [*anékso*]

anniversary aniversario *m.* [*anibersárjo*]: *wedding -,* aniversario de boda [*de bóda*]

announce (to) anunciar *r.* [*anunθjár*], participar *r.* [*partiθipár*], **-ment** anuncio *m.* [*anúnθjo*], participación *f.* [*partiθipaθjón*]

annual *a.* anual [*anwál*]; **-ly** *adv.* anualmente [*anwalménte*]

anorak anorak *m.* [*anorák*]

another *a.-pron.* otro(a) [*ótro*]: *- beer,* otra cerveza [*ótra θerbéθa*]; *- one,* otro(a) [*ótro*]

anovulatory anovulatorio *m.* [*anobulatórjo*]

answer (to) contestar *r.* [*kontestár*], responder *r.* [*rrespondér*]: *to - the telephone,* contestar al teléfono [*kontestár al teléfono*] ‖ **2.** *n.* respuesta *f.* [*rrespwésta*], contestación *f.* [*kontestaθjón*]

antacid antiácido *m.* [*antiáθido*]

ante: *- shave lotion,* loción *f* para antes del afeitado [*loθjón pára ántes del afeitádo*]

antibiotic antibiótico *m.* [*antibjótiko*]

anticyclone anticiclón *m.* [*antiθiklón*]

anti-dandruff *a.* anticaspa [*antikáspa*]: *- shampoo* champú *m.* contra la caspa [*tchampú kóntra la káspa*]

antidote contraveneno *m.* [*kontrabenéno*]

antifreeze anticongelante *m.* [*antikonxelánte*]

antihistamine antihistamínico *m.* [*antiistamíniko*]

antiphonary antifonario *m.* [*antifonárjo*]

antiquarian *a.* anticuario(a) [*antikwárjo*] ‖ **2.** *n.* anticuario(a) *m.-f.*

antiquated *a.* anticuado(a) [*antikwádo*]

antique *a.* antiguo(a) [*antíguo*]: *- coins,* monedas *f.pl.* antiguas [*monédas antíguas*]; *- firearms* armas *f.pl.* de fuego antiguas [*ármas de fwégo*]; *- maps* mapas *m. pl.* antiguos [*mápas*]; ‖ **2.** *n.* antigüedad *f.* [*antig-wedád*]; **- dealer,** anticuario *m.* [*an-tikwárjo*]; **- shop** tienda *f.* de antigüedades [*tjénda de antigwedádes*]

antiquity antigüedad *f.* [*antigwedád*] ‖ **2.** monumento *m.* antiguo [*monuménto antígwo*]

antiseptic antiséptico *m.* [*antiséptiko*]; **- mouthwash** antiséptico bucal [*bukál*]

antispasmodic antiespasmódico *m.* [*antiespasmódiko*]

anus ano *m.* [*áno*]

anxiety ansiedad *f.* [*ansjedád*]

any *a.-pron.* cualquier(a) [*kwalkjér*], algún (alguna) [*algún, algúna*] (questions) ‖ **2.** ningun(a) [*ningún, ningúna*] (negative sentences)

anybody *pron.* alguien [*álgjen*] (questions) ‖ **2.** nadie [*nádje*] (negative sentences)

anything *pron.* algo [*álgo*] (questions) ‖ **2.** nada [*náda*] (negative sentences)

anyway *adv.* de todas formas [*de tódas fórmas*]

anywhere *adv.* en alguna parte [*en algúna párte*] (questions) ‖ **2.** en ninguna parte [*en ningúna párte*] (negative sentences)

aorta aorta *f.* [*aórta*]

apart *adv.* aparte [*apárte*]; **-ment** apartamento *m.* [*apartaménto*]: **- with bathroom,** apartamento con cuarto de baño [*kon kwárto de bánjo*]; **- with dining room,** apartamento con comedor [*kon komedór*]; **- with kitchen,** apartamento con cocina [*koθína*]; **- with balcony,** apartamento con terraza [*kon terráθa*]

aperitif aperitivo *m.* [*aperitíbo*]: **- snack** tapa *f.* [*tápa*]

aperture abertura *f.* [*abertúra*]

apiece *adv.* cada uno(a) [*káda úno*]

apparatus aparato *m.* [*aparáto*]

appeal atractivo *m.* [*atraktíbo*]: **sex -,** atractivo sexual [*sekswál*]

appear (to) aparecer (zc) [*apareθér*]

appendicitis apendicitis *f.* [*apendiθítis*]

appendix apéndice *m.* [*apéndiθe*]

appetite apetito *m.* [*apetíto*], **-zer** aperitivo *m.* [*aperitíbo*], tapa *f.* [*tápa*]

apple manzana *f.* [*manθána*]; **- pie** tarta *f.* de manzana [*tárta de*]; **- compote** compota *f.* de manzanas [*kompóta de*]; **- tart** tarta *f.* de manzana [*tárta*]

apply (to) poner *irr.* [*ponér*]: **to - an ointment,** aplicar *r.* una pomada [*úna pomáda*]

approximate *a.* aproximado(a) [*aproksimádo*]; **-ly** *adv.* aproximadamente [*aproksimadaménte*]

apricot albaricoque *m.* [*albarikóke*]: **- jam** mermelada *f.* de albaricoque [*merméláda de*]

April abril *m.* [*abríl*]

apron delantal *m.* [*delantál*]

aquamarine aguamarina *f.* [*agwamárina*]

aquaplane esquí *m.* acuático [*eskí akwátiko*]

aquatic(al) *a.* acuático(a) [*akwátiko*]

aqueduct acueducto *m.* [*akwedúkto*]

arc arco *m.* [*árko*]; **-ade** arcada *f.* [*arkáda*], pasaje *m.* [*pasáxe*]

arch arco *m.* [*árko*]

archaelogical *a.* arqueológico(a) [*arkeolóxiko*]

archbishop arzobispo *m.* [*arθobíspo*]

archipelago archipiélago *m.* [*artchipjélago*]

architect arquitecto(a) *m.-f.* [*arkitékto*]; **-ural** *a.* arquitectónico(a) [*arkitektóniko*]; **-ure** arquitectura *f.* [*arkitektúra*]

archway arcada *f.* [*arkáda*]

area área *f.* [*área*], zona *f.* [*θóna*]: **in this -,** en esta zona [*en ésta*]

arena plaza *f.* de toros [*pláθa de tóros*] (bullfight)

arm brazo *m.* [*bráθo*], **-band** brazal *m.* [*braθál*]; **-chair** sillón *m.* [*siljón*]

armour armadura *f.* [*armadúra*]

aroma aroma *f.* [*aróma*], **-tic** *a.* aromático (a) [*aromátiko*]

around *adv.* alrededor [*alrrededór*] ‖ **2.** *prep.* alrededor de [*alrrededór de*]: **- the world,** alrededor del mundo [*del múndo*] ‖ **3.** aproximadamente [*aproksimadaménte*]: **- seven o'clock**, a las siete aproximadamente [*a las sjéte*]

arquebus arcabuz *m.* [*arkabúθ*]

arrange (to) arreglar *r.* [*arreglár*]; **-d** *a.* arreglado(a) [*arregládo*]; **-ment** arreglo *m.* [*arréglo*]; **-s** preparativos *m.pl.* [*preparatíbos*]

arrival llegada *f.* [*ljegáda*]

arrive (to) llegar *r.* [*ljegár*] (at, in, etc./a)

art arte *f.* [*árte*]: **work of -,** obra *f.* de arte [*óbra de*]; **-book** libro *m.* de arte [*líbro de*]; **- gallery** galería *f.* de arte [*galería*]

artery arteria *f.* [*artérja*]

arterial *a.* arterial [*arterjál*]

arthritis artritis *f.* [*artrítis*]

artichoke alcachofa *f.* [*alkatchófa*]; **fried -s,** alcachofas *pl.* fritas [*frítas*]; **- in vinegar,** alcachofas *pl.* a la vinagreta [*alkatchófas a la binagréta*]

article artículo *m.* [*artíkulo*]: **- of clothing**, prenda *f.* de vestir [*prénda de bestír*]

artificial *a.* artificial [*artifiθjál*]: **- pearl** perla *f.* artificial [*pérla artifiθjál*]; **- stone** piedra *f.* falsa [*pjédra fálsa*]

artist artista *m.-f.* [*artísta*]; **-ic** *a.* artístico(a) [*artístiko*]

as *adv.* como [*kómo*]; **as ... as**; tan ... como [*tan...kómo*]: **my room is - big - yours,** mi habitación es tan grande como la tuya [*mi abitaθjón es tan gránde kómo la túja*] ‖ **2.** *conj.* mientras [*mjéntras*], cuando [*kwándo*] ‖ **3.** ya que [*ja ke*]

ascend (to) ascender (ie) [*asθendér*] (a)

ash ceniza *f.* [*θeníθa*]; **-tray** cenicero *m.* [*θeniθéro*]

ask (to) preguntar *r.* [*preguntár*] (for/por) ‖ **2.** pedir (i) [*pedír*] (for/u.c.)

asleep *a.* dormido(a) [*dormído*]: **to be -,** estar *irr.* dormido(a) [*estár*]

asparagus espárrago *m.* [*espárrago*]; **- tips** puntas *f.pl.* de espárragos [*púntas de*]

aspect aspecto *m.* [*aspékto*]

asphalt asfalto *m.* [*asfálto*]

asphyxiation asfixia *f.* [*asfíksja*]

aspic gelatina *f.* [*xelatína*]

aspirin aspirina *f.* [*aspirína*]

assemble (to) montar *r.* [*montár*]

assist (to) asistir *r.* [*asistír*], ayudar *r.* [*ajudár*] (so./a); **-ance** asistencia *f.* [*asisténθja*], ayuda *f* [*ajúda*]; **-ant** aprendiz(a) *m.-f.* [*aprendíθ*], ayudante *m.-f.* [*ajudánte*] ‖ **2. shop -,** dependiente *m.* [*dependjénte*]; dependienta *f.* [*dependjénta*]

assort/ed *a.* variado(a) [*barjádo*]: **- biscuits** surtido *m.* de galletas [*surtído de galjétas*]; **- cheeses** quesos *m.pl.* variados [*késos barjádos*]; **- hors d'oeuvres** entremeses *m.pl.* variados [*entreméses barjádos*]; **-ment** surtido *m.* [*surtído*]

asthma asma *m.* [*ásma*]

astringent *a* astringente [*astrinxénte*]: **- lotion** loción *f.* astringente [*loθjón*]

at *prep.* en [*en*], a [*a*], de [*de*], con [*kon*]; junto a [*xúnto a*]: **- home,** en casa [*en kása*]; **- seven o'clock**, a las siete [*a las sjéte*]

athletics atletismo *m.* [*atletísmo*]

attack ataque *m.* [*atáke*], agresión *f.* [*agresjón*]: **heart -,** infarto *m.* [*infárto*] ‖ **2.** *vb* atacar *r.* [*atakár*]

attend (to) atender (ie) [*atendér*] (so./a); servir (i) [*serbír*] ‖ **2. to - mass,** oir *irr.* misa [*oír mísa*]; **-ant** acomodador(a) *m.-f.* [*akomodadór*] (cinema)

attractive *a.* atractivo(a) [*atraktíbo*]

aubergine berenjena *f.* [*berenxéna*], **fried -s,** berenjenas fritas [*frítas*]; **roasted -s,** berenjenas asadas [*asádas*]; **stuffed -s,** berenjenas rellenas [*rreljénas*]

auction subasta *f.* [*subásta*]

August agosto *m.* [*agósto*]

aunt tía *f.* [*tía*]

austral *a.* austral [*austrál*]

Australia Australia *f.* [*austrálja*]

authentic *a.* auténtico(a) [*auténtiko*]

author autor(a) *m.-f.* [*autór*]

automatic *a.* automático(a) [*automátiko*]; **-ally** *adv.* automáticamente [*automatikaménte*]

automobile automóvil *m.* [*automóbil*], coche *m.* [*kótche*]

autumn otoño *m.* [*otónjo*]

auxiliary *a.* auxiliar [*auksiljár*]

available *a.* disponible [*disponíble*]: **to be -,** estar *irr.* disponible [*estár*]

avenue avenida *f.* [*abenída*]

avocado aguacate *m.* [*agwakáte*]

await (to) esperar *r* [*esperár*]

awake (to) despertar (ie) [*despertár*] ‖ **2.** *a.* **to be -,** estar *irr.* despierto(a) [*despjérto*]

away *adv.* fuera [*fwéra*]

axle eje *m.* [*éxe*], **back -,** eje trasero [*traséro*]; **front -,** eje delantero [*delantéro*]

B

baby bebé *m.* [*bebé*]; **- eels** angulas *f. pl.* [*angúlas*]; **- marrows** calabacines *m. pl.* [*kalabaθínes*]; **- octopus** pulpitos *m. pl.* [*pulpítos*]; **- squids** chipirones *m. pl.* [*tchipirónes*]; **-sitter** canguro *m.-f.* [*kangúro*]

bacillus bacilo *m.* [*baθílo*]

back espalda *f.* [*espálda*] ‖ **2. to be -**, estar *irr.* de vuelta [*estár de bwélta*]; **-ache** dolor *m.* de espalda [*dolór de espálda*]; **-pack** mochila *f.* [*motchíla*]; **-ward** *a.* hacia atrás [*áθja atrás*]; **-yard** patio *m.* trasero [*pátjo traséro*]

bacon beicon *m.* [*béikon*], tocino *m.* [*toθíno*]

bacterium bacteria *f.* [*baktérja*]

bad *a.* malo(a) [*málo*] ‖ **2.** mal (before masc. nouns); **-ly** *adv.* mal

bag bolsa *f.* [*bólsa*], bolso *m.* [*bólso*], saco *m.* [*sáko*]

baggage equipaje *m.* [*ekipáxe*]

bait cebo *m.* [*θébo*]

bake (to) cocer (ue) [*koθér*], asar *r.* en el horno [*asár en el órno*]; **-d** *a.* cocido(a) [*koθído*], asado(a) en el horno [*asádo en el órno*]; **-r** panadero *m.* [*panadéro*]; **-r's** panadería *f.* [*panadería*]

baking: - powder, levadura *f.* en polvo [*lebadúra en pólbo*]

balcony balcón *m.* [*balkón*], terraza *f.* [*terráθa*] ‖ **2.** anfiteatro *m.* [*anfiteátro*]

Balearic *a.* balear [*baleár*]; **the - Islands**, las Islas Baleares [*las íslas baleáres*]

ball pelota *f.* [*pelóta*] (tennis, etc.), balón *m.* [*balón*] (football, etc.); bola *f.* [*bóla*] (golf, etc.) ‖ **2.** baile *m.* [*báile*] (party); **- bearing** cojinete *m.* [*koxinéte*]; **- cartridges** cartuchos *m.pl.* de bala [*kartútchos de bála*]

ballet ballet *m.* [*balé*]; **- dancer** bailarín *m.* [*bailarín*] ‖ **2.** bailarina *f.* [*bailarína*]

balloon globo *m.* [*glóbo*]

ballpoint: - pen, bolígrafo *m.* [*bolígrafo*]

ballroom salón *m.* de baile [*salón de báile*]

balsam bálsamo *m.* [*bálsamo*]

banana plátano *m.* [*plátano*]

band banda *f.* [*bánda*] ‖ **2.** cinta *f.* [*θínta*]; **elastic -,** goma *f.* elástica [*góma elástika*]

bandage venda *f.* [*bénda*]

bank banco *m.* [*bánko*]; **-book** libreta *f.* de ahorros [*libréta de aórros*]; **-er** banquero *m.* [*bankéro*]; **-note** billete *m.* de banco [*biljéte de bánko*]; **- transfer** transferencia *f.* bancaria [*transferénθja bankárja*]

banquet banquete *m.* [*bankéte*]

bar barra *f.* [*bárra*] ‖ **2.** bar *m.* [*bar*] ‖ **3.** bar *m.* de tapas [*de tápas*] (light snacks) ‖ **4. - of chocolate,** tableta *f.* de chocolate [*tabléta de tchokoláte*]; **-man** barman *m.* [*bárman*]; **-stool** taburete *m.* [*taburéte*]

barbecue barbacoa *f.* [*barbakóa*], **-d: - steak,** churrasco *m.* [*tchurrásko*]

barber barbero *m.* [*barbéro*]; **-'s shop** barbería *f.* [*barbería*]

bargain ocasión *f.* [*okasjón*] (sales)

bar/maid camarera *f.* [*kamaréra*]; **-man** camarero *m.* [*kamaréro*]

barometer barómetro *m.* [*barómetro*]

baroque *a.* barroco(a) [*barróko*]

barrel barril *m.* [*barríl*]

barstool taburete *m.* [*taburéte*]

basic *a.* básico(a) [*básiko*]

basilica basílica *f.* [*basílika*]

basket cesto *m.* [*θésto*]; cesta *f.* [*θésta*] (shopping); **-ball** baloncesto *m.* [*balonθésto*]; **- match,** partido *m.* de baloncesto [*partído de*]

Basque *a.* vasco(a) [*básko*]; **- Country** País Vasco [*país*] ‖ **2.** *n.* vasco(a) *m.-f.* [*básko*]

bass róbalo *m.* [*rróbalo*], lubina *f.* [*lubína*]

batavian: - endive, escarola *f.* [*eskaróla*]

bath baño *m.* [*bánjo*]; **-robe** albornoz *m.* [*albornóθ*], bata *f.* [*báta*]; **-room** cuarto *m.* de baño [*kwárto de bánjo*]; **- fittings** saneamiento *m.* [*saneamjénto*]; **-salt** sal *f.* de baño [*sal de*]; **-towel** toalla *f.* de baño [*toálja de*]; **-tub** bañera *f.* [*banjéra*]

bath/e (to) bañar(se) *r.* [*banjár(se)*]; **-er** bañista *m.* [*banjísta*]; **-ing: - costume** bañador *m.* [*banjadór*]; **- hut** caseta *f.* [*kaséta*]; **- suit** bañador *m.* [*banjadór*]

batter: in -, rebozado(a) [*rreboθádo*] (fish, etc.)

battery batería *f.* [*batería*]; pila *f.* [*píla*]

bay bahía *f.* [*baía*]; **- leaf** laurel *m.* [*lauré*]

be (to) *vb. y vb. aux.* ser *irr.* [*ser*] (see grammar) ‖ **2.** estar *irr.* [*estár*] (see grammar)

beach playa f. [*plája*]; **to be on the -**, estar en la playa [*estár en la*]; **- chair** tumbona f. [*tumbóna*]

bean haba f. [*ába*]; **broad -**, alubia [*alúbja*]; **French -**, judía f. [*xudía*]; **green -**, judía f. verde [*xudía bérde*]; **haricot -**, alubia f. [*alúbja*]

beard barba f. [*bárba*]

beat (to) batir r. [*batír*] (eggs, etc.)

beautiful a. hermoso(a) [*ermóso*], bello(a) [*béljo*]

beauty belleza f. [*beljéθa*]; **- saloon** salón m. de belleza [*salón de beljéθa*]

because conj. porque [*porké*] || **2.** prep. **- of,** debido a [*debido a*]

bed cama f. [*káma*]; **double -**, cama de matrimonio [*de matrimónjo*]; **extra -**, cama supletoria [*supletórja*]; **single -**, cama individual [*indibidwál*]; **to go to -**, acostarse (ue) [*akostárse*], ir irr. a la cama [*ir a la káma*]; **- and breakfast** cama f. con desayuno [*káma kon desajúno*]; **-linen** ropa f. de cama [*rrópa de káma*]; **-room** dormitorio m. [*dormitórjo*]; **- table** mesita f. de noche [*mesíta de nótche*]; **-warming pan** mundillo m. [*mundíljo*]

beef buey m. [*bwei*], carne f. de buey [*kárne de*]; **roast -**, carne de buey asada [*asáda*]; rosbif m. [*rrósbif*]; **-chop** chuleta f. de buey [*tchuléta de*]; **-steak** bistec m. [*bisték*]

beer cerveza f. [*θerbéθa*]; **black -**, cerveza negra [*négra*]; **draught -**, cerveza de barril [*de barríl*]; **Lager-**, cerveza blanca [*blánka*]; **glass of -**, caña f. [*kánja*]; **-bar** cervecería f. [*θerbeθería*]; **-glass** vaso m. de cerveza [*báso de θerbéθa*]; **-house** cervecería f. [*θerbeθería*]

beetroot remolacha f. [*rremolátcha*]

before adv. antes [*ántes*] || **2.** delante [*delánte*] (local) || **3.** prep. antes de [*de*] || **3.** conj. antes de que [*ántes de ke*]

beg (to) pedir (i) [*pedír*], solicitar r. [*soliθitár*]

begin (to) empezar (ie) [*empeθár*], comenzar (ie) [*komenθár*]; **to - to do sth.,** empezar a hacer u.c. [*empeθár a aθér úna kósa*]; **-ner** principiante m./f. [*prinθipjánte*]; **-ning** comienzo m. [*komjénθo*]; principio m. [*prinθípjo*]; **at the - of the year,** a principios de año [*a prinθípjos de ánjo*]; **from the -**, desde el principio [*désde el*]

behalf: on - of, en nombre de [*en nómbre de*]

behind prep. detrás de [*detrás de*]; **- the hotel,** detrás del hotel [*del otél*]

beige a. beige [*béis*]

believe (to) creer r. [*kreér*]; **I - it**, me lo creo [*me lo kréo*]

bell campana f. [*kampána*] || **2.** cascabel m. [*kaskabél*] || **3.** timbre m. [*tímbre*]; **to ring the -**, tocar r. el timbre [*tokár el*]; **-boy** botones m. [*botónes*]

bellows fuelle m. [*fwélje*]; **- catch** dispositivo m. de fuelle [*dispositíbo de*]

belly vientre m. [*bjéntre*], barriga f. [*barríga*]; **-ache** dolor m. de vientre [*dolór de bjéntre*]

belong (to) pertenecer (zc) [*perteneθér*] (to/a), ser irr. [*ser*] (to/de): **it belongs to my father,** es de mi padre [*es de mi pádre*]; **-ings** efectos m.pl. personales [*eféktos personáles*]

below prep. debajo de [*debáxo de*]

belt cinturón m. [*θinturón*] || **2. seat -**, cinturón de seguridad [*de seguridád*]; **to fasten the -s,** abrocharse r. los cinturones de seguridad [*abrochárse los θinturónes de seguridád*] || **3.** Mech. correa f. de transmisión [*korréa de transmisjón*]

bench banco m. [*bánko*] || **2. - with backrest,** escaño m. [*eskánjo*]

bend curva f. [*kúrba*], recodo m. [*rrekódo*]

beneath prep. debajo de [*debáxo de*]

beret boina f. [*bóina*]

besom escoba f. [*eskóba*]

best a. el (la) mejor [*el mexór*] (superl.)

bet (to) apostar (ue) [*apostár*] || **2.** n. apuesta f. [*apwésta*]

better a. mejor [*mexór*] (comp.)

between prep. entre [*éntre*] (with nomin.): **- you and me,** entre tú y yo [*éntre tu i jo*]

beverage bebida f. [*bebída*]; **alcoholic -**, bebida alcohólica [*alkoólika*]; **non-alcoholic -**, bebida sin alcohol [*sin alkoól*]

beyond prep. más allá de [*mas aljá de*]

Bible biblia f. [*bíblja*]

bicarbonate bicarbonato m. [*bikarbonáto*]

bicycle bicicleta f. [*biθikléta*]; **to go by -**, ir irr. en bicicleta [*ir en biθikléta*]

big a. grande [*gránde*] || **2.** gran [*gran*] (before the noun)

bikini bikini m. [*bikíni*]

bill nota f. [*nóta*], cuenta f. [*kwénta*] || **2.** factura f. [*faktúra*] (invoice)

billiard billar m. [*biljár*]; **- cue** taco m. de billar [*táko de*]; **- room** sala f. de billar [*sála de*]

bin: *rubbish* -, cubo *m.* de basura [*kúbo de basúra*]

bingo bingo *m.* [*bíngo*]; - **hall** sala *f.* de bingo [*sála de bíngo*]

birth parto *m.* [*párto*]; nacimiento *m.* [*naθimjénto*]; *date of* -, fecha *f.* de nacimiento [*fétcha de*]; *place of* -, lugar *m.* de nacimiento [*lugár de*]; - **certificate** partida *f.* de nacimiento [*partída de*]; -**day** cumpleaños *m.* [*kumpleáŋos*]

biscuit galleta *f.* [*galjéta*] ‖ **2.** bizcocho *m.* [*biθkótcho*]

bishop obispo *m.* [*obíspo*]

bite mordedura *f* [*mordedúra*], picadura *f.* [*pikadúra*] (insect)

bitter *a* amargo(a) [*amárgo*]: - **marmalade** mermelada *f.* de naranja amarga [*mermeláda de naránxa amárga*]; - **sweet** *a.* agridulce [*agridúlθe*] ‖ **2.** *n.* bíter *m.* [*bíter*] (drink)

bivouac vivac *m.* [*bibák*] ‖ **2.** *vb.* vivaquear *v.* [*bibakeár*]

black *a.* negro(a) [*négro*]: - **and white** en blanco y negro [*en blánko i négro*]; - **coffee** café *m.* solo [*kafé sólo*]; - **pepper** pimienta *f.* negra [*pimjénta*]; - **pudding** morcilla *f.* [*morθílja*]; -**berry** zarzamora *f.* [*θarθamóra*]

bladder vejiga *f.* [*bexíga*]

blank *a.* en blanco [*en blánko*]

blanket manta *f.* [*mánta*]; - **cape** poncho *m.* [*póntcho*]

blazer chaqueta *f.* (de) sport [*tchakéta de sport*]

bleach (to) decolorar *r.* [*dekolorár*] ‖ **2.** *n.* lejía *f.* [*lexía*]; -**ing** decoloración *f.* [*dekoloraθjón*]

bleed (to) sangrar *r.* [*sangrár*]; -**ing** hemorragia *f.* [*emorráxja*]

blend mezcla *f.* [*méθkla*]; -**er** licuadora *f.* [*likuadóra*]; *hand* -, batidora *f.* [*batidóra*]

blind *a.* ciego(a) [*θjégo*]; - **man** ciego *m.;* - **woman** ciega *f.* [*θjéga*]

blister ampolla *f.* [*ampólja*]

block bloque *m.* [*blóke*], taco *m.* [*táko*] (of wood); -**ed** *a.* atascado(a) [*ataskádo*]

blond *a.* rubio [*rrúbjo*]

blood sangre *f.* [*sángre*]; - **pressure** presión *f.* sanguínea [*presjón sangínea*]; - **transfusion** transfusión *f.* de sangre [*transfusjón de sángre*]

blouse blusa *f.* [*blúsa*]

blow (to) soplar *r.* [*soplár*] (wind); - **out** reventón *m.* [*rrebentón*]; - **up** ampliación *f.* [*ampljaθjón*]

blue *a.* azul [*aθúl*]; - **fish** pescado *m.* azul [*peskádo*]; -**berry** arándano *m.* [*arándano*]

blunderbuss trabuco *m.* [*trabúko*]

boar jabalí *m.* [*xabalí*]; -**'s head** cabeza *f.* de jabalí [*kabéθa de*]

board pensión *f.* [*pensjón*]; *full* -, pensión completa [*kompléta*]; *half* -, media pensión [*médja*]

boarding: -**card** tarjeta *f.* de embarque [*tarxéta de embárke*]; - **house** pensión *f.* [*pensjón*]

boat barco *m.* [*bárko*]; bote *m.* [*bóte*], barca *f.* [*bárka*]; *fishing* -, barco *m.* de pesca [*bárko de péska*]; *sailing* -, barco *m.* de vela [*bárko de béla*]; -**hook** bichero *m.* [*bitchéro*]; -**trailer** portabarcas *m.* [*portabárkas*]; -**yard** astillero *m.* [*astiljéro*]

body cuerpo *m.* [*kuérpo*]; - **massage** masaje *m.* corporal [*masáxe korporál*]; -**wave** moldeado *m.* [*moldeádo*] (hair); -**work** carrocería *f.* [*karroθería*]

boil (to) hervir (ie) [*erbír*] ‖ **2.** *n.* forúnculo *m.* [*forúnkulo*]; -**ed** *a.* hervido(a) [*erbído*], cocido(a) [*koθído*]; *lightly* - *(in water),* pasado(a) por agua [*pasádo por água*] (eggs, etc.); -**er** caldera *f.* [*kaldéra*]; -**ing:** - **point** punto *m.* de ebullición [*púnto de ebulliθjón*]

Bologna: - *sausage,* mortadela *f.* [*mortadéla*]

bolt cerrojo *m.* [*θerróxo*], pestillo *m.* [*pestíljo*]; - **ring** cáncamo *m.* [*kánkamo*]

bonbon caramelo *m.* [*karamélo*]

bone hueso *m.* [*uéso*]

bonnet capó *m.* [*kapó*]

book (to) reservar *r.* [*rreserbár*] (room, etc.); ‖ **2.** *n.* libro *m.* [*líbro*]: *address* -, agenda *f.* [*axénda*]; *telephone* -, guía *f.* telefónica [*gía telefónika*]; -**ed** *a.* reservado(a) [*rreserbádo*]; - *up,* completo(a) [*kompléto*] (flight, etc.); -**ing** reserva *f.* [*rresérba*]; - *office,* taquilla *f.* de billetes (pasajes) [*takílja de biljétes* (*pasáxes*)]; -**shop** librería *f.* [*librería*]; -**seller** librero *m.* [*libréro*]; -**stall** quiosco *m.* [*kjósko*]

boot bota *f.* [*bóta*]; -**black** limpiabotas *m.* [*limpjabótas*]

booth cabina *f.* [*kabína*]: *telephone* -, cabina *f.* de teléfono [*de teléfono*] ‖ **2.** puesto *m.* [*puésto*] (market)

border orilla *f.* [*orílja*], borde *m.* [*bórde*] ‖ **2.** frontera *f.* [*frontéra*] (of a country)

borer taladradora *f.* [*taladradóra*]

borrow (to) tomar *r.* prestado [*tomár prestádo*]

both *a.* ambos(as) [*ámbos*] || **2.** *pron.* **- of,** ambos(as), los(las) dos [*los dos*]

bottle botella *f.* [*botélja*]; frasco *m.* [*frásko*] (medicine, perfume, etc.): **a - of wine,** una botella de vino [*úna botélja de bíno*]; **feeding -,** biberón *m.* [*biberón*]; **-d** *a.* embotellado(a) [*emboteljádo*]; **- opener** abrebotellas *m.* [*abrebotéljas*]

bouillabaise bullabesa *f.* [*buljabésa*]

bouillon caldo *m.* [*káldo*]; **- cube** pastilla *f.* de caldo [*pastílja de*]

boulevard bulevar *m.* [*bulebár*], paseo *m.* [*paséo*]

bouquet ramo *m.* [*rrámo*] || **2.** aroma *m.* [*aróma*] (wine)

bourbon whisky *m.* americano [*wíski amerikáno*]

boutique boutique *f.* [*butík*], tienda *f.* [*tjénda*]

bow lazo *m.* [*láθo*] || **2.** bóveda *f.* [*bóbeda*] (Arch.); **- tie** corbata *f.* de lazo [*korbáta de láθo*], pajarita *f.* [*paxaríta*]

bowel intestino *m.* [*intestíno*]; **- movement** deposición *f.* [*deposiθjón*]

bowl tazón *m.* [*taθón*], plato *m.* hondo [*pláto óndo*] (soup) || **2.** jofaina *f.* [*xofáina*]

bowling bolos *m.pl.* [*bólos*]; **- alley** bolera *f.* [*boléra*]

box caja *f.* [*káxa*]; **jewellery -,** joyero *m.* [*xojéro*]; **letter -,** buzón *m.* [*buθón*]; **- of matches,** caja de cerillas [*de θeríljas*]; **post office -,** apartado *m.* de correos [*apartádo de korréos*] || **2.** *Theat.* palco *m.* [*pálko*]; **-ing** boxeo *m.* [*bokséo*]; **- match,** combate *m.* de boxeo [*kombáte de*]

boy niño *m.* [*nínjo*], chico *m.* [*tchíko*], muchacho *m.* [*mutchátcho*]; **-friend** novio *m.* [*nóbjo*]

bracelet brazalete *m.* [*braθaléte*], pulsera *f.* [*pulséra*]

braces tirantes *m.pl.* [*tirántes*]

brain(s) seso(s) *m.pl.* [*sésos*]: **fried -,** sesos a la romana [*a la rromána*]

braised *a.* guisado(a) [*gisádo*] (fish, meat)

brake freno *m.* [*fréno*]; **- blocks** pastillas *f. pl.* de freno [*pastíljas de*]; **- fluid** líquido *m.* de los frenos [*líkido de los*]; **- lights** luces *f. pl.* de freno [*lúθes de*]; **- pedal** pedal *m.* de freno [*pedál de*]; **- shoes** zapatas *f. pl.* [*θapátas*]

braking frenado *m.* [*frenádo*]

branch ramo *m.* [*rrámo*] || **2.** sucursal *f.* [*sukursál*]

brandy coñac *m.* [*konják*]

brass latón *m.* [*latón*]

bread pan *m.* [*pan*]: **English -,** pan inglés [*inglés*]; **French -,** pan francés [*franθés*]; **loaf of -** barra *f.* de pan [*bárra de*]; **round -,** pan redondo [*rredóndo*]; **sliced -,** pan de molde [*de mólde*]; **slice of -,** rebanada *f.* de pan [*rrebanáda de*]; **sticks of -,** bastones *m.pl.* [*bastónes*] (thick), palitos *m.pl.* [*palítos*] (thin); **toasted -,** pan *m.* tostado [*pan tostádo*]; **twisted -,** trenzas *f.pl.* [*trénθas*]; **Vienna -,** pan *m.* de Viena [*pan de bjéna*]; **wholemeal -,** pan integral [*integrál*]; **- crumbed** *a.* rebozado(a) [*rreboθádo*]; **- crumbs** pan *m.* rallado [*pan rraljádo*]; **-roll** panecillo *m.* [*paneθíljo*]; **-shop** panadería *f.* [*panadería*]

break (to) romper(se) *r.* [*rrompérse*] || **2.** *n.* pausa *f.* [*páusa*], descanso *m.* [*deskánso*]; **-down** avería *f.* [*abería*]; **-fast (to)** desayunar *r.* [*desajunár*] || **2.** *n.* desayuno *m.* [*desajúno*]: **to have -,** desayunar *r.* [*desajunár*]

bream besugo *m.* [*besúgo*]: **baked -,** besugo al horno [*besúgo al órno*]; **gilt-head -,** dorada *f.* [*doráda*]

breast pecho *m.* [*pétcho*] || **2.** pechuga *f.* [*petchúga*] (of chicken); **- of mutton** paletilla *f.* de carnero [*paletílja de karnéro*]

breath respiración *f.* [*rrespiraθjón*]; **-e (to)** respirar *r.* [*rrespirár*]; **-ing** respiración *f.* [*rrespiraθjón*]

breeze brisa *f.* [*brísa*]: **sea -,** brisa del mar [*del mar*]

brewery fábrica *f.* de cerveza [*fábrika de θerbéθa*]

brick ladrillo *m.* [*ladríljo*]

bridal *a.* nupcial [*nupθjál*]; **- wear shop** boutique *f.* para novias [*butík pára nóbjas*] (shop)

bride novia *f.* [*nóbja*]

bridge puente *m.* [*pwénte*]

brief *a.* breve [*brébe*]; **- case** cartera *f.* [*kartéra*]

bright *a.* brillante [*briljánte*] || **2.** claro(a) [*kláro*], despejado(a) [*despexádo*]

brilliant brillante *m.* [*briljánte*]; **-ine** brillantina *f.* [*briljantína*]

bring (to) traer *irr.* [*traér*] || **2.** llevar *r.* [*ljebár*]

Britain (Great) Gran Bretaña *f.* [*gran bretánja*]

British *a.* británico(a) [*britániko*]: **he is -,** es británico [*es*] || **2.** *n.pl.* **the -,** los británicos [*los británikos*]

broad *a.* ancho(a) [*ántcho*]; **- beans** habas *f. pl.* [*ábas*], alubias *f. pl.* [*alúbjas*]; **- stewed with pork,** habas *f. pl.* a la catalana [*ábas a la katalána*]; **-casting: - station,** emisora de radio *f.* [*emisóra de rrádjo*]

brocade brocado *m.* [*brokádo*]

broccoli brécol *m.* [*brékol*], bróculi *m.* [*brókuli*]

brochette brocheta *f.* [*brotchéta*]

broken *a.* roto(a) [*rróto*]; **- down** *a.* averiado(a) [*aberjádo*], estropeado(a) [*estropeádo*] (machine)

bronchitis bronquitis *f.* [*bronkítis*]

bronchopneumonia bronconeu-monía *f.* [*bronkoneumonía*]

bronze bronce *m.* [*brónθe*]; **of -,** de bronce [*de*]

brooch broche *m* [*brótche*]

broom escoba *f.* [*eskóba*]

broth caldo *m.* [*káldo*]; **chicken -,** caldo de gallina [*de galjína*]; **vegetable -,** caldo de verdura [*de berdúra*]

brother hermano *m.* [*ermáno*]; **- in-law** cuñado *m.* [*kunjádo*]

brow ceja *f.* [*θéxa*]

brown *a.* marrón [*marrón*] ‖ **2.** castaño(a) [*kastánjo*] (hair) ‖ **3.** moreno(a) [*moréno*] (sun-tanned)

bruise morado *m.* [*morádo*], contusión *f.* [*kontusjón*]; **-d** *a.* magullado(a) [*magujládo*]

brush (to) cepillar *r.* [*θepiljár*] ‖ **2.** *n.* cepillo *m.* [*θepíljo*] ‖ **3.** brocha *f.* [*brótcha*]; **shaving -,** brocha de afeitar [*de afeitár*] ‖ **4.** *Auto.* escobilla *f.* [*eskobílja*]; **-less: - shaving,** espuma *f.* de afeitar [*espúma de afeitár*]

Brussels Bruselas *f.* [*brusélas*]; **- sprouts** coles *f.pl.* de Bruselas [*kóles de*]

bucket cubo *m.* [*kúbo*]

buckle hebilla *f.* [*ebílja*]

bud capullo *m.* [*kapúljo*]

buffet bar *m.* [*bar*], cantina *f.* [*kantína*] ‖ **2.** bufet *m.* libre [*bufét líbre*]; **- car** coche *m.* restaurante [*kótche rrestauránte*]

build (to) construir (y) [*konstruír*], edificar *r.* [*edifikár*]; **-ing** edificio *m.* [*edifiθjo*], construcción *f.* [*konstrukθjón*]; **- site,** solar *m.* [*solár*]

bulb bombilla *f.* [*bombílja*]

bull toro *m.* [*tóro*]; **-fight** corrida *f.* de toros [*korrida de*]; **- poster,** cartel *m.* de toros [*kartél de tóros*]; **-fighter** torero *m.* [*toréro*]; **-'s cape,** capa *f.* de torero [*kápa de*]; **-'s hat,** montera *f.* [*montéra*]; **-'s sword,** estoque *m.* [*estóke*]; **-fighting** toreo *m.* [*toréo*]; **-meat** carne *f.* de toro [*kárne de tóro*]; **-ring** plaza *f.* de toros [*plá θa de tóros*]

bumper parachoques *m.* [*paratchókes*]

bun bollo *m.* [*bóljo*]; magdalena *f.* [*madaléna*]

bunch manojo *m.* [*manóxo*]; **- of grapes** racimo *m.* de uvas [*rra θimo de úbas*] ‖ **2.** ramo *m.* [*rrámo*] (flowers)

bundle bulto *m.* [*búlto*]

bung tapón *m.* [*tapón*] (of barrel)

bunk litera *f.* [*litéra*]

buoy boya *f.* [*bója*]

bureau escritorio *m.* [*eskritórjo*]

burn (to) quemar *r.* [*kemár*] ‖ **2.** *n.* quemadura *f.* [*kemadúra*]; **-t** *a.* quemado(a) [*kemádo*]

burst (to) reventarse (ie) [*rrebentárse*] ‖ **2.** *n.* reventón *m.* [*rrebentón*]

bus autobús *m.* [*autobús*]; **- driver** conductor *m.* de autobús [*konduktór de*]; **- station** terminal *f.* de autobuses [*terminál de autobúses*]; **- stop** parada *f.* de autobús [*paráda de*]; **- ticket** billete *m.* de autobús [*biljéte de*]

business negocio *m.* [*negóθjo*]; **-man** hombre *m.* de negocios [*ombre de negóθjos*]; **- trip** viaje *m.* de negocios [*bjáxe de*]; **-woman** mujer *f.* de negocios [*muxér de*]

busy *a.* ocupado(a) [*okupádo*]

but *conj.* pero [*péro*]

butane butano *m.* [*butáno*]

butcher carnicero *m.* [*karni θéro*]; **-'s** carnicería *f.* [*karni θería*]

butler mayordomo *m.* [*majordómo*]

butter mantequilla *f.* [*mantekílja*]

buttocks nalgas *f.pl.* [*nálgas*]

button botón *m.* [*botón*]; **-hole** ojal *m.* [*oxál*]

buy (to) comprar *r.* [*komprár*]; **-er** comprador(a) *m.- f.* [*kompradór*]

by *prep.* por [*por*]

bye ¡adiós! [*adjós*], ¡hasta la vista! [*ásta la bísta*]

by-road carretera *f.* secundaria [*karretéra sekundárja*]

C

cab cabriolé m. [*kabrjolé*] || **2.** taxi m. [*táksi*]

cabaret cabaré m. [*kabaré*]

cabbage col f. [*kol*], repollo m. [*rrepóljo*]; **red -**, col lombarda [*kol lombárda*]; **- soup** (*with broad beans and pork*) potaje m. gallego [*potáxe galjégo*]

cabin camarote m. [*kamaróte*] || **2.** cabina f. [*kabína*]

cabinet armario m. [*armárjo*], bargueño m. [*bargénjo*]

cable (to) telegrafiar r. [*telegrafjár*] || **2.** n. cable m. [*káble*]; **- flash** flas m. de cordón [*flas de kordón*]

cafe café m. [*kafé*] || **2.** cafetería f. [*kafetería*]; **c.-theatre** café-teatro m. [*kafé-teátro*]

caffeine cafeína f. [*kafeína*]; **- free** descafeinado(a) [*deskafeinádo*]

cake pastel m. [*pastél*], tarta f. [*tárta*]; **cream filled -**, brazo m. de gitano [*bráθo de xitáno*]; **sponge -**, bizcocho m. [*biθkótcho*]; **-shop** pastelería f. [*pastelería*]

calculator calculadora f. [*kalkuladóra*]

calendar calendario m. [*kalendárjo*]

calf ternera f. [*ternéra*]; **-'s tongue** lengua f. de ternera [*léngua de*]

call (to) llamar r. [*ljamár*] || **2.** llamar por teléfono [*por teléfono*], telefonear r. [*telefoneár*] || **3.** n. llamada f. [*ljamáda*]; **intercity -,** llamada interurbana [*interurbána*]; **trunk -,** conferencia f. [*konferénθja*]

calm a. tranquilo(a) [*trankílo*] || **2.** n. calma f. [*kálma*]

calorie caloría f. [*kaloría*]

cam: - shaft, árbol m. de levas [*árbol de lébas*]

cambric batista f. [*batísta*]

camellia camelia f. [*kamélja*]

camembert (cheese) queso m. de camembert [*késo de kamembért*]

cameo camafeo m. [*kamaféo*]

camera cámara f. fotográfica [*kámara fotográfika*], máquina f. de fotografiar [*mákina de fotografjár*]

camomile manzanilla f. [*manθanílja*]; **-tea** infusión f. de manzanilla [*infusjón de*]

camp: - site, camping m. [*kámping*]; **-ing. - goods**, artículos m. pl. de camping [*artíkulos de*]

can vb. aux. poder irr. [*poder*] (to be able): **I can't do it,** no puedo hacerlo [*no pwédo aθérlo*] || **2.** saber irr. [*sabér*] (to know how to do): **we can't speak Spanish,** no sabemos (hablar) español [*no sabémos ablár espanjól*] (see grammar) || **3.** n. bidón m. [*bidón*]

canape canapé m. [*kanapé*]

Canary Islands Islas f.pl. Canarias [*íslas kanárjas*]

cancel (to) cancelar r. [*kanθelár*], anular r. [*anulár*]; **-lation** cancelación f. [*kanθelaθjón*], anulación f. [*anulaθjón*]

cancer cáncer m. [*kánθer*]

candelabra candelabro m. [*kandelábro*]

candle vela f. [*béla*]

candy confite m. [*konfíte*]

cane caña f. [*kánja*]; **- sugar** azúcar m. de caña [*aθúkar de kánja*]

canned a. enlatado(a) [*enlatádo*], envasado(a) [*embasádo*]; **- food** comida f. de lata [*komída de láta*], conservas f. pl. [*konsérbas*]

canoe canoa f. [*kanóa*]

canteen cantina f. [*kantína*]

cap gorra f. [*górra*], gorro m. [*górro*]

cape capa f. [*kápa*], capelina f. [*kapelína*] || **2.** Geo. cabo m. [*kábo*]

caper alcaparra f. [*alkapárra*]

capital capital f. [*kapitál*] || **2.** Arch. capitel m. [*kapitél*] || **3.** capital m. [*kapitál*] (money)

capon capón m. [*kapón*]

capstan cabrestante m. [*kabrestánte*]

capsule cápsula f. [*kápsula*]

car coche m. [*kótche*], automóvil m. [*automóbil*]; **dining -,** coche restaurante [*kótche rrestauránte*]; **sleeping -,** coche cama [*kótche káma*]; **- accessories** accesorios m. pl. del coche [*akθesórjos del*]; **- documents** documentación f. del coche [*dokumentaθjón del*]; **- keys** llaves f. pl. del coche [*ljábes del*]; **- wash** túnel m. de lavado [*túnel de labádo*]

carafe garrafa f. [*garráfa*]

caramel caramelo m. [*karamélo*]; **- custard** flan m. [*flan*]

carat quilate m. [*kiláte*]

carbine carabina f. [*karabína*]

carbohydrate hidrato m. de carbono [*idráto de karbóno*]

carbon: - paper, papel m. carbón [*papél karbón*]; **-ated** a. efervescente [*eferbesθénte*]

carburettor carburador m. [*karburadór*]

card tarjeta *f.* [*tarxéta*], ficha *f.* [*fítcha*]: ***credit* -,** tarjeta *f.* de crédito [*tarxéta de krédito*] ‖ **2.** carta *f.* [*kárta*], naipe *m.* [*náipe*] (game) ‖ **3.** cartulina *f.* [*kartulína*] (material); **-board** cartón *m.* [*kartón*]; **- box,** caja *f.* de cartón [*káxa de*]

cardiac *a.* cardíaco(a) [*kardíako*]

cardigan chaqueta *f.* de punto [*tchakéta de púnto*]

cargo carga *f.* [*kárga*]

caries caries *f.* [*kárjes*]

carillon carrillón *m.* [*karrillón*]

carmine carmín *m.* [*karmín*]

carnation clavel *m.* [*klabél*]

carp carpa *f.* [*kárpa*]

carpet alfombra *f.* [*alfómbra*]: ***fitted* -,** moqueta *f.* [*mokéta*]

carrier transportista *m.-f.* [*transportísta*]

carrot zanahoria *f.* [*θanaórja*]

carry (to) llevar *r.* [*ljebár*], transportar *r.* [*transportár*]

cart carro *m.* [*kárro*], carretilla *f.* [*karretílja*]

carte: *a la* **-,** a la carta [*a la kárta*]

carton cartón *m.* [*kartón*]; **- of cigarettes** cartón de cigarrillos [*de θigarríljos*] ‖ **2.** bote *m.* [*bóte*] (cream, etc.)

cartoons dibujos *m. pl.* animados [*dibúxos animádos*]

cartridge cartucho *m.* [*kartútcho*]

carved: **- *figure*,** imagen *f.* de talla [*imáxen de tálja*]

carving talla *f.* [*tálja*]

cash caja *f.* [*káxa*] ‖ **2.** efectivo *m.* [*efektíbo*]; **to pay -,** pagar *r.* al contado [*pagár al kontádo*]; **- desk** caja *f.*; **-ier** cajero *m.* [*kaxéro*]

casino casino *m.* [*kasíno*]

cassette casete *f.* [*kaséte*]

castanet castañuela *f.* [*kastanjwéla*]

Castile Castilla *f.* [*kastílja*]

Castilian *a.* castellano(a) [*kasteljáno*] ‖ **2.** *n.* castellano(a) *m.-f.* (person) ‖ **3.** castellano *m.* (language)

cast: *c.-iron* de hierro fundido [*de jérro fundído*]

castle castillo *m.* [*kastíljo*]

cat gato *m.* [*gáto*]

catarrh catarro *m.* [*katárro*]

cathedral catedral *f.* [*katedrál*]

cauliflower coliflor *f.* [*koliflór*]

caviar caviar *m.* [*kabjár*]; **- cakes** pasteles *m.pl.* de caviar [*pastéles de*]

cayenne: **- *pepper*,** pimentón *m.* [*pimentón*]

ceiling techo *m.* [*tétcho*]

celery apio *m.* [*ápjo*]

cello violoncelo *m.* [*bjolonθélo*]

cellophane celofán *m.* [*θelofán*]

cement cemento *m.* [*θeménto*]

cent céntimo *m.* [*θéntimo*]

centigrade *a.* centígrado(a) [*θentígrado*]

centimetre centímetro *m.* [*θentímetro*]

central *a.* central [*θentrál*]

centre centro *m.* [*θéntro*]: *the* **- of *Madrid*,** el centro de Madrid [*el θéntro de madríd*]; ***shopping* -,** centro comercial [*θéntro komerθjál*] ‖ **2. to - the *image*,** encuadrar *r.* la imagen [*enkwadrár la imáxen*]

ceramic *a.* cerámico(a) [*θerámico*]; **-s** cerámica *f.* [*θerámika*]

cereal cereal *m.* [*θereál*]

certain *a.* seguro(a) [*segúro*]; cierto(a) [*θjérto*]

certificate certificado *m.* [*θertifikádo*], diploma *m.* [*diplóma*] (education): ***birth* -,** partida *f.* de nacimiento [*partída de naθimjénto*]; ***medical* -,** certificado *m.* médico [*θertifikádo médiko*]

certify (to) certificar *r.* [*θertifikár*]

cervical *a.* cervical [*θerbikál*]

chain cadena *f.* [*kadéna*]

chair silla *f.* [*sílja*]: ***arm*-,** sillón *m.* [*siljón*]; ***lounge* -,** tumbona *f.* [*tumbóna*]

chalet chalé *m.* [*tchalé*]

chalk tiza *f.* [*tíθa*]

chamber cámara *f.* [*kámara*], **-maid** camarera *f.* (de habitación) [*kamaréra de abitaθjón*]; **- of commerce** cámara *f.* de comercio [*de komérθjo*]; **- orchestra** orquesta *f.* de cámara [*orkésta de*]

champagne champán *m.* [*tchampán*]: ***brut* -,** champán brut [*brut*]; ***dry* -,** champán seco [*séko*], ***medium dry* -,** champán semiseco [*semiséko*]; ***Spanish* -,** cava *m.* [*kába*]

champion campeón *m.* [*kampeón*] ‖ **2.** campeona *f.* [*kampeóna*], **-ship** campeonato *m.* [*kampeonáto*]

chance posibilidad *f.* [*posibilidád*], oportunidad *f.* [*oportunidád*]

chandelier araña *f.* [*arája*]

change (to) cambiar *r.* [*kambjár*]: **to - Pounds into Euros,** cambiar libras en euros [*líbras en éuros*] ‖ **2.** hacer *irr.* trasbordo [*aθér trasbórdo*] (as of plains, platforms, etc.) ‖ **3. to - colour,** desteñir (i) [*destenjír*] ‖ **4.** *n.* cambio *m.* [*kámbjo*] ‖ **5.** trasbordo *m.* [*trasbórdo*] (as of vehicles) ‖ **6. -s** mudas *f. pl.* [*múdas*]

channel canal *m.* [*kanál*]

charge (to) cargar *r.* [*kargár*] ‖ **2.** cobrar *r.* [*kobrár*] ‖ **3.** *n.* **hire** *-,* alquiler *m.* [*alkilér*]; **reversed** *-,* cobro *m.* revertido [*kóbro rrebertído*]; - **account** cuenta *f.* corriente [*kwénta korrjénte*]

charter: *- flight,* vuelo *m.* chárter [*bwélo tchárter*]

chassis chasis *m.* [*tchásis*]

chauffeur chófer *m.* [*tchófer*]

cheap *a.* barato(a) [*baráto*]

check (to) facturar *r.* [*fakturár*] (luggage); **-ed** *-* a cuadros [*a kwádros*]; **- in** registro *m.* [*rrexístro*]; **- desk,** recepción *f.* [*rreθepθjón*] (hotel); mostrador *m.* de facturación [*mostradór de fakturaθjón*] (airport, etc.); **-up** chequeo *m.* [*tchekéo*]

cheek mejilla *f.* [*mexílja*]; **-bone** pómulo *m.* [*pómulo*]

cheerful *a.* alegre [*alégre*], animado(a) [*animádo*]

cheese queso *m.* [*késo*]; *Camembert* -, queso de camembert [*de kamembért*]; *soft* -, queso tierno [*tjérno*]; *dry* -, queso seco [*séko*]; *Dutch* -, queso de Holanda [*de olánda*]; *Edam* -, queso de bola [*de bóla*]; *Emmenthal* -, queso Emmental [*eméntál*]; *grated* -, queso rallado [*rraljádo*]; *Gruyère* -, queso de Gruyère [*de grujér*]; *- in portions,* queso en porciones [*en porθjónes*]; *Manchego* -, queso manchego [*mantchégo*]; *Parmesan* -, queso parmesano [*parmesáno*]; *- cake* pastel *m. pl.* de queso [*pastél de ké-so*], tarta *f.* de queso [*tárta de*]; **-s: assorted** -, quesos *pl.* variados [*barjádos*]; **- tart** tarta *f.* de queso [*tárta de*]

chemical *a.* químico(a) [*kímiko*]

chemist *a.* farmacéutico(a) [*farmaθéutiko*] ‖ **2.** *n.* farmacéutico(a) *m.-f.* ‖ **3.** **-'s** farmacia *f.* [*farmáθja*]

cheque cheque *m.* [*tchéke*], talón *m.* [*talón*]; *traveller's* -, cheque de viaje [*tchéke de bjáxe*]; **-book** talonario *m.* [*talonárjo*]

cherimoya chirimoya *f.* [*tchirimója*]

cherry cereza *f.* [*θeréθa*]; **- jam** mermelada *f.* de cereza [*mermeláda de*]

chess ajedrez *m.* [*axedréθ*]

chest pecho *m.* [*pétcho*], tórax *m.* [*tóraks*] ‖ **2.** arca *f.* [*árka*]; **-nut** castaña *f.* [*kastánja*]

chewing gum chicle *m.* [*tchíkle*]

chic *a.* elegante [*elegánte*]

chicken pollo *m.* [*póljo*]; *braised* -, pollo guisado [*gisádo*]; *fried* -, pollo frito [*fríto*]; *roast* -, pollo asado

[*asádo*]; *spit roasted* -, pollo a l'ast [*a last*]; *stuffed* -, pollo relleno [*rreljéno*]; **- giblets** menudillos *m. pl.* de gallina [*menudíljos de galjína*]

chickpea garbanzo *m.* [*garbánθo*]: *boiled* **-s,** garbanzos *pl.* cocidos [*koθídos*]

chicory achicoria *f.* [*atchikórja*]

chiffon gasa *f.* [*gása*]

chignon: *- slide,* aguja *f.* de moño [*agúxa de mónjo*]

child niño *m.* [*nínjo*]

children niños *m. pl.* [*nínjos*]; **-'s hats** sombreros *m. pl.* para niños [*sombré-ros pára*]; **-'s nursery** guardería *f.* infantil [*gwardería infantíl*]; **-'s wear** ropa *f.* infantil [*rrópa infantíl*]; **shop,** tienda *f.* de ropa infantil [*tjén-da de*]

chimney chimenea *f.* [*tchimenéa*]

chin barbilla *f.* [*barbílja*]

chinaware loza *f.* [*lóθa*], porcelana *f.* [*porθelána*]

chips patatas *f.pl.* fritas [*patátas frítas*]

chlorophyl clorofila *f.* [*klorofíla*]; **- shampoo** champú *m.* de clorofila [*tchampú de klorofíla*]

chocolate chocolate *m.* [*tchokoláte*]: *bar of* -, tableta *f.* de chocolate [*ta-bléta de*]; *French style* -, chocolate a la francesa [*tchokoláte a la franθésa*]; *Spanish style* -, chocolate a la española [*a la espanjóla*]; *Swiss style* -, chocolate a la suiza [*a la swíθa*]; **-s** bombones *m. pl.* [*bombónes*] **- truffles** trufas *f. pl.* [*trúfas*]

choir coro *m.* [*kóro*]

cholera cólera *m.* [*kólera*]

cholesterol colesterol *m.* [*kolesteról*]

choose (to) elegir (i) [*elexír*], escoger *r.* [*eskoxér*]

chop chuleta *f.* [*tchuléta*]: *grilled* **-s,** chuletas *pl.* a la parrilla [*tchulétas a la parrílja*]; *lamb* **-s,** chuletas de cordero [*de kordéro*]; *pork* **-s,** chuletas de cerdo [*de θérdo*]; *veal* **-s,** chuletas de ternera [*de ternéra*]

choppy *a.* movido(a) [*mobído*]

Christmas Navidad *f.* [*nabidád*]

chrom/e cromo *m.* [*krómo*], **-ium** cromo *m.* [*krómo*]; **- plated** *a.* cromado(a) [*kromádo*]

chronic *a.* crónico(a) [*króniko*]

chronometer cronómetro *m.* [*kronó-metro*]

chrysanthemum crisantemo *m.* [*kri-santémo*]

church iglesia *f.* [*iglésja*]

cider sidra *f.* [*sídra*]

cigar puro *m.* [*púro*]

cigarette cigarrillo *m.* [*θigarríljo*]: **carton of -s,** cartón *m.* de cigarrillos [*kartón de θigarríljos*]; **filter tip -,** cigarrillo con filtro [*kon fíltro*]; **packet of -s,** paquete *m.* de cigarrillos [*pakéte de θigarríljos*]; **filterless,** cigarrillo sin filtro [*sin fíltro*]; **- case** pitillera *f.* [*pitiljéra*]; **- holder** boquilla *f.* [*bokílja*]; **- lighter** encendedor *m.* [*enθendedór*], mechero *m.* [*metchéro*]; **- paper** papel *m.* de fumar [*papél de fumár*]

cine camera tomavistas *m.* [*tomabístas*]

cinema cine *m.* [*θíne*]; **-scope** cinerama *m.* [*θineráma*]

cinnamon canela *f.* [*kanéla*]

circle círculo *m.* [*θírkulo*]

circuit recorrido *m.* [*rrekorrído*] ‖ **2.** circuito *m.* [*θirkwíto*] (elect.): **short -,** cortocircuito *m.* [*kortoθirkwíto*]

circulat/ion circulación *f.* [*θirkulaθjón*]; **-ory** *a.* circulatorio(a) [*θirkulatórjo*]

circumference circunferencia *f.* [*θirkumferénθja*]

circumstance circunstancia *f.* [*θirkumstánθja*]

circus circo *m.* [*θírko*]

cistern cisterna *f.* [*θistérna*]

citric *a.* cítrico(a) [*θítriko*]

city ciudad *f.* [*θjudád*]; **- centre** centro *m.* de la ciudad [*θéntro de la θjudád*]

civil *a.* civil [*θibíl*]

claim (to) reclamar *r.* [*rrreklamár*] ‖ **2.** *n.* reclamación *f.* [*rreklamaθjón*]

clam almeja *f.* [*alméxa*]; **-s in brine,** almejas *pl.* al natural [*alméxas al naturál*]; **steamed -s,** almejas a la marinera [*a la marinéra*]

clamp fijación *f.* [*fixaθjón*]

claret: -wine, vino *m.* clarete [*bíno klaréte*]

clasp cierre *m.* [*θjérre*]

class clase *f.* [*kláse*]: **economy -,** clase turista [*turísta*]; **first -,** (de) primera clase [*de priméra kláse*]; **second -,** (de) segunda clase [*segúnda kláse*]; **-ical** *a.* clásico(a) [*klásiko*]

claustrophobia claustrofobia *f.* [*klaustrofóbja*]

clean (to) limpiar *r.* [*limpjár*]: **to - with paraffin,** petrolear *r.* [*petroleár*] ‖ **2.** *a.* limpio(a) [*límpjo*], **-er's** tintorería *f.* [*tintorería*]; **-ing** limpieza *f.* [*limpjéθa*]; **- lady,** señora *f.* de la limpieza [*senjóra de la*]; **- materials,**

artículos *m.pl.* de limpieza [*artíkulos de limpjéθa*]

cleansing limpieza *f.* [*limpjéθa*] (skin, etc); **- cream** crema *f.* limpiadora [*kréma limpjadóra*]; **- lotion** loción *f.* limpiadora [*loθjón limpjadóra*]

clear *a.* claro(a) [*kláro*], despejado(a) [*despexádo*] (sky)

clementine clementina *f.* [*klementína*]

clerk empleado *m.* [*empleádo*], dependiente *m.* [*dependjénte*] (in shops, etc.)

clever *a.* inteligente [*intelixénte*], listo(a) [*lísto*]

client cliente *m.-f.* [*kljénte*]

cliff acantilado *m.* [*akantiládo*]

climate clima *m.* [*klíma*]

climb (to) escalar *r.* [*eskalár*] ‖ **2.** *n.* escalada *f.* [*eskaláda*]; **-er** escalador *m.* [*eskaladór*]; **-ing** alpinismo *m.* [*alpinísmo*]; **- boots,** botas *f.pl.* de montaña [*bótas de montáña*]; **- trousers,** pantalón *m.* de montaña [*pantalón de*]

clinic clínica *f.* [*klínika*]: **dental -,** clínica dental [*dentál*]; **-al** *a.* clínico(a) [*klíniko*]

clip clip *m.* [*klip*], grapa *f.* [*grápa*]; **-per: nail -,** cortaúñas *m.* [*kortaúnjas*]

cloak capa *f.* [*kápa*]; **-room** guardarropa *f.* [*guardarrópa*]

clock reloj *m.* [*rrelóx*]: **alarm -,** despertador *m.* [*despertadór*] ‖ **2.** hora *f.* [*óra*]: **it is five o'clock,** son las cinco (horas) [*son las θínko*]; **-maker's** relojería *f.* [*rreloxería*] (shop)

clog chinela *f.* [*tchinéla*], zueco *m.* [*θwéko*]

cloister claustro *m.* [*kláustro*]

clos/e (to) cerrar (ie) [*θerrár*]; **-ed** *a.* cerrado(a) [*θerrádo*]; **-ing** cierre *m.* [*θjérre*]; **- time,** hora *f.* de cierre [*óra de*]

cloth tela *f.* [*téla*], paño *m.* [*pánjo*], tejido *m.* [*texído*]; **- bound** *a.* en tela [*en téla*] (books, etc.); **- badge** insignia *f.* de tela [*insígnja de*]; **- emblem** emblema *m.* de tela [*embléma de*]; **-es** ropa *f.* [*rrópa*]: **coloured -,** ropa de color [*de kolór*]; **- pegs** pinzas *f. pl.* de tender la ropa [*pínθas de tendér la*]; **-ing** ropa *f.* [*rrópa*], vestidos *m. pl.* [*bestídos*]; **- list,** lista *f.* de ropa [*lísta de*]

cloud nube *f.* [*núbe*]; **-less** *a.* despejado(a) [*despexádo*]; **-y** *a.* nublado(a) [*nubládo*]

clove clavo *m.* [*klábo*] ‖ **2. of garlic** diente *m.* de ajo [*djénte de áxo*]

clown payaso *m*. [*pajáso*]
club club *m*. [*klub*] (society) ‖ **2.** club *m*. [*klub*], boite *f*. [*bwat*] (public)
clutch embrague *m*. [*embráge*] (car); **- plate** disco *m*. de embrague [*dísko de*]; **- pedal** pedal *m*. de embrague [*pedál de*]
coach autocar *m*. [*autokár*] ‖ **2.** coche *m*. [*kótche*], vagón *m*. [*bagón*] (rail)
coagulant coagulante *m*. [*koagulánte*]
coal carbón *m*. [*karbón*]
coast costa *f*. [*kósta*]; **on the -**. en la costa [*en la*]; **-al** *a*. costero(a) [*kostéro*], de la costa [*de la*]; **-guard** guardacostas *m*. [*gwardakóstas*]
coat chaqueta *f*. [*tchakéta*], abrigo *m*. [*abrígo*], **-ed: - with bread crumbs** rebozado(a) [*rreboθádo*]; **-hanger** percha *f*. [*pértcha*]
cockle berberecho *m*. [*berberétcho*]
cocktail cóctel *m*. [*kóktel*]; **fruit -,** macedonia *f*. de frutas [*maθedónja de frútas*]; **prawn -,** cóctel *m*. de gambas [*kóktel de gámbas*]; **- cherry** guinda *f*. [*gínda*]
cocoa cacao *m*. [*kakáo*]
coconut coco *m*. [*kóko*]
cod bacalao *m*. [*bakaláo*]; **- fried with garlic,** bacalao a la vizcaína [*a la biθkaína*]; **- with tomato,** bacalao con tomate [*kon tomáte*]; **-e** código *m*. [*kódigo*]; **-fish** bacalao *m*. [*bakaláo*]
coffee café *m*. [*kafé*]; **black -,** café solo [*sólo*]; **iced -,** café helado [*eládo*]; **- served with ground-ice,** granizado *m*. de café [*graniθádo de kafé*]; **instant -,** café instantáneo [*kafé instantáneo*]; **white -,** café con leche [*kon létche*], **- with a little milk,** cortado *m*. [*kortádo*]; **decaffeinated -,** café descafeinado [*deskafeinádo*]; **- bar** cafetería *f*. [*kafetería*]; **- cup** taza *f*. para café [*táθa pára kafé*]; **- grinder** molinillo *m*. de café [*moliníljo de*]; **- machine** cafetera *f*. [*kafetéra*], máquina *f*. de café [*mákina de*]; **- shop** cafetería *f*. [*kafetería*]
cog rueda *f*. dentada [*rrwéda dentáda*]
cognac coñac *m*. [*konják*]
coil bobina *f*. [*bobína*]
coin moneda *f*. [*monéda*]
cold *a*. frío(a) [*frío*]; **- dish** plato *m*. frío [*pláto frío*]; **- drink** refresco *m*. [*rrefrésko*]; **- front** frente *m*. frío [*frénte frío*]; **- meats** fiambres *m pl*. [*fjámbres*] ‖ **2.** frío *m*. [*frío*], tener *irr*. frío [*tenér frío*]; **I am -,** tengo frío [*téngo*] ‖ **3.** **it's -,** hace frío [*áθe*]

colic cólico *m*. [*kóliko*]
colitis colitis *f*. [*kolítis*]
collapse colapso *m*. [*kolápso*]
collar collar *m*. [*koljár*] (dog); **-bone** clavícula *f*. [*klabíkula*]
collect (to) coleccionar *r*. [*kolekθjonár*] ‖ **2. to - payment,** cobrar *r*. [*kobrár*]; **-ion** cobro *m*. [*kóbro*] ‖ **3.** *n*. recogida *f*. [*rrekoxída*] ‖ **4.** colección *f*. [*kolekθjón*] (stamps, etc.)
college colegio *m*. [*koléxjo*]
colour color *m*. [*kolór*] ‖ **2.** en color [*en*]
coma coma *m*. [*kóma*]
comb peine *m*. [*péine*], peineta *f*. [*peinéta*]
comb (to) peinar *r*. [*peinár*]
come (to) venir *irr*. [*benír*]; **to - from,** venir *irr*. de [*benír de*]. ser *irr*. de [*ser de*] ‖ **2. to - out well (badly),** salir (g) bien (mal) [*salír bjen (mal)*]
comedy comedia *f*. [*komédja*]
comfort comodidad *f*. [*komodidád*], **-able** *a*. cómodo(a) [*komódo*]
comic cómico(a) *m.-f*. [*kómiko*] ‖ **2.** tebeo *m*. [*tebéo*] ‖ **3.** *a*. cómico(a) [*kómiko*]
commerce comercio *m*. [*komérθjo*]
commercial *a*. comercial [*komerθjál*]
commission comisión *f*. [*komisjón*]
common *a*. común [*komún*]; **Common Market,** Mercado *m*. Común [*merkádo komún*]
communication comunicación *f*. [*komunikaθjón*]
compact *a*. compacto(a) [*kompákto*], **- disc** disco *m*. compacto [*dísko kompákto*]; CD *m*. [*θedé*]
companion compañero(a) *m.-f*. [*kompanjéro*]
company compañía *f*. [*kompanjía*] ‖ **2.** empresa *f*. [*emprésa*]
compare (to) comparar *r*. [*komparár*] (to, with/con)
compartment compartimiento *m*. [*kompartimjénto*], departamento *m*. [*departaménto*]
compass brújula *f*. [*brúxula*]
compatriot compatriota *m.-f*. [*kompatrjóta*]
compensation compensación *f*. [*kompensaθjón*]; indemnización *f*. [*indemniθaθjón*]
competit/ion competición *f*. [*kompetiθjón*] ‖ **2.** Com. competencia *f*. [*kompeténθja*]; **-ive** *a*. competitivo(a) [*kompetitíbo*]
compilation recopilación *f* [*rrekopilaθjón*]

complain (to) quejarse *r.* [*kexárse*]

complaint queja *f.* [*kéxa*]; **-s book** libro *m.* de reclamaciones [*líbro de rreklamaθjónes*]

complete *a.* completo(a) [*kompléto*]; **-ly** *adv.* completamente [*kompletaménte*]

compos/er compositor *m.* [*kompositór*]; **-ition** composición *f.* [*komposiθjón*]

compote compota *f.* [*kompóta*]; **apple -,** compota de manzana [*de manθána*]; **strawberry -,** compota *f.* de fresa [*de frésa*]

compress compresa *f.* [*komprésa*]; **-or** compresor *m.* [*kompresór*]

computer ordenador *m.* [*ordenadór*]; **personal -,** ordenador *m.* personal [*personál*]; **PC** *m.* [*peθé*]

concentrated *a.* concentrado(a) [*konθentrádo*]

concert concierto *m.* [*konθjérto*]; **- hall** sala *f.* de conciertos [*sála de konθjértos*]

condensed *a.* condensado(a) [*kondensádo*]; **- milk** leche *f.* condensada [*létche*]

condenser condensador *m.* [*kondensadór*]

condiment condimento *m.* [*kondiménto*]

condom preservativo *m.* [*preserbatíbo*]

conductor conductor *m.* [*konduktór*] ‖ **2.** cobrador *m.* [*kobradór*] (tram) ‖ **3.** director *m.* [*direktór*] (orchestra)

confection/ery repostería *f.* [*reposterɩ́a*]; **-er's** confitería *f.* [*konfiterɩ́a*]

conference conferencia *f.* [*konferénθja*]

confess (to) confesarse (ie) [*konfesárse*]; **-ion** confesión *f.* [*konfesjón*]; **- box,** confesionario *m.* [*konfesjonárjo*]

confirm (to) confirmar *r.* [*konfirmár*]; **-ation** confirmación *f.* [*konfirmaθjón*]; **- of reservation,** confirmación de reserva [*de resérba*]

conger: -eel congrio *m.* [*kóngrjo*]

congress congreso *m.* [*kongréso*]

connect (to) unir *r.* [*unír*], conectar *r.* [*konektár*]; **-ing: - rod,** biela *f.* [*bjéla*]; **-ion** enlace *m.* [*enláθe*], conexión f. [*koneksjón*] ‖ **2.** correspondencia *f.* [*korrespondénθja*] (rail)

conserv/ation conservación *f.* [*konserbaθjón*]; **-e (to)** conservar *r.* [*konserbár*] ‖ **2.** *n.* conserva *f.* [*konsérba*]

consignment envío *m.* [*embío*]; **- note** nota *f.* de envío [*nóta de*]

consist (to) consistir *r.* [*konsistír*] (of/en)

consommé consomé *m.* [*konsomé*]

constant *a.* constante [*konstánte*], continuo(a) [*kontínwo*]

constipation estreñimiento *m.* [*estreɲimjénto*]

construction construcción *f.* [*konstrukθjón*]

consulate consulado *m.* [*konsuládo*]

consulting: - room, consulta *f.* [*konsúlta*]

consumption consumo *m.* [*konsúmo*] ‖ **2.** consumición *f.* [*konsumiθjón*]

contact contacto *m.* [*kontákto*]; **- lenses** lentillas *f.pl.* [*lentíljas*]

contagion contagio *m.* [*kontáxjo*]

contagious *a.* contagioso(a) [*kontaxjóso*]

container contenedor *m.* [*kontenedór*]

contamination contaminación *f.* [*kontaminaθjón*]

content contenido *m.* [*kontenído*] ‖ **2.** *a.* contento(a) [*konténto*]

continental *a.* continental [*kontinentál*]; **- breakfast** desayuno *m.* continental [*desajúno kontinentál*]

continue (to) continuar *r.* [*kontinwár*], seguir (i) [*segír*]; **to - to do sth.,** seguir (continuar) haciendo u.c. [*aθjéndo úna kósa*]

contraceptive anticonceptivo *m.* [*antikonθeptíbo*]

contract contrato *m.* [*kontráto*]

control (to) controlar *r.* [*kontrolár*] ‖ **2.** *n.* control *m.* [*kontról*]

contusion contusión *f.* [*kontusjón*]

convent convento *m.* [*kombénto*]

convention convención *f.* [*kombenθjón*]

conversation conversación *f.* [*kombersaθjón*]

converter convertidor *m.* [*kombertidór*]

cook (to) guisar *r.* [*gisár*], cocinar *r.* [*koθinár*] ‖ **2.** cocer (ue) [*koθér*] ‖ **3.** cocinero(a) *m.-f.* [*koθinéro*]; **-ed** *a.* guisado(a) [*gisádo*], cocido(a) [*koθído*]; **- vegetables,** legumbres *f. pl.* cocidas [*legúmbres koθídas*]; **-er** cocina *f.* [*koθína*]; **gas -,** cocina de gas [*de gas*]; **-ing** cocina *f.* [*koθína*], gastronomía *f.* [*gastronomía*]; **Spanish -,** la cocina española [*la koθína espanjóla*]; **- pans,** batería *f.* de cocina [*batería de*]; **- stove,** hornillo *m.* [*orníljo*], horno *m.* [*órno*]

cool *a.* fresco(a) [*frésko*], templado(a) [*templádo*]; **it's -,** hace fresquito [*áθe freskíto*] ‖ **2.** frío(a) [*frío*]; **-ing: - system,** sistema *m.* de refrigeración [*sistéma de rrefrixeraθjón*]

copper cobre *m.* [*kóbre*]; **of -,** de cobre [*de*]; **- lamp** lámpara *f.* de cobre [*lámpara de*]

copy copia *f.* [*kópja*]: **- paper,** papel *m.* carbón [*papél karbón*] ‖ **2.** ejemplar *m.* [*exemplár*] (book)

coral coral *m.* [*korál*]

cord cordel *m.* [*kordél*], cuerda *f.* [*kwérda*] ‖ **2.** cordón *m.* [*kordón*]

cordovan: - bat, sombrero *m.* cordobés [*sombréro kordobés*]

corduroy pana *f.* [*pána*]

cork corcho *m.* [*kórtcho*] ‖ **2.** tapón *m.* de corcho [*tapón del*]: **- screw** sacacorchos [*sakakórtchos*]

corn trigo *m.* [*trígo*] ‖ **2.** callo *m.* [*káljo*]: **- salve** callicida *f.* [*kaljiθida*]

cornea córnea *f.* [*kórnea*]

corner esquina *f.* [*eskína*] (outside) ‖ **2.** rincón *m.* [*rrinkón*] (inside)

cornflakes copos *m.pl.* de maíz [*kópos de maiθ*]

correct *a.* correcto(a) [*korrékto*]

correspondence correspondencia *f.* [*korrespondénθja*]

corridor pasillo *m.* [*pasíljo*]

corset faja *f.* [*fáxa*]: **-ry** corsetería *f.* [*korsetería*]

cosmetic cosmético *m.* [*kosmétiko*] ‖ **2.** *a.* cosmético(a) [*kosmétiko*]

cost (to) costar (ue) [*kostár*], valer *irr.* [*balér*]: **how much does it -?** ¿cuánto vale? [*kwánto bále*] ‖ **2.** *n.* coste *m.* [*kóste*], gasto *m.* [*gásto*]: **at - price,** a precio de coste [*a préθjo de kóste*]

costume traje *m.* (chaqueta) [*tráxe tchakéta*]: **bathing -,** bañador *m.* [*banjadór*]

cot cuna *f.* [*kúna*], camita *f.* [*kamíta*]

cottage casa *f.* de campo [*kása de kámpo*]

cotton algodón *m.* [*algodón*]

couch sofá *m.* [*sofá*]

cough tos *f.* [*tos*]: **- syrup,** jarabe *m.* contra la tos [*xarábe kóntra la*]: **to have a -,** tener *irr.* tos [*tenér tos*]

count (to) contar (ue) [*kontár*]

counter mostrador *m.* [*mostradór*]; ventanilla *f.* [*bentanílja*] (bank, etc.)

country país *m.* [*país*]: **of the -,** del país [*del*]: **- ham** jamón *m.* del país [*xamón del*]: **- scene** paisaje *m.* [*paisáxe*]: **-side** campo *m.* [*kámpo*]

couple pareja *f.* [*paréxa*]

courgette calabacín *m.* [*kalabaθín*]

courier mensajero *m.* [*mensaxéro*]: **- service** servicio *m.* de mensajeros [*serbjθjo de mensaxéros*]

course plato *m.* [*pláto*]: **first -,** primer plato [*primér*]: **second -,** segundo plato [*segúndo*]

court pista *f.* [*písta*] (tennis, etc.) ‖ **2.** tribunal *m.* [*tribunál*]: **-yard** patio *m.* [*pátjo*]

cousin primo(a) *m.-f.* [*prímo*]

cove cala *f.* [*kála*]

cover (to) cubrir *irr.* [*kubrír*] ‖ **2.** *n.* cubierto *m.* [*kubjérto*] ‖ **3** cubierta *f.* [*kubjérta*] (book, etc.)

cow vaca *f.* [*báka*]

crab cangrejo *m.* [*kangréxo*]

crackling chicharrones *m.pl.* [*tchitcharrónes*]

cradle cuna *f.* [*kúna*]

cramp calambre *m.* [*kalámbre*]

crampon crampón *m.* [*krampón*]

crank: - shaft, cigüeñal *m.* [*θigwenjál*]

crash choque *m.* [*tchóke*], accidente *m.* [*akθidénte*]: **car -,** accidente de coche [*de kótche*]

crawfish cigala *f.* [*θigála*]

crayfish langostino *m.* [*langostíno*]

cream nata *f.* [*náta*]; crema *f.* [*kréma*]: **cheese -,** crema *f.* de queso [*de késo*]: **- filled cake,** brazo *m.* de gitano [*bráθo de xitáno*]: **ice -,** helado *m.* [*eládo*]: **whipped -,** nata *f.* montada [*náta montáda*]: **- base** crema *f.* base [*kréma báse*]: **- buns** lioneses *f.pl.* de trufa [*ljonésas de trúfa*]: **- drops** chocolatinas *f.* [*tchokolatínas*]: **-less** *a.* descremado(a) [*deskremádo*], desnatado(a) [*desnatádo*]: **- milk,** leche *f.* desnatada [*létche*]: **- truffles** trufas *f. pl.* heladas [*trúfas eládas*]

crease: - resistant, inarrugable [*inarrugáble*]

credit crédito *m.* [*krédito*]: **- card** tarjeta *f.* de crédito [*tarxéta de krédito*]; tarjeta *f.* de compras [*tarxéta de kómpras*] (of department stores)

crest cresta *f.* [*krésta*] (wave, etc.)

crew tripulación *f.* [*tripulaθjón*]: **ground -,** personal *m.* de tierra [*personál de tjérra*] (airport)

crisp: potato -s, patatas *f.pl.* fritas [*patátas frítas*]

croissant croissant *m.* [*kruasánt*]

croquet: - set, juego *m.* de croquet [*xuégo de króket*]

croquette croqueta *f.* [*krokéta*]: **chicken -,** croqueta de pollo [*de póljo*]: **cod -,** croqueta de bacalao [*de bakaláo*]: **fish -,** croqueta *f.* de pescado [*de peskádo*]: **ham -,** croqueta de jamón [*de xamón*]: **meat -,** croqueta de carne [*de kárne*]: **potato -,** croqueta de patata [*de patáta*]

cross (to) cruzar *r.* [*kruθár*], atravesar (ie) [*atrabesár*] ‖ **2.** *n.* cruz *f.* [*kruθ*]: **Red Cross**, Cruz Roja [*kruθ rróxa*]: **- roads** cruce *m.* [*krúθe*]: **-ing** travesía *f.* [*trabesía*]: **-word** crucigrama *m.* [*kruθigráma*]

crotchet: - hook, ganchillo *m.* [*gantchíljo*]

croupier crupier *m.* [*krupjé*]

crown corona *f.* [*koróna*]

crude *a.* crudo(a) [*krúdo*]

cruet: - set, vinagreras *f.pl.* [*binagréras*]

cruise crucero *m.* [*kruθéro*]

crumb miga *f.* [*míga*]

crunchy *a.* crujiente [*kruxjénte*]

crust corteza *f.* [*kortéθa*]

crustacean crustáceo *m.* [*krustáθeo*]

cry (to) llorar *r.* [*ljorár*]

crystal cristal *m.* [*kristál*]: **- lamp** lámpara *f.* de cristal [*lámpara de*]

cube cubo *m.* [*kúbo*]: terrón *m.* [*terrón*]: **- of sugar**, terrón *m.* de azúcar [*de aθúkar*] ‖ **2.** pastilla *f.* [*pastílja*]

cubic *a.* cúbico(a) [*kúbiko*]

cucumber pepino *m.* [*pepíno*]: **- salad** ensalada *f.* de pepinos [*ensaláda de pepínos*]

cue taco *m.* [*táko*] (billiard)

cuff puño *m.* [*púnjo*] (of shirts): **- links** gemelos *m.pl.* [*xemélos*]

culinary *a.* culinario(a) [*kulinárjo*]

cultivated *a.* cultivado(a) [*kultibádo*]: **- pearl** perla *f.* cultivada [*pérla kultibáda*]

cultur/al *a.* cultural [*kulturál*]: **-e** cultura *f.* [*kultúra*]

cumin comino *m.* [*komíno*]

cup taza *f.* [*táθa*]: **- of coffee**, taza *f.* de café [*táθa de kafé*] ‖ **2.** copa *f.* [*kópa*] (sports): **-board** armario *m.* [*armárjo*]

curaçao curasao *m.* [*kurasáo*]

curd cuajada *f.* [*kuaxáda*]

cure (to) curar *r.* [*kurár*]

curl rizo *m.* [*rríθo*]

currant corriente *f.* [*korrjénte*]: **electric -**, corriente eléctrica [*eléktrika*]: **- account** cuenta *f* corriente [*kuénta*]: **-s** pasas *f.pl.* [*pásas*]: **red -**, grosellas *f.pl.* [*groséljas*]

cushion cojín *m.* [*koxín*], almohadón *m.* [*almoadón*]: **air -**, cojín de aire [*koxín de áire*]

custard crema *f.* [*kréma*], natillas *f.pl.* [*natíljas*]: **- of cream**, natillas *f.* de crema [*ljonésas de*]: **- apple** chirimoya *f.* [*tchirimója*] (fruit)

customer cliente *m.-f.* [*kljénte*]

customs aduana *f.* [*adwána*] ‖ **2.** derechos *m.pl.* de aduana [*derétchos de*]: **- control** control *m.* de aduana [*kontról de*]: **- officer** aduanero *m.* [*adwanéro*]

cut (to) cortar *r.* [*kortár*]: **to - low in the neck**, escotar *r.* [*eskotár*] ‖ **2.** *n.* corte *m.* [*kórte*]

cutlery cubertería *f.* [*kubertería*]: cubiertos *m.pl.* [*kubjértos*]

cutlet chuleta *f.* [*tchuléta*]

cuttlefish sepia *f.* [*sépja*]

cycl/e bicicleta *f.* [*biθikléta*]: **-ing** ciclismo *m.* [*θiklísmo*]: **-ist** ciclista *m.-f.* [*θiklísta*]

cylinder cilindro *m.* [*θilíndro*]: **- block** bloque *m.* del cilindro [*blóke del*]

D

dahlia dalia *f.* [*dália*]
daily *a.* diario(a) [*djário*]; - **newspa-per** diario *m.* || **2.** *adv.* diariamente [*djarjaménte*]
dairy lechería *f.* [*letchería*]; - **maid** lechera *f.* [*letchéra*]; - **man** lechero *m.* [*letchéro*]; - **produce** productos *m. pl.* lácteos [*prodúktos lákteos*]
daisy margarita *f.* [*margaríta*]
damag/e (to) dañar *r.* [*danjár*], perjudicar *r.* [*perxudikár*] || **2.** averiarse *r.* [*aberjárse*] || **2.** *n.* daño *m.* [*dánjo*], perjuicio *m.* [*perxwíθjo*]; -**ing** *a.* perjudicial [*perxudiθjál*]
damp *a* húmedo(a) [*úmedo*], mojado(a) [*moxádo*] || **2.** *n.* humedad *f.* [*umedád*]
dance (to) bailar *r.* [*bailár*] || **2.** *n.* baile *m.* [*báile*]; - **hall** salón *m.* de baile [*salón de*]; -**r** bailarín *m* [*bailarín*] || **3.** bailarina *f.* [*bailarína*] || **4.** bailaor(a) *m.-f.* [*bailaór*] (Flamenco)
dandruff caspa *f.* [*káspa*]
danger peligro *m.* [*pelígro*]; riesgo *m.* [*rrjésgo*]; -**ous** *a.* peligroso(a) [*peligróso*]; arriesgado(a) [*arrjesgádo*]
daring *a.* atrevido(a) [*atrebído*]; osado(a) [*osádo*]
dark *a.* oscuro(a) [*oskúro*] || **2.** moreno(a) [*moréno*] (a person), -**en (to)** oscurecer (zc) [*oskureθér*]; -**ness** oscuridad *f.* [*oskuridád*]
darn zurcido *m.* [*θurθído*]; -**ing**: - **thread**, hilo *m.* de zurcir [*ílo de θurθír*]
date fecha *f.* [*fétcha*]; **sell-by -**, fecha de caducidad [*de kaduθidád*]; - **of birth** fecha de nacimiento [*de naθimjénto*] || **2.** cita *f.* [*θíta*] || **3.** Bot. dátil *m.* [*dátil*]; -**d** *a.* anticuado(a) [*antikwádo*]; pasado(a) de moda [*pasádo de móda*]
daughter hija *f.* [*íxa*], **d.-in-law** hija política [*polítika*]
davit pescante *m.* [*peskánte*]
dawn alba *f.* [*álba*], amanecer *m.* [*amaneθér*]
day día *m.* [*día*]; **the - after tomor-row,** pasado mañana [*pasádo manjána*]; **the - before yesterday,** anteayer [*anteajér*]; - **break** amanecer *m.* [*amaneθér*]; **at -,** al amanecer [*al*]; -**light** luz *f.* del día [*luθ del día*]; -**time** día *m.* [*día*]; **in the -,** de día

[*de día*]; - **trip** excursión *f.* (viaje *m.*) de un día [*ekskursjón (bjáxe) de un día*]
dead *a.* muerto(a) [*muérto*] || **2.** *n.* muerto(a) *m.-f.*
deaf *a.* sordo(a) [*sórdo*], **d.-and-dumb** sordomudo(a) [*sordomúdo*]
dear *a.* caro(a) [*káro*] || **2.** querido(a) [*kerído*] (in letters): - **Jaime,** querido Jaime [*kerído xáime*]; - **Sir,** Muy Sr. mío [*mui senjór mío*] (letter)
debate (to) debatir *r.* [*debatír*], discutir *r.* [*diskutír*] || **2.** *n.* debate *m.* [*debáte*], discusión *f.* [*diskusjón*]
debit débito *m.* [*débito*]; - **balance** saldo *m.* negativo [*sáldo negatíbo*]
debt deuda *f.* [*déuda*]
decade década *f.* [*dékada*]
decaffeinated *a.* descafeinado(a) [*deskafeinádo*]; **a - coffee,** un café descafeinado [*un kafé*]
decay caries *f.* [*kárjes*]
deceive (to) engañar *r.* [*enganjár*]
decelerate (to) reducir (zc) la velocidad [*reduθír la beloθidád*]
December diciembre *m.* [*diθjémbre*]
decent *a.* decente [*deθénte*]
decide (to) decidir *r.* [*deθidír*]
decis/ion decisión *f.* [*deθisjón*]: **to ma-ke a -,** tomar *r.* una decisión [*tomár úna*]; -**ive** *a.* decidido(a) [*deθidído*], decisivo(a) [*deθisíbo*]
deck cubierta *f.* [*kubjérta*]: **on -,** en cubierta [*en*]; - **chair** tumbona *f.* [*tumbóna*]
declare (to) declarar *r.* [*deklarár*]: **I have nothing to -!** ¡No tengo nada que declarar! [*no téngo náda ke*] (customs)
declaration declaración *f.* [*deklaraθjón*]
décolleté *a.* escoltado(a) [*eskoltádo*]
decompression descompresión *f.* [*deskompresjón*]
decor decoración *f.* [*dekoraθjón*]; -**ate (to)** decorar *r.* [*dekorár*]; -**ation** decoración *f.* [*dekoraθjón*]
decoy reclamo *m.* [*rreklámo*]
deduce (to) deducir (zc) [*deduθír*] (from/de), descontar (ue) [*deskontár*] (de)
deduction deducción *f.* [*deduk θjón*], descuento *m.* [*deskwénto*] (from/de)
deep *a.* profundo(a) [*profúndo*]: **it's five metres -,** tiene diez metros de profundidad [*tjéne djeθ métros de profundidád*]; -**ly** *adv.* profundamente [*profundaménte*]

deer ciervo *m.* [θjérbo], venado *m.* [benádo]; **jugged -,** civet *m.* de ciervo [θíßët de]

defeat (to) derrotar *r.* [derrotár] ‖ **2.** *n.* derrota *f.* [derróta]

defect defecto *m.* [defékto]; **-ive** *a.* defectuoso(a) [defektwóso]

deficit déficit *m.* [défiθit]

degree grado *m.* [grádo]

dehydrated *a.* deshidratado(a) [desidratádo]

delay (to) retrasar *r.* [rretrasár]; **to be delayed,** llevar *r.* retraso [ljebár rretráso] ‖ **2.** *n.* retraso *m.* [rretráso]

delegation delegación *f.* [delegaθjón]

delicate *a.* delicado(a) [delikádo]; **- clothes** ropa *f.* delicada [rrópa]

delicious *a.* delicioso(a) [deliθjóso]

delightful *a.* encantador(a) [enkantadór], agradable [agradáble]

deliver (to) entregar *r.* [entregár] (goods); **-y** entrega *f.* [entréga]; **- note,** albarán *m.* de entrega [albarán de entréga]; **- service,** servicio *m.* a domicilio [serbíθjo a domiθíljo]

demand (to) reclamar *r.* [rreklamár] ‖ **2.** *n.* reclamación *f.* [rreklamaθjón]

demonstration demostración *f.* [demostraθjón] ‖ **2.** manifestación *f.* [manifestaθjón] (Pol.)

denims pantalones *m.pl.* vaqueros [pantalónes bakéros]

dense *a.* denso(a) [dénso], espeso(a) [espéso]

dent/al *a.* dental [dentál]; **-ifrice** dentífrico *m.* [dentífriko]; **-ist** dentista *m.-f.* [dentísta]; **-ure** dentadura *f.* postiza [dentadúra postíθa]

deodorant desodorante *m.* [desodoránte]

depart (to) salir (g) [salír], partir *r.* [partír] (from/de)

department departamento *m.* [departaménto]; **- store** grandes almacenes *m. pl.* [grándes almaθénes]

departure salida *f.* [salída], partida *f.* [partída] (from/de)

depilatory depilatorio *m.* [depilatórjo]; **cream -,** depilatorio en crema [en kréma]; **liquid -,** depilatorio líquido [líkido]

deposit (to) depositar *r.* [depositár] ‖ **2.** *n.* depósito *m.* [depósito], fianza *f.* [fjánθa]; **- account** cuenta *f.* de ahorros [kwénta de aórros] ‖ **3.** *n.* entrada *f.* [entráda], señal *f.* [senjál], garantía *f.* [garantía] (purchase)

depress/ant sedante *m.* [sedánte]; **-ed** *a.* deprimido(a) [deprimído]; **-ion** depresión *f.* [depresjón]; **-ive** *a.* depresivo(a) [depresíßo]

depth profundidad *f.* [profundidád]; **-meter** profundímetro [profundímetro]

dermatitis dermatitis *f.* [dermatítis]

descen/d (to) bajar *r.* [baxár], descender (ie) [desθendér]; **-t** bajada *f.* [baxáda], descenso *m.* [desθénso]

desert desierto *m.* [desjérto]

design (to) diseñar *r.* [disenjár], crear *r.* [kreár] ‖ **2.** *n.* diseño *m.* [disénjo], creación *f.* [kreaθjón]; **-er** diseñador(a) [disenjadór]; **fashion -,** modisto(a) *m.-f.* [modísto]

desire (to) desear *r.* [deseár] ‖ **2.** *n.* deseo *m.* [deséo]

desk escritorio *m.* [eskritórjo] ‖ **2. information -,** mostrador *m.* (oficina *f.*) de información [mostradór (ofiθína) de informaθjón]; **- clerk** recepcionista *m.-f.* [rreθepθjonísta]

dessert postre *m.* [póstre]; **- wine** vino *m.* dulce [bíno dúlθe], vino de postre [bíno de póstre]; **- spoon** cuchara *f.* de postre [kutchára de]

destination destino *m.* [destíno] (trains, etc.)

detail detalle *m.* [detálje]

detective: - novel, novela *f.* policíaca [nobéla poliθíaka]

detergent detergente *m.* [deterxénte]

detour desvío *m.* [desbío]

devaluation devaluación *f.* [debalwaθjón]

devalue (to) devaluar *r.* [debalwár]

develop (to) revelar *r.* [rrebelár] (photo); **-ing** revelado *m.* [rrebeládo] (photo) ‖ **2.** *n.* desarrollo *m.* [desarróljo]; **housing development** zona *f.* residencial [θóna rresidenθjál], urbanización *f.* [urbaniθaθjón]

deviation desviación *f.* [desbjaθjón] (from/de)

diabet/es diabetes *f.* [djabétes]; **-ic** *a.* diabético(a) [djabétiko] ‖ **2.** *n.* diabético(a) *m.-f.* [djabétiko]

diagnosis diagnóstico *m.* [djagnóstiko]

diagonal *a.* diagonal [djagonál]; **-ly** *adv.* diagonalmente [djagonalménte]

dial (to) marcar *r.* [markár] (a telephone number) ‖ **2.** *n.* esfera *f.* [esféra] (watch) ‖ **3.** *n.* disco *m.* marcador [dísko markadór] (telephone); **-ling: - code,** prefijo *m.* [prefíxo]

dialect dialecto *m.* [djalékto]

diamond diamante *m.* [djamánte]

diaphragm diafragma *m.* [djafrágma]

diarrhoea diarrea *f.* [*djarréa*]

diary agenda *f.* [*axénda*] ‖ **2.** diario *m.* [*djárjo*]

dice dados *m.pl.* [*dádos*]

dictionary diccionario *m.* [*dikθjonárjo*]

die (to) morir (ue) [*morír*]

diesel: - ***engine,*** motor *m.* (de) Diesel [*motór de diésel*]; - ***oil,*** Diesel [*diésel*]

diet régimen *m.* [*rréximen*], dieta [*djéta*]; ***to be on a*** -, estar *irr.* a régimen [*estár a rréximen*]; **-ary** *a.* de régimen [*de rréximen*]; dietético(a) [*djetétiko*]

differen/ce diferencia *f.* [*diferénθja*]; **-t** *a.* diferente [*diferénte*], distinto(a) [*distínto*]; **-tial** diferencial *m.* [*diferenθjál*].

difficult *a.* difícil [*difíθil*]; **-y** dificultad *f.* [*difikultád*]

digestion digestión *f.* [*dixestjón*]

digital *a.* digital [*dixitál*]

dimension dimensión *f.* [*dimensjón*]

din/e (to) cenar *r.* [*θenár*]; ***to - out,*** salir (g) a cenar [*salír a θenár*]; **-ing:** - ***car,*** vagón-restaurante *m.* [*bagón rrestauránte*]; - ***room,*** comedor *m.* [*komedór*]

dinner cena *f.* [*θéna*]; - ***jacket*** esmokin *m.* [*esmókin*]; - ***time*** hora *f.* de (comer) cenar [*óra de θenár*]

dipped: - ***lights,*** luces *f.pl.* de cruce [*lúθes de krúθe*]

direct *a.* directo(a) [*dirékto*]; - ***contact flash*** flas *m.* de contacto directo [*flas de kontákto dirékto*]; **-ion** dirección *f.* [*direkθjón*]; **-ly** *adv.* directamente [*direktaménte*]; **-or** director *m.* [*direktór*]

dirty *a.* sucio(a) [*súθjo*], manchado(a) [*mantchádo*]; ***to get -,*** ensuciarse *r.* [*ensuθjárse*]

disagreeable *a.* desagradable [*desagradáble*]

disappear (to) desaparecer (zc) [*desapareθér*]

disc disco *m.* [*dísko*], disquete *m.* [*diskéte*] (computer)

disconnect (to) desconectar *r.* [*deskonektár*]

discotheque discoteca *f.* [*disketéka*]

discount descuento *m.* [*deskwénto*], rebaja *f.* [*rrebáxa*]

discret/e *a.* discreto(a) [*diskréto*]; **-ion** discreción *f.* [*diskreθjón*]

disembarkation desembarco *m.* [*desembárko*] (persons)

dish plato *m.* [*pláto*]; ***large -,*** fuente *f.* [*fwénte*]; ***to wash the -es*** fregar

(ie) los platos [*fregár los plátos*]; **-washer** lavaplatos *m.* [*labaplátos*]

disinfect (to) desinfectar *r.* [*desinfektár*]; **-ant** *a.* desinfectante [*desinfektánte*]; **-ed** *a.* desinfectado(a) [*desinfektádo*]

diskette disquete *m.* [*diskéte*]

dislocation luxación *f.* [*luksaθjón*]

dismantle (to) desmontar *r.* [*desmontár*]

dismount (to) apearse *r.* [*apeárse*] (from/de)

dispensary centro *m.* de salud [*θéntro de salúd*]

display exposición *f.* [*eksposiθjón*]; ***window -,*** escaparate [*eskaparáte*]

distan/ce distancia *f.* [*distánθja*]; ***to be at a -,*** estar *irr.* lejos [*estár léxos*]; - ***adjustor*** ajuste *m.* de distancias [*axúste de*]; - **meter** telémetro *m.* [*telémetro*]; **-t** *a.* lejano(a) [*lexáno*]

distill/ation destilación *f.* [*destilaθjón*]; **-ed** *a.* destilado(a) [*destiládo*]; - ***water,*** agua *f.* destilada [*ágwa*]; **-ery** destilería *f.* [*destilería*]

distribut/e (to) repartir *r.* [*repartír*], distribuir *r.* [*distribwír*]; **-ion** distribución *f.* [*distribuθjón*], reparto *m.* [*rrepárto*] ‖ **2.** delco *m.* [*délko*] (car): - ***cable,*** cable *m.* del delco [*káble del délko*]; - ***cap,*** tapa *f.* del delco [*tápa del délko*]; **-or** distribuidor *m.* [*distribwidór*]; repartidor *m.* [*rrepartidór*]

district distrito *m.* [*distríto*]; ***postal -,*** distrito postal [*postál*] ‖ **2.** barrio *m.* [*bárrjo*] (of a town)

ditch cuneta *f.* [*kunéta*] (road)

dive (to) bucear *r.* [*bußeár*] ‖ **2.** *n.* buceo *m.* [*bußéo*], inmersión *f.* [*imersjón*]; **-r** buzo *m.* [*búßo*], buceador(a) *m.-f.* [*bußeadór*]

diver/sion diversión *f.* [*dibersjón*] ‖ **2.** desvío *m.* [*desbío*]; **-t (to)** desviar *r.* [*desbjár*]

dividend dividendo *m.* [*dibidéndo*]

diving buceo *m.* [*bußéo*]; - ***suit*** escafandra *f.* [*eskafándra*]

division sección *f.* [*sekθjón*]

divorce (to) divorciarse *r.* [*diborθjárse*] ‖ **2.** *n.* divorcio *m.* [*dibórθjo*]

dizziness vértigo *m.* [*bértigo*]

do (to) hacer *irr.* [*aθér*] ‖ **2.** *aux.* ***to do*** is not translated in interrogative and negative sentences: ***how - you -?*** ¿cómo está(n) Vd(s)? [*kómo está ustéd*]; ***what - you -?*** ¿qué profesión tiene? [*ke profesjón tjéne*]; **d.-it-yourself** bricolaje *m.* [*brikoláxe*]; - ***shop,*** tienda *f.* de bricolaje [*tjénda de*]

dock (to) atracar *r.* [*atrakár*] (ship) ‖ **2.** *n.* desembarcadero *m.* [*desembarkadéro*], muelle *m.* [*muélje*]

doctor médico(a) *m.-f.* [*médiko*], doctor(a) *m.-f.* [*doktór*]

document documento *m.* [*dokuménto*]; **-s** documentación *f.* [*dokumentaθjón*]

dodgem cars auto-choques *m. pl.* [*autotchókes*]

dog perro *m.* [*pérro*]; **- collar** collar *m.* de perro [*koljár de pérro*]; **hot -** perrito caliente [*perríto kaljénte*]

doll muñeca *f.* [*munjéka*]

dollar dólar *m.* [*dólar*]

dolphin delfín *m.* [*delfín*]

domestic *a.* doméstico(a) [*doméstiko*]; **- articles** artículos *m. pl.* para el hogar [*artíkulos pára el ogár*]; **- flights** vuelos *m. pl.* nacionales [*bwélos naθjonáles*]

donation donativo *m.* [*donatíbo*] ‖ **2.** donación *f.* [*donaθjón*]

done *a.* hecho(a) [*étcho*], cocido(a) [*koθído*]; **well -**, muy hecho(a) [*mui étcho*]

donkey burro *m.* [*búrro*]

door puerta *f.* [*pwérta*]; **back -**, puerta trasera [*traséra*]; **front -**, puerta principal [*prinθipál*]; **- bell** timbre *m.* [*tímbre*]; **-man** portero *m.* [*portéro*]; **-way** portal *m.* [*portál*], entrada *f.* [*entráda*]

dose dosis *f.* [*dósis*]

dossier dossier *m.* [*dosjér*]

double *a.* doble [*dóble*]

doubt duda *f.* [*dúda*]

dough masa *f.* [*mása*], pasta *f.* [*pásta*]; **-nut** buñuelo *m.* [*bunjwélo*], dónut *m.* [*dónut*]

down *adv.* abajo [*abáxo*], hacia abajo [*áθja*]; **-hill** *a.* de descenso [*de desθénso*]; cuesta abajo [*kwésta abáxo*]; **-stairs** *adv.* abajo [*abáxo*], escalera abajo [*eskaléra abáxo*]; **to go -**, bajar *r.* la escalera [*baxár la eskaléra*]; **-town** *adv.* en el centro de la ciudad [*en el θéntro de la θjudád*]

dozen docena *f.* [*doθéna*]; **a - oysters,** una docena de ostras [*úna doθéna de óstras*]; **half a - eggs,** media docena de huevos [*médja doθéna de wébos*]

drain desagüe *m.* [*deságwe*]

drama drama *m.* [*dráma*]; **-tic** *a.* dramático(a) [*dramátiko*]

draper's tienda *f.* de lencería [*tjénda de lenθería*]

draught: - beer, cerveza *f.* de barril [*θerbéθa de barríl*]

draw (to) dibujar *r.* [*dibuxár*]; **-ing** dibujo *m.* [*dibúxo*]; **- block,** bloc *m.* de dibujo [*blok de*]; **- room,** sala *f.* de estar [*sála de estár*], salón *m.* [*salón*]

dream (to) soñar (ue) [*sonjár*] (of/con) ‖ **2.** *n.* sueño *m.* [*swénjo*]

dress (to) vestirse (i) [*bestírse*] ‖ **2.** *n.* vestido *m.* [*bestído*], traje *m.* [*tráxe*]; **evening -**, traje *m.* de etiqueta [*tráxe de etikéta*], vestido *m.* de noche [*bestído de nótche*]; **-ing -ing** aliño *m.* [*alínjo*], salsa *f.* [*sálsa*] (for salad) ‖ **2. - gown,** albornoz *m.* [*albornóθ*], bata *f.* [*báta*]; **- table,** tocador *m.* [*tokadór*]; **-maker** modisto(a) *m.-f.* [*modísto*]; **-making** costura *f.* [*kostúra*]; **- materials** tejidos *m.pl.* [*texídos*]

dried *a.* secado(a) [*sekádo*]; paso(a) [*páso*]; **- figs** higos *m. pl.* secos [*ígos sékos*]; **- milk** leche *f.* en polvo [*létche en pólbo*]

drill (to) taladrar *r.* [*taladrár*] ‖ **2.** *n.* taladro *m.* [*taládro*]

drink (to) beber *r.* [*bebér*] ‖ **2.** *n.* bebida *f.* [*bebída*]; **alcoholic -**, bebida alcohólica [*alkoólika*]; **non alcoholic -**, bebida sin alcohol [*sin alkoól*]; **warm -**, bebida caliente [*kaljénte*] ‖ **3.** trago *m.* [*trágo*]; **to take a -**, echar *r.* un trago [*etchár un trágo*]; **-able** *a.* potable [*potáble*]; **-ing: - water,** agua potable [*ágwa potáble*]; **-s kiosk** quiosco *m.* de bebidas [*kjósko de bebídas*]

driv/e (to) conducir (zc) (un coche) [*konduθír (un kótche)*] (a car, etc.); **-er** conductor *m.* [*konduktór*]; **-ing: - licence,** permiso (carné) *m.* de conducir [*permíso (karné) de konduθír*]; **- mirror,** espejo *m.* retrovisor [*espéxo rretrobisór*]; **- school,** autoescuela *f.* [*autoeskwéla*]

drop (to) dejar *r.* caer [*dexár kaér*], soltar (ue) [*soltár*] ‖ **2.** *n.* gota *f.* [*góta*]

drown (to) ahogarse *r.* [*aogárse*]

drug droga *f.* [*dróga*], medicamento *m.* [*medikaménto*]

drum tambor *m.* [*tambór*]

drunken *a.* borracho(a) [*borrátcho*]; **-ess** embriaguez *f.* [*embrjagéθ*]

dry (to) secar(se) *r.* [*sekárse*] ‖ **2.** *a.* seco(a) [*séko*]; **- beans,** judías *f.pl.* secas [*xudías sékas*]; **- fruit,** fruta *f.* seca [*frúta séka*]; **- sangría,** sangría *f.* seca [*sangría séka*]; **- wine** vino *m.* seco [*bíno séko*]; **- clean (to)** limpiar *r.* en seco [*limpjár en séko*]; **- cleaning** lavado *m.* en seco [*labádo en séko*]; **-er** secador *m.* [*sekadór*]

duck pato *m.* [*páto*]: - *a l'orange,* pato a la naranja [*a la naránxa*]; **roast -,** pato asado [*asádo*]
dumb *a.* mudo(a) [*múdo*]
dummy chupete *m.* [*tchupéte*]
duodenal *a.* duodenal [*dwodenál*]
during *prep.* durante [*duránte*]

Dutch *a.* holandés [*olandés*]; - **cheese** queso *m.* de Holanda [*késo de olánda*]
duty-free *a.* libre de impuestos [*líbre de impuéstos*]
dye (to) teñir(se) (i) [*tenjírse*] ‖ **2.** *n.* tinte *m.* [*tínte*], color *m.* [*kolór*]
dynamo dinamo *m.* [*dinámo*]

E

each *a.* cada [*káda*]; todos(as) [*tódos*];
- **day** todos los días [*tódos los días*] ‖
2. *pron.* cada uno(a) [*káda úno*]
ear oreja *f.* [*oréxa*] ‖ **2.** oído *m.* [*oído*]
(sense)
early *a.* temprano(a) [*tempráno*] ‖ **2.**
adv. temprano, a principios [*a prinθípjos*]; - **in May,** a principios de mayo
[*a prinθípjos de májo*]
earn (to) ganar *r.* [*ganár*]; **to - money,**
ganar dinero [*dinéro*]; **-ings** ingresos
m.pl. [*ingrésos*]
ear/piece auricular *m.* [*aurikulár*];
-ring pendiente *m.* [*pendjénte*]
earth tierra *f.* [*tjérra*]; **-en** *a.* de tierra
[*de*]; **-ware** de barro [*de bárro*]
easiness facilidad *f.* [*faθilidád*]
east este *m.* [*éste*] ‖ **2.** *adv.* al este [*al*],
hacia el este [*áθja al éste*]; **-ern** *a.* del
este [*del*], oriental [*orjentál*]; **-wards**
adv. hacia el este [*áθja el éste*]
eas/y *a.* fácil [*fáθil*], sencillo(a) [*senθíljo*];
- **payments** facilidades *f. pl.* de pago
[*faθilidádes de págo*]; **-ily** *adv.* fácil-
mente [*faθilménte*]
eat (to) comer *r.* [*komér*]; **to - one's
breakfast,** desayunar *r.* [*desajunár*];
to - out, comer fuera [*komér fuéra*];
-able *a.* comestible [*komestíble*]
eau: - **de Cologne,** agua *f.* de colonia
[*ágwa de kolónja*], colonia *f.*
ebony *a.* de ébano [*de ébano*]
ecolog/ical *a.* ecológico(a) [*ekolóxiko*];
-y ecología *f.* [*ekoloxía*]
econom/ical *a.* económico(a) [*ekonó-
miko*], barato(a) [*baráto*]; **-ize** ahorrar
r. [*aorrár*]; **-y** economía *f.* [*eko-
nomía*]; - **class,** clase *f.* turista [*kláse
turísta*]
eczema eczema *m.* [*ekθéma*]
edge borde *m.* [*bórde*] ‖ **2.** filo *m.* [*fílo*]
(knife, etc.)
edi/fice edificio *m.* [*edifíθjo*]; **-fy (to)**
edificar *r.* [*edifikár*], construir [*konstruír*]
edition edición *f.* [*ediθjón*]
eel anguila *f.* [*angíla*]; **baby -s,** angulas
f. pl. [*angúlas*]; **fried baby -s,** angulas a la cazuela [*a la kaθwéla*];
smoked -, anguila *f.* ahumada [*angíla aumáda*]
effect efecto *m.* [*efékto*]; **in -,** efectivamente [*efektibaménte*]; **-s: personal -,**

efectos *m. pl.* personales [*eféktos personáles*], cosas *f. pl.* personales [*kósas
personáles*]
effervescent *a.* efervescente [*eferbesθénte*]
egg huevo *m.* [*wébo*]; - **baked in batter**
huevo al plato [*al pláto*]; **boiled -,**
huevo pasado por agua [*pasádo por
ágwa*]; **fried -,** huevo frito [*fríto*];
hard-boiled -, huevo duro [*dúro*];
poached -, huevo escalfado [*eskalfá-
do*]; **scrambled -,** huevo revuelto
[*rebwélto*]; **stuffed -,** huevo relleno
[*reljéno*]; - **custard** natillas *f. pl.* [*natíljas*]; - **plant** berenjena *f.* [*berenxéna*]; - **shampoo** champú *m.* de
huevo [*tchampú de wébo*]; **-shell** cáscara *f.* de huevo [*káskara de*]
eight *a.* ocho [*ótcho*]; **-een** dieciocho
[*djeθiótcho*]; **-y** ochenta [*otchénta*]
elastic *a.* elástico(a) [*elástiko*]; - **band**
goma *f.* elástica [*góma elástika*]
elastoplast tiritas *f.pl.* [*tirítas*]
elbow codo *m.* [*kódo*]
eld/er *a.* mayor [*majór*]; **-est** mayor;
her - daughter, su hija mayor [*su
íxa majór*]
electric(al) *a.* eléctrico(a) [*eléktriko*];
- **current** corriente *f.* eléctrica [*korrjénte*]; - **goods** electrodomésticos
m.pl. [*electrodoméstikos*]; - **motor**
electromotor *m.* [*elektromotór*]; **-s** ins-
talación *f.* eléctrica [*instalaθjón eléktrika*] - **system** sistema *m.* eléctrico [*sistéma*]
electricity electricidad *f.* [*electriθidád*];
- **supply** suministro *m.* eléctrico [*su-
minístro eléktriko*]
electrocardiogram electrocardiogra-
ma *m.* [*elektrokardjográma*]
electronic *a.* electrónico(a) [*elektróniko*]; - **flash** flas *m.* electrónico [*flas
elektróniko*]; **-s** electrónica *f.* [*elektró-
nika*]
elegan/ce elegancia *f.* [*elegánθja*]; **-t** *a.*
elegante [*elegánte*]
element elemento *m.* [*eleménto*]; **-al** *a.*
elemental [*elementál*], básico(a)
[*básiko*]
elevator montacargas *m.* [*montakárgas*]
eleven *a.* once [*ónθe*]
else *adv.* otro [*ótro*]; **someone -,** otro(a),
otra persona [*ótra persóna*]; **some-
thing -,** otra cosa [*ótra kósa*] ‖ **2.** más
[*mas*]; **anything -,** algo más [*álgo
mas*]; **anyone -,** alguien más [*álgjen
mas*]; **-where** *adv.* en otra parte [*en
ótra párte*], en otro lugar [*en ótro lugár*]

embark (to) embarcar(se) r. [embar-kárse]; **-ation** embarque m. [em-bárke]

embolism embolia f. [embólja]

embossed a. en relieve [en rreljébe], repujado(a) [rrepuxáðo]; **of - lea-ther,** de cuero repujado [de kwéro rrepuxáðo]

embroidery bordado m. [bordáðo]; **of -,** bordado(a); **- thread** hilo m. de bordar [ílo de bordár]

emerald esmeralda f. [esmerálda] ‖ **2.** a. (color) esmeralda [kolór]

emergency emergencia f. [emerxénθja]; **- exit** salida f. de emergencia [salída de] ‖ **2.** Med. urgencia f. [urxénθja]

emetic vomitivo m. [bomitíbo]

emission emisión f. [emisjón]

emotion emoción f. [emoθjón]; **-al** a. emocional [emoθjonál]

employ (to) emplear r. [empleár] (work) ‖ **2.** emplear, usar r. [usár]; **-ee** empleado(a) m.-f. [empleáðo]; **-ment** empleo m. [empléo], colocación f. [kolokaθjón]; **- agency,** agencia f. de colocación [axénθja de kolokaθjón]

empty (to) vaciar r. [baθjár] ‖ **2.** a. vacío(a) [baθío]

emulsion emulsión f. [emulsjón]

enamel (to) esmaltar r. [esmaltár] ‖ **2.** n. esmalte m. [esmálte]

encephalitis encefalitis f. [enθefalítis]

enclose (to) adjuntar r. [adxuntár] (document, etc.); **-d** a. adjunto(a) [adxúnto]; **the - letter,** la carta adjunta [la kárta adxúnta]

end (to) terminar r. [terminár] ‖ **2.** acabar r. [akabár], finalizar r. [finaliθár] ‖ **3.** n. fin m. [fin], final m. [finál] ‖ **4.** extremo m. [ekstrémo]

endive endibia f. [endíbja]; **batavian -,** escarola f. [eskaróla]

endorse (to) endosar r. [endosár]; **-ment** endoso m. [endóso]

energy energía f. [enerxía]

engin/e máquina f. [mákina], motor m. [motór] ‖ **2.** locomotora f. [lokomotó-ra]; **- block** bloque m. del motor [blóke del]; **- driver** maquinista m. [makinísta] (rail); **-eer** ingeniero m. [inxenjéro] ‖ **2.** maquinista m. [maki-nísta]; **-eering** ingeniería f. [inxenje-ría]

England Inglaterra f. [inglatérra]

English a. inglés (inglesa) [inglés (in-glésa)] ‖ **2.** n. the -, los ingleses m.pl. [los ingléses] ‖ **3.** inglés m. [in-glés] (language): **to speak -,** hablar

r. inglés [ablár]; **-man** inglés m. [in-glés]: **he is an -,** es inglés [es]; **- speaking** a. de habla inglesa [de ábla inglésa]; **-woman** inglesa f. [inglésa]: **she is an -,** es inglesa [es]

engraving grabado m. [grabáðo]; grabación f. [grabaθjón]

enlarge (to) ampliar r. [ampljár] (photo); **-ment** ampliación f. [am-pljaθjón]

enough a. bastante [bastánte], suficiente [sufiθjénte] ‖ **2.** adv. bastante [bastán-te], suficientemente [sufiθjenteménte]

ensemble conjunto m. [konxúnto]

enter (to) entrar r. [entrár] (en)

entertainment diversión f. [dibersjón]

entire a. entero(a) [entéro], todo(a) [tó-do]; **-ly** adv. enteramente [entera-ménte], del todo [del tódo]

entrance entrada f. [entráda]; **- hall** vestíbulo m. [bestíbulo]

entrecot entrecot m. [entrekót]; **beef -,** entrecot m. de buey [de bwei]; **grilled -,** entrecot a la parrilla [a la parrílja]; **veal -,** entrecot de ternera [de ternéra]

entry entrada f. [entráda]; **- fee** entrada f. (ticket)

envelop (to) envolver (ue) [embolbér]; **-e** sobre m. [sóbre]: **airmail -,** sobre aéreo [aéreo]

epidemic epidemia f. [epidémja]

epilep/sy epilepsia f. [epilépsja]; **-tic** epiléptico(a) m.-f. [epiléptiko]

epoch época f. [époka]

equipment equipo m. [ekípo]

erection erección f. [erekθjón]

erotic a. erótico(a) [erótiko]

eruption erupción f. [erupθjón]

escalator escalera f. mecánica [eskaléra mekánika]

escalope escalope m. [eskalópe]; **- Mi-lanese** escalope a la milanesa [a la milanésa]; **- Viennese** escalope a la vienesa [a la bjenésa]

especial a. especial [espeθjál]; **-ly** adv. especialmente [espeθjalménte], sobre todo [sóbre tódo]

esplanade paseo m. (marítimo) [paséo (maritímo)]

espresso café m. exprés [kafé eksprés]

establish (to) establecer (zc) [estable-θér] ‖ **2. to - oneself,** establecerse [estableθérse]; **-ment** establecimiento m. [estableθimjénto]

estate finca f. [fínka]; **housing -,** urbani-zación f. [urbaniθaθjón]; **- agent** agen-cia f. inmobiliaria [axénθja inmobiljárja]

etching aguafuerte *m.* [*aguafuérte*]
eucalyptus eucalipto *m.* [*eukalípto*]
Euro euro *m.* [*éuro*]
Europe Europa *f.* [*európa*]
European *a.* europea(a) [*európéo*]:
- **Union** Unión *f.* Európea [*unjón*] ∥
2. *n.* europeo(a) *m.-f.* [*európéo*]
evacuat/e (to) evacuar *r.* [*ebakwár*];
-**ion** evacuación *f.* [*ebakwaθjón*]
evaporation evaporación *f.* [*ebaporaθjón*]
eve víspera *f.* [*bíspera*]
even *a.* liso(a) [*líso*], llano(a) [*ljáno*] ∥ 2.
adv. incluso [*inklúso*], hasta [*ásta*]
evening tarde *f.* [*tárde*], noche *f.*
[*nótche*]: **good -,** buenas tardes [*buénas tárdes*], buenas noches [*buénas
nótches*]: **tomorrow -,** mañana por
la tarde [*manjána por la tárde*]: **yesterday -,** ayer por la tarde [*ajér por
la tárde*] ∥ 2. velada *f.* [*beláda*]:
- **dress** traje *m.* de noche [*de nótche*]
(woman); traje de etiqueta [*de etikéta*]
(man); - **gown** vestido *m.* de noche
[*bestído de*]: - **performance** función
f. (sesión *f.*) de noche [*funθjón
(sesjón) de nótche*]
event suceso *m.* [*suθéso*]
ever *adv.* nunca [*núnka*], jamás [*xamás*]
∥ 2. alguna vez [*algúna beθ*]
every *a.* cada [*káda*], todos(as) [*tódos*]:
- **day** cada día [*káda día*], todos los
días [*todos los días*], -**body** *pron.* todo
el mundo [*tódo el múndo*], todos(as)
[*tódos*]: -**thing** *pron.* todo [*tódo*];
-**where** *adv.* en todas partes [*en tódas pártes*]
exact *a.* exacto(a) [*eksákto*]; -**ly** *adv.*
exactamente [*eksaktaménte*]
examination examen *m.* [*eksámen*] ∥
2. *Med.* reconocimiento *m.* [*rrekono-
θimjénto*]
excellent *a.* excelente [*eksθelénte*]
except *prep.* excepto [*eksθépto*], salvo
[*sálbo*]: -**ion** excepción *f.* [*eksθepθjón*]:
-**ional** *a.* excepcional [*eksθepθjonál*]
excess exceso *m.* [*eksθéso*]: - **luggage**
exceso de equipaje [*de ekipáxe*]
exchange cambio *m.* [*kámbjo*]:
foreign -, divisas *f. pl.* [*dibísas*]:
rate of -, tipo de cambio [*típo
de kámbjo*] ∥ 2. **telephone -,** central *f.* telefónica [*θentrál telefónika*]
exclusive *a.* exclusivo(a) [*eksklusíbo*], -**ly**
adv. exclusivamente [*eksklusibaménte*]

excursion excursión *f.* [*ekskursjón*]:
- **centre** centro *m.* excursionista [*θéntro ekskursjonísta*]: - **fare** tarifa *f.* de
excursión [*tarífa de ekskursjón*]: -**ist**
excursionista *m.-f.* [*ekskursjonísta*]
excuse (to) excusar *r.* [*ekskusár*] ∥ 2.
excuse me, disculpe(me) [*diskúlpe*]
∥ 3. *n.* excusa *f.* [*ekskúsa*]
exempt *a.* exento(a) [*eksénto*], libre [*líbre*] (from/de): - **from taxes,** libre
(exento) de impuestos [*libre (eksénto)
de impuéstos*]
exhaust escape *m.* [*eskápe*]: - **pipe** tubo *m.* de escape [*túbo de*]
exit salida *f.* [*salída*]: **emergency -,** salida de emergencia [*de emerxénθja*]
expect (to) esperar *r.* [*esperár*]
expens/e gasto *m.* [*gásto*]: - **account**
cuenta *f.* de gastos [*kuénta de gástos*]:
-**ive** *a.* caro(a) [*káro*]
explosion explosión *f.* [*eksplosjón*]
export (to) exportar *r.* [*eksportár*] ∥ 2. *n.*
exportación *f.* [*eksportaθjón*], - **licence**
licencia *f.* de exportación [*liθénθja de
eksportaθjón*]
exposure exposición *f.* [*eksposiθjón*]:
- **meter** fotómetro *m.* [*fotómetro*]:
- **time** tiempo *m.* de exposición
[*tjémpo de eksposiθjón*]
express expreso *m.* [*ekspréso*] (rail) ∥
2. *adv.* urgente [*urxénte*]: **to send
sth. -,** enviar *r.* u.c. urgente [*embjár
úna kósa urxénte*]
exquisite *a.* exquisito(a) [*ekskisíto*]
extension *Tel.* extensión *f.* [*ekstensjón*]
exterior *a.* exterior [*eksterjór*]
extinguisher extintor *m.* [*ekstintór*]
extra *a.* extra [*ekstra*], adicional [*adiθjonál*]
extract extracto *m.* [*ekstrákto*]
extraordinar/y *a.* extraordinario(a)
[*ekstraordinárjo*], -**ily** *adv.* extraordi-
nariamente [*ekstraordinarjaménte*]
extreme *a.* extremo(a) [*ekstrémo*]: -**ly**
adv. extremadamente [*ekstremada-
ménte*]: sumamente [*sumaménte*]
eye ojo *m.* [*óxo*]: -**brow** ceja *f.* [*θéxa*]:
-**lash** pestaña *f.* [*pestánja*]: -**let** ojete
m. [*oxéte*]: -**lid** párpado *m.* [*párpado*]: -**liner** lápiz *m.* de ojos [*lápiθ de
óxos*]: -**shadow** sombra *f.* para los
ojos [*sómbra pára los óxos*], -**sight** visión *f.* [*bisjón*], vista *f.* [*bísta*];
-**wash** colirio *m.* [*kolírjo*]

F

fabric tejido *m.* [*texído*], tela *f.* [*téla*]
fabulous *a.* fabuloso(a) [*fabulóso*]
façade fachada *f.* [*fatcháda*]
face cara *f.* [*kára*]; **- cloth** paño *m.* [*pánjo*]; **-pack** mascarilla *f.* facial [*maskarílja faθjál*]; **- powders** polvos *m. pl.* faciales [*pólbos faθjáles*]
facial *a.* facial [*faθjál*]; **- massage** masaje *m.* facial [*masáxe faθjál*]
facilit/ies instalaciones *f. pl.* [*instalaθjónes*]; **cooking -,** derecho *m.* a cocina [*derétcho a koθína*]; **sports -,** instalaciones *f. pl.* deportivas [*instalaθjónes deportíbas*]; **-y** facilidad *f.* [*faθilidád*]
factory fábrica *f.* [*fábrika*]
faculty facultad *f.* [*fakultád*]
faded *a.* descolorido(a) [*deskolorído*], desteñido(a) [*destenjído*]
fail (to) fallar *r.* [*faljár*]; fracasar *r.* [*frakasár*]; **-ure** fracaso *m.* [*frakáso*]; fallo *m.* [*fáljo*]; **heart -,** paro *m.* cardíaco [*páro kardíako*]
faint (to) desmayarse [*desmajárse*]; **-ing** desmayo *m.* [*desmájo*]; **-ness** desmayo *m.* [*desmájo*], desfallecimiento *m.* [*desfaljeθimjénto*]
fair feria *f.* [*férja*] || **2.** *a.* rubio(a) [*rrúbjo*], blanco(a) [*blánko*] (skin); **-ground** recinto *m.* de feria [*rreθínto de férja*]
fall (to) caer(se) *irr.* [*kaérse*]; **to - asleep,** dormirse (ue) [*dormírse*]; **to - ill,** caer *irr.* enfermo(a) [*kaér enf.rmo*] || **2.** *n.* caída *f.* [*kaída*]
fals/e *a.* falso(a) [*fálso*]; **-ification** falsificación *f.* [*falsifikaθjón*]; **-ify** falsificar *r.* [*falsifikár*]
familiar *a.* familiar [*familjár*]
family familia *f.* [*familja*]; **- doctor** médico *m.* de familia [*médiko de familja*]
famous *a.* famoso(a) [*famóso*]
fan (to) abanicar *r.* [*abanikár*]; **- oneself,** abanicarse *r.* [*abanikárse*] || **2.** *n.* aficionado(a) *m.-f.* [*afiθjonádo*] || **3.** abanico *m.* [*abaníko*] || **4.** ventilador *m.* [*bentiladór*]; **- belt** correa *f.* del ventilador [*korréa del*]; **-light** claraboya *f.* [*klarbója*]
fancy capricho *m.* [*kaprítcho*]; **- goods** caprichos *m. pl.* [*kaprítchos*]
fantas/tic(al) *a.* fantástico(a) [*fantástiko*]; **-y** fantasía *f.* [*fantasía*]

far *adv.* lejos [*léxos*] (from/de); **not - from here,** no muy lejos de aquí [*no mui léxos de akí*]; **very - from here,** muy lejos de aquí [*mui léxos de akí*]
fare tarifa *f.* [*tarífa*], precio *m.* de billete (pasaje) [*préθjo de biljéte (pasáxe)*]; **-well!** *interj.* ¡adiós! [*adjós*]
farm granja *f.* [*gránxa*]; **-er** granjero(a) [*granxéro*]; **-house** granja *f.* [*gránxa*]; **-yard** corral *m.* [*korrál*]
fashion moda *f.* [*móda*]; **to be in -,** estar *irr.* de moda [*estár de móda*]; **to be out of -,** estar *irr.* pasado(a) de moda [*estár pasádo de*]; **- designer** diseñador(a) *m.-f.* de moda [*disenjadór de móda*]; **- parade** desfile *m.* de moda [*desfíle de móda*]; **-able** *a.* **to be -,** estar *irr.* de moda [*estár de móda*]
fast *a.* firme [*fírme*], seguro(a) [*segúro*] || **2.** rápido(a) [*rrápido*] || **3.** *adv.* rápidamente [*rrapidaménte*], deprisa [*deprísa*]; **-en (to)** abrochar *r.* [*abrotchár*] (seat belts)
fat grasa *f.* [*grása*], **cooking -,** manteca *f.* [*mantéka*] || **2.** *a.* gordo(a) [*górdo*]; **to get -,** engordar *r.* [*engordár*]
father padre *m.* [*pádre*]; **f.-in-law** padre político [*polítiko*], suegro *m.* [*swégro*]
fatty *a.* graso(a) [*gráso*]
fault falta *f.* [*fálta*], defecto *m.* [*defékto*] || **2.** tara *f.* [*tára*] (goods)
favour favor *m.* [*fabór*]; **do me the - of,** hágame el favor de (hacer u.c.) [*ágame el fabór de (aθér úna kósa)*]; **-able** *a.* favorable [*faboráble*]; **-ite** *a.* favorito(a) [*faboríto*], preferido(a) [*preferído*]
fax fax *m.* [*faks*]
fear (to) tener *irr.* miedo (a u.c. o u.p.) [*tenér mjédo a úna kósa o úna persóna*]; temer *r.* [*temér*] (for/por) || **2.** *n.* miedo *m.* [*mjédo*], temor *m.* [*temór*] (of/a)
feast fiesta *f.* [*fjésta*]; **- day** día *m.* de fiesta [*día de fjésta*]
feather pluma *f.* [*plúma*]; **- bed** colchón *m.* de plumas [*koltchón de plúmas*]
February febrero *m.* [*febréro*]; **in -,** en febrero [*en*]
fee honorarios *m. pl.* [*onorárjos*]
feed comida *f.* [*komída*]; **-ing** alimentación *f.* [*alimentaθjón*]; **- bottle,** biberón *m.* [*biberón*]
feel sentir (ie) [*sentír*]; **-ing** sentimiento *m.* [*sentimjénto*] || **2.** sensación *f.* [*sensaθjón*], impresión *f.* [*impresjón*]
feet pies *m. pl.* [*pjes*]
feminine *a.* femenino(a) [*femeníno*]

femur fémur *m.* [*fémur*]

fence cerca *f.* [*θérka*], valla *f.* [*bálja*]

fermentation fermentación *f.* [*fermentaθjón*]

ferry ferry *m.* [*férri*]. transbordador *m.* [*transbordadór*]

fertil/e *a.* fértil [*fértil*]; **-izer** fertilizante *m.* [*fertiliθánte*]

festiv/al festival *m.* [*festibál*]; fiesta *f.* [*fjésta*]; **-ity** fiesta *f.* [*fjésta*]

fetch (to) ir *irr.* a buscar [*ir a buskár*], recoger *r.* [*rrekoxér*]

fever fiebre *f.* [*fjébre*]

few *a.-pron.* algunos(as) [*algúnos*], unos(as) cuantos(as) [*únos kwántos*]

fiancé prometido *m.* [*prometído*]; **-e** prometida *f.* [*prometída*]

fibre fibra *f.* [*fíbra*]

fiction novela *f.* [*nobéla*] ‖ **2.** ficción *f.* [*fikθjón*]

field campo *m.* [*kámpo*]

fifteen *a.* quince [*kínθe*]; **-th** *a.* decimoquinto(a) [*deθimokínto*] ‖ **2.** quince [*kínθe*]: **the - of May,** el quince de mayo [*el kínθe de májo*]

fifth *a.* quinto(a) [*kínto*] ‖ **2.** cinco [*θínko*]: **the - of May,** el cinco de mayo [*el θínko de májo*]

fifty *a.* cincuenta [*θinkwénta*]

fig higo *m.* [*ígo*]: **dried -s,** higos *pl.* secos [*ígos sékos*]

figure figura *f.* [*figúra*] ‖ **2.** número *m.* [*número*], cifra *f.* [*θífra*] (math.)

file (to) limar *r.* [*limár*]: **to - one's nails,** limarse las uñas [*limárse las únjas*] ‖ **2.** *n.* lima *f.* [*líma*] (tool) ‖ **3** carpeta *f.* [*karpéta*] ‖ **4** archivo *m.* [*artchíbo*], expediente *m.* [*ekspedjénte*] (archive)

fill (to) llenar *r.* [*ljenár*] (with/de): **to - in,** rellenar *r.* [*rreljenár*]: **to - in a form,** rellenar un impreso [*rreljenár un impréso*]

fillet filete *m.* [*filéte*]: **anglerfish -,** filete de rape [*de rrápe*]: **beef -,** filete de buey [*de bwéi*]: **grouper -,** filete de mero [*de méro*], **hake -,** filete de merluza [*de merlúθa*] **pork -,** filete de cerdo [*de θérdo*]: **sole -,** filete de lenguado [*de lengwádo*]: **sole - fried in batter,** filete de lenguado a la romana [*a la rromána*]: **sole - meunière,** filete de lenguado al vino blanco [*al bíno blánko*]: **veal -,** filete de ternera [*de ternéra*]

filling llenado *m.* [*ljenádo*] ‖ **2.** relleno *m.* [*rreljéno*]: **- station** gasolinera *f.* [*gasolinéra*]

film (to) filmar *r.* [*filmár*], rodar (ue) una película [*rrodár úna pelíkula*] ‖ **2.** *n.* film *m.* [*film*], película *f.* [*pelíkula*]: **colour -,** película en color [*en kolór*]; **black and white -,** película en blanco y negro [*en blánko i négro*]; **- counter** contador *m.* de fotografías [*kontadór de fotografías*]; **- loader** carga *f.* de la película [*kárga de la pelíkula*]

filter (to) filtrar(se) *r.* [*filtrárse*] ‖ **2.** *n.* filtro *m.* [*fíltro*]: **colour -,** filtro de color [*de kolór*], **oil -,** filtro de aceite [*de aθéite*]; **-tip** boquilla *f.* [*bokílja*], filtro *m.* [*fíltro*]

fin aleta *f.* [*aléta*]

final *a.* final [*finál*], último(a) [*último*] **-ly** *adv.* finalmente [*finalménte*], por fin [*por fin*]

financ/es fondos *m.pl.* [*fóndos*], **-ial** *a.* financiero(a) [*finanθjéro*]; **-ing** financiación *f.* [*finanθjaθjón*]

find (to) encontrar (ue) [*enkontrár*]

fine *a.* fino(a) [*fíno*] ‖ **2.** bien [*bjen*]: **to be -,** estar [*estár*] ‖ **3.** bueno(a) [*buéno*]: **it is -,** hace buen tiempo [*áθe bwen tjémpo*]

finger dedo *m.* [*dédo*]; **-nail** uña *f.* [*únja*]; **-tip** punta *f.* del dedo [*púnta del dédo*]

finish (to) acabar *r.* [*akabár*], terminar *r.* [*terminár*]; **-ed** *a.* acabado(a) [*akabádo*]: **hand -,** acabado(a) a mano [*akabádo a máno*]; **- product,** producto *m.* acabado [*prodúkto akabádo*]

fire fuego *m.* [*fwégo*], lumbre *f.* [*lúmbre*] ‖ **2.** estufa *f.* [*estúfa*]: **electric -,** estufa eléctrica [*eléktrika*]; **gas -,** estufa de gas [*de gas*] ‖ **3.** incendio *m.* [*inθéndjo*]; **- alarm** alarma *f.* de incendios [*alárma de inθéndjos*]; **- brigade** bomberos *m.pl.* [*bombéros*]; **- exit** salida *f.* de emergencia [*salída de emerxénθja*]; **- extinguisher** extintor *m.* [*ekstintór*]; **-man** bombero *m.* [*bombéro*]; **- place** chimenea *f.* [*tchimenéa*]; **-wood** leña *f.* [*lénja*]; **-works** fuegos *m.pl.* artificiales [*fwégos artifiθjáles*]

firm *a.* firme [*fírme*]

first *a.* primer(o) (a) [*priméro*]: **at -,** al principio [*al prinθípjo*] ‖ **2.** uno (úno); **the - of May,** el uno de mayo [*el úno de májo*]; **- aid** primeros auxilios *m.pl.* [*priméros auksíljos*]; **- kit,** botiquín *m.* [*botikín*]; **- class** primera clase *f.* [*priméra kláse*]; **- floor** primer piso *m.* [*primér píso*], primera planta *f.*

[*priméra plánta*]; - **gear** primera (marcha) *f.* [*priméra mártcha*]; -**ly** *adv.* primero [*priméro*], en primer lugar [*en primér lugár*]; - **performance** estreno *m.* [*estréno*]

fish (to) pescar *r.* [*peskár*] ‖ **2.** *n.* pez *m.* [*peθ*] (animal) ‖ **3.** pescado *m.* [*peskádo*] (food); **boiled -,** pescado hervido [*erbído*]; **fried -,** pescado frito [*fríto*]; - **fried in batter,** fritura *f.* de pescado [*fritúra de peskádo*]; **grilled -,** pescado a la parrilla [*peskádo a la parrílja*]; - **grilled on the grid,** pescado a la plancha [*a la plántcha*]; - **stew** zarzuela *f.* de pescado [*θarθwéla de peskádo*]; -**bone** espina *f.* [*espína*]; -**erman** pescador *m.* [*peskadór*]; -**ing** pesca *f.* [*péska*]; **to go -,** ir *irr.* a pescar [*ir a peskár*]; - **bag,** bolsa *f.* portapeces [*bólsa portapéθes*]; - **licence,** permiso *m.* de pesca [*permíso de péska*]; - **net** red *f.* de pesca [*rred de péska*]; - **rod,** caña *f.* de pescar [*kánja de peskár*]; - **tackle,** aparejos *m.pl.* de pesca [*aparéxos de péska*]; - **monger** pescador(a) *m.-f.* [*peskadór*]; -**'s,** pescadería *f.* [*peskadería*]

fist puño *m.* [*púnjo*]

fit (to) ir *irr.* bien [*ir bjen*] (size) ‖ **2** retocar *r.* [*rretokár*] ‖ **3.** *n. Med.* ataque *m.* [*atáke*]; -**ness** estado *m.* físico [*estádo físiko*]; -**s** convulsiones *f. pl.* [*kombulsjónes*]; -**ted** *a.* ajustado(a) [*axustádo*]; -**ting** prueba *f.* [*prwéba*]; - **room,** probador *m.* [*probadór*]

five *a.* cinco [*θínko*]

fives frontón *m.* [*frontón*]

flank tapa *f.* [*tápa*]

flannel franela *f.* [*franéla*]

flash flas *m.* [*flas*]; - **bulb** flas de bombilla [*de bombílja*]

flask frasco *m.* [*frásko*]

flat *a.* plano(a) [*pláno*], llano(a) [*ljáno*] ‖ **2.** piso *m.* [*píso*], apartamento *m.* [*apartaménto*]

flavour (to) condimentar *r.* [*kondimentár*]; -**ing** condimento *m.* [*kondiménto*]

flight vuelo *m.* [*bwélo*]; **charter -,** vuelo chárter [*tchárter*]

flint piedra *f.* de encendedor [*pjédra de enθendedór*]

float flotador *m.* [*flotadór*]

floor planta *f.* [*plánta*], piso *m.* [*píso*] ‖ **2.** suelo *m.* [*swélo*]; **first -,** primera planta *f.* [*priméra*]; **ground -,** planta baja [*báxa*]; - **cloth** bayeta *f.* [*bajéta*]

floppy disquete *m.* [*diskéte*] (computer)

florist florista *m.-f.* [*florísta*]; -**'s** floristería *f.* [*floristería*]

flour harina *f.* [*arína*]

flower flor *f.* [*flor*]; -**pot** maceta *f.* [*maθéta*]; - **vase** florero *m.* [*floréro*]

flu gripe *f.* [*grípe*]

fluent *a.* con soltura [*kon soltúra*]; **she speaks - Spanish,** habla el español con soltura [*ábla el espanjól kon soltúra*]

fly (to) volar (ue) [*bolár*], ir *irr.* en avión [*ir en abjón*] ‖ **2.** *n.* mosca *f.* [*móska*]; - **spray** spray *m.* insecticida [*esprái insektiθída*]; -**over** paso *m.* elevado [*páso elebádo*]

foam espuma *f.* [*espúma*]; **shaving -,** espuma de afeitar [*de afeitár*]; - **bath** espuma de baño [*de bánjo*]

focal: - distance, distancia *f.* focal [*distánθja fokál*]; - **point** foco *m.* [*fóko*]

focus (to) enfocar *r.* [*enfokár*] ‖ **2.** *n.* enfoque *m.* [*enfóke*]

fogged *a.* velado(a) [*beládo*]

foie-gras foie-gras *m.* [*fwagrás*], paté *m.* [*paté*]; - **pies** pasteles *m. pl.* de foie-gras [*pastéles de*]

foil hoja *f.* [*óxa*] (metal): **aluminium -,** papel *m.* de aluminio [*papél de alumínjo*]

fold (to) doblar *r.* [*doblár*], plegar (ie) [*plegár*]. **do not -!,** ¡no doblar! [*no doblár*] ‖ **2.** *n.* pliegue *m.* [*pljége*], doblez *f.* [*dobléθ*]

folding plegable [*plegáble*]; - **chair** silla *f.* plegable [*sílja*]; - **screen** biombo *m.* [*bjómbo*]; - **table** mesa *f.* plegable [*mésa*]

folklore: - music, música *f.* folklórica [*músika folklórika*]

follow (to) seguir (i) [*segír*]; -**er** seguidor(a) *m.-f.* [*segidór*]

food comida *f.* [*komída*]; - **shop** tienda *f.* de comestibles [*tjénda de komestíbles*], colmado *m.* [*kolmádo*]; - **department** sección *f.* de alimentación [*sekθjón de alimentaθjón*]; - **stuffs** comestibles *m.pl.* [*komestíbles*]

foot pie *m.* [*pje*], pata *f.* [*páta*]; - **warming pan** brasero *m.* [*braséro*]; -**ball** fútbol *m.* [*fútbol*]; - **match,** partido *m.* de fútbol [*partído de*]; - **player,** futbolista *m.* [*futbolísta*], jugador *m.* de fútbol [*xugadór de fútbol*]; - **board** estribo *m.* [*estríbo*]; - **bridge** puente *m.* para peatones [*pwénte pára peatónes*]; -**path** sendero *m.* [*sendéro*]; -**wear** calzado *m.* [*kalθádo*]

for *prep.* para [*pára*]; - **my father,** para mi padre [*mi pádre*] ‖ **2.** por [*por*];

- ***two pounds,*** por dos libras [*dos libras*] (exchange)

force fuerza *f.* [*fuérθa*]

fore/arm antebrazo *m.* [*antebráθo*]; **-cast** previsión *f.* [*prebisjón*], parte *m.* [*párte*]; **weather -,** parte meteorológico [*meteorolóxiko*]; **-head** frente *f.* [*frénte*]

foreign *a.* extranjero(a) [*ekstranxéro*]; **- exchange** divisas *f. pl.* [*dibísas*], oficina *f.* de cambio [*ofiθina de kámbjo*]; **- language** idioma *m.* extranjero [*idjóma*]; **-er** extranjero(a) *m.-f.*

forest bosque *m.* [*bóske*]; **- fire** incendio *m.* forestal [*inθéndjo forestál*]

forever *adv.* siempre [*sjémpre*], para siempre [*pára*]

forget (to) olvidar *r.* [*olbidár*], olvidarse *r.* (sth./de u.c.) [*olbidárse de úna kósa*]

fork tenedor *m.* [*tenedór*] ‖ **2.** bifurcación *f.* [*bifurkaθjón*] (road)

form forma *f.* [*fórma*] ‖ **2.** impreso *m.* [*impréso*]

format formato *m.* [*formáto*]

former *a.* anterior [*anterjór*]; **-ly** *adv.* antes [*ántes*]

fortnight quincena *f.* [*kinθéna*]

fortune suerte *f.* [*swérte*]

forty *a.* cuarenta [*kwarénta*]

forward *adv.* hacia adelante [*áθja adelánte*]

fountain fuente *f.* [*fwénte*], surtidor *m.* [*surtidór*]; **- pen** estilográfica *f.* [*estilográfika*]

four *a.* cuatro [*kwátro*]; **-teen** *a.* catorce [*katórθe*]; **-th** *a.* cuarto(a) [*kwárto*]; **the - of May,** el cuatro de mayo [*el kwátro de májo*]

fracture (to) fracturar *r.* [*frakturár*]; **to - an arm,** fracturarse un *brazo* [*frakturárse un bráθo*] ‖ **2.** *n.* fractura *f.* [*fraktúra*]

frame marco *m.* [*márko*] (door, window, etc.)

France Francia *f.* [*fránθja*]

frank *a.* franco(a) [*fránko*], sincero(a) [*sinθéro*]

Frankfurter salchicha *f.* de Frankfurt [*saltchítcha de Fránkfurt*]

fraud timo *m.* [*tímo*], fraude *m.* [*fráude*]

free *a.* libre [*líbre*]; **- port** puerto *m.* franco [*pwérto fránko*] ‖ **2.** gratuito(a) [*gratwíto*]; **- sample** muestra *f.* gratuita [*mwéstra gratwíta*]

freeze (to) congelar *r.* [*konxelár*] (food); **-r** congelador *m.* [*konxeladór*]

freight transporte *m.* [*transpórte*] ‖ **2.** carga *f.* [*kárga*]; **air -,** carga aérea [*kárga aérea*]

French *a.* francés (francesa) [*franθés (franθésa)*] ‖ **2.** *n.* francés *m.* [*franθés*] (language); **- bean** judía *f.* [*xudía*]; **- dressing** vinagreta *f.* [*binagréta*]; **-man** francés *m.* [*franθés*]; **-woman** francesa *f.* [*franθésa*]

fresco fresco *m.* [*frésko*] (art)

fresh *a.* fresco(a) [*frésko*]; **- fish** pescado *m.* fresco [*peskádo frésko*]; **-ening: - lotion,** loción *f.* refrescante [*loθjón rrefreskánte*]

Friday viernes *m.* [*bjérnes*]; **on -,** el viernes [*el*]

fridge nevera *f.* [*nebéra*]

fried *a.* frito(a) [*fríto*]; **- eggs** huevos *m.pl.* fritos [*wébos frítos*]; **- fish (assortment)** fritura *f.* de pescado [*fritúra de peskádo*]; **- meat (assortment)** fritura *f.* de carne [*fritúra de kárne*]

friend amigo(a) *m.-f.* [*amígo*]; **boy -,** novio *m.* [*nóbjo*]; **girl -,** novia *f.* [*nóbja*]; **-ly** *a.* simpático(a) [*simpátiko*], amable [*amáble*]

fringe flequillo *m.* [*flekíljo*]

fritter churro *m.* [*tchúrro*], buñuelo *m.* [*bunjwélo*]

from *prep.* de [*de*], desde [*désde*]; **- Spanish into English,** del español al inglés [*del espanjól al inglés*] ‖ **2.** desde [*désde*], a partir de [*a partír de*]; **- now on,** a partir de ahora [*a partír de aóra*]; **- one o'clock,** desde la una [*désde la úna*]

front delantera *f.* [*delantéra*]; parte *f.* delantera [*párte delantéra*]; **in - of the building,** delante del edificio [*del edifiθjo*]; ‖ **2.** *a.* delantero(a) [*delantéro*], de delante [*de delánte*]; **-age** fachada *f.* [*fatcháda*]; **-al** *a.* frontal [*frontál*]; **- axle** eje *m.* delantero [*éxe delantéro*]; **- door** puerta *f.* de entrada [*pwérta de entráda*]

frontier frontera *f.* [*frontéra*] ‖ **2.** *a.* fronterizo(a) [*fronteríθo*]

frost helada *f.* [*eláda*]

frozen *a.* congelado(a) [*konxeládo*]; **- fish** pescado *m.* congelado [*peskádo*]; **- meat** carne *f.* congelada [*kárne*]

fruit fruta *f.* [*frúta*]; **frosted -,** fruta escarchada [*eskartcháda*]; **preserved -,** confitura *f.* [*confitúra*]; **- in season** fruta *f.* de temporada [*de temporáda*]; **- dish** frutero *m.* [*frutéro*]; **- salad** macedonia *f.* de frutas [*maθedónja de*]; **-shop** frutería *f.* [*frutería*]

fry (to) freír (i) [*freír*]; **-ing: - pan,** sartén *f.* [*sartén*]

fuel combustible *m.* [*kombustíble*];
- **tank** depósito *m.* de combustible
[*de kombustíble*]

full *a.* lleno(a) [*ljéno*], completo(a)
[*kompléto*]; **at - speed,** a toda velocidad [*a tóda beloθidád*]; - **of,**
lleno(a) de [*ljéno de*]; - **board** pensión *f.* completa [*pensjón kompléta*];
-**time** jornada *f.* completa [*xornáda
kompléta*]; -**y** *adv.* completamente
[*kompletaménte*]

fumigat/e (to) fumigar *r.* [*fumigár*];
-**ion** fumigación *f.* [*fumigaθjón*]

fun broma *f.* [*bróma*] ‖ **2.** diversión
[*dibersjón*]; - **fair** parque *m.* de atracciones [*párke de atrakθjónes*]

function (to) funcionar *r.* [*funθjonár*] ‖
2. *n.* función *f.* [*funθjón*]; -**al** *a.* fun-
cional [*funθjonál*]; -**ary** funcionario(a)
m.-f. [*funθjonárjo*]

fund fondo *m.* [*fóndo*]

funicular funicular *m.* [*funikulár*]

funny *a.* divertido(a) [*dibertído*], gracio-
so(a) [*graθjóso*]

fur piel *f.* [*pjel*]; - **coat** abrigo *m.* de pie-
les [*abrígo de pjéles*]; - **shop** peletería
f. [*peletería*]

furious *a.* furioso(a) [*furjóso*]

furnish (to) amueblar *r.* [*amweblár*]
(with/con) ‖ **2.** suministrar *r.* [*suminis-
trár*] (supply)

furniture muebles *m.pl.* [*mwébles*];
piece of -, mueble *m.* [*mwéble*];
- **polish** limpiamuebles *m.* [*limpja-
mwébles*]; - **shop** tienda *f.* de muebles
[*tjénda de mwébles*]

furrier's peletería *f.* [*peletería*]

fuse fusible *m.* [*fusíble*]; - **box** caja *f.* de
fusibles [*káxa de fusíbles*]; -**d** *a.* fundi-
do(a) [*fundído*]

future futuro *m.* [*futúro*]; **in the -,** en el
futuro [*en el*] ‖ **2.** *a.* futuro(a) [*futúro*]; *his - wife,* su futura esposa [*su
futúra espósa*]

G

gabardine gabardina *f.* [*gabardína*]

gala gala *f.* [*gála*], festival *m.* [*festibál*]

gallant *a.* galante [*galánte*]

gallery galería *f.* [*galería*]; *art* -, galería *f.* de arte [*de árte*]

gallop galope *m.* [*galópe*]

galosh chanclo *m.* [*tchánklo*]

gambling juego *m.* [*xwéɵo*]; **- house** casa *f.* de juego [*kása de xwéɵo*]

game juego *m.* [*xwéɵo*] ‖ **2.** caza *f.* [*káɵa*] (hunting); *big* -, caza mayor [*káɵa majór*]; **- bag** morral *m.* [*morrál*]; **- reserve** coto *m.* de caza [*kóto de káɵa*]

gangrene *Med.* gangrena *f.* [*gangréna*]

gangway pasarela *f.* [*pasaréla*]

garage garaje *m.* [*garáxe*] ‖ **2.** taller *m.* de reparaciones [*taljér de reparaɵjónes*] (repairs) ‖ **3.** gasolinera *f.* [*gasolinéra*] (filling station)

garden jardín *m.* [*xardín*]:*vegetable* -, huerto *m.* [*wérto*]; **- centre** vivero *m.* [*bibéro*] **- furniture** muebles *m. pl.* de jardín [*mwébles de xardín*]; **-er** jardinero *m.* [*xardinéro*]

gardenia gardenia *f.* [*gardénja*]

garlic ajo *m.* [*áxo*]:*clove of* -, diente *m.* de ajo [*djénte de*]; **- sauce** alioli *m.* [*aljóli*], salsa *f.* de ajo [*sálsa de áxo*]

garment vestido *m.* [*bestído*], prenda *f.* de vestir [*prénda de bestír*]

garnish *Gast.* guarnición *f.* [*gwarniɵjón*]

gas gas *m.* [*gas*]:*butane* -, gas butano [*butáno*]; *natural* -, gas natural [*naturál*]; **- cooker** cocina *f.* de gas [*koɵína de*]; **- fire** estufa *f.* de gas [*estúfa de*]

gas(oline) gasolina *f.* [*gasolína*]

gastri/c *a.* gástrico(a) [*gástriko*]; **-tis** gastritis *f.* [*gastrítis*]

gastronom/ic *a.* gastronómico(a) [*gastronómiko*]; **-y** gastronomía *f.* [*gastronomía*]

gate puerta *f.* [*pwérta*], portal *m.* [*portál*] ‖ **2.** puerta *f.* (de salida) [*pwérta de salída*] (airport); **-way** entrada *f.* [*entráda*]

gauze gasa *f.* [*gása*]

gay *a.* gay [*gai*], homosexual [*omosekswál*]

gear marcha *f.* [*mártcha*]; **- box** caja *f.* de cambios [*káxa de kámbjos*]

gel gel *m.* [*xel*]

gelatine gelatina *f.* [*xelatína*]

gem gema *f.* [*xéma*]

general *a.* general [*xenerál*]; **- store** tienda *f.* de comestibles [*tjénda de komestíbles*]

generator generador *m.* [*xeneradór*]

genitals genitales *m.pl.* [*xenitáles*]

gentleman caballero *m.* [*kabaljéro*]

genuine *a.* auténtico(a) [*auténtiko*]

geograph/ic(al) *a.* geográfico(a) [*xeográfiko*]; **-y** geografía *f.* [*xeografía*]

geranium geranio *m.* [*xeránjo*]

get (to) obtener *irr.* [*obtenér*], recibir *r.* [*rreɵibír*] ‖ **2.** coger *r.* [*koxér*]; *to - down (off),* apearse *r.* [*apeárse*] (de); *to - out,* bajar *r.* [*baxár*] (of/de); *to - on* subir *r.* [*subír*] *(into/a)* (car, etc.) ‖ **3.** *to - sun-tanned,* broncearse *r.* [*bronɵeárse*] ‖ **4.** *to - up,* levantarse *r.* [*lebantárse*]

Gibraltar Gibraltar [*xibraltár*]:*the Rock of* -, el Peñón *m.* de Gibraltar [*el penjón de*]; **-ian** gibraltareño(a) *m.-f.* [*xibraltarénjo*]

gift regalo *m.* [*rregálo*]; **- cheque** cheque *m.* de regalo [*tchéke de*]; **-s** artículos *m. pl.* de regalo [*artíkulos de*]; **- shop** tienda *f.* de artículos de regalo [*tjénda de artíkulos de*]

gilt *a.* dorado(a) [*doráfo*]

gin ginebra *f.* [*xinébra*]; **- and cola** cuba libre *m.* de ginebra [*kúba líbre de xinébra*]; **- and tonic** ginebra *f.* con tónica [*xinébra kon tónika*], gin *m.* tonic [*tchin tónik*]

ginger jengibre *m.* [*xenxíbre*]

gipsy gitano(a) *m.-f.* [*xitáno*]

girl muchacha *f.* [*mutchátcha*], chica *f.* [*tchíka*]; **- friend** novia *f.* [*nóbja*]

giro giro *m.* postal [*xíro postál*]

give (to) dar *irr.* [*dar*] ‖ **2.** poner *irr.* [*ponér*]:*to - an injection,* poner una inyección [*úna injekɵjón*]; *to - a serum,* poner un suero [*un swéro*]; *to - a vaccination,* poner una vacuna [*úna bakúna*]

gizzard molleja *f.* [*moljéxa*]

glacé *a. Gast.* escarchado(a) [*eskartchádo*], confitado(a) [*konfitádo*]

glacier glaciar *m.* [*glaɵjár*]

glad *a.* contento(a) [*konténto*]:*to be* -, alegrarse *r.* [*alegrárse*] (of/de)

gladiolus gladiolo *m.* [*gladjólo*]

glass vidrio *m.* [*bídrjo*], cristal *m.* [*kristál*]; *of* -, de vidrio [*de bídrjo*] ‖ **2.** vaso *m.* [*báso*] (drinking glass); *small* -, copa *f.* [*kópa*]: *a - of water,* un vaso *m.* de agua [*un báso* de ágwa]; **- cleaner** limpiacristales m. [limpjakristáles]; **- door** puerta f. de cristal [pwérta de kristál]; **-es** gafas f.pl. [gáfas]; **- lamp** lámpara f. de vidrio [lámpara de bídrjo]; **-ware** cristalería f. [kristalería], artículos m.pl. de cristal [artíkulos de kristál]

lazed a. vidriado(a) [bidrjádo] || **2.** barnizado(a) [barniθádo] (varnish)

lobe globo m. [glóbo], bola f. [bóla]; **-trotter** trotamundos m.-f. [trotamúndos]

lossy a. brillante [briljánte]

love guante m. [gwánte]

lucose glucosa f. [glukósa]

lue cola f. (de pegar) [kóla de pegár], pegamento m. [pegaménto]

lycerine glicerina f. [gliθerína]

o (to) ir irr. [ir] (to/a): **to - away,** marcharse r. [martchárse]; **to - by car (train),** ir irr. en coche (tren) [ir en kótche (tren)]; **to - down,** bajar r. [baxár]; **to - on foot,** ir irr. a pie [ir a pje]; **to - out,** salir [salír] (of/de); **to - shopping** ir irr. de compras [ir de kómpras]; **to - up,** subir r. [subír] (to/a)

oal gol m. [gol] || **2.** portería f. [portería] (sports); **-keeper** portero m. [portéro]; **- mouth** portería f. [portería]

oat cabra f. [kábra], cabritillo m. [kabritíljo]; **roast -,** cabritillo asado [asádo]; **-skin** piel f. de cabra [pjel de kábra]

old oro m. [óro]; **of -,** de oro [de]; **-en** a. de oro [de óro] || 2 a. dorado(a) [dorádo] (colour); **g. -plated** a. chapado(a) en oro [tchapádo en óro]

olf golf m. [golf]; **to play -,** jugar (ue) al golf [xugár al]; **- ball** pelota f. de golf [pelóta de golf]; **- club** club m. de golf [klub de]; **- course** campo m. de golf [kámpo de]; **-er** jugador(a) m.-f. de golf [xugadór de golf]; **- stick** palo m. de golf [pálo de]

ood a. buen(o)(a) [bwéno]; **-bye** adiós [adjós]; **- afternoon,** buenas tardes [bwénas tárdes]; **- evening,** buenas tardes; buenas noches [bwénas nótches]; **- morning,** buenos días [bwénos días]; **- night,** buenas noches [bwénas nótches]; **to say -,** despedirse (i) [despedírse] (to/de); **g.-looking** a. guapo(a) [gwápo]

oose ganso m. [gánso]; **- barnacles** percebes m.pl. [perθébes]

orgeous a. magnífico(a) [magnífiko], estupendo (a) [estupéndo]

Gothic a. gótico(a) [gótiko]

gown vestido m. [bestído] || **2.** bata f. [báta]

grace gracia f. [gráθja], elegancia f. [elegánθja]; **-ful** a. lleno(a) de gracia [ljéno de gráθja], elegante [elegánte]; **-fully** adv. con gracia [kon gráθja], con elegancia [kon elegánθja]

gradual a. gradual [gradwál]; **-ly** adv. poco a poco [póko a póko], gradualmente [gradwalménte]

grain grano m. [gráno] || **2.** cereales m. pl. [θereáles]

grammar gramática f. [gramátika]: **Spanish -,** gramática española [gramátika espanjóla]; **- book** manual m. de gramática [manwál de gramátika]

gramme gramo m. [grámo]

grand a. gran(de) [gránde]; **-child** nieto(a) m.-f. [njéto]; **-daughter** nieta f. [njéta] **-father** abuelo m. [abwélo]; **-mother** abuela f. [abwéla]; **-parents** abuelos m. pl. [abwélos]; **-son** nieto m. [njéto]

granulated a. granulado(a) [granuládo]

grape uva f. [úba]: **a bunch of -s,** un racimo m. de uvas [un rraθímo de úbas]; **black -,** uva negra [négra]; **white -,** uva blanca [blánka]; **muscatel -,** uva moscatel [moskatél]; **-fruit** pomelo m. [pomélo]; **- juice** zumo m. de pomelo [θúmo de pomélo]

grass hierba f. [jérba]; **-land** prado m. [prádo] || **2.** pasto m. [pásto]

grate (to) rallar r. [rraljár]; **-d** a. rallado(a) [rraljádo]

gratin: au -, gratinado(a) [gratinádo]

gratis adv. gratis [grátis], gratuitamente [gratwitaménte]

gratuitous a. gratuito(a) [gratwíto]; **-ly** adv. gratuitamente [gratwitaménte]

gravel grava f. [grába], gravilla f. [grabílja]

grazing pasto m. [pásto]

greas/e (to) engrasar r. [engrasár] || **2.** n. grasa f. [grása] **-ing** engrase m. [engráse]; **-y** a. graso(a) [gráso] (food), grasiento(a) [grasjénto]

great a. gran(de) [grán(de)]: **Great Britain,** Gran Bretaña [gran bretánja]; **-coat** gabán m. [gabán]

green a. verde [bérde]; **- bean** judía f. verde [xudía]; **- card** carta f. verde [kárta]; **-grocer** verdulero m. [berduléro]; **-'s** verdulería f. [berdulería]; **- house** invernadero m. [imbernadéro]; **- olives** aceitunas f. pl. verdes [aθeitúnas bérdes]; **- pepper** pimiento *m.* verde [*pimjénto*]; - **salad** ensalada *f.* verde [*ensaláda*] - **vegetables** verdura *f.* [*berdúra*]; **assorted** -, verdura *f.* variada [*barjáda*]; **boiled** -, verdura hervida [*berdúra erbída*]; **fried** -, verdura salteada [*salteáda*]

greeting saludo *m.* [*salúdo*]; -**s: -card** tarjeta *f.* de felicitación [*tarxéta de feliθitaθjón*]

grey *a.* gris [*gris*]; - **mullet** mújol *m.* [*múxol*]

grill (to) asar *r.* a la parrilla [*asár a la parrílja*] ‖ **2.** *n.* parrilla *f.* [*parrílja*] (iron); parrillada *f.* [*parriljáda*] (dish): **mixed fish** -, parrillada de pescado [*de peskádo*]; **mixed meat** -, parrillada de carne [*de kárne*]; **-ed** *a.* a la parrilla [*a la parrílja*]; a la brasa [*a la brása*]

grocer/ies comestibles *m. pl.* [*komestíbles*]; -'**s** tienda *f.* de ultramarinos [*tjénda de ultramarínos*], colmado *m.* [*kolmádo*] (shop); -**y** tienda *f.* de ultramarinos *m.* [*ultrmarínos*]; tienda *f.* de comestibles [*tjénda de komestíbles*]

grog ponche *m.* [*póntche*]

ground tierra *f.* [*tjérra*], suelo *m.* [*swélo*]; - **floor** planta *f.* baja [*plánta báxa*]; -**nut** cacahuete *m.* [*kakawéte*]; **sports** - terreno (campo) *m.* de juego [*terréno (kámpo) de xwégo*]; - **pepper** pimienta *f.* molida [*pimjénta molída*]

group grupo *m.* [*grúpo*], conjunto *m.* [*konxúnto*]

grouper mero *m.* [*méro*]

grow (to) cultivar *r.* [*kultivar*] ‖ **2.** crecer (zc) [*kreθér*]; **to - up,** hacerse *irr.* mayor [*aθérse majór*]; -**n: - up** adulto(a) *m.-f.* [*adúlto*]: **the - ups,** los mayores [*los majóres*]

guard guardia *m.* [*gwárdja*]

guest invitado(a) *m.-f.* [*imbitádo*] ‖ **2.** cliente(a) *m.-f.* [*kljénte*]

guide guía *f.* [*gía*] (book) ‖ **2. tour** -, guía *m.-f.* ‖ **3.** cartelera *f.* [*karteléra*] (theatres, cinemas, etc.)

guitar guitarra *f.* [*gitárra*], -**ist** guitarrista *m.-f.* [*gitarrísta*]

gulf golfo *m.* [*gólfo*]

gull gaviota *f.* [*gabjóta*]

gum goma *f.* [*góma*]; **chewing** -, goma de mascar [*de maskár*]

gun escopeta *f.* [*eskopéta*], fusil *m.* [*fusíl*]; - **licence** permiso *m.* de armas [*permíso de ármas*]; -**smith's** armería *f.* [*armería*]

guy tipo *m.* [*típo*], tío *m.* [*tío*]

gymnastics gimnasia *f.* [*ximnásja*]

gynaecologist ginecólogo(a) *m.-f.* [*xinekólogo*]

gypsy gitano(a) *m.-f.* [*xitáno*]; - **dress** vestido *m.* de gitana [*bestído de xitána*]

haberdasher's mercería f. [merʌería]
habitual a. habitual [habitwál], acostumbrado(a) [akostumbrádo], **-ly** adv. habitualmente [abitwalménte], por costumbre [por kostúmbre]
haemorr/hage hemorragia f. [emorráxia], **-hoids** hemorroides f. pl. [emorróides]
haggle (to) regatear r. [rregateár]
hail granizo m. [graníθo]
hair pelo m. [pélo], cabello m. [kabéljo]; -**brush** cepillo m. para el cabello [θepíljo pára el kabéljo]; -**cut** corte m. de pelo [kórte de pélo]; -**do** peinado m. [peinádo]; -**dresser** peluquero m. [pelukéro]; -**dresser's** peluquería f. [pelukería]; -**dryer** secador (de pelo) [sekadór de pélo]; -**lacquer** laca f. para el cabello [láka pára el kabéljo]; -**less** a. calvo(a) [kálbo]; -**pin** horquilla f. [orkílja], aguja f. para el pelo [agúxa pára el pélo]; **h.-remover** depilatorio m. [depilatórjo]; -**slide** pasador m. [pasadór]; -**spray** laca f. para el pelo [láka pára el pélo]; -**style** peinado m. [peinádo], corte m. de pelo [kórte de pélo]; -**tonic** quina f. [kína]
hake merluza f. [merlúθa]; **baked -**, merluza al horno [al órno]; **fried -**, merluza frita [fríta]; -**fried in batter**, merluza a la romana [a la rromána]; -**with parsley sauce**, merluza a la vizcaína [a la biθkaína]
half a. medio(a) [médjo]; -**a kilo**, medio kilo m. [kílo]; -**a litre**, medio litro m. [lítro] || **2.** n. mitad f. [mitád]; **a -**, la mitad (of/de); -**baked** medio cocido(a) [médjo koθído], medio hecho(a) [médjo étcho]; -**board** media pensión f. [médja pensjón]; -**fare** medio billete m. [médjo biljéte]; **h.-time** descanso m. [deskánso] (sports)
halibut mero m. [méro]
hall vestíbulo m. [bestíbulo] (entrance room), sala f. [sála]; **town -**, ayuntamiento m. [ajuntamjénto]; -**mark** contraste m. [kontráste]
hallo interj. ¡hola! [óla]
halt salto m. [álto]
ham jamón m. [xamón]; **cooked -**, jamón en dulce [en dúlθe]; **country -**, jamón del país [del país]; **cured-**, jamón serrano [serráno]

hamburger hamburguesa f. [amburgésa]
hammer martillo m. [martíljo]
hand mano f. [máno], **-bag** bolso m. [bólso], **-ball** balonmano m. [balonmáno]; **-book** manual m. [manwál]; **-brake** freno m. de mano [fréno de mano]; **-icraft** artesanía f. [artesanía] || **2.** objetos m. pl. de artesanía [obxétos de] (articles); **-kerchief** pañuelo m. [panjwélo]; **-le** asa f. [ása] || **2.** pomo m. [pómo] (door, etc.); **-made** a. de artesanía [de artesanía], hecho(a) a mano [étcho a máno]; **h.-me-down** de segunda mano [de segúnda máno]; **- set** aparato m. [aparáto]; **-written** escrito(a) a mano [eskríto a máno]
hang (to) colgar (ue) [kolgár] || **2. to - up**, colgar (ue) el auricular [el aurikulár]; **-er** percha f. [pértcha], **-ing: - bridge**, puente m. colgante [pwénte kolgánte]
happen (to) suceder r. [suθedér], pasar r. [pasár]
happy a. feliz [felíθ] (to be/ser)
harbour puerto m. [pwérto]
hard a. duro(a) [dúro], sólido(a) [sólido]; **h.-boiled** a. duro(a) [dúro] (egg); **-ly** adv. apenas [apénas]; **-ware** ferretería f. [ferretería] (articles, shop)
hare liebre f. [ljébre]; **braised -**, liebre guisada [gisáda]; **jugged -**, civet m. de liebre [θibét de]; **roast -**, liebre asada [asáda]
haricot judía f. (verde) [xudía bérde] (bean); **boiled -s**, judías pl. hervidas [xudías erbídas]
harpoon arpón m. [arpón]
haste prisa f. [prísa]; **to be in -**, tener irr. prisa [tenér]; **-n (to)** darse irr. prisa [dárse prísa]
hat sombrero m. [sombréro], **-band** cinta f. de sombrero [θínta de]; **-pin** alfiler f. de sombrero [alfilér de]; **-shop** sombrerería f. [sombrerería]
hatchet hacha f. [átcha]
haute couture alta costura f. [álta kostúra]
have (to) tener irr. [tenér]; **to - an accident**, sufrir r. un accidente [sufrír un akθidénte] || **2.** tomar r. [tomár]; **to - a cup of tea**, tomar una taza de té [úna táθa de te] || **3. to - to do**, deber r. hacer [debér aθér]
haversack mochila f. [motchíla]
hazel: - nut, avellana f. [abeljána]
he pron. pers. él [el]

head cabeza *f.* [*kabéθa*]; **-ache** dolor *m.* de cabeza [*dolór de*]; **-light** luz *f.* de carretera [*luθ de karretéra*]; **- office** oficina *f.* central [*ofiθína θentrál*]; **-quarters (of the Guardia Civil)** cuartel *m.* (de la Guardia Civil) [*kwartél de la gwárdja θibíl*]; **-set** auriculares *m.pl.* [*aurikuláres*]; **-waiter** maitre *m.* [*métre*]

health salud *f.* [*salúd*]; **-y** *a.* sano(a) [*sáno*]; saludable [*saludáble*]

hear (to) oír *irr.* [*oír*] ‖ **2.** escuchar *r.* [*eskutchár*]; **-ing** oído *m.* [*oído*]

heart corazón *m.* [*koraθón*]; **- attack** infarto *m.* de miocardio [*infárto de mjokardjo*]; **- failure** colapso *m.* cardíaco [*kolápso kardíako*]

heat (to) calentar (ie) [*kalentár*]; **to - up**, calentarse (ie) [*kalentárse*] ‖ **2.** *n.* calor *m.* [*kalór*]; **-er** calentador *m.* [*kalentadór*]; **gas -**, calentador de gas [*de gas*]; **water -**, calentador de agua [*de água*]; **-ing** calefacción *f.* [*kalefakθjón*]; **central -**, calefacción central [*θentrál*]; **-ing system** sistema *m.* de calefacción [*sistéma de kalefakθjón*]

heavy *a.* pesado(a) [*pesádo*]

hectare hectárea *f.* [*ektárea*]

heel talón *m.* [*talón*], tacón *m.* [*takón*] (shoe)

height altura *f.* [*altúra*]

helicopter helicóptero *m.* [*elikóptero*]

hello *interj.* ¡hola! [*óla*]

helmet casco *m.* [*kásko*]

help (to) ayudar *r.* [*ajudár*] ‖ **2.** *n.* ayuda *f.* [*ajúda*], socorro *m.* [*sokórro*]

hem dobladillo *m.* [*dobladíljo*]

hepatitis hepatitis *f.* [*epatítis*]

her *pron. pers. ac.* la [*la*] ‖ **2.** *dat.* le [*le*] ‖ **3.** ella [*élja*] (with prep.) ‖ **4.** *a. pos.* su(s) [*su*]

herb hierba *f.* [*jérba*]; **-al** *a.* de hierbas [*de jérbas*]; **- cheese** queso *m.* de hierbas [*késo de jérbas*]; **- tea** infusión *f.* de hierbas [*infusjón de jérbas*]

here *adv.* aquí [*akí*]

hermetic *a.* hermético(a) [*ermétiko*]; **-ally** *adv.* herméticamente [*hermetikaménte*]

herring arenque *m.* [*arénke*]; **pickled -**, arenque salado [*saládo*]

high *a.* alto(a) [*álto*], elevado(a) [*elebádo*]; **- fidelity** alta fidelidad *f.* [*álta fidelidád*]; **-lands** tierras *f. pl.* altas [*tjérras áltas*]; **h.-heeled** *a.* de tacón alto [*de takón álto*]; **-lights** reflejo *m.* [*refléxo*]; **h.-speed** *a.* de gran velocidad [*de gran beloθidád*]; **- tide** marea

f. alta [*maréa álta*]; **-way** carretera *f.* [*karretéra*], autopista *f.* [*autopísta*]

hike excursión *f.* [*ekskursjón*]; **to -**, hacer *irr.* una excursión [*aθér úna*]; **-r** excursionista *m.-f.* [*ekskursjonísta*]

hill colina *f.* [*kolína*]; **-side** ladera *f.* [*ladéra*]

him *pron. pers. ac.* lo, le [*lo*, *le*] ‖ **2.** *dat.* le [*le*] ‖ **3.** [*él*] (with prep.)

hindquarter espaldilla *f.* [*espaldílja*]

hinge bisagra *f.* [*biságra*]

hip cadera *f.* [*kadéra*]; **-bone** hueso *m.* de la cadera [*wéso de la*]

hire (to) alquilar *r.* [*alkilár*] ‖ **2.** *n.* alquiler *m.* [*alkilér*]; **car -**, alquiler *m.* de coches [*de kótches*]; **-d** *a.* alquilado(a) [*alkiládo*]

his *a. pos.* su(s) (su) [*su*] ‖ **2.** *pron. pos.* suyo(a) [*sújo*], suyos(as) *pl.* [*sújos*]

Hispanic *a.* hispánico(a) [*ispániko*]

histor/ic(al) *a.* histórico(a) [*istóriko*]; **-y** historia *f.* [*istórja*]

hitch-hik/e (to) hacer *irr.* autostop [*aθér autostóp*]; **-er** autostopista *m.-f.* [*autostopísta*]; **-ing** autostop *m.* [*autostóp*]

hobby pasatiempo *m.* [*pasatjémpo*], afición *f.* [*afiθjón*]

hock jarrete *m.* [*xarréte*]

hockey hockey *m.* [*ókei*]

hold (to) tener *irr.* (en la mano) [*tenér en la máno*], agarrar *r.* [*agarrár*] ‖ **2.** poseer *r.* [*poseér*] (control) ‖ **3. - on!** ¡No cuelgue! [*no kwélge*] (telephone)

hole agujero *m.* [*aguxéro*] ‖ **2.** hoyo *m.* [*ójo*] (golf) ‖ **3.** bache *m.* [*bátche*] (road)

holiday día *m.* festivo [*día festíbo*]; **bank -**, día festivo oficial [*ofiθjál*]; **h.-maker** turista *m.-f.* [*turísta*], veraneante *m.-f.* [*veraneánte*] (summer); **- resort** lugar *m.* de vacaciones [*lugár de bakaθjónes*], centro *m.* turístico [*θéntro turístiko*]; **-s** vacaciones *f. pl.* [*bakaθjónes*]; **to be on -**, estar *irr.* de vacaciones [*estár de*]

holy *a.* santo(a) [*sánto*]; **- Week** Semana *f.* Santa [*semána sánta*]

home hogar *m.* [*ogár*], casa *f.* [*kása*]; domicilio *m.* [*domiθíljo*]; **to go -**, ir *intr.* a casa [*ir a*]; **to be at -**, estar *irr.* en casa [*estár en*]; **- cooking** cocina *f.* casera [*komída kaséra*]; **h.-made** *a.* hecho(a) en casa [*étcho en kása*]; **-wards** *adv.* hacia casa [*áθja kása*]

honey miel *f.* [*mjel*]; **-moon** luna *f.* de miel [*lúna de mjel*], viaje *m.* de novios [*bjáxe de nóbjos*]

hood capucha *f.* [*kapútcha*] ‖ **2.** capota *f.* [*kapóta*] (car)

hook gancho *m.* [*gántcho*] ‖ **2.** anzuelo *m.* [*anθwélo*] (fishing); **-s and eyes** corchetes *m. pl.* [*kortchétes*]

hope (to) esperar *r.* [*esperár*]: *I - not,* espero que no [*espéro ke no*]; *I - so,* espero que sí [*sí*] ‖ **2.** *n.* esperanza *f.* [*esperánθa*]; **-ful** *a.* esperanzador(a) [*esperanθadór*]; **-less** *a.* desesperado(a) [*desesperádo*]; perdido(a) [*perdído*]

horizon horizonte *m.* [*oriθónte*]; **-tal** *a.* horizontal [*oriθontál*]; **-tally** *adv.* horizontalmente [*oriθontalménte*]

hormon/al *a.* hormonal [*ormonál*]; **-e** hormona *f.* [*ormóna*]; **- cream** crema *f.* de hormonas [*kréma de ormónas*]

horn cuerno *m.* [*kwérno*] ‖ **2.** bocina *f.* [*boθína*]

horology relojería *f.* [*rreloxería*]

hors d'oeuvres entremeses *m.pl.* [*entreméses*]; *mixed -,* entremeses variados [*barjádos*]

horse caballo *m.* [*kabáljo*]; **-back:** *on -,* a caballo [*a kabáljo*]; **- chestnut** castaña *f.* (de Indias) [*kastánja de índjas*]; **- doctor** veterinario(a) *m.-f.* [*beterinárjo*]; **-man** jinete *m.* [*xinéte*]; **- meat** carne *f.* de caballo [*kárne de*]; **- race** carrera *f.* de caballos [*karréra de*]; **- radish** rábano *m.* picante [*rrábano pikánte*]; **-trials** concurso *m.* de hípica [*konkúrso de ípika*]; **-woman** amazona *f.* [*amaθóna*]

horticulture horticultura *f.* [*ortikultúra*]

hospital hospital *m.* [*ospitál*]; **-ize** hospitalizar *r.* [*ospitaliθár*]

hostel hostal *m.* [*ostál*], residencia *f.* [*rresidénθja*]; *youth -,* albergue *m.* (para la juventud) [*albérge pára la xubentúd*]

hostess camarera *f.* [*kamaréra*] ‖ **2.** azafata *f.* [*aθafáta*]

hot *a.* caliente [*kaljénte*], caluroso(a) [*kaluróso*]; *it is -,* hace calor [*áθe kalór*]; *to be -,* tener *irr.* calor [*tenér kalór*]; **- dog** perrito *f.* caliente [*perríto*]; **- meal** comida *f.* caliente [*komída*]; **-pot** estofado *m.* [*estofádo*]; **- water** agua *f.* caliente [*água kaljénte*]

hotel hotel *m.* [*otél*]; **h.-keeper** hotelero *m.* [*oteléro*]; **- manager** director *m* de hotel [*direktór de otél*]

hour hora *f.* [*óra*]; *a quarter of an -,* un cuarto de hora [*un kwárto de óra*]; *half an -,* media hora [*médja óra*];

house casa *f.* [*kása*], edificio *m.* [*edifíθjo*]; domicilio *m.* [*domiθíljo*]: *at our -,* en nuestra casa [*en nwéstra kása*]; **-boat** casa *f.* flotante [*flotánte*]; **-hold** casa *f.* [*kása*], hogar *m.* [*ogár*]; **- goods,** menaje *m.* [*menáxe*]; **-keeper** ama *f.* de llaves [*áma de ljábes*]; **- keys** llaves *f.pl.* de la casa (del piso) [*ljábes de la kása (del píso)*]; **-maid** criada *f.* [*krjáda*]; **-wife** ama *f.* de casa [*áma de kása*]; **-work** trabajo *m.* doméstico [*trabáxo doméstiko*]

housing: - estate, urbanización *f.* [*urbaniθaθjón*]

how? *pron. interr.* ¿cómo? [*kómo*]; **- are you?** ¿cómo estás (estáis)? [*kómo estás (estáis)*]; **- do you do?** ¿cómo está (están) Vd. (Vds.)? [*kómo está (están) ustéd (ustédes)*]; **- many?** ¿cuántos(as)? [*kwántos*]; **- much?** ¿cuánto(a)? [*kwánto*]; **- old are you?** ¿qué edad tienes? [*ke edád tjénes*], ¿qué edad tiene Vd.? [*ke edád tjéne ustéd*]

huge *a.* enorme [*enórme*], inmenso(a) [*iménso*]

human *a.* humano(a) [*umáno*]; **- being** ser *m.* humano [*ser umáno*]

humid *a.* húmedo(a) [*úmedo*]; **-ity** humedad *f.* [*umedád*]

humour humor *m.* [*umór*]: *to be in bad (good) -,* tener *irr.* mal (buen) humor [*tenér mal (buen) umór*]

hundred *a.* cien [*θjen*] (before the noun), ciento [*θjénto*]: *five -,* quinientos(as) [*kinjéntos*]; *a - Euros,* cien euros *m. pl.* [*θjen éuros*]; *two - Euros,* doscientas euros [*dosθjéntas éuros*]

hung/er hambre *f.* [*ámbre*]; **-ry** *a.* hambriento(a) [*ambrjénto*]: *to be -,* tener *irr.* hambre [*tenér ámbre*]

hunt (to) cazar *r.* [*kaθár*] ‖ **2.** *n.* caza *f.* [*káθa*]; **-er** cazador *m.* [*kaθadór*]

hunting caza *f.* [*káθa*]; cacería *f.* [*kaθería*]; **- ground** coto *m.* de caza [*kóto de káθa*]; **- horn** cuerno *m.* de caza [*kwérno de káθa*]; **- party** cacería *f.* [*kaθería*]; **- scene** escena *f.* de caza [*esθéna de káθa*]

hurricane huracán *m.* [*urakán*]

hurry (to) darse *irr.* prisa [*dárse prísa*]: **- up!** ¡date prisa! [*dáte prísa*] ‖ **2.** *n.* prisa *f.* [*prísa*]: *to be in a -,* tener *irr* prisa [*tenér*]

hurt (to) herir (ie) [*erír*] ‖ **2.** doler (ue)
  [*dolér*] ‖ **3.** *n.* herida *f.* [*erída*], lesión
  f. [*lesjón*]
husband marido *m.* [*marído*], esposo
  m. [*espóso*]
hyacinth jacinto *m.* [*xaθínto*]
hydraulic *a.* hidráulico(a) [*idráuliko*]:
  - brake freno *m.* hidráulico [*fréno*];
  - suspension suspensión *f.* hidráuli-
  ca [*suspensjón idráulika*]

hydro/electric *a.* hidroeléctrico(a)
  [*idroeléktriko*]; **-gen** hidrógeno *m.*
  [*idróxeno*]; **-plane** hidroavión *m.*
  [*idroabjón*]
hygien/e higiene *f.* [*ixjéne*]; **-ic** *a.* higié-
  nico(a) [*ixjéniko*]
hyper/market hipermercado *m.* [*iper-
  merkádo*]; **-tension** hipertensión *f.*
  [*ipertensjón*]
hysterical *a.* histérico(a) [*istériko*]

I

I *pron. pers.* yo [*jó*]
Iberian *a.* ibérico(a) [*ibériko*]
ice hielo *m.* [*jélo*]; **-box** nevera *f.* [*nebé-ra*]; **- cream** helado *m.* [*eládo*]: **cho-colate -,** helado de chocolate [*de tchokoláte*]; **egg and cream -,** hela-do de biscuit [*de biskwít*]; **mixed -,** helado variado [*barjádo*]; **straw-berry -,** helado de fresa [*de frésa*]; **vanilla -,** helado de vainilla [*de bai-nílja*]; **i.-cold** *a.* helado(a) [*eládo*]; **- cube** cubito *m.* de hielo [*kubíto de jélo*]; **-ed** *a.* helado(a) [*eládo*]: **- coffee,** granizado *m.* de café [*graniθádo de kafé*]; **- lemonade,** granizado de limón [*de limón*]; **i.-skate** patín *m.* de hielo [*patín de jélo*]
icon icono *m.* [*ikóno*]; **-oclastic** *a.* ico-noclasta [*ikonoklásta*]
icy *a.* helado(a) [*eládo*], cubierto(a) de hielo [*kubjérto de jélo*]
idea idea *f.* [*idéa*]: **I've got an -,** tengo una idea [*téngo úna idéa*]
identi/cal *a.* idéntico(a) [*idéntiko*]; **-fication** identificación *f.* [*identifika-θjón*]; **-fy** identificar *r.* [*identifikár*]; **-ty** identidad *f.* [*identidád*]; **- card** docu-mento *m.* de identidad [*dokuménto de*]
idiot idiota *m.-f.* [*idjóta*]
if *conj.* si [*si*]
ignition encendido *m.* [*enθendído*] (motor, etc.); **- cable** cable *m.* de encendido [*káble de*]; **- coil** bobina *f.* de encendido [*bobína de*]; **- key** llave *f.* de contacto [*ljábe de kontákto*]; **- switch** interruptor *m.* de encendido [*interruptór de*]; **- system** sistema *m.* de encendido [*sistéma de*]
ill *a.* enfermo(a) [*enférmo*]: **to fall -,** caer *irr.* enfermo [*kaér*]; **-ness** enfer-medad *f.* [*enfermedád*]
illumination iluminación *f.* [*ilumina-θjón*]
illusionist ilusionista *m.-f.* [*ilusjonísta*]
illustration ilustración *f.* [*ilustraθjón*]
image imagen *f.* [*imáxen*]
imitat/e (to) imitar *r.* [*imitár*], copiar *r.* [*kopjár*]; **-ion** imitación *f.* [*imitaθjón*], copia *f.* [*kópja*] ‖ **2.** *a.* de imitación [*de imitaθjón*]
immediate *a.* inmediato(a) [*inmedjáto*]; **-ly** *adv.* inmediatamente [*inmedjata-ménte*]

immense *a.* inmenso(a) [*inménso*]
immersion inmersión *f.* [*inmersjón*]; **- course** curso *m.* intensivo [*kúrso intensíbo*]
immobile *a.* inmóvil [*inmóbil*]
impermeable *a.* impermeable [*imper-meáble*]
import (to) importar *r.* [*importár*] ‖ **2.** *n.* importación *f.* [*importaθjón*]
important *a.* importante [*importánte*]
importer importador(a) *m.-f.* [*importa-dór*]
impossible *a.* imposible [*imposíble*]
impotent *a.* impotente [*impoténte*]
impression/ism impresionismo *m.* [*impresjonísmo*]; **-ist** impresionista *m.-f.* [*impresjonísta*]
improbable *a.* improbable [*improbáble*]
improve (to) mejorar *r.* [*mexorár*], **-ment** mejora *f.* [*mexóra*]
in *prep.* en [*en*], dentro de [*déntro de*]: **- Spain,** en España [*en espánja*]; **- London,** en Londres [*en lóndres*]; **- January,** en enero [*en enéro*]; **- the morning,** por la mañana [*por la manjána*]; **- twenty minutes,** dentro de veinte minutos [*déntro de béinte minútos*]
inauguration inauguración *f.* [*inaugu-raθjón*]
inch pulgada *f.* [*pulgáda*]
incident incidente *m.* [*inθidénte*]
includ/e incluir (y) [*inklwír*]; **-ed** inclui-do(a) [*inklwído*], comprendido(a) [*komprendído*], **-ing** incluso [*in-klúso*], inclusive [*inklusíbe*]
incom/e ingresos *m. pl.* [*ingrésos*]; **-ing** de llegada [*de ljegáda*] (train, air, etc.): **- passengers,** los pasajeros que lle-gan [*los pasaxéros ke ljégan*]
incubation incubación *f.* [*inkubaθjón*]
incurable *a.* incurable [*inkuráble*]
indeed *adv.* realmente [*rrealménte*], efectivamente [*efectibaménte*], en efecto [*en efékto*]
index índice *m.* [*índiθe*]: **- finger** dedo *m.* índice [*dédo*]
indicat/e (to) indicar *r.* [*indikár*]; **-or.** **- lights,** intermitentes *m. pl.* [*intermi-téntes*]
indigestion indigestión *f.* [*indixestjón*]
indiscretion indiscreción *f.* [*indiskreθjón*]
individual *a.* individual [*indibidwál*]
indoor *a.* interior [*interjór*]: **- pool** pis-cina *f.* cubierta [*pisθína kubjérta*]
industr/ial industrial *a.* [*industrjál*], profesional [*profesjonál*]; **-y** industria *f.* [*indústrja*]

ineffective *a.* ineficaz [*inefikáθ*]

infantil *a.* infantil [*infantíl*]

infect (to) infectar *r.* [*infektár*], contagiar *r.* [*kontaxjár*] (persons); **-ed** *a.* infectado(a) [*infektádo*]; **-ion** infección *f.* [*infekθjón*], contagio *m.* [*kontáxjo*] (persons); **-ious** *a.* infeccioso(a) [*infekθjóso*], contagioso(a) [*kontaxjóso*] (persons)

inferior *a.* inferior [*inferjór*] (to/a); **-ity** inferioridad *f.* [*inferjoridád*]

infirmary hospital *m.* [*ospitál*] ‖ **2.** enfermería *f.* [*enfermería*]

inflam/e (to) inflamarse *r.* [*inflamárse*]; **-ed** *a.* inflamado(a) [*inflamádo*]; **-mation** inflamación *f.* [*inflamaθjón*]

influenza gripe *f.* [*grípe*]

inform (to) informar *r.* [*informár*] (de); **-ation** información *f.* [*informaθjón*]; *hotel -,* información hotelera [*oteléra*]; **-** *desk,* mostrador *m.* de información [*mostradór de*]; información *f.* [*informaθjón*]; **-ative** *a.* informativo(a) [*informatíbo*]

infusion infusión *f.* [*infusjón*]; **-** *of camomile,* infusión de manzanilla [*de manθanílja*]; **-** *of peppermint,* infusión de menta [*de ménta*]

inhabitant habitante *m.* [*abitánte*]

inject (to) inyectar *r.* [*injektár*]; **-ion** inyección *f.* [*injekθjón*]

injur/e (to) herir (ie) [*erír*], lesionar *r.* [*lesjonár*]; **-ed** *a.* herido(a) [*erído*], lesionado(a) [*lesjonádo*]; **-y** herida *f.* [*erída*], lesión *f.* [*lesjón*]

ink tinta *f.* [*tínta*]; **-well** tintero *m.* [*tintéro*]; **-y** *a.* manchado(a) de tinta [*mantchádo de tínta*]

inland *a.* del interior [*del interjór*]

inn posada *f.* [*posáda*], fonda *f.* [*fónda*]; **-keeper** posadero *m.* [*posadéro*]

inner *a.* interior [*interjór*]; **-** *tube* cámara *f.* de aire [*kámara de áire*]

inscription inscripción *f.* [*inskripθjón*]

insomnio insomnio *m.* [*insómnjo*]

inspect (to) revisar *r.* [*rrebisár*], inspeccionar *r.* [*inspekθjonár*]; **-or** revisor *m.* [*rrebisór*]

instant instante *m.* [*instánte*]; **-** *cocoa* cacao *m.* instantáneo [*kakáo instantáneo*]; **-** *coffee* café *m.* instantáneo [*kafé*]; **-aneous** *a.* instantáneo(a) [*instantáneo*]

instead: **-** *of,* prep. en lugar de [*en lugár de*]

instinct instinto *m.* [*instínto*]

institute instituto *m.* [*institúto*], colegio *m.* [*koléxjo*]

instruct/or instructor *m.* [*instruktór*], monitor *m.* [*monitór*]; **-ress** instructora *f.* [*instruktóra*], monitora *f.* [*monitóra*]

instrument instrumento *m.* [*instruménto*]

insufficien/cy insuficiencia *f.* [*insufiθjénθja*]; **-t** *a.* insuficiente [*insufiθjénte*]

insular *a.* insular [*insulár*]

insulat/ing: **-** *tape,* cinta *f.* aislante [*θínta aislánte*]; **-ion** aislamiento *m.* [*aislamjénto*]

insulin insulina *f.* [*insulína*]

insur/ance seguro *m.* [*segúro*]; **-** *policy* póliza *f.* de seguro [*póliθa de*]; **-e (to)** asegurar *r.* [*asegurár*] (against/contra); **-ed** *a.* asegurado(a) [*asegurádo*]

intake entrada *f.* [*entráda*], toma *f.* [*tóma*] (electricity, etc.)

intensive *a.* intensivo(a) [*intensíbo*]; **-** *care* cuidados *m.pl.* intensivos [*kwidádos intensíbos*]

interactive *a.* interactivo(a) [*interaktíbo*]

intercom interfono *m.* [*interfóno*]

intercontinental *a.* intercontinental [*interkontinentál*]

interest (to) interesar *r.* [*interesár*] ‖ **2.** *n.* interés *m.* [*interés*] (in/en); **-ed** *a.* interesado(a) [*interesádo*]; **-ing** *a.* interesante [*interesánte*]

interference interferencia *f.* [*interferénθja*]

interior *a.* interior [*interjór*] ‖ **2.** *n.* interior *m.*; **-** *design* diseño *m.* de interiores [*disénjo de interjóres*], interiorismo *m.* [*interjorísmo*]

intermedi/ary intermediario(a) *m.-f.* [*intermedjárjo*], **-ate** *a.* intermediario(a) [*intermedjárjo*], intermedio(a) [*intermédjo*]; **-** *ring,* anillo *m.* intermedio [*aníljo*]

interminable *a.* interminable [*intermináb

le*]

intermittent *a.* intermitente [*intermiténte*]

internal *a.* interno(a) [*intérno*], interior [*interjór*]

international *a.* internacional [*internaθjonál*]; **-** *departures* salidas *f.pl.* internacionales [*salídas internaθjonáles*]; **-** *driving licence* permiso *m.* internacional de conducir [*permíso de konduθír*]; **-** *flights* vuelos *m.* pl. internacionales [*bwélos internaθjonáles*]; **-** *luggage office* consigna *f.* internacional [*konsígna*]

interpret/ation interpretación *f.* [*interpretaθjón*]; **-er** intérprete *m.-f.* [*intérprete*]

interval intervalo *m.* [*interbálo*] ‖ **2.** descanso *m.* [*deskánso*], intermedio *m.* [*intermédjo*] (theatre, etc.)

intestin/al *a.* intestinal [*intestinál*]; **-e** intestino *m.* [*intestíno*]

into *prep.* en [*en*], a [*a*]; **to go - the house**, entrar *r.* en la casa [*entrár en la kása*], ir *irr.* a la casa [*ir a la kása*]; **to translate - Spanish,** traducir (zc) al español [*traduθír al espanjol*]

intoxication intoxicación *f.* [*intoksikaθjón*]

intramuscular *a.* intramuscular [*intramuskulár*]

intravenous *a.* intravenoso(a) [*intrabenóso*]

intricate *a.* complicado(a) [*komplikádo*]

introduction introducción *f.* [*introdukθjón*]

invalid *a.* inválido(a) [*imbálido*]; **- chair** silla *f.* de ruedas [*sílja de rrwédas*]

invention invento *m.* [*imbénto*]

invest (to) invertir (ie) [*imbertír*]; **-ment** inversión *f.* [*imbersjón*]

invitation invitación *f.* [*imbitaθjón*] (a)

invite (to) invitar *r.* [*imbitár*] (to/a)

invoice factura *f.* (comercial) [*faktúra*]

involve (to) envolver (ue) [*embolbér*]

Ireland Irlanda *f.* [*irlánda*]

Irish *a.* irlandés (irlandesa) [*irlandés, (irlandésa)*] ‖ **2.** *n.* irlandés *m.* irlandesa *f.* ‖ **3. - coffee** café *m.* irlandés [*kafé irlandés*]

iron (to) planchar *r.* [*plantchár*] ‖ **2.** *n.* plancha f. [*plántcha*]: **steam -,** plancha *f.* de vapor [*plántcha de bapór*] ‖ **3.** hierro *m.* [*jérro*]: **of wrought -,** de hierro forjado [*de jérro forxádo*]; **-ing: - board**, tabla *f.* de planchar [*tábla de plantchár*]; **-monger's** ferretería *f.* [*ferretería*]

irrigation riego *m.* [*rrjégo*], regadío *m.* [*rregadío*]; **- system** sistema *m.* de regadío [*sistéma de*]

island isla *f.* [*ísla*]

isle isla *f.* [*ísla*]

isolation aislamiento *m.* [*aislamjénto*]

it *pron. pers. nom.* él, ella (ello) [*el, élja, (éljo)*] ‖ **2.** *ac.* lo [*lo*] ‖ **3.** *dat.* le [*le*]

itching picor *m.* [*pikór*]

item artículo *m.* [*artíkulo*], pieza *f.* [*pjéθa*]

its *a. pos.* su(s) [*su*] ‖ **2.** *pron. pos.* suyo(a) [*sújo*]; suyos(as) *pl.* [*sújos*]

ivory marfil *m.* [*marfíl*]

J

jacket chaqueta *f.* [*tchakéta*], americana *f.* [*amerikána*]

jam mermelada *f.* [*mermeláda*]; **raspberry** -, mermelada de frambuesa [*de frambwésa*]; **strawberry** -, mermelada de fresa [*de frésa*] || **2.** atasco *m.* [*atásko*] (traffic)

January enero *m.* [*enéro*]

jasmine jazmín *m.* [*xaθmín*]

jeans vaqueros *m. pl.* [*bakéros*]; tejanos *m.pl.* [*texános*]

jeep (coche) todo terreno *m.* [(*kótche*) *tódo terréno*]

jelly jalea *f.* [*xaléa*], gelatina *f.* [*xelatína*]

jellyfish medusa *f.* [*medúsa*]

jersey jersey *m.* [*xerséi*]

jet azabache *m.* [*aθabátche*] || **2.** Aer. (avión *m.*) reactor *m.* [(*abjón*) *rreaktór*]

jewel joya *f.* [*xója*]; **-ler** joyero *m.* [*xojéro*]; **-'s** joyería *f.* [*xojería*]; **-lery** joyas *f. pl.* [*xójas*] || **2.** joyería *f.* [*xojería*]

job *m.* trabajo *m.* [*trabáxo*]

jockey jinete *m.* [*xinéte*]

join (to) juntar *r.* [*xuntár*]; **-t** juntura *f.* [*juntúra*], articulación *f.* [*artikulaθjón*] (Anat.)

joke broma *f.* [*bróma*]; chiste *m.* [*tchíste*]

journal diario *m.* [*djárjo*]

journey (to) viajar *r.* [*bjaxár*] || **2.** *n.* viaje *m.* [*bjáxe*]

joy alegría *f.* [*alegría*]; **-ful** *a.* alegre [*alégre*]

jug jarro *m.* [*xárro*], jarra *f.* [*xárra*]; cántaro *m.* [*kántaro*]; **-ged: - deer,** civet *m.* de ciervo [*θibét de θjérbo*]; **- hare,** civet de liebre [*de ljébre*]

juic/e jugo *m.* [*xúgo*], zumo *m.* [*θúmo*]; **apple -,** zumo de manzana [*de manθána*]; **apricot -,** zumo de albaricoque [*de albarikóke*]; **fruit -,** zumo de fruta [*de frúta*]; **grapefruit -,** zumo de pomelo [*de pomélo*]; **lemon -,** zumo de limón [*de limón*]; **orange -,** zumo de naranja [*de naránxa*]; **peach -,** zumo de melocotón [*de melokotón*]; **pear -,** zumo de pera [*de péra*]; **tomato -,** zumo de tomate [*de tomáte*]; **-y** *a.* jugoso(a) [*xugóso*]

July julio *m.* [*xúljo*]; **in -,** en julio [*en xúljo*]

jump (to) saltar *r.* [*saltár*] || **2.** *n.* salto *m.* [*sálto*]; **high -,** salto de altura [*de altúra*]

June junio *m.* [*xúnjo*]; **in -,** en junio [*en xúnjo*]

K

keel quilla *f.* [*kílja*]

keep (to) guardar *r.* [*gwardár*]. mantener (ie) [*mantenér*]; *to - a look-out,* vigilar *r.* [*bixilár*] ‖ **2. - still!** ¡estáte quieto(a)! [*estáte kjéto*]; **-er** guardia *m.-f.* [*gwárdja*]. vigilante *m.- f.* [*bixilánte*]

kerb bordillo *m.* [*bordíljo*]

ketchup ketchup *m.* [*kétchup*], salsa *f.* de tomate [*sálsa de tomáte*]

key llave *f.* [*ljábe*]. **-board** teclado *m.* [*tekládo*]; **-hole** entrada *f.* de la cerradura [*entráda de la θerradúra*]; **- ring** llavero *m.* [*ljabéro*]

kick: - starter, pedal *m.* de arranque [*pedál de arránke*]

kidney riñón *m.* [*rrinjón*]; **-s in wine,** riñones *pl.* al jerez [*rrinjónes al xeréθ*]; **lamb's -s,** riñones de cordero [*de kordéro*]; **pig's -s,** riñones de cerdo [*de θérdo*]; **- sauté,** riñones salteados [*salteádos*]; **- bean** alubia *f.* [*alúbja*]. judía *f.* [*xudía*]

kilo(gramme) kilo *m.* [*kílo*]

kilo/metre kilómetro *m.* [*kilómetro*]; **-watt** kilovatio *m.* [*kilobátjo*]

kind *a.* amable [*amáble*] ‖ **2.** *n.* tipo *m.* [*típo*]. clase *f.* [*kláse*]; *what kind of house ...?* ¿qué clase (tipo) de casa...? [*ke kláse (típo) de kása*]; **-liness** amabilidad *f.* [*amabilidád*]; **-ly** *adv.* amablemente [*amableménte*]; **-ness** amabilidad *f.* [*amabilidád*]

kindergarten parvulario *m.* [*parbulárjo*]

kiosk quiosco *m.* [*kjósko*]

kirsch kirsch *m.* [*kirch*]

kiss (to) besar *t.* [*besár*] ‖ **2.** *n.* beso *m.* [*béso*]

kit equipo *m.* [*ekípo*]; *first aid -,* botiquín *m.* [*botikín*]; *tool-,* caja *f.* de herramientas [*káxa de erramjéntas*]

kitchen cocina *f.* [*koθína*]; **- cloth** paño *m.* de cocina [*pánjo de*]; **- furniture** muebles *m. pl.* de cocina [*muébles de*]; **-ware** batería *f.* de cocina [*batería de*]

kiwi kiwi *m.* [*kiwi*]

knee rodilla *f.* [*rrodílja*]

knickers bragas *f.pl.* [*brágas*]

knife cuchillo *m.* [*kutchíljo*]. navaja *f.* [*nabáxa*]

knit (to) tejer *r.* [*texér*] ‖ **2.** hacer *irr.* punto [*aθér púnto*]; **-ting** punto *m.* [*púnto*]; **k.-wear** géneros *m. pl.* de punto [*xéneros de púnto*]

knock golpe *m.* [*gólpe*]

know (to) conocer (zc) [*konoθér*], saber *irr.* [*sabér*]

L

label etiqueta *f.* [*etikéta*]: **green -**, etiqueta verde [*bérde*]

lace encaje *m.* [*enkáxe*], puntilla *f.* [*puntílja*]: **hand-made -**, puntilla *f.* a mano [*a máno*]; **machine-made -**, puntilla a máquina [*a mákina*]; **-s** cordones *m.pl.* [*kordónes*]

lack (to) faltar *r.* [*faltár*]

lacquer laca *f.* [*láka*]

lady señora *f.* [*senjóra*], dama *f.* [*dáma*]

lake lago *m.* [*lágo*]

lamb cordero *m.* [*kordéro*], carne *f.* de cordero [*kárne de*]: **braised -**, cordero guisado [*gisádo*]; **roast(ed) -**, cordero asado [*kordéro asádo*]; **- chops** chuletas de cordero [*tchulétas de*]; **grilled -**, chuletas de cordero a la parrilla [*a la parrílja*]; **-s fry** criadillas *f. pl.* (de cordero) [*krjadíljas*]; **-'s wool** lana *f.* de cordero [*lána de kordéro*]

lamp lámpara *f.* [*lámpara*], faro *m.* [*fáro*] (car): **oil -**, quinque *m.* [*kinké*]; **street -**, farol *m.* [*faról*]; **votive -**, lámpara *f.* votiva [*lámpara botíba*]; **-shade** pantalla *f.* [*pantálja*]

land (to) aterrizar *r.* [*aterriθár*] (plane), desembarcar *r.* [*desembarkár*] (ship) ‖ **2.** *n.* tierra *f.* [*tjérra*]: **by -**, por tierra [*por*] ‖ **3.** país *m.* [*país*] (country); **-ing** aterrizaje *m.* [*aterriθáxe*] (plane), desembarco *m.* [*desembárko*] (passengers); **-scape** paisaje *m.* [*paisáxe*]

language lengua *f.* [*léngwa*], idioma *m.* [*idjóma*]: **the Spanish -**, el (idioma) español [*el (idjóma) espanjól*]

lapel solapa *f.* [*solápa*]

lard manteca *f.* (de cerdo) [*mantéka de θérdo*]

large *a.* grande [*gránde*], importante [*importánte*]: **a - size**, una talla grande [*úna tálja gránde*]

laryngitis laringitis *f.* [*larinxítis*]

last *a.* último(a) [*último*]: **- night**, anoche [*anótche*]; **- Monday**, el lunes pasado [*el lúnes pasádo*] ‖ **2.** *n.* horma *f.* [*órma*] (shoes)

lat/e *a.* tardío (a) [*tardío*] ‖ **2.** *adv.* tarde [*tárde*]: **to be -**, llegar *r.* tarde [*ljegár*]; tardar *r.* [*tardár*]; **-er** *adv.* más tarde [*mas tárde*], después [*despwés*]: **one year -**, un año después [*un ánjo despwés*]; **see you -!** ¡te veo después! [*te béo despwés*], ¡hasta luego! [*ásta lwégo*]

lateral *a.* lateral [*laterál*]

laugh (to) reír(se) (i) [*rreírse*] (at/de); **-ter** risa *f.* [*rrísa*]

launch lancha *f.* [*lántcha*] (Naut.)

laundry lavandería *f.* [*labandería*] ‖ **2.** ropa *f.* sucia [*rrópa súθja*]; **- basket** cesto *m.* de la ropa sucia [*θésto de la rrópa súθja*]

laurel laurel *m.* [*laurél*]

lavatory lavabo *m.* [*labábo*]; **- paper** papel *m.* higiénico [*papél ixjéniko*]

lawyer abogado(a) *m.-f.* [*abogádo*]

laxative laxante *m.* [*laksánte*]

lay (to) poner *irr.* [*ponér*] colocar *r.* [*kolokár*]; **-out** diseño *m.* [*disénjo*], maqueta *f.* [*makéta*]

lazy *a.* perezoso(a) [*pereθóso*]

lead (to) llevar *r.* [*ljebár*], conducir (zc) [*konduθír*], dirigir *r.* [*dirixír*] ‖ **2.** *n.* plomo *m.* [*plómo*]; **l.-free** sin plomo [*sin plómo*] (petrol)

leaf hoja *f.* [*óxa*]; **-let** folleto *m.* [*foljéto*]; **- spring** resorte *m.* [*rresórte*]

league liga *f.* [*líga*] (sport)

leak agujero *m.* [*aguxéro*] ‖ **2.** escape *m.* [*eskápe*]

learn (to) aprender *r.* [*aprendér*]; **to - Spanish**, aprender español [*espanjól*]; **to - to swim**, aprender a nadar [*aprendér a nadár*]; **-er** principiante *m.-f.* [*prinθipjánte*]

leasing arrendamiento *m.* [*arrendamjénto*], alquiler *m.* [*alkilér*] ‖ **2.** leasing *m.* [*lísing*] (financial)

leather cuero *m.* [*kwéro*], piel *f.* [*pjél*]: **- bottle** bota *f.* de vino [*bóta de bíno*]; **- bound** *a.* en piel [*en*]; **- clothing** confecciones *f. pl.* en ante (cuero) [*konfekθjónes en ánte (kwéro)*]

leave (to) dejar *r.* [*dexár*], abandonar *r.* [*abandonár*]: **to - the window open**, dejar *r.* la ventana abierta [*dexár la bentána abjérta*] ‖ **2.** salir *irr.* [*salír*], partir *r.* [*partír*] (de); **-ing** salida *f.* [*salída*], partida *f.* [*partída*]

leek puerro *m.* [*pwérro*]

left *a.* izquierdo(a) [*iθkjérdo*] ‖ **2.** *n.* izquierda *f.* [*iθkjérda*]: **to the -**, a la izquierda [*a la*]; **l.-handed** *a.* zurdo(a) [*θúrdo*]; **l.-luggage office** consigna *f.* [*konsígna*]

leg pierna *f.* [*pjérna*] ‖ **2.** pata *f.* [*páta*] (animals, furnitures) ‖ **3.** muslo *m.* [*múslo*] (chicken, etc.): **- of chicken**, muslo *m.* de pollo [*múslo de póljo*]; **- of mutton**, pierna *f.* de cordero [*pjérna de kordéro*]

legal *a.* legal [*legál*]

leisure tiempo *m.* libre [*tjémpo líbre*], ocio *m.* [*óθjo*]

lemon limón *m.* [*limón*]; **-ade** limonada *f.* [*limonáda*]; **iced -**, granizado *m.* de limón [*graniθádo de limón*]; **white -**, gaseosa *f.* [*gaseósa*]; **- juice** zumo *m.* de limón [*θúmo de limón*]; **- squeezer** exprimidor *m.* de limones [*eksprimidór de limónes*]; **- tea** té *m.* con limón [*te kon limón*]

lend (to) prestar *r.* [*prestár*], dejar *r.* [*dexár*] (money, etc.)

length longitud *f.* [*lonxitúd*]; **-en (to)** alargar *r.* [*alargár*]

lens lentes *f. pl.* [*léntes*]; **contact -**, lentes *f. pl.* de contacto [*léntes de kontákto*], lentillas *f. pl.* [*lentíljas*]

lentil lenteja *f.* [*lentéxa*]; **boiled -s**, lentejas *pl.* cocidas [*koθídas*]; **- soup** sopa *f.* de lentejas [*sópa de lentéxas*]

less *adv.* menos [*ménos*]

lesson clase *f.* [*kláse*], lección *f.* [*lekθjón*]; **the English -**, la clase (lección) de inglés [*la kláse (lekθjón) de inglés*]

let (to) dejar *r.* [*dexár*] || **2.** alquilar *r.* [*alkilár*]

letter carta *f.* [*kárta*]; **- box** buzón *m.* [*buθón*]; **- cabinet** taquillón *m.* [*takiljón*]; **- paper** papel *m.* de carta [*papél de kárta*]

lettuce lechuga *f.* [*letchúga*]

level nivel *m.* [*nibél*]; **- crossing** paso *m.* a nivel [*páso a nibél*]

lever palanca *f.* [*palánka*]

liaison enlace *m.* [*enláθe*]

library biblioteca *f.* [*bibljotéka*]; **mobile -**, biblioteca móvil [*móbil*]; **public -**, biblioteca pública [*públika*]

licence licencia *f.* [*liθénθja*], permiso *m.* [*permíso*]

lie (to) tender(se) (ie) [*tendérse*], acostarse (ue) [*akostárse*]; **to - down (in the sun)**, tumbarse *r.* (al sol) [*tumbárse (al sol)*] || **2.** estar *irr.* acostado(a) (echado(a)) [*estár akostádo (etchádo)*] (state) || **3.** estar *irr.* (situado) [*estár (situádo)*] (to be situated), encontrarse (ue) [*enkontrárse*] (in/en)

life vida *f.* [*bída*]; **still -**, bodegón *m.* [*bodegón*]; **- belt** cinturón *m.* salvavidas [*θinturón salbabídas*]; **-boat** bote *m.* salvavidas [*bóte*]; **-guard** socorrista *m.-f.* [*sokorrísta*]; **- insurance** seguro *m.* de vida [*segúro de bída*]; **- jacket** chaleco *m.* salvavidas [*tchaléko salbabídas*]

lift ascensor *m.* [*asθensór*]; **goods -**, montacargas *m.* [*montakárgas*]; **ski -**, telesquí *m.* [*teleskí*]

ligament ligamento *m.* [*ligaménto*]

light *a.* claro(a) [*kláro*] || **2.** ligero(a) [*lixéro*] || **3.** *n.* luz *f.* [*luθ*], lámpara *f.* [*lámpara*]; **-bulb** bombilla *f.* [*bombílja*]; **-en (to)** iluminar *r.* [*iluminár*] || **4.** aligerar *r.* [*alixerár*]; **-er** encendedor *m.* [*enθendedór*], mechero *m.* [*metchéro*]; **-house** faro *m.* [*fáro*]; **-ing** alumbrado *m.* [*alumbrádo*]; **-meter** fotómetro *m.* [*fotómetro*]; **-ning** relámpago *m.* [*rrelámpago*]; **- rod**, pararrayos *m.* [*pararrájos*]; **-s** faros *m. pl.* [*fáros*]; **parking -**, luces *f. pl.* de estacionamiento [*lúθes de estaθjonamjénto*]; **traffic -**, semáforo *m.* [*semáforo*]

like (to) querer (ie) [*kerér*], gustar *r.* [*gustár*]; **I - it**, me gusta [*me gústa*] || **2.** *adv.* como [*kómo*]

"li-lo" colchón *m.* hinchable [*koltchón intcháble*]

lily azucena *f.* [*aθuθéna*]; **iris -**, lirio *m.* [*lírjo*]

lime lima *f.* [*líma*]; **- juice** zumo *m.* de lima [*θúmo de líma*]

limit (to) limitar *r.* [*limitár*] || **2.** *n.* límite *m.* [*límite*]; **speed -**, límite de velocidad [*límite de beloθidád*]; **-ation** limitación *f.* [*limitaθjón*]; **-ed** *a.* limitado(a) [*limitádo*]

limousine limusina *f.* [*limusína*]

limpet lapa *f.* [*lápa*]

linden: - tea, tila *f.* [*tíla*]

line línea *f.* [*línea*], raya *f.* [*rrája*] || **2.** hilo *m.* [*ílo*]; **fishing -**, sedal *m.* [*sedál*], hilo *m.* de pescar [*ílo de peskár*] || **3.** cuerda *f.* [*kwérda*], cabo *m.* [*kábo*]; **plastic -**, cabo de plástico [*de plástiko*]

linen lienzo *m.* [*ljénθo*], lino *m.* [*líno*] || **2.** lencería *f.* [*lenθería*]

liniment linimento *m.* [*liniménto*]

lining forro *m.* [*fórro*] || **2. - pencil**, lápiz *m.* perfilador [*lápiθ perfiladór*]

link (to) enlazar *r.* [*enlaθár*], conectar *r.* [*konektár*] || **2.** *n.* enlace *m.* [*enláθe*], conexión *f.* [*koneksjón*] (air, etc.)

lip labio *m.* [*lábjo*]; **- brush** pincel *m.* para los labios [*pinθél pára los lábjos*]; **- stick** lápiz *m.* de labios [*lápiθ de lábjos*]

liqueur licor *m.* [*likór*]; **aniseed -**, licor de anís [*de anís*]; **orange -**, licor de naranja [*de naránxa*]; **peppermint -**, licor de menta [*de ménta*]

liquid *a.* líquido(a) [*líkido*] ‖ **2.** *n.* líquido *m.* [*líkido*]; - **detergent** detergente *m.* líquido [*deterxénte*]; - **make-up** maquillaje *m.* líquido [*makiljáxe líkido*]; - **soap** jabón *m.* líquido [*xabón líkido*]

list lista *f.* [*lísta*], relación *f.* [*rrelaθjón*] ‖ **2.** catálogo *m.* [*katálogo*]; **price -,** lista de precios [*de préθjos*]; **waiting -,** lista de espera [*de espéra*]; **wine -,** carta *f.* de vinos [*kárta de bínos*]; - **price** precio *m.* de catálogo [*préθjo de katálogo*]

listen (to) escuchar *r.* [*eskutchár*]

lit *a.* encendido(a) [*enθendído*]

literature literatura *f.* [*literatúra*]

lithography litografía *f.* [*litografía*]

litre litro *m.* [*lítro*]; ‖ **2. two -s of wine,** dos litros de vino [*dos lítros de bíno*]

little *a.* pequeño(a) [*pekénjo*] ‖ **2.** poco(a) [*póko*] ‖ **3. a -,** algo [*álgo*] (de), un poco [*un póko*] (de)

liv/e (to) vivir *r.* [*bibír*] ‖ **2.** *a.* vivo(a) [*bíbo*] ‖ **3.** *adv.* en directo [*en dirékto*]

liver hígado *m.* [*ígado*]; **beef -,** hígado de buey [*de buei*]; **braised -,** hígado guisado [*gisádo*]; **chicken -,** hígado de pollo [*de póljo*]; **fried -,** hígado frito [*fríto*]; **pork -,** hígado de cerdo [*de θérdo*]; **veal -,** hígado de ternera [*de ternéra*]; - **with garlic,** hígado al ajillo [*al axíljo*]

living. - room, sala *f.* de estar [*sála de estár*], living *m.* [*líbing*]

load (to) cargar *r.* [*kargár*]; **to - the camera,** cargar la cámara [*la kámara*] ‖ **2.** *n.* carga *f.* [*kárga*]

loaf pan *m.* [*pan*]; **round -,** pan redondo [*rredóndo*]

loan (to) prestar *r.* [*prestár*] (money) ‖ **2.** *n.* préstamo *m.* [*préstamo*]

lobby vestíbulo *m.* [*bestíbulo*]

lobster bogavante *m.* [*bogabánte*]; **spiny -,** langosta *f.* [*langósta*]

local *a.* local [*lokál*] ‖ **2.** urbano(a) [*urbáno*]

location situación *f.* [*situaθjón*], ubicación *f.* [*ubikaθjón*]

lock cerradura *f.* [*θerradúra*]; **-er** taquilla *f.* [*takílja*]

locomotive locomotora *f.* [*lokomotóra*]

lodg/e (to) alojarse *r.* [*aloxárse*]; **-ing** alojamiento *m.* [*aloxamjénto*]

loin lomo *m.* [*lómo*], solomillo *m.* [*solomíljo*]; - **of pork,** lomo *m.* de cerdo [*lómo de θérdo*]

lollipop pirulí *m.* [*pirulí*], chupa-chup *m.* [*tchupatchúp*]

long *a.* largo(a) [*lárgo*]: **how - is it?** ¿cuánto tiene de largo? [*kwánto tjéne de lárgo*]: **how - have you been waiting?** ¿cuánto tiempo llevas esperando? [*kwánto tjémpo ljébas esperándo*] ‖ **2.** *n.* longitud *f.* [*lonxitúd*]; - **jump** salto *m.* de longitud [*sálto de*]; - **range lens** teleobjetivo *m.* [*teleobxetíbo*]

look (to) mirar *r.* [*mirár*], considerar *r.* [*konsiderár*]: **to - after,** cuidar *r.* [*kwidár*]: **to - at,** mirar *r.* [*mirár*]: **to - for,** buscar *r.* [*buskár*] ‖ **2.** *n.* mirada *f.* [*miráda*] ‖ **3.** aspecto *m.* [*aspékto*]; - **out** vigilante *m.* [*bixilánte*]

loop anilla *f.* [*anílja*]

loose *a.* suelto(a) [*swélto*], flojo(a) [*flóxo*]; **1.- fitting** holgado(a) [*olgádo*]; **-n (to)** aflojar *r.* [*afloxár*], soltar (ue) [*soltár*]

lorry camión *m.* [*kamjón*]; - **driver** camionero *m.* [*kamjonéro*]

lose (to) perder (ie) [*perdér*]

loss pérdida *f.* [*pérdida*]

lost *a.* perdido(a) [*perdído*]; - **property** objetos *m. pl.* perdidos [*obxétos perdídos*]

lot: a -, mucho *adv.* [*mútcho*] ‖ **2. a - of** mucho(a) *a.:* - **a - of money,** mucho dinero [*dinéro*]; **thanks a lot!** ¡muchísimas gracias! [*mutchísimas gráθjas*]

lotion loción *f.* [*loθjón*]

lottery lotería *f.* [*lotería*]; - **ticket** billete *m.* de lotería [*biljéte de*]

lotto lotería *f.* primitiva [*lotería primitíba*]

loud *a.* fuerte [*fwérte*], alto(a) [*álto*] (sound); **-speaker** altavoz *m.* [*altaboθ*]

lounge salón *m.* (de descanso) [*salón de deskánso*], sala *f.* de estar [*sála de estár*]: **departure -,** sala de espera [*sála de espéra*] (airport)

louse piojo *m.* [*pjóxo*]

love (to) amar *r.* [*amár*], querer (ie) [*kerér*] ‖ **2.** gustar *r.* [*gustár*]: **he loves money,** le gusta el dinero [*le gústa el dinéro*] ‖ **3.** *n.* amor *m.* [*amór*], cariño *m.* [*karínjo*]; **-ly** *a.* encantador(a) [*enkantadór*]; **-r** amante *m.-f.* [*amánte*]

low *a.* bajo(a) [*báxo*], reducido(a) [*rreduθído*]; - **price,** precio *m.* bajo (reducido) [*préθjo báxo (rreduθído)*]; - **tide** marea *f.* baja [*maréa báxa*] ‖ **2.** *adv.* bajo [*báxo*]; **-er** *a.* inferior [*inferjór*]; **l.-level** *a.* de bajo nivel [*de báxo nibél*]; **l.-necked** *a.* escotado(a) [*eskotádo*]

lozenge gragea *f.* [*graxéa*]
lubricat/e (to) engrasar *r.* [*engrasár*];
-ion engrase *m.* [*engráse*]; **-or** engra-
sador *m.* [*engrasadór*]
luck suerte *f.* [*swérte*]; **-y** *a.* afortunado(a)
[*afortunádo*]; **-ily** *adv.* afortunada-
mente [*afortunadaménte*]
luggage equipaje *m.* [*ekipáxe*]; **left-
room,** consigna *f.* [*konsígna*]; **- conveyor** cinta *f.* de equipaje [*θínta de
ekipáxe*]; **- locker** consigna automáti-
ca [*automátika*]; **- office** consigna
lumbago lumbago *m.* [*lumbágo*]

lumber trastos *m. pl.* viejos [*trástos bjé-
xos*]; **- room** trastero *m.* [*trastéro*]
lump terrón *m.* [*terrón*]; **- sugar** azúcar
m. en terrones [*aθúkar en terrónes*]
lunch (to) almorzar (ue) [*almorθár*],
comer *r.* [*komér*] ‖ **2.** *n.* almuerzo *m.*
[*almwérθo*], comida *f.* [*komída*]; **- hour**
hora *f.* de comer [*óra de komér*]
lung pulmón *m.* [*pulmón*]
lustre brillo *m* [*bríljo*]
luxur/ious *a.* de lujo [*de lúxo*], lujo-
sos(a) [*luxóso*]; **-y** lujo *m.* [*lúxo*]
lye lejía *f.* [*lexía*]

M

macaroni macarrones *m.pl.* [*makarrónes*]; **- cheese** macarrones gratinados [*makarrónes gratinádos*]

machine máquina *f.* [*mákina*]; **drinks -,** máquina *f.* de bebidas [*de bebídas*]; **washing -,** lavadora *f.* [*labadóra*]

mackerel caballa *f.* [*kabálja*]

made *a.* hecho(a) [*étcho*], fabricado(a) [*fabrikádo*]; **- in Spain** fabricado(a) en España [*fabrikádo en espánja*]; **m.-to-measure** hecho(a) a medida [*étcho a medída*]

magazine almacén *m.* [*almaθén*] ‖ **2.** revista *f.* [*rrebísta*]

magnet imán *m.* [*imán*]; **-ic** *a.* magnético(a) [*magnétiko*]; **- tape** cinta *f.* magnetofónica [*θínta magnetofónika*]

magnolia magnolia *f.* [*magnólja*]

mahogany *a.* de caoba [*de kaóba*]

maid doncella *f.* [*donθélja*], criada *f.* [*krjáda*] ‖ **2.** camarera *f.* [*kamaréra*] (hotel); **-'s uniforms,** uniformes *m.pl.* de servicio [*unifórmes de serbíθjo*]; **- servant** criada *f.* [*krjáda*]

mail (to) echar *r.* al correo [*etchár al korréo*], enviar por correo [*embjár por*] ‖ **2.** *n.* correo *m.* [*korréo*], correspondencia *f.* [*korrespondénθja*]; **air -,** correo aéreo [*korréo aéreo*]; **by -,** por correo [*por korréo*]; **-box** buzón *m.* [*buθón*]

main *a.* principal [*prinθipál*], central [*θentrál*]; **- course** plato *m.* principal [*pláto*]; **- road** carretera *f.* principal [*karretéra*]; **- street** calle *f.* principal (mayor) [*kálje prinθipál (majór)*]; **- station** estación *f.* central [*estaθjón θentrál*]; **-ly** *adv.* principalmente [*prinθipálménte*], sobre todo [*sóbre tódo*]; **-tain (to)** mantener (ie) [*mantenér*], conservar *r.* [*konserbár*]; **-tenance** mantenimiento *m.* [*mantenimjénto*]

maize maíz *m.* [*maíθ*]

majolica *a.* de majólica [*de maxólika*]

major *a.* mayor [*majór*], principal [*prinθipál*] ‖ **2.** *n.* mayor *m.*

make (to) hacer *irr.* [*aθér*] ‖ **2.** fabricar *r.* [*fabrikár*], producir (zc) [*produθír*] ‖ **3. to - appear more dense,** crepar *r.* [*krepár*]; **to - copies,** sacar *r.* copias [*sakár kópjas*]; **to - to measure,** hacer *irr.* a medida [*aθér a medída*]; **to - up,** maquillar *r.* [*maki-*]

ljár] ‖ **4.** *n.* hechura *f.* [*etchúra*] ‖ **5.** marca *f.* [*márka*], modelo *m.* [*modélo*]; **m.-up** maquillaje *m.* [*makiljáxe*]; **- bag,** neceser *m.* [*neθesér*]; **- compact,** maquillaje *m.* compacto [*kompákto*]; **- remover,** desmaquillador *m.* [*desmakiljadór*]

making fabricación *f.* [*fabrikaθjón*], confección *f.* [*konfekθjón*] (clothes)

male *a.* macho [*mátcho*] (animal), varón [*barón*] (person)

malt malta *f.* [*málta*]; **- whisky** whisky *m.* de málta [*wíski de*]

man hombre *m.* [*ómbre*]

manage/ment dirección *f.* [*direkθjón*], gerencia *f.* [*xerénθja*]; **-r** director *m.* [*direktór*], gerente *m.* [*xerénte*]

mandarin mandarina *f.* [*mandarína*]

mango mango *m.* [*mángo*]

manicure manicura *f.* [*manikúra*]

Manila: - shawl, mantón *m.* de Manila [*mantón de maníla*]

mannequin modelo *f.* [*modélo*]

mantilla mantilla *f.* [*mantílja*]

mantle manto *m.* [*mánto*], capa *f.* [*kápa*]

manual *a.* manual [*manwál*] ‖ **2.** *n* manual *m.* [*manwál*]

manufacture (to) fabricar *r.* [*fabrikár*], confeccionar *r.* [*konfekθjonár*] (clothes) ‖ **2.** *n.* fabricación *f.* [*fabrikaθjón*], confección *f.* [*konfekθjón*] (clothes); **-r** fabricante *m.-f.* [*fabrikánte*]

many *a.* muchos(as) *pl.* [*mútchos*]

manzanilla ; **- sherry** manzanilla *f.* [*manθanílja*]

map mapa *m.* [*mápa*], carta *f.* [*kárta*]; plano *m.* [*pláno*]

marble mármol *m.* [*mármol*]

March marzo *m.* [*márθo*]

margarine margarina *f.* [*margarína*]

marguerite margarita *f.* [*margaríta*]

maritime *a.* marítimo(a) [*marítimo*]

marionette marioneta *f.* [*marjonéta*]

marjoram mejorana *f.* [*mexorána*], orégano *m.* [*orégano*]

marker rotulador *m.* [*rrotuladór*]

market mercado *m.* [*merkádo*]; **flea -,** mercadillo *m.* [*merkadíljo*]; **second-hand -,** mercado de ocasión [*de okasjón*]; **-place** mercado *m.* [*merkádo*], plaza *f.* [*pláθa*]

marmalade mermelada *f.* [*mermeláda*]; **orange -,** mermelada de naranja [*de naránxa*]

marquee carpa *f.* [*kárpa*], entoldado *m.* [*entoldádo*]

marquetry marquetería f. [*marketería*]

marriage matrimonio m. [*matrimónjo*]

married a. casado(a) [*kasádo*]; **to be -**, estar *irr.* casado [*estár kasádo*]; **to get -**, casarse r. [*kasárse*] (to/con)

marrow: baby -, calabacín m. [*kalabaín*]

marry (to) casarse r. [*kasárse*] (so./con alg.)

marzipan mazapán m. [*maθapán*]

mascara mascarilla f. [*maskarílja*]; rímel m. [*rrímel*]; **cream -**, mascarilla f. en crema [*maskarílja en kréma*]

mask máscara f. [*máskara*]

mass misa f. [*mísa*]

mass/age masaje m. [*masáxe*]; **-eur** masajista m. [*masaxísta*]; **-euse** masajista f. [*masaxísta*]

mast mástil m. [*mastíl*], palo m. [*pálo*]

mat felpudo m. [*felpúdo*] (door) ‖ **2.** tapete m. [*tapéte*] (table)

match cerilla f. [*θerílja*] ‖ **2.** partido m. [*partído*], combate m. [*kombáte*] (sport); **-box** caja f. de cerillas [*káxa de θeríljas*]

material material m. [*materjál*]

matinée sesión f. (función f.) de tarde [*sesjón (funθjón) de tárde*]

matt a. mate [*máte*]

matter materia f. [*matérja*], asunto m. [*asúnto*]; **printed -**, impresos m. pl. [*imprésos*] ‖ **2.** *interj.* **what is the -?** ¿qué pasa? [*ke pása*]

mattress colchón m. [*koltchón*]; **-es** colchonería f. [*kotchonería*]

mature a. maduro(a) [*madúro*]

maximum a. máximo(a) [*máksimo*]; **-load** carga f. máxima [*kárga*]; **- speed** velocidad f. máxima [*beloθidád*]

May mayo m. [*májo*]; **in -**, en mayo (en)

mayonnaise (salsa) f. mayonesa f. [*sálsa majonésa*]

mayor alcalde m. [*alkálde*] ‖ **2.** alcaldesa f. [*alkaldésa*]

me *pron. pers. dat./acus.*, me [*me*]

meal comida f. [*komída*] ‖ **2.** harina f. [*arína*], **-time** hora f. de comer [*óra de komér*]

mean (to) significar r. [*signifikár*], querer *irr.* decir [*kerér deθír*]; **what does it -?** ¿qué quiere decir? [*ke kjére deθír*] ‖ **2.** a. medio(a) [*médjo*]; **- temperature,** temperatura f. media [*temperatúra médja*]; **-ing** sentido m. [*sentído*], significado m. [*signifikádo*]; **what is the - of this?** ¿qué quiere decir (ésto)? [*ke kjére deθír (ésto)*]; **-s** medio m. [*médjo*]; **- of**

transport, medio m. de transporte [*médjo de transpórte*]

measur/e (to) medir (i) [*medír*] ‖ **2.** n. medida f. [*medída*]; dimensión f. [*dimensjón*]; **made to -**, hecho(a) a medida [*étcho a*]; **-ment** medida f. [*medída*] ‖ **2.** medición f. [*mediθjón*]; **-ing** medición f. [*mediθjón*]; **- tape**, cinta f. métrica [*θínta métrika*]

meat carne f. [*kárne*]; **beef -**, carne de buey [*de bwei*]; **braised -** carne guisada [*gisáda*]; **grilled -**, carne a la brasa (plancha) [*a la brása (plántcha)*]; **lamb -**, carne de cordero [*de kordéro*]; **minced -**, carne picada [*pikáda*]; **pork -**, carne de cerdo [*de θérdo*]; **roasted -**, carne asada [*asáda*], **stewed -**, carne estofada [*estofáda*]; **- ball** albóndiga f. [*albóndiga*]; **- pie** pastel m. de carne [*pastél de kárne*], empanada f. de carne [*empanáda*]

mechanic mecánico m. [*mekániko*] ‖ **2.** a. mecánico(a) [*mekániko*]; **-al** a. mecánico(a) [*mekániko*]

medal medalla f. [*medálja*]

medallion medallón m. [*medaljón*]

medic/al a. médico(a) [*médiko*]; **- auxiliary** practicante m. [*praktikánte*]; **- service** servicio m. médico [*serbíθjo médiko*]; **-ation** medicación f. [*medikaθjón*]

medicament medicamento m. [*medikaménto*], medicina f. [*mediθína*]

medicine medicina f. [*mediθína*], medicamento m. [*medikaménto*] ‖ **2.** medicina f. [*mediθína*] (science)

Mediterranean a. mediterráneo(a) [*mediterráneo*]; **the -**, el Mediterráneo m.

medium a. medio(a) [*médjo*], mediano(a) [*medjáno*]; **m.-dry** semiseco(a) [*semiséko*]; **m.-sized** de tamaño medio [*de tamánjo médjo*]

meet (to) encontrar (ue) [*enkontrár*] ‖ **2.** encontrarse (ue) [*enkontrárse*] (so./con alg.); **-ing** reunión f. [*reunjón*]; **- point**, punto m. de encuentro [*púnto de enkwéntro*] ‖ **2.** entrevista f. [*entrebísta*]

mellow a. maduro(a) [*madúro*]

melon melón m. [*melón*]; **water -**, sandía f. [*sandía*]

member miembro m. [*mjémbro*]

membrane membrana f. [*membrána*]

memory memoria f. [*memórja*]; **loss of -**, amnesia f. [*amnésja*]

mend (to) arreglar r. [*arreglár*], reparar r. [*rreparár*]; **-ed** a. arreglado(a)

men hombres *pl.* [*ómbres*]; -**'s shop** boutique *f.* de caballeros [*butik de kabaljéros*]; -**'s wear** confección *f.* para caballeros [*konfekθjón pára*]

mental *a.* mental [*mentál*]; -**ity** mentalidad *f.* [*mentalidád*]; -**ly** *adv.* mentalmente [*mentalménte*]

mention (to) mencionar *r.* [*menθjonár*]

menu menú *m.* [*menú*], minuta *f.* [*minúta*]; **today's** -, menú del día [*menú del día*]; **tourist** -, menú turístico [*menú turístiko*]

mercerised: - silk, sedalina *f.* [*sedalína*]

merchan/dise mercancía *f.* [*merkanθía*], género *m.* [*xénero*]; -**t** comerciante *m.* [*komerθjánte*]

mercury mercurio *m.* [*merkúrjo*]

mere *a.* mero(a) [*méro*], simple [*símple*]; -**ly** *ad.* simplemente [*simplaménte*]

meringue merengue *m.* [*merénge*]

merriment diversión *f.* [*dibersjón*]

merry *a.* divertido(a) [*dibertído*]; alegre [*alégre*]; **to make** -, divertirse (ie) [*dibertírse*]; **m.-go-round** tiovivo *m.* [*tjobíbo*]

mesh engranaje *m.* [*engranáxe*]

mess/age mensaje *m.* [*mensáxe*], recado *m.* [*rrekádo*]; -**enger** mensajero(a) *m.-f.* [*mensaxéro*]

metabol/ic *a.* metabólico(a) [*metabólika*]; -**ism** metabolismo *m.* [*metabolísmo*]

metal metal *m.* [*metál*]; **of** -, de metal [*de*]; - **badges** insignias *f. pl.* metálicas [*insígnjas metálikas*]; -**lic** *a.* metálico(a) [*metáliko*]; -**work** objetos *m. pl.* de metal [*obxétos de metál*]

meteorolog/ical *a.* meteorológico(a) [*meteorolóxiko*]; -**y** meteorología *f.* [*meteoroloxía*]

meter contador *m.* [*kontadór*]; **gas** -, contador de gas [*de gas*]; **electricity** -, contador eléctrico [*eléktriko*]; **parking** - parquímetro *m.* [*parkímetro*]

metre metro *m.* [*métro*]; **cubic** -, metro cúbico [*kúbiko*]; **square** -, metro cuadrado [*kwadrádo*]

metropolitan *a.* metropolitano(a) [*metropolitáno*]

micro/phone micrófono [*mikrófono*]; -**wave** microonda *f.* [*mikroónda*]; - **oven**, microondas *m.* [*mikroóndas*]

mid *a.* medio(a) [*médjo*]; -**day** mediodía *m.* [*médjodía*]; **at** -, al mediodía [*al*]

middle medio *m.* [*médjo*]; **in the** - **of,** en medio de [*en médjo de*] ‖ **2. in** the - **of May,** a mediados de mayo [*a medjádos de májo*]

midnight medianoche *f.* [*medjanótche*]; **at** -, a medianoche [*a*]

migraine jaqueca *f.* [*xakéka*]

mild *a.* templado(a) [*templádo*] (climate), suave [*swábe*] (taste, etc.); -**ness** suavidad *f.* [*swabidád*]

mile milla *f.* [*mílja*]; **nautical** -, milla *f.* marina [*mílja marína*]; -**age** kilometraje *m.* [*kilometráxe*]

milk leche *f.* [*létche*]; **condensed** -, leche condensada [*kondensáda*]; **fresh** -, leche fresca [*fréska*]; - **of almonds,** leche de almendras [*de alméndras*]; - **of crushed almonds,** horchata *f.* de almendras [*ortcháta de alméndras*]; - **of crushed tiger nuts**, horchata de chufa [*de tchúfa*]; **powdered** -, leche *f.* en polvo [*létche en pólbo*]; **skimmed** -, leche descremada (desnatada) [*létche deskremáda (desnatáda)*]; - **without cream** leche *f.* descremada [*létche deskremáda*] - **chocolate** chocolate *m.* con leche [*tchokoláte kon létche*]; -**man** repartidor *m.* de leche [*repartidór de létche*]; - **products** productos *m. pl.* lácteos [*prodúktos lákteos*]; - **shake** batido *m.* [*batído*]

mill (to) moler (ue) [*molér*] ‖ **2.** *n.* molino *m.* [*molíno*], molinillo *m.* [*moliníljo*] (coffee)

millimetre milímetro *m.* [*milímetro*]

million millón *m.* [*miljón*]

milometer cuentakilómetros *m.* [*kwentakilómetros*]

minced *a.* picado(a) [*pikádo*]; - **meat** carne *f.* picada [*kárne*]

mind mente *f.* [*ménte*]

mine *pron. pos.* mío(a) [*mío*]; **a friend of** -, un amigo mío [*un amígo mío*]

mineral *a.* mineral [*minerál*]; - **water** agua *f.* mineral [*água minerál*]; - **still** -, agua mineral sin gas [*sin gas*]; **sparkling** -, agua mineral con gas [*kon gas*]

miniature miniatura *f.* [*minjatúra*]; **in** -, en miniatura [*en minjatúra*]; - **golf** minigolf *m.* [*minigólf*]

mini/bus microbús *m.* [*mikrobús*]; -**mum** *a.* mínimo(a) [*mínimo*] ‖ **2.** *n.* mínimo *m.* [*mínimo*]; - **speed,** velocidad *f.* mínima [*beloθidád mínima*]; -**skirt** minifalda *f.* [*minifálda*]

mink visón *m.* [*bisón*]; - **coat** abrigo *m.* de visón [*abrígo de*]

minor *a.* menor [*menór*], más pequeño(a) [*mas pekénjo*]

Minorca Menorca *f.* [*menórka*]; **-n** *a.* menorquín (menorquina) [*menorkín*] ‖ **2.** *n.* menorquín (menorquina) *m.-f.* [*menorkín*]

minority minoría *f.* [*minoría*]

mint menta *f.* [*ménta*]; *infusion of -*, infusión *f.* de menta [*infusjón de*]

minus *prep.-a.* menos [*ménos*] (math.) ‖ **2.** *- two degrees*, dos grados bajo cero [*dos grádos báxo θéro*]

minute minuto *m.* [*minúto*] ‖ **2.** nota *f.* [*nóta*], minuta *f.* [*minúta*]

mirror espejo *m.* [*espéxo*]; *driving -*, retrovisor *m.* [*rretrobisór*]

miss señorita *f.* [*senjoríta*]

mist niebla *f.* [*njébla*]

mister señor *m.* [*senjór*]

mix (to) mezclar *r.* [*meθklár*] ‖ **2.** *n.* mezcla *f.* [*méθkla*]; **-ed** *a.* surtido(a) [*surtído*], variado(a) [*barjádo*]; **-er** batidora *f.* [*batidóra*]

mobile *a.* móvil [*móbil*]; *- home* caravana *f.* [*karabána*]

moccasin mocasín *m.* [*mokasín*]

mode moda *f.* [*móda*]; **-l** modelo *m.-f.* [*modélo*]

modern *a.* moderno(a) [*modérno*]; **-ism** modernismo *m.* [*modernísmo*]; **-ist** *a.* modernista [*modernísta*]

modi/fication modificación *f.* [*modifikaθjón*]; **-fy (to)** modificar *r.* [*modifikár*]

module módulo *m.* [*módulo*]

moist *a.* húmedo(a) [*úmedo*], mojado(a) [*moxádo*]; **-ure** humedad *f.* [*umedád*]

mollusc molusco *m.* [*molúsko*]

moment momento *m.* [*moménto*]; *at the -*, en este momento [*en éste*]; *in a -*, dentro de un momento [*déntro de un*]

monastery monasterio *m.* [*monastérjo*]

Monday lunes *m.* [*lúnes*]

money dinero *m.* [*dinéro*]; **-box** hucha *f.* [*útcha*]; *- order* giro *m.* postal [*xíro postál*]

monitor monitor *m.* [*monitór*]

month mes *m.* [*mes*]; **-ly** *a.* mensual [*menswál*] ‖ **2.** *adv.* mensualmente [*menswalménte*]

monument monumento *m.* [*monuménto*]

moorish: *- gun*, espingarda *f.* [*espingárda*]

mop fregona *f.* [*fregóna*]

moped vespino *m.* [*bespíno*]

more *a.-adv.* más [*mas*]; *- than a thousand...*, más de mil... [*mas de mil*]; *- than you*, más que tú [*mas ke tu*]

morning mañana *f.* [*manjána*]; *good -*, buenos días [*buénos días*]

mortal *a.* mortal [*mortál*]

mortar mortero *m.* [*mortéro*]

mosaic mosaico *m.* [*mosáiko*]

mosquito mosquito *m.* [*moskíto*]

most *a.* la mayoría de [*la mayoría de*]; *- people*, la mayoría de la gente [*de la xénte*]

mother madre *f.* [*mádre*]; **m.-in law** madre política [*polítika*]; suegra *f.* [*swégra*] (fam.); **m.-of pearl** nácar *m.* [*nákar*]; **m.-to-be** futura mamá *f.* [*futúra mamá*]

motor motor *m.* [*motór*]; **-bike** moto *f.* [*móto*]; **-boat** lancha *f.* (motora) [*lántcha motóra*]; **-cycling** motorismo *m.* [*motorísmo*]; **-ing** automovilismo *m.* [*automobilísmo*]; **-ist** automovilista *m.* [*automobilísta*]; *- racing* carreras *f.pl.* de coches [*karréras de kótches*], automovilismo *m.* [*automobilísmo*]; **-way** autopista *f.* [*autopísta*]

mould molde *m.* [*mólde*]

mountain montaña *f.* [*montánja*]; *- climber* alpinista *m.* [*alpinísta*]; **-eering** alpinismo *m.* [*alpinísmo*]; *- face* pared *f.* [*paréd*]; *- hut* refugio *m.* de montaña [*rrefúxjo de montánja*]; **-ous** *a.* montañoso(a) [*montanjóso*]; *- view* vista *f.* a la montaña [*bísta a la*]

mounting montura *f.* [*montúra*]

moustache bigote *m.* [*bigóte*]

mouth boca *f.* [*bóka*]; **-piece** boquilla *f.* [*bokílja*]

move (to) mover(se) (ue) [*mobérse*]; **-d** *a.* movido(a) [*mobído*]; **-ment** movimiento *m.* [*mobimjénto*]

movie película *f.* [*pelíkula*]; *- camera* cámara *f.* de filmar [*kámara de filmár*]

moving *a.* en movimiento [*en mobimjénto*], en marcha [*en mártcha*]; *- staircase* escalera *f.* mecánica [*eskaléra mekánika*]

much *a.* mucho(a) [*mútcho*] ‖ **2.** *adv.* mucho [*mútcho*]

mud barro *m.* [*bárro*]; **-guards** guardabarros *m. pl.* [*gwardabárros*]

mullet mújol *m.* [*múxol*]; *red -*, salmonete *m.* [*salmonéte*]

multi/coloured *a.* policromado(a) [*polikromádo*]; **-national** *a.* multinacional [*multinaθjonál*]

multi/ple *a.* múltiple [*múltiple*]; **-ply (to)** multiplicar *r.* [*multiplikár*] (by/por); **-purpose** *a.* (de) multiuso [*(de) multiúso*]; **-tude** multitud *f.* [*multitúd*]

mural mural *m.* [*murál*], pintura *f.* mural [*pintúra*]

muscatel moscatel *m.* [*moskatél*]

muscle músculo *m.* [*múskulo*]

muscular *a.* muscular [*muskulár*]

museum museo *m.* [*muséo*]

mushroom champiñón *m.* [*tchampinjón*], seta *f.* [*séta*]; *fried -s,* setas *pl.* fritas [*sétas frítas*]; *grilled -s,* setas a la brasa [*a la brása*]; *-s in garlic,* setas al ajillo [*al axíljo*]

music música *f.* [*músika*]; **-al** *a.* musical [*musikál*]; *- comedy,* zarzuela *f.* [*θarθwéla*]; *- instrument,* instrumento *m.* musical [*instruménto musikál*]; *- box* cajita *f.* de música [*kaxíta de músika*]; *- hall* sala *f.* de espectáculos [*sála de espektákulos*]

musician músico(a) *m.-f.* [*músiko*]

musket mosquete *m.* [*moskéte*]

mussel mejillón *m.* [*mexiljón*], almeja *f.* [*almέxa*]; *-s in brine,* almejas *pl.* al natural [*almέxas al naturál*];

steamed -s, almejas a la marinera [*a la marinéra*]

must *mod. vb.* deber *r.* [*debér*]; tener *irr.* que [*tenér ke*]; *I - pay,* tengo que pagar [*téngo ke pagár*]

mustard mostaza *f.* [*mostáθa*]

mute *a.* mudo(a) [*múdo*] ‖ **2.** *n.* mudo(a) *m.-f.* ‖ **3.** *deaf -,* sordomudo(a) *m.-f.* [*sordomúdo*]

mutton carnero *m.* [*karnéro*], carne *f.* de carnero [*kárne de karnéro*]: *braised -,* carnero guisado [*gisádo*]; *roast -,* carnero asado [*asádo*]; *- chop* chuleta *f.* de carnero [*tchuléta de karnéro*]

mutual *a.* mutuo(a) [*mútwo*], recíproco(a) [*reθíproko*]; **-ly** *adv.* mutuamente [*mutwaménte*]

my *a. pos.* mi(s) [*mi*]; *I wash - hands,* me lavo las manos [*me lábo las mános*]

mytholog/ical *a.* mitológico(a) [*mitolóxiko*]; **-y** mitología *f.* [*mitoloxía*]

N

nail clavo *m*. [*klábo*] ‖ **2.** uña *f*. [*únja*]; **-brush** cepillo *m*. de uñas [*θepíljo de únjas*]; **- clippers** cortaúñas *m*. [*kortaúnjas*]; **-file** lima *f*. de uñas [*líma de únjas*]; **- polish** esmalte *m*. de uñas [*esmálte de únjas*]; **n.-scissors** tijeras *f*. *pl*. para las uñas [*tixéras pára las únjas*]; **- varnish** esmalte *m*. de uñas [*esmálte de*]; **- hardener,** fijaesmalte *m*. [*fixaesmálte*]; **- remover,** quitaesmalte *m*. [*kitaesmálte*]

naked *a*. desnudo(a) [*desnúdo*]

name nombre *m*. [*nómbre*]; apellido *m*. [*apeljído*] (surname) ‖ **2. my - is Pedro,** me llamo Pedro [*me ljámo pédro*]; **what's your -?** ¿cómo te llamas? [*kómo te ljámas*], ¿cómo se llama (Vd.)? [*kómo se ljáma ustéd*]; **- day** santo *m*. [*sánto*], día *m*. de santo [*día de*]

nanny niñera *f*. [*ninjéra*]

nap siesta *f*. [*sjésta*]; **to have a -,** dormir (ue) la siesta [*dormír la*]

napkin servilleta *f*. [*serbiljéta*]

nappy pañal *m*. [*panjál*]; **to change a -,** cambiar un pañal [*kambiár un*]

narcotic narcótico *m*. [*narkótiko*] ‖ **2.** *a*. narcótico(a) [*narkótiko*]

narrow *a*. estrecho(a) [*estrétcho*]

nasal *a*. nasal [*nasál*]

nasty *a*. desagradable [*desagradáble*]

national *a*. nacional [*naθjonál*]; **- park** parque *m*. nacional [*párke naθjonál*]; **-ity** nacionalidad *f*. [*naθjonalidád*]

native *a*. natal [*natál*]; **- language** lengua *f*. materna [*léngua matérna*]

natural *a*. natural [*naturál*]; **- gas** gas *m*. natural [*gas*]; **-ly** *adv*. naturalmente [*naturalménte*], desde luego [*désde lwégo*]

nature naturaleza *f*. [*naturaléθa*]

nausea náuseas *f*. *pl*. [*náuseas*]

nautic(al) *a*. náutico(a) [*náutiko*]; **- mile** milla *f*. marítima [*mílja marítima*]; **- sports** deportes *m*. *pl*. náuticos [*depórtes náutikos*]

naval *a*. naval [*nabál*]

navel ombligo *m*. [*omblígo*]

navi/gable *a*. navegable [*nabegáble*]; **-gate (to)** navegar *r*. [*nabegár*]; **-gation** navegación *f*. [*nabegaθjón*]

navy marina *f*. [*marína*]; **merchant -,** marina mercante [*merkánte*]

near *a*. cercano(a) [*θerkáno*] ‖ **2.** *prep*. cerca de [*θérka de*]; **- here,** cerca de aquí [*de akí*]; **- the coast,** cerca de la costa [*la kósta*]; **-by** *a*. cercano(a) [*θerkáno*]; **-ly** *adv*. casi [*kási*]; **-ness** proximidad *f*. [*proksimidád*], cercanía *f*. [*θerkanía*]; **n.-sighted** *a*. corto(a) de vista [*kórto de bísta*], miope [*miópe*]

necessar/y *a*. necesario(a) [*neθesárjo*]; **-ily** *adv*. necesariamente [*neθesarjaménte*]

neck cuello *m*. [*kwéljo*]; **low -,** escote *m*. [*eskóte*]; **roll -,** cuello *m*. de cisne [*kwéljo de θisne*] ‖ **2.** garganta *f*. [*gargánta*]; **-lace** gargantilla *f*. [*gargantílja*]; **-line** escote *m*. [*eskóte*]

nectar néctar *m*. [*nektár*]; **-ine** nectarina *f*. [*nektarína*]

need (to) necesitar *r*. [*neθesitár*], faltar *r*. [*faltár*] ‖ **2.** *n*. necesidad *f*. [*neθesidád*]

need/le aguja *f*. [*agúxa*], aguja de coser [*de kosér*]; **stocking -,** aguja de hacer media [*de aθér médja*]; **-less** *a*. innecesario(a) [*ineθesárjo*]; inútil [*inútil*]; **-lessly** *adv*. innecesariamente [*ineθesarjaménte*]; inútilmente [*inutilménte*]; **-work** costura *f*. [*kostúra*]

negat/ion negación *f*. [*negaθjón*]; **-ive** *a*. negativo(a) [*negatíbo*]; **in -,** en negativo [*en*] ‖ **2.** *n*. negativo [*negatíbo*] (photo); **-ively** *adv*. negativamente [*negatibaménte*]

negligée salto *m*. de cama [*sálto de káma*]

negro negro(a) *m*.-*f*. [*négro*]

neighbour *a*. vecino(a) [*beθíno*] ‖ **2.** *n*. vecino(a) *m*.-*f*.; **-hood** vecindad [*beθindád*], barrio *m*. [*bárrjo*]

neither *adv*. tampoco [*tampóko*]

nephew sobrino *m*. [*sobríno*]

nerv/e nervio *m*. [*nérbjo*]; **- centre** centro *m*. nervioso [*θéntro nerbjóso*]; **-ous** *a*. nervioso(a) [*nerbjóso*]; **- system,** sistema *m*. nervioso [*sistéma nerbjóso*]; **-ousness** nerviosismo *m*. [*nerbjosísmo*]

net red *f*. [*rred*]; **fishing -,** red de pescar [*rred de peskár*]; **hair -,** redecilla *f*. [*rredeθílja*]; **mosquito -,** mosquitero *m*. [*moskitéro*] ‖ **2.** *a*. neto(a) [*néto*]; **- price,** precio *m*. neto [*préθjo néto*]; **- weight,** peso *m*. neto [*péso*]; **-work** red *f*. [*rred*]; **road -,** red de carreteras [*de karretéras*]

neu/ralgia neuralgia *f*. [*neurálxja*]; **-rosis** neurosis *f*. [*neurósis*]

neuter *a*. neutro(a) [*néwtro*]

never *adv.* nunca [*núnka*], jamás [*xamás*]; **-theless** *adv.* sin embargo [*sin embárgo*]

new *a.* nuevo(a) [*nuébo*]; *a - car,* un coche nuevo [*un kótche*]; **-born** recién *m.* nacido [*reθién naθído*]; **-comer** recién *m.* llegado [*reθién ljegádo*]; **-lyweds** recién *m. pl.* casados [*reθién kasádos*]; **N.-Year** Año *m.* nuevo [*ánjo nuébo*]

news noticias *f. pl.* [*notiθjas*]; **latest -,** actualidades *f. pl.* [*aktwalidádes*]; **- bulletin** noticiario *m.* [*notiθjárjo*]; **-paper** periódico *m.* [*perjódiko*], diario *m.* [*djárjo*] (daily); **- stand,** quiosco *m.* de periódicos [*kjósko de perjódikos*]

next *a.* próximo(a) [*próksimo*], de al lado [*de al ládo*]; **the - house,** la casa de al lado [*la kása de al ládo*], la casa siguiente [*sigjénte*]; **- week,** la semana que viene [*la semána ke bjéne*]; **- door** de al lado [*de al ládo*]

nice *a.* bonito(a) [*boníto*]; **n.-looking** guapo(a) [*gwápo*]

nickname apodo *m.* [*apódo*]

night noche *f.* [*nótche*]; *all -,* toda la noche [*tóda la nótche*]; *at -,* por la noche [*por la nótche*]; *good -!* ¡buenas noches! [*buénas nótches*]; *last -,* anoche [*anótche*]; **-club** club *m.* nocturno [*klub noktúrno*]; **-dress** camisón *m.* [*kamisón*]; **-life** vida *f.* nocturna [*bída noktúrna*]; **-ly** *a.* nocturno(a) [*noktúrno*], de noche [*de nótche*]; **n.-time** noche *f.* [*nótche*]

nine *a.* nueve [*nuébe*]; **-teen** *a.* diecinueve [*djeθinuébe*]; **-ty** *a.* noventa [*nobénta*]

ninth *a.* noveno(a) [*nobéno*]

nip trago *m.* [*trágo*]

no *adv.* no [*no*]; **-body** *pron.* nadie [*nádje*]; **- else,** nadie más [*nádje mas*]

nocturnal *a.* nocturno(a) [*noktúrno*]

nois/e ruido *m.* [*rrwído*]; **-eless** *a.* silencioso(a) [*silenθjóso*]; **-y** *a.* ruidoso(a) [*rrwidóso*]

nominal *a.* nominal [*nominál*]

non-alcoholic *a.* sin alcohol [*sin alkoól*]; **- drink** bebida *f.* sin alcohol [*bebída*]

none *pron.* ninguno(a) [*ningúno*]

nonsense tontería *f.* [*tontería*], disparate *m.* [*disparáte*]

nonstop *a.* sin escala(s) [*sin eskála*]; **- flight** vuelo *m.* sin escala(s) [*buélo sin*]

noodle pasta *f.* (de sopa) [*pásta de sópa*], fideo *m.* [*fidéo*]; **- soup** sopa *f.* de fideos [*sópa de fidéos*]

noon mediodía *f.* [*medjodía*]

no-one *pron.* nadie [*nádje*]

normal *a.* normal [*normál*]; **-ly** *adv.* normalmente [*normalménte*]

north norte *m.* [*nórte*]; **-east** noreste *m.* [*noréste*]; **-ern** del norte [*del nórte*]; **-west** noroeste *m.* [*noroéste*]

nose nariz *f.* [*nariθ*]; **-bleed** hemorragia *f.* nasal [*emorráxja nasál*]

not *adv.* no [*no*]; **he is - here,** no está aquí [*no está akí*]; **- at all,** en absoluto [*en absolúto*]

notary notario *m.* [*notárjo*]

note (to) anotar *r.* [*anotár*], apuntar *r.* [*apuntár*] ‖ **2.** notar *r.* [*notár*] ‖ **3.** *n.* nota *f.* [*nóta*] ‖ **4.** billete *m.* de banco [*biljéte de bánko*]; **-book** cuaderno *m.* [*kwadérno*]; **-case** billetero *m.* [*biljetéro*]

nothing *pron.* nada [*náda*]

notice (to) darse *irr.* cuenta [*dárse kwénta*] (sth/de) ‖ **2.** *n.* aviso *m.* [*abíso*]; **-board** tablón *m.* de anuncios [*tablón de anúnθjos*]

noti/fication aviso *m.* [*abíso*], notificación [*notifikaθjón*]; **- of postal order,** aviso *m.* de giro postal [*de xíro postál*]; **- of telegram,** aviso de telegrama [*de telegráma*]; **-fy (to)** notificar *r.* [*notifikár*]

nougat turrón *m.* [*turrón*]

nourish (to) nutrir *r.* [*nutrír*], alimentar *r.* [*alimentár*]; **-ing** *a.* nutritivo(a) [*nutritíbo*]; **- cream,** crema *f.* nutritiva [*kréma nutritíba*]

novel novela *f.* [*nobéla*]

November noviembre *m.* [*nobjémbre*]; *in -,* en noviembre [*en nobjémbre*]

now *adv.* ahora [*aóra*]; *from - on,* a partir de ahora [*a partír de*]; *right -,* ahora mismo [*mísmo*]; *until -,* hasta ahora [*ásta*]; **-adays** *adv.* actualmente [*aktwalménte*], en la actualidad [*en la aktwalidád*]

nowhere *adv.* en ninguna parte [*en ningúna párte*]

nude *a.* desnudo(a) [*desnúdo*]

number número *m.* [*número*]; **telephone -,** número *m.* de teléfono [*de teléfono*]; **-plate** (placa *f.* de) matrícula *f.* [*pláka de matríkula*]

nuptial *a.* nupcial [*nupθjál*]

nurse enfermera *f.* [*enferméra*] ‖ **2.** niñera *f.* [*ninjéra*]; **-ry** guardería *f.* (infantil) [*gwardería infantíl*]

nut nuez *f.* [*nweθ*]; ***bazel* -,** avellana *f.*
[*abeljána*]; ***pea-s,*** cacahuetes *m. pl.*
[*kakawétes*]; ***salted pea-s,*** cacahuetes
salados [*saládos*]; ***toasted pea-s,***
cacahuetes tostados [*tostádos*]; **-cracker**
cascanueces *m.* [*kaskanwéθes*]; **-meg**

nuez *f.* moscada [*nweθ moskáda*] ‖ **2.**
tuerca *f.* [*twérka*] (mechanical)
nutrition nutrición *f.* [*nutriθjón*], alimentación *f.* [*alimentaθjón*]
nutshell cáscara *f.* [*káskara*]
nylon nilón *m.* [*nilón*]

O

oak roble *m.* [*rróble*]: **cork -,** alcornoque *m.* [*alkornóke*]; **- wood,** robledal *m.* [*robledál*]

oar remo *m.* [*rrémo*], pala *f.* de remo [*pála de*]; **-man** remero *m.* [*reméro*]; **-woman** remera *m.* [*reméra*]

oat avena *f.* [*abéna*]; **-meal** harina *f.* de avena [*arína de*]; **-s** copos *m. pl.* de avena [*kópos de*]

obelisk obelisco *m.* [*obelísko*]

obes/e *a.* obeso(a) [*obéso*]; **-ity** obesidad *f.* [*obesidád*]

object objeto *m.* [*obxéto*], cosa *f.* [*kósa*]; **-ion** objeción *f.* [*obxeθjón*]; **-ive** objetivo *m.* [*obxetíbo*]; **-or** objetor *m.* [*obxetór*]; **conscientious -,** objetor de conciencia [*obxetór de konθjénθja*]

obligat/ion obligación *f.* [*obligaθjón*]; **-ory** *a.* obligatorio(a) [*obligatórjo*]

oblige (to) obligar *r.* [*obligár*] (to do/a hacer)

oblique *a.* oblicuo(a) [*oblíkwo*], inclinado(a) [*inklinádo*]; **-ly** *adv.* oblicuamente *m.* [*oblikwaménte*]

obscur/e *a.* oscuro [*oskúro*]; **-ity** *n.* oscuridad *f.* [*oskuridád*]

observ/ation observación *f.* [*obserbaθjón*]; **- balloon,** globo *m.* sonda [*glóbo sónda*]; **-atory** observatorio *m.* [*obserbatórjo*]; **-e (to)** observar *r.* [*obserbár*]

obstacle obstáculo *m.* [*obstákulo*]; **- race,** carrera *f.* de obstáculos [*karréra de*]

obtain (to) obtener *irr.* [*obtenér*], conseguir [*konsegír*]

obvious *a.* evidente [*ebidénte*], obvio(a) [*óbjo*]

occasion ocasión *f.* [*okasjón*]; **-al** *a.* eventual [*ebentwál*]; **-ally** *adv.* en ocasiones [*en okasjónes*], ocasionalmente [*okasjonalménte*]

occu/pant inquilino(a) *m.-f.* [*inkilíno*] (house, etc.); **-pation** ocupación *f.* [*okupaθjón*]; **-py (to)** ocupar *r.* [*okupár*]

occur (to) ocurrir *r.* [*okurrír*], suceder *r.* [*suθedér*]

ocean océano *m.* [*oθéano*]

o'clock *adv.*, **it's one -,** es la una [*es la úna*]; **it's ten -,** son las diez [*son las djeθ*]; **at one (ten) o'clock,** a la una (a las diez) [*a la úna (a las djeθ)*]

October octubre *m.* [*oktúbre*]; **in -,** en octubre [*en*]

octopus pulpo *m.* [*púlpo*]: **baby -,** pulpito *m.* [*pulpíto*]

odontologist *n.* dentista [*dentísta*], odontólogo(a) [*odontólogo*]

odor olor *m.* [*olór*]; **-iferous** *a.* oloroso(a) [*oloróso*]; **-less** inodoro(a) [*inodóro*]

of *prep.* de [*de*]; **a bottle - beer,** una botella de cerveza [*(úna botélja) de θerbéθa*]

offal menudillos *m. pl.* [*menudíljos*], asaduras *f. pl.* [*asadúras*]; **- shop** tienda *f.* de despojos [*tjénda de despóxos*]

offens/e infracción *m.* [*infrakθjón*], delito *m.* [*delíto*]; **- ive** *a.* ofensivo(a) [*ofensíbo*], insultante [*insultánte*]

offer (to) ofrecer (zc) [*ofreθér*] ‖ **2.** *Com.* ofertar *r.* [*ofertár*] ‖ **3.** ofrecimiento *m.* [*ofreθimjénto*] ‖ **4.** *Com.* oferta *f.* [*oférta*]

offic/e oficina *f.* [*ofiθína*], despacho *m.* [*despátcho*]; **- hours** horas *f. pl.* de oficina [*óras de ofiθína*]; **-er** oficial *m.-f.* [*ofiθjál*]; **customs -,** aduanero(a) *m.-f.* [*adwanéro*] ‖ **2.** *a.* oficial [*ofiθjál*]

often *adv.* a menudo [*a menúdo*]

oil aceite *m.* [*aθéite*]: **olive -,** aceite de oliva [*de olíba*]; **-can** aceitera *f.* [*aθejtéra*]; **- consumption** consumo *m.* de aceite [*konsúmo de*]; **- filter** filtro *m.* de aceite [*fíltro de*]; **- level** nivel *m.* de aceite [*nibél de*]; **- painting** cuadro *m.* al óleo [*kwádro al óleo*] ‖ **2.** *vb.* **(to)** engrasar *r.* [*engrasár*], lubricar *r.* [*lubrikár*]; **-y** *a.* aceitoso(a) [*aθeitóso*]

ointment ungüento *m.* [*ungwénto*], pomada *f.* [*pomáda*]

okay *interj.* está bien [*está bjen*], de acuerdo [*de akwérdo*]

old *a.* viejo(a) [*bjéxo*] ‖ **2. to be twenty years -,** tener veinte años [*tenér béinte ánjos*]; **how - is he?** ¿qué edad tiene? [*ke edád tjéne*] ‖ **3.** antiguo(a) [*antígwo*]; **-er** *a.* mayor [*majór*]; **o.-fashioned** *a.* anticuado(a) [*antikwádo*], pasado(a) de moda [*pasádo de móda*]

olive aceituna *f.* [*aθeitúna*]: **black -s,** aceitunas *pl.* negras [*négras*]; **green -s,** aceitunas verdes [*bérdes*]; **stuffed -s,** aceitunas rellenas [*rreljénas*]; **-s with stones,** aceitunas con hueso [*kon wéso*]

omelette tortilla *f.* [*tortílja*]: **asparagus -,** tortilla de espárragos [*de espá-*

rragos]; **French -,** tortilla francesa [*franθésa*]; **ham -,** tortilla de jamón [*de xamón*]; **pea -,** tortilla de guisantes [*de gisántes*]; **Spanish -,** tortilla de patatas [*de patátas*], tortilla a la española [*a la espanjóla*]; **spinach -,** tortilla de espinacas [*de espinákas*].

on *prep.* en [*en*], sobre [*sóbre*], encima de [*enθíma de*] ‖ **2.** *Temp.* **- Friday,** el viernes [*el bjérnes*]; **- May 5th,** el cinco de mayo [*el θínko de májo*]

once *adv.* una vez [*úna beθ*] ‖ **2. at -,** en seguida [*en segída*]

one *a.* un(a) [*un*] ‖ **2.** *pron.* uno(a) [*úno*]; **o.-way** de dirección única [*de direkθjón únika*] (street); de ida [*de ída*] (ticket)

onion cebolla *f.* [*θebólja*]; **- soup** sopa *f.* de cebolla [*sópa de θebólja*]

only *a.* único(a) [*úniko*] ‖ **2.** *adv.* sólo [*sólo*], solamente [*solaménte*]

opal ópalo *m.* [*ópalo*]

opaque *a.* opaco(a) [*opáko*]

open (to) abrir *r.* [*abrír*] ‖ **2.** *a.* abierto(a) [*abjérto*]; **to be -,** estar *irr.* abierto(a) [*estár abjérto*]; **- air** *a.* al aire libre [*al áire líbre*]; **- ticket,** billete *m.* abierto [*biljéte abjérto*]; **-ing** apertura *f.* [*apertúra*]

opera ópera *f.* [*ópera*]; **ligth -,** opereta *f.* [*operéta*]; **- glasses** gemelos *m. pl.* [*xemélos*]; **- house** teatro *m.* de la ópera [*teátro de la ópera*]

operat/e (to) funcionar *r.* [*funθjonár*] ‖ **2.** *Med.* operar *r.* [*operár*] ‖ **3.** accionar *r.* [*akθjonár*], hacer *irr.* funcionar [*aθér funθjonár*]; **-ion** funcionamiento *m.* [*funθjonamjénto*] ‖ **4.** *Med.* operación *f.* [*operaθjón*]; **-or** operador(a) *m.-f.* [*operadór*], telefonista *m.-f.* [*telefonísta*]

ophthalmologist oftalmólogo(a) *m.-f.* [*oftalmólogo*], oculista *m.-f.* [*okulísta*]

opinion opinión *f.* [*opinjón*]; **- poll,** sondeo *m.* de opinión [*sondéo de*], encuesta [*enkuésta*]

opium opio *m.* [*ópjo*]

opportun/e *a.* oportuno(a) [*oportúno*]; **-ity** oportunidad *f.* [*oportunidád*]

optic/al *a.* óptico(a) [*óptiko*]; **-s** óptica *f.* [*óptika*]

or *conj.* o (u) [*o*]

orange naranja *f.* [*naránxa*]; **- juice** zumo *m.* de naranja [*θúmo de*] ‖ **2.** *a.* de color naranja [*de kolór naránxa*]; **-ade** naranjada *f.* [*naranxáda*]

orchestra orquesta *f.* [*orkésta*]

orchid orquídea *f.* [*orkídea*]

order (to) pedir (i) [*pedír*], encargar *r.* [*enkargár*] ‖ **2.** *n.* orden *m.* [*órden*] ‖ **3.** pedido *m.* [*pedído*], encargo *m.* [*enkárgo*]

ordinary *a.* corriente [*korrjénte*]

oregano orégano *m.* [*orégano*]

organ órgano *m.* [*órgano*]; **-ic** *a.* orgánico(a) [*orgániko*]; **-ize (to)** organizar *r.* [*organiθár*]; **-ization** organización *f.* [*organiθaθjón*]

orgasm orgasmo *m.* [*orgásmo*]

origin origen *m.* [*órigen*], procedencia *f.* [*proθedénθja*]; **country of -,** país *m.* de origen [*país de oríxen*]; **-al** *a.* original [*orixinál*]

ornament ornamento *m.* [*ornaménto*]; **-al** *a.* ornamental [*ornamentál*]

orthopaedics ortopedia *f.* [*ortopédja*]

other *a.* otro(a) [*ótro*]; **-wise** *adv.* de otra manera [*de ótra manéra*]

ounce onza *f.* [*ónθa*]

our *pron. a. pos.* nuestro(a) [*nuéstro*]

out *adv.* fuera [*fuéra*], afuera [*afuéra*]; **- of focus,** desenfocado(a) [*desenfokádo*]; **-board** fueraborda *m.* [*fuerabórda*]; **-dated** *a.* anticuado(a) [*antikwádo*]; **-fit** equipo *m.* [*ekípo*]; **-fitter's** tienda *f.* de confección para caballeros [*tjénda de konfekθjón pára kabaljéros*]; **-side** *a.* exterior [*eksterjór*] ‖ **2.** *prep.* fuera de [*fuéra de*]; **- the building,** fuera del edificio [*fuéra del edifíθjo*]; **-skirts** afueras *f. pl.* [*afuéras*]; **-standing** *a.* destacado(a) [*destakádo*]; **-ward** *a.* exterior [*eksterjór*]; **- journey,** viaje *m.* de ida *f.* [*bjáxe de ída*]

oval *a.* ovalado(a) [*obaládo*]

oven horno *m.* [*órno*]

over *prep.* arriba de [*arríba de*], por encima de [*por enθíma de*] ‖ **2.** más de [*mas de*] (more); **-all** bata *f.* [*báta*]; **-s** mono *m.* [*móno*]; **-cast** *a.* nublado(a) [*nubládo*]; **-coat** abrigo *m.* [*abrígo*]; **-done** *a.* muy hecho(a) [*mui étcho*], demasiado cocido(a) [*demasjádo koθído*]; **-dose** sobredosis *f.* [*sobredósis*]; **-eat (to)** comer *r.* demasiado [*komér demasjádo*]; **-exposed** *a.* quemado(a) [*kemádo*], **-night** *adv.* por la noche [*por la nótche*]; **-seas** ultramar *m.* [*ultramár*]; **-shoe** chanclo *m.* [*tchánklo*]; **-sized** *a.* demasiado grande [*demasjádo gránde*]; **-take (to)** adelantar *r.* [*adelantár*] (car)

owe (to) deber *r.* [*debér*] (to/a), adeudar *r.* [*adeudár*] (to/a)

own (to) poseer *r.* [*poseér*] ‖ **2.** *a.* propio(a) [*própjo*]; **-er** propietario(a) *m.-f.* [*propjetárjo*], dueño(a) *m.-f.* [*duénjo*]

ox buey *m.* [*buei*]; **-tail** rabo *m.* de buey [*rrábo de*]

oxide óxido *m.* [*óksido*]

oxygen oxígeno *m.* [*oksíxeno*]: **- mask,** mascarilla *f.* de oxígeno [*maskarílja de*]; **-ated** *a.* oxigenado(a) [*oksixenádo*]: **- water,** agua *f.* oxigenada [*ágwa oksixenáda*]

oyster ostra *f.* [*óstra*]

P

pace marcha *f.* [*mártcha*], velocidad *f.* [*belobidád*]; **-maker** marcapasos *m.* [*markapásos*] (Med.)

pack (to) empaquetar *r.* [*empaketár*], embalar *r.* [*embalár*] ‖ **2.** hacer *irr.* (la maleta) [*aθer la maléta*] (suitcase) ‖ **3.** *n.* bulto *m.* [*búlto*], mochila *f.* [*motchíla*]; **-age** paquete *m.* [*pakéte*], bulto *m.* [*búlto*]; **-et** paquete *m.* [*pakéte*]: **- of cigarettes,** paquete de cigarillos [*de θigarríljos*]; **- of potato chips,** bolsa *f.* de patatas fritas [*bólsa de patátas frítas*]; **- soup** sopa *f.* de sobre [*sópa de sóbre*]

pad almohadilla *f.* [*almoadílja*] ‖ **2.** zapata *f.* [*θapáta*] (break): **shoulder -,** hombrera *f.* [*ombréra*]

paddle pala *f.* [*pála*], remo *m.* [*rrémo*]

paediatrician pediatra *m.-f.* [*pedjátra*]

page (to) llamar *r.* por altavoz [*ljamár por altaboθ*] ‖ **2.** *n.* botones *m.* [*botónes*] (club) ‖ **3.** página *f.* [*páxina*]; **-ant** desfile *m.* [*desfíle*], cabalgata *f.* [*kabalgáta*] (on horses): **-boy** botones *m.* [*botónes*] (hotel)

pain dolor *m.* [*dolór*]; **-ful** *a.* doloroso(a) [*doloróso*]; **-killer** calmante *m.* [*kalmánte*]

paint pintura *f.* [*pintúra*]: **coat of -,** capa *f.* de pintura [*kápa de pintúra*]; **-brush** pincel *m.* [*pinθél*], brocha *f.* [*brótcha*] (wall); **-er** pintor *m.* [*pintór*]; **-ing** pintura *f.* [*pintúra*]: **oil -,** pintura al óleo [*al óleo*]; **- remover** quitapinturas *m.* [*kitapintúras*]

pair par *m.* [*par*]: **a - of,** un par de [*un par de*] (shoes) ‖ **2.** pareja *f.* [*paréxa*] (persons)

palace palacio *m.* [*paláθjo*]

palate paladar *m.* [*paladár*]

pale *a.* pálido(a) [*pálido*] ‖ **2.** claro(a) [*kláro*] (colour) ‖ **3.** rubio(a) [*rrúbjo*] (beer, etc.)

palette paleta *f.* [*paléta*]; **- knife** espátula *f.* [*espátula*]

palm palma *f.* [*pálma*]; **- tree** palmera *f.* [*palméra*] ‖ **2.** palma *f.* [*pálma*] (hand)

pan cacerola *f.* [*kaθeróla*], cazuela *f.* [*kaθwéla*] ‖ **2. frying -,** sartén *f.* [*sartén*] ‖ **3. pots and -s,** batería *f.* (de cocina) [*batería (de koθína)*]; **-cake** crepe *f.* [*krep*]

panel panel *m.* [*panél*] ‖ **2.** tablero *m.* [*tabléro*] (control, etc.) ‖ **3. - beater's,** chapistería *f.* [*tchapistería*]

panoram/a panorama *m.* [*panoráma*]; **-ic** *a.* panorámico(a) [*panorámiko*]

pansy pensamiento *m.* [*pensamjénto*]

panties bragas *f.pl.* [*brágas*]

pantry despensa *f.* [*despénsa*]

paper papel *m.* [*papél*]: **toilet -,** papel higiénico [*papél ixjéniko*]; **writing -,** papel de carta [*papél de kárta*] ‖ **2.** periódico *m.* [*perjódiko*] (newspaper): **- in rústica** [*en rrústika*]; **-clip** sujetapapeles *m.* [*suxetapapéles*]; **-s** papeles *m. pl.* [*papéles*], documentos *m.pl.* [*dokuméntos*]: **identity -,** documentación *f.* [*dokumentaθjón*]; **- towel** toallita *f.* de papel [*toaljíta de papél*]

paprika pimentón *m.* [*pimentón*]

parade desfile *m.* [*desfíle*]: **fashion -,** desfile de moda [*de móda*]

paraffin parafina *f.* [*parafína*]; **- lamp** lámpara *f.* de petróleo [*lámpara de petróleo*]

parallel *a.* paralelo(a) [*paralélo*] (to/con, a)

paraly/se (to) paralizar *r.* [*paraliθár*]; **-sis** parálisis *f.* [*parálisis*]; **-tic** *a.* paralítico(a) [*paralítiko*]

parasite parásito *m.* [*parásito*]

parasol sombrilla *f.* [*sombrílja*], parasol *m.* [*parasól*]

parcel paquete *m.* [*pakéte*]

parchment pergamino *m.* [*pergamíno*]

pardon (to) perdonar *r.* [*perdonár*] ‖ **2.** *n.* perdón *m.* [*perdón*]

parents padres *m.pl.* [*pádres*]

parish parroquia *f.* [*parrókja*]

park (to) aparcar *r.* [*aparkár*] ‖ **2.** *n.* parque *m.* [*párke*]: **amusement -,** parque de atracciones [*párke de atrakθjónes*]; **-ing** aparcamiento *m.* [*aparkamjénto*]: **- attendant,** guardacoches *m.* [*gwardacótches*]; **- lights,** luces *f.pl.* de posición [*lúθes de posiθjón*]; **no -!** ¡prohibido aparcar! [*proibído aparkár*]; **-meter** parquímetro *m.* [*parkímetro*]

Parmesan: - cheese, queso *m.* parmesano [*késo parmesáno*]

parsley perejil *m.* [*perexíl*]

parquet parqué *m.* [*parké*]

part parte *f.* [*párte*]: **a - of,** (una) parte de [*úna parte de*] ‖ **2.** pieza *f.* [*pjéθa*]: **spare -,** pieza de repuesto [*de rrepwésto*] ‖ **3.** papel *m.* [*papél*] (theatre); **-ial** *a.* parcial [*parθjál*]; **-ially** *adv.* parcialmente [*parθjalménte*]

participat/e (to) participar *r.* [*partiθi-pár*] (in/en); **-ion** participación *f.* [*partiθipaθjón*]

particular *a.* particular [*partikulár*], especial [*espeθjál*]; **-ly** *adv.* particularmente [*particularménte*], especialmente [*espeθjalménte*]

parting raya *f.* [*rrája*]

partly *adv.* en parte [*en párte*], parcialmente [*parθjalménte*]

partner compañero(a) [*kompanjéro*], socio(a) [*sóθjo*]

partridge perdiz *f.* [*perdíθ*]

party fiesta *f.* [*fjésta*]

pass (to) pasar *r.* [*pasár*] ‖ **2.** *n.* puerto *m.* [*pwérto*] (mountain) ‖ **3.** abono *m.* [*abóno*], pase *m.* [*páse*] (bus, etc.); **-age** paso *m.* [*páso*] ‖ **4.** pasaje *m.* [*pasáxe*] (ticket)

passenger pasajero(a) *m.-f.* [*pasaxéro*], viajero(a) [*bjaxéro*]

passing paso *m.* [*páso*] (time, etc.) ‖ **2.** adelantamiento *m.* [*adelantamjénto*] (car)

passport pasaporte *m.* [*pasapórte*]; **- control** control *m.* de pasaportes [*kontról de pasapórtes*]

past pasado *m.* [*pasádo*]; **in the -,** antes [*ántes*], en el pasado [*en el pasádo*] ‖ **2.** *a.* pasado(a) [*pasádo*], anterior [*anterjór*] ‖ **3. it is ten - eight,** son las ocho y diez [*son las ótcho i djéθ*]

paste pasta *f.* [*pásta*]; **tomato -,** tomate *m.* concentrado [*konθentrádo*]

pastel pastel *m.* [*pastél*]; **- drawing** pintura *f.* al pastel [*pintúra al*]

pastille pastilla *f.* [*pastílja*]

pastime pasatiempo *m.* [*pasatjémpo*]

pastry pasteles *m. pl.* [*pastéles*]; pastelería *f.* [*pastelería*]; **- buns** lionesas *f. pl.* [*ljonésas*]

pasty empanada *f.* [*empanáda*]

patch parche *m.* [*pártche*] ‖ **2.** mancha *f.* [*mántcha*]

pâté paté *m.* [*paté*]

patent (leather) charol *m.* [*tcharól*]

paternal *a.* paterno(a) [*patérno*]

path camino *m.* [*kamíno*], sendero *m.* [*sendéro*]

patient paciente *m.-f.* [*paθjénte*]

patina pátina *f.* [*pátina*]

pause pausa *f.* [*páusa*], descanso *m.* [*deskánso*]

pavement pavimento *m.* [*pabiménto*], acera *f.* [*aθéra*]

pavillion pabellón *m.* [*pabeljón*]

paving pavimento *m.* [*pabiménto*]; **-stone** baldosa *f.* [*baldósa*]

pawnshop casa *f.* de empeños [*kása de empénjos*]

pay (to) pagar *r.* [*pagár*]; **to - in,** ingresar *r.* [*ingresár*]; **-day** día *m.* de pago [*día de págo*]; **-ment** pago *m.* [*págo*], cobro *m.* [*kóbro*]; **- in,** imposición *f.* [*imposiθjón*]; **advance -,** anticipo *m.* [*antiθípo*]; **cash -,** pago al contado [*págo al kontádo*]; **-off** liquidación *f.* [*likidaθjón*]

pea guisante *m.* [*gisánte*]

peach melocotón *m.* [*melokotón*]; **-es in syrup,** melocotones *pl.* en almíbar [*melokotónes en almíbar*]; **- jam** mermelada *f.* de melocotón [*mermeláda de*]; **- juice** zumo *m.* de melocotón [*θúmo de*]

peanut cacahuete *m.* [*kakawéte*]; **salted -s,** cacahuetes *pl.* salados [*kakawétes saládos*]; **toasted -s,** cacahuetes tostados [*tostádos*]

pear pera *f.* [*péra*]

pearl perla *f.* [*pérla*]; **string of -s,** collar *m.* de perlas [*koljár de pérlas*]

pedal pedal *m.* [*pedál*]

pedestrian peatón *m.* [*peatón*], peatona *f.* [*peatóna*]; **- crossing** paso *m.* de peatones [*páso de peatónes*]

pedicure pedicura *f.* [*pedikúra*]

peel piel *f.* [*pjel*], corteza *f.* [*kortéθa*]

peg clavija *f.* [*klabíxa*]

pellets perdigones *m.pl.* [*perdigónes*]

pelota pelota *f.* vasca [*pelóta báska*]

pen pluma *f.* [*plúma*]; **ballpoint -,** bolígrafo *m.* [*bolígrafo*]; **fountain -,** pluma *f.* estilográfica [*plúma estilográfika*]

pencil lápiz *m.* [*lápiθ*]

pennant banderín *m.* [*banderín*]

penicillin penicilina *f.* [*peniθilína*]

peninsula península *f.* [*península*]; **the Iberian -,** la Península Ibérica [*la península ibérika*]; **-r** *a.* peninsular [*peninsulár*]

penis pene *m.* [*péne*]

penknife cortaplumas *m.* [*kortaplúmas*]

pension pensión *f.* [*pensjón*]; **-er** jubilado(a) *m.-f.* [*xubiládo*]

penthouse sobreático *m.* [*sobreátiko*]

penultimate *a.* penúltimo(a) [*penúltimo*]

people gente *f.* [*xénte*], personas *f.pl.* [*persónas*]; **- say that...,** dicen que...[*díθen ke*]

pepper pimienta *f.* [*pimjénta*]; **black -,** pimienta negra [*négra*]; **red -,** pimentón *m.* [*pimentón*]; **white -,** pimienta *f.* blanca [*pimjénta blánka*]; **-corn**

pimienta en grano [*en gráno*]; - **mill** molinillo *m.* de pimienta [*moliníljo de pimjénta*]; -**mint** menta *f.* [*ménta*]; **iced -**, granizado *m.* de menta [*graniθáɗo ɗe*]; - **tea** infusión *f.* de menta [*imfusjón de ménta*]

per *prep.* por [*por*]; - **cent,** por cien(to) [*por θjénto*]; - **day,** por día [*por día*]; - **person,** por persona [*por persóna*]; -**centage** porcentaje *m.* [*porθentáxe*]

perch perca *f.* [*pérka*]

perfect *a.* perfecto(a) [*perfékto*]; -**ly** *adv.* perfectamente [*perfektaménte*]; -**ion** perfección *f.* [*perfekθjón*]

perforat/ed *a.* perforado(a) [*perforáɗo*]; -**ion** perforación *f.* [*perforaθjón*]

performance sesión *f.* [*sesjón*], función *f.* [*funθjón*], representación *f.* [*representaθjón*]; **evening -,** sesión *f.* de tarde [*de tárɗe*]; **morning -,** sesión matinal [*matinál*]; **night -,** sesión de noche [*de nótche*]

perfume perfume *m.* [*perfúme*]; - **shop** perfumería *f.* [*perfumería*]; -**ry** perfumería *f.* [*perfumería*]

perhaps *adv.* quizás [*kiθas*], tal vez [*tal beθ*]

period período *m.* [*período*], época *f.* [*époka*]; -**ic** *a.* periódico(a) [*perjóɗiko*]

permanent *a.* permanente [*permanénte*]; - **wave** permanente *f.* [*permanénte*] (hair)

permission permiso *m.* [*permíso*], licencia *f.* [*liθénθja*]

permit (to) permitir *r.* [*permitír*] ‖ **2.** *n.* permiso *m.* [*permíso*]

person persona *f.* [*persóna*], -**al** *a.* personal [*personál*], particular [*partikulár*]; - **documents,** documentación *f.* personal [*dokumentaθjón personál*]; - **effects,** efectos *m. pl.* personales [*eféktos personáles*]; -**ally** *adv.* personalmente [*personalménte*]; -**ality** personalidad *f.* [*personalidáɗ*]; -**nel** personal *m.* [*personál*]

pesetas pesetas *f.pl.* [*pesétas*]

petrol gasolina *f.* [*gasolína*]; **two star -,** gasolina normal [*normál*]; **four star -,** (gasolina) súper *m.* [*súper*]; - **consumption** consumo *m.* de gasolina [*konsúmo ɗe*]; - **engine** motor *m.* de gasolina [*motór ɗe*]; - **pump** bomba *f.* de gasolina [*bómba ɗe*]; - **station** gasolinera *f.* [*gasolinéra*]; estación *f.* de servicio [*estaθjón de serbíθjo*]; - **tank** depósito *m.* de gasolina [*depósito ɗe*]; - **tube** tubo *m.* de gasolina [*túbo ɗe*]

petroleum petróleo *m.* [*petróleo*]

pharmaceutical *a.* farmacéutico(a) [*farmaθéutiko*] ‖ **2.** *n.* fármaco *m.* [*fármako*]

pharmacy farmacia *f.* [*farmáθja*]

pharyn/gitis faringitis *f.* [*farinxítis*]; -**x** faringe *f.* [*farínxe*]

pheasant faisán *m.* [*faisán*]

phone (to) telefonear *r.* [*telefoneár*], llamar *r.* por teléfono [*ljamár por teléfono*] ‖ **2.** *n.* teléfono *m.* [*teléfono*]; - **book,** guía *f.* telefónica [*gía telefónika*]

phonetic *a.* fonético(a) [*fonétiko*]; -**s** fonética *f.* [*fonétika*]

photo foto *f.* [*fóto*]; - **booth,** fotomatón *m.* [*fotomatón*]

photocop/ier fotocopiadora *f.* [*fotokopjaɗóra*]; -**y (to)** fotocopiar *r.* [*fotokopjár*] ‖ **2.** *n.* fotocopia *f.* [*fotokopja*]

photoelectric *a.* fotoeléctrico(a) [*fotoeléktriko*]; - **cell** célula *f.* fotoeléctrica [*θélula*]

photograph (to) fotografiar *r.* [*fotografjár*] ‖ **2.** *n.* foto(grafía) *f.* [*fotografía*]; **to take -s,** sacar *r.* (hacer *irr.*) fotos [*sakár (aθér) fótos*]; -**er** fotógrafo *m.* [*fotógrafo*]; -**ic** *a.* fotográfico(a) [*fotográfiko*]; - **camera,** cámara fotográfica [*kámara fotográfika*]; - **material shop,** tienda *f.* de material fotográfiko [*tjénda de materjál fotográfiko*]; -**y** fotografía *f.* [*fotografía*]

phrase frase *f.* [*fráse*]; - **book** manual *m.* de conversación [*manuál de kombersaθjón*], libro de frases (hechas) [*libro de fráses (étchas)*]

physical *a.* físico(a) [*fisiko*] ‖ **2.** *n.* reconocimiento *m.* médico [*rekonoθimiénto médiko*], chequeo [*tchekéo*]

piano piano *m.* [*pjáno*]; **to play the -,** tocar *r.* el piano [*tokár el pjáno*]

pick (to): - up, recoger *r.* [*rrekoxér*], ir *irr.* a buscar [*ir a buskár*] ‖ **2. to - up the ear-piece,** descolgar (ue) el auricular [*deskolgár el aurikulár*] ‖ **3.** *n.* pico *m.* [*píko*]; **hand -,** piolet *m.* [*pjolét*]; - **axe** piqueta *f.* [*pikéta*]; -**le** escabeche *m.* [*eskabétche*]

picnic merienda *f.* en el campo [*merjénda en el kámpo*], merienda al aire libre [*al áire líbre*]

pictur/e cuadro *m.* [*kuáɗro*] ‖ **2.** foto *f.* [*fóto*], ilustración *f.* [*ilustraθjón*]; - **book** libro *m.* ilustrado [*libro ilustráɗo*]; - **frame** marco *m.* [*márko*]; - **postcard** tarjeta *f.* postal [*tarxéta postál*], postal *f.* [*postál*]; - **slide** diapositiva *f.* [*djapositiba*], transparencia *f.* [*transparénøja*]; **-esque** *a.* pintoresco(a) [*pintorésko*]

pie pastel *m.* [*pastél*]: empanada *f.* [*empanáda*]; empanadilla *f.* [*empanadílja*]: **cheese -,** empanada (empanadilla) de queso [*de késo*]; **meat -,** empanada (empanadilla) de carne [*de kárne*]; **tunny -,** empanada (empanadilla) de atún [*de atún*]

piece pieza *f.* [*pjéøa*], trozo *m.* [*tróøo*]: **- of furniture,** mueble *m.* [*muéble*]

pier embarcadero *m.* [*embarkadéro*], muelle *m.* [*muélje*]

pig cerdo *m.* [*θérdo*] ‖ **2.** lechón *m.* [*letchón*]

pigeon pichón *m.* [*pitchón*], paloma *f.* [*palóma*]

pile (to) amontonar *r.* [*amontonár*] ‖ **2.** *n.* montón *m.* [*montón*] ‖ **3. -fabric,** tela *f.* de rizo [*téla de rríθo*] ‖ **4.** *Arch.* pilar *m.* [*pilár*]; **-d** *a.* amontonado(a) [*amontonádo*]; **- up,** acumulado(a) [*akumuládo*]; **-s** hemorroides *m. pl.* [*emorróides*]

pilgrim peregrino(a) *m.-f.* [*peregríno*]; **-age** peregrinación *f.* [*peregrinaøjón*]

pill píldora *f.* [*píldora*]: **the -,** la píldora (anticonceptiva) [*la píldora (antikonøeptíba)*]; **-box** pastillero *f.* [*pastiljéro*]

pillar pilar *m.* [*pilár*], columna *f.* [*kolúmna*]: **- box,** buzón *f.* [*buθón*]

pillion asiento *m.* trasero [*asjénto traséro*] (Auto)

pilot (to) pilotar *r.* [*pilotár*] ‖ **2.** *n.* piloto *m.* [*pilóto*]

pin alfiler *f.* [*alfilér*]: **drawing -,** chincheta *f.* [*tchintchéta*]; **hair -,** horquilla *f.* [*orkílja*]; **safety -,** imperdible *m.* [*imperdíble*] ‖ **2.** clavija *f.* [*klabíxa*], perno *m.* [*pérno*]

pincers tenazas *f.pl.* [*tenáθas*] ‖ **2.** pinzas *f.pl.* [*pínθas*]

pine pino *m.* [*pino*]; **-apple** piña *f.* [*pínja*]: **- juice,** zumo *m.* de piña [*θúmo de*]; **- nut** piñón *m.* [*pinjón*]

ping-pong ping-pong *m.* [*pingpóng*], tenis *m.* de mesa [*ténis de mésa*]; **- set** juego *m.* de ping-pong [*xwégo de*]

pinion piñón *m.* [*pinjón*]

pink *a.* rosa [*rrósa*], rosado(a) [*rrosádo*] ‖ **2.** *n.* clavelina *f.* [*klabelína*]

pinnace balandro *m.* [*balándro*], bote [*bóte*]

pipe pipa *f.* [*pípa*]: **to smoke a -,** fumar *r.* en pipa [*fumár en pípa*]; **- cleaners** escobillas *f.pl.* de pipa [*eskobíljas de*]; **-line** tubería *f.* [*tubería*]

piping cañería *f.* [*kanjería*] ‖ **2.** cordoncillo *m.* [*kordonθíljo*]

pirogue piragua *f.* [*pirágua*]

piss (to) mear *r.* [*meár*] ‖ **2.** *n.* meada *f.* [*meáda*]

pistachio pistacho *m.* [*pistátcho*]

pistol pistola *f.* [*pistóla*]

piston pistón *m.* [*pistón*], émbolo *m.* [*émbolo*]

pit stalls platea *f.* [*platéa*]

pity lástima *f.* [*lástima*]: **what a -!,** ¡qué lástima! [*ke lástima*]

pivot pivote *m.* [*pibóte*]

pizza pizza *f.* [*pítsa*]

placard cartel *m.* [*kartél*], letrero *m.* [*letréro*]

place plaza *f.* [*pláθa*] ‖ **2.** sitio *m.* [*sítjo*], lugar *m.* [*lugár*]: **- of residence,** domicilio *m.* [*domiθíljo*]: **to take -,** tener *irr.* lugar [*tenér lugár*], celebrarse *r.* [*θelebrárse*]

plain *a.* claro(a) [*kláro*], llano(a) [*ljáno*]: **in - clothes,** de civil [*de θibíl*], de paisano [*de pajsáno*] ‖ **2.** *n.* llanura *f.* [*ljanúra*], llano *m.* [*ljáno*]

plait trenza *f.* [*trénθa*]

plan plano *m.* [*pláno*] ‖ **2.** plan *m.* [*plan*], proyecto *m.* [*projékto*]

plane avión *m.* [*abjón*]

planet planeta *m.* [*planéta*]; **-arium** planetario *m.* [*planetárjo*]

plant (to) plantar *r.* [*plantár*] ‖ **2.** *n.* planta *f.* [*plánta*]: **- pot** maceta *f.* [*maθéta*] ‖ **3.** planta *f.* [*plánta*], fábrica *f.* [*fábrika*] (factory); **-ation** plantación [*plantaθjón*]

plaque placa *f.* [*pláka*]

plaster enyesado *m.* [*enjesádo*] ‖ **2. sticking -,** esparadrapo *m.* [*esparadrápo*]

plastic plástico *m.* [*plástiko*] ‖ **2.** *a.* de plástico [*de plástiko*]; **- surgery** cirugía *f.* estética [*θirugía estética*]

plasticine plastilina *f.* [*plastilína*]

plate plato *m.* [*pláto*]: **dinner -,** plato llano [*ljáno*]: **quarter -,** plato de postre [*de póstre*]; **soup -,** plato de sopa [*de sópa*] ‖ **2.** placa *f.* [*pláka*]: **number -,** matrícula *f.* [*matríkula*] (car)

platform plataforma *f.* [*platafórma*] ‖ **2.** andén *m.* [*andén*]

platinum platino *m.* [*platíno*]; **-blonde** *a.* rubio platino [*rrúbjo platíno*]

play (to) jugar (ue) [*xugár*] ‖ **2.** *n.* juego *m.* [*xwégo*]; **-er** jugador *m.* [*xugadór*]; **-room** cuarto *m.* de juego [*kwárto de xwégo*]‖ **3.** *n.* obra *f.* de teatro [*óbra* de teatro] (theatre); **-bill** cartel m. [kártel]; **-house** teatro m. [teátro]

pleasant a. agradable [agradáble]

pleas/e (to) gustar r. [gustár] || **2.** adv. por favor [por fabór]; **-ed** a. contento(a) [konténto], satisfecho(a) [satisfétcho]: **to be -,** estar irr. contento [estár konténto] (with/con); **-ing** a. grato(a) [gráto], agradable [agradáble]; **-ure** gusto m. [gústo], placer m. [plaθér]; **- boat,** barco m. de recreo [bárko de rrekréo]; **- ground,** parque m. de atracciones [párke de atrakθjónes]

pleat pliegue m. [pljége], doblez f. [dobléθ]; **-ed** a. plisado(a) [plisádo]

plenty abundancia f. [abundánθja] || **2.** pron. muchos(as) [mútchos]; **- of** muchos(as) [mútchos]

plimsoll zapatilla f. [θapatílja], playera f. [plajéra], tenis m. [ténis]

plot parcela f. [parθéla], solar m. [solár] (building)

plug bujía f. [buxía] (car) || **2.** enchufe m. [entchúfe]: **to -,** enchufar r. [entchufár] || **3.** tapón m. [tapón]; **-hole** desagüe m. [deságwe]

plum ciruela f. [θirwéla]; **- jam** mermelada f. de ciruela [mermeláda de]; **- juice** zumo m. de ciruela [θúmo de]

plumb/er fontanero(a) m.-f. [fontanéro]; **-ing** fontanería f. [fontanería]

plunge (to) zambullirse r. [θambuljírse] || **2.** n. chapuzón m. [tchapuθón], zambullida f. [θambuljída]

plus adv. más [mas]

pneumatic a. neumático(a) [neumátiko]; **- brakes** frenos m. pl. neumáticos [frénos neumátikos]; **- gun** fusil m. neumático [fusíl neumátiko]

pneumonia neumonía f. [neumonía]

poach (to) escalfar r. [eskalfár], cocer a fuego lento [koθér a fwégo lénto]: **-ed egg,** huevo m. escalfado [wébo eskalfádo]

pocket bolsillo m. [bolsíljo]; **- book** libro m. de bolsillo [líbro de]; **- handkerchief** pañuelo m. de bolsillo [panjwélo de]; **-knife** navaja f. [nabáxa]

poe/m poesía f. [poesía], **-t** poeta m.-f. [poéta]; **-try** poesía f. [poesía]

point punto m. [púnto]; **- of sale** punto de venta [de bénta], **-s** platinos m. pl. [platínos] (of a car)

pointed a. en punta [en púnta], puntiagudo(a) [puntiagúdo]

poison (to) envenenar r. [embenenár], intoxicar [intoksikár], contaminar

[kontaminár] || **2.** n. veneno m. [benéno]; **-ous** a. venenoso [benenóso]

pole: - vault, salto con pértiga [sálto kon pértiga]

police policía f. [poliθía]; **- inspector** inspector m. de policía [inspektór de poliθía]; **-man** policía m. [poliθía], guardia m. urbano [gwárdja urbáno]; **- station** comisaría f. [komisaría]

polo: - neck sweater, suéter m. de cuello cisne [suéter de kwéljo θísne]

pomegranate granada f. [granáda]

porcelain porcelana f. [porθelána]: **of -,** de porcelana [de]

pore poro m. [póro]

pork cerdo m. [θérdo], carne f. de cerdo [kárne de], **roast -,** carne de cerdo asada [kárne de θérdo asáda]; **lean -,** carne magra [mágra]; **salted -,** tocino m. [toθíno]; **- butcher's** chacinería f. [tchaθinería]; **- chop** chuleta f. de cerdo [tchuléta de θérdo]; **- loin** lomo m. de cerdo [lómo de]; **- rib** costilla f. de cerdo [kostílja de]; **- sausage** butifarra f. [butifárra], embutido m. [embutído]: **black -,** butifarra negra [négra]; **fried -,** butifarra frita [fríta]; **grilled -,** butifarra a la brasa [a la brása]; **white -,** butifarra blanca [blánka]

porridge gachas f. de avena [gátchas de abéna]

port puerto m. [pwérto] || **2.** vino m. de Oporto [bíno de opórto]

porter mozo m. [móθo]

portion porción f. [porθjón], ración f. [rraθjón]

portrait retrato m. [rretráto]

positive a. positivo(a) [positíbo]

possible a. posible [posíble]

post correo m. [korréo]; **-box** apartado m. de correos [apartádo de korréos], **-card** (tarjeta f.) postal f. [tarxéta postál]; **-man** cartero m. [kartéro]; **- office** oficina f. de correos [ofiθína de korréos]: **general -,** central f. de correos [θentrál de]; **sub -,** estafeta f. de correos [estaféta de]; **- savings bank;** caja f. postal de ahorros [káxa postál de aórros]

postage franqueo m. [frankéo]; **- stamp** sello m. (de correos) [séljo de korréos]

postal a. postal [postál]; **- district** distrito m. postal [distríto]; **- order** giro m. postal [xíro]

poste: - restante, lista f. de correos [lísta de korréos]

poster cartel *m*. [*kartél*]
posy ramillete *m*. [*ramiljéte*]
potable *a*. potable [*potáble*]
pot: *flower* -, maceta *f*. [*maθéta*]
potage potaje *m*. [*potáxe*]
potato patata *f*. [*patáta*]: *boiled* **-s**, patatas *pl*. hervidas [*patátas erbídas*]; *chillied* **-s,** patatas bravas [*brábas*]; *fried* -, patatas fritas [*frítas*]; *stuffed* **-,** patatas rellenas [*reljénas*]; **- crisp** patatas *f.pl*. fritas [*patátas frítas*]; **- puree** puré *m*. de patatas [*puré de patátas*]
potent *a*. potente [*poténte*]
pottery cerámica *f*. [*θerámika*]: **of -,** de cerámica [*de*]
pouch zurrón *m*. [*θurrón*]
poultry: **- shop,** pollería *f*. [*poljería*]
pound libra *f*. [*líbra*]; **- Sterling** libra esterlina [*esterlína*]
powder polvo *m*. [*pólbo*] ‖ **2.** polvos *pl*. (de tocador) [*pólbos (de tokadór)*] (make-up); **- bowl** polvera *f*. [*polbéra*]; **- compacts** polvos *m. pl*. compactos [*pólbos kompáktos*]; **- puff** borla *f*. [*bórla*]
power potencia *f*. [*poténθja*]; **-house** central *f*. eléctrica [*θentrál eléktrika*]
prams carrocería *f*. [*karroθería*] (of a car)
prawn gamba *f*. [*gámba*]; *large (Dublin Bay)* -, cigala *f*. [*θigála*]; **- cocktail,** cóctel *m*. de gambas [*kóktel de gámbas*]; **-s:** *grilled on the grid,* gambas a la plancha [*gámbas a la plántcha*]; **-with garlic,** gambas al ajillo [*al axíljo*]
precious *a*. precioso(a) [*preθjóso*]; **- stone** piedra *f*. preciosa [*pjédra*]
prefabricated *a*. prefabricado(a) [*prefabrikádo*]
preface prólogo *m*. [*prólogo*]
prefer (to) preferir (ie) [*preferír*] (to. a)
prefix prefijo *m*. [*prefíxo*]
pregnan/cy embarazo *m*. [*embaráθo*]; **-t** embarazada *f*. [*embaraθáda*]
preparation preparación *f*. [*preparaθjón*] ‖ **2.** preparativo *m*. [*preparatíbo*]
prepare (to) preparar *r*. [*preparár*]
prepackaged *a*. empaquetado [*empaketádo*]
prescribe (to) recetar *r*. [*rreθetár*] (Med.)
prescription receta *f*. [*rreθéta*]
presence presencia *f*. [*presénθja*]
present (to) presentar *r*. [*presentár*]; **to - oneself,** presentarse [*presentárse*] ‖ **2.** *a*. presente [*presénte*]. **to be -,** estar *irr*. presente [*estár*] ‖ **3.** *n*. regalo *m*. [*rregálo*]; **-s** objetos *m. pl*. de regalo [*obxétos de*]

preservative conservante *m*. [*konserbánte*]
preserve confitura *f*. [*konfitúra*]; **-d** *a*. en almíbar [*en almíbar*]; **- fruit,** confitura *f*. [*konfitúra*]
president presidente *m*. [*presidénte*]
press prensa *f*. [*prénsa*]; **-ure** presión *f*. [*presjón*]
pretty *a*. bonito(a) [*boníto*]
price precio *m*. [*préθjo*]
prickly: **- pear,** higo *m*. chumbo [*ígo tchúmbo*]
priest sacerdote *m*. [*saθerdóte*]
prince príncipe *m*. [*prínθipe*]
princess princesa *f*. [*prinθésa*]
print (to) imprimir *r*. [*imprimír*]; **-ed** *a*. impreso(a) [*impréso*]; estampado(a) [*estampádo*]; **- matter,** impreso *m*. [*impréso*]; **-ing** impresión *f*. [*impresjón*]
prison cárcel *f*. [*kárθel*]
private *a*. privado(a) [*pribádo*]; **- beach** playa *f*. privada [*plája*]; **- car** coche *m*. particular [*kótche partikulár*]; **- shoot** coto *m*. [*kóto*]
probable *a*. probable [*probáble*]
problem problema *m*. [*probléma*]
product producto *m*. [*prodúkto*]
profession profesión *f*. [*profesjón*]
professor catedrático *m*. [*katedrátiko*]
programme programa *m*. [*prográma*]
project (to) proyectar *r*. [*projektár*]; **-or** proyector *m*. [*projektór*]
propose (to) proponer *irr*. [*proponér*]
prostitute prostituta *f*. [*prostitúta*]
Provence: **- sauce,** salsa *f*. provenzal [*sálsa probenθál*]
province provincia *f*. [*probínθja*]
prune ciruela *f*. pasa [*θiruéla pása*]
ptisan tisana *f*. [*tisána*]
pub pub *m*. [*pab*], cervecería *f*. [*θerbeθería*], taberna *f*. [*tabérna*]
public público *m*. [*públiko*]; **-ation** publicación *f*. [*publikaθjón*]
pudding pudin *m*. [*púdin*]
puff: **- pastry,** pasta *f*. de hojaldre [*pásta de oxáldre*]
puffed: **- out,** *a*. ahuecado(a) [*awekádo*]
pull (to) tirar *r*. [*tirár*] (de); **-over** jersey *m*. [*xerséi*]
pulse pulso *m*. [*púlso*]
pump bomba *f*. [*bómba*]; **-s** zapatillas *f. pl*. [*θapatíljas*]
punch ponche *m*. [*póntche*]
punctual *a*. puntual [*puntuál*]; **-ly** *adv*. puntualmente [*puntualménte*]
puncture pinchazo *m*. [*pintcháθo*]
pupil alumno(a) *m.-f*. [*alúmno*]
puppet muñeco(a) *m.-f*. [*munjéko*]

pure *a.* puro(a) [*púro*]
puree puré *m.* [*puré*]: - *of broad beans,* puré de habas [*de ábas*]; - *of peas,* puré de guisantes [*de gisántes*]; - *of potatoes,* puré de patatas [*de patátas*]; - *of spinach,* puré de espinacas [*de espinákas*]
purgative purga *f.* [*púrga*]
purge (to) purgar *r.* [*purgár*] (Med.)

purse bolsa *f.* [*bólsa*], bolsillo *m.* [*bolsíljo*] ‖ **2.** portamonedas *f. pl.* [*portamonédas*]
pus pus *f.* [*pus*] (Med.)
push (to) empujar *r.* [*empuxár*]
put (to) poner *irr.* [*ponér*]: *to - on (a shoe),* calzar *r.* [*kalθár*], ponerse *irr.* (un zapato) [*ponérse un θapáto*]
pyjamas pijama *m.* [*pixáma*]

quail codorniz *f.* [*kodorniθ*]
quality calidad *f.* [*kalidád*]
quantity cantidad *f.* [*kantidád*]
quarter cuarto *m.* [*kwárto*]; *a -,* un cuarto [*un kwárto*] (of/de); *a - of a kilo,* un cuarto de kilo [*de kílo*]; *three -s*

of a kilo, tres cuartos de kilo [*tres kwártos de kílo*]
quartet cuarteto *m.* [*kwartéto*]
quay muelle *m.* [*mwélje*]
queen reina *f.* [*rréina*]
question pregunta *f.* [*pregúnta*] *m.* ‖ **2.** cuestión *f.* [*kwestjón*] (problema)
quick *a.* rápido(a) [*rrápido*]; **-ly** *adv.* deprisa [*deprísa*]
quiet *a.* quieto(a) [*kjéto*], tranquilo(a) [*trankílo*]
quite *adv.* bastante [*bastánte*]

R

rabbit conejo *m.* [*konéxo*]: **braised -**, conejo guisado [*gisádo*]; **grilled -**, conejo a la brasa [*a la brása*]; **roasted -**, conejo asado [*asádo*]; **stewed -**, conejo guisado [*gisádo*]; **- with garlic**, conejo al ajillo [*al axíljo*]

race carrera *f.* [*karréra*]; **- course** hipódromo *m.* [*ipódromo*]

radiator radiador *m.* [*rradjadór*]

radio radio *f.* [*rrádjo*]; **-graph** radiografía *f.* [*rradjografía*]; **- set** aparato *m.* de radio [*aparáto de*]

radish rábano *m.* [*rrábano*]: **horse -**, rábano picante [*pikánte*]

rage rabia *f.* [*rrábja*]

ragout ragú *m* [*rragú*]: **deer -**, ragú de ciervo [*de θjérbo*]; **hare -**, ragú de liebre [*de ljébre*]; **mutton -**, ragú de cordero [*de kordéro*]

rail rail *m.* [*rraíl*]; **-way** ferrocarril *m.* [*ferrokarríl*]

rain (to) llover (ue) [*ljobér*]: **it's raining,** está lloviendo [*está ljobjéndo*] || **2.** lluvia *f.* [*ljúbja*]; **-coat** gabardina *f.* [*gabardína*]; **-storm** chubasco *m.* [*tchubásko*]

raise (to) levantar *r.* [*lebantár*] || **2.** subir *r.* [*subír*] (prices) || **3.** *n.* subida *f.* [*subída*] (prices)

raisin pasa *f.* [*pása*]

ranch rancho *m.* [*rrántcho*]

range gama *f.* [*gáma*]: **- of speeds,** gama de velocidades [*de beloθidádes*]

raquet raqueta *f.* [*rrakéta*]

rare *a.* raro(a) [*rráro*] || **2.** escaso(a) [*eskáso*]

raspberry frambuesa *f.* [*frambwésa*]; **- jam** mermelada *f.* de frambuesa [*mermeláda de*]

rate tarifa *f.* [*tarífa*] || **2.** tanto *m.* (por ciento) [*tánto (por θjénto)*]

rather *adv.* bastante [*bastánte*]

ration ración *f.* [*rraθjón*] (of/de)

rattle sonajero *m.* [*sonaxéro*]

ravioli raviolis *m. pl.* [*rrabjólis*]

raw *a.* crudo(a) [*krúdo*]

ray rayo *f.* [*rrája*] || **2.** *n.* rayo *m.* [*rrájo*]

razor navaja *f.* de afeitar [*nabáxa de afeitár*]: **safety -**, maquinilla *f.* de afeitar [*makinílja de*]; **- blade** hoja *f.* de afeitar [*óxa de*]

read (to) leer *r.* [*leér*]; **-er** lector(a) *m.-f.* [*lektór*]; **-ing** lectura *f.* [*lektúra*]

ready *a.* listo(a) [*lísto*], preparado(a) [*preparádo*]; **r.-made** *a.* confeccionado(a) [*konfekθjonádo*]; **- clothes,** ropa *f.* de confección [*rrópa de konfékθjon*]; **- clothing shop for ladies,** tienda *f.* de confección para señoras [*tjénda de konfekθjón pára senjóras*]

real *a.* verdadero(a) [*berdadéro*], auténtico(a) [*auténtiko*]; **-ly** *adv.* realmente [*rrealménte*], verdaderamente [*berdaderaménte*]

rear *a.* trasero(a) [*traséro*]; **- light** luz *f.* trasera [*luθ traséra*]

rebuild (to) reconstruir (y) [*rrekonstrwír*]

receipt recepción *f.* [*rreθepθjón*] || **2.** recibo *m.* [*rreθíbo*]

receive (to) recibir *r.* [*rreθibír*]; tomar *r.* [*tomár*]; **-r** auricular *m.* [*aurikulár*] (phone)

recent *a.* reciente [*rreθjénte*]; **-ly** *adv.* recientemente [*rreθjenteménte*]

reception recepción *f.* [*rreθepθjón*]; **-ist** recepcionista *m.-f.* [*rreθepθjonísta*]

recital recital *m.* [*rreθitál*]

recommend (to) recomendar (ie) [*rrekomendár*]; **-ation** recomendación *f.* [*rrekomendaθjón*]

reconstituent reconstituyente *m.* [*rrekonstitujénte*]

record disco *m.* [*dísko*]; **-er: tape -**, magnetófono [*magnetófono*]

red *a.* rojo(a) [*rróxo*] || **2.** tinto [*tínto*]: **- wine,** vino *m.* tinto [*bíno*]; **- cabbage** col *f.* lombarda [*kol lombárda*]; **- mullets** salmonetes *m. pl.* [*salmonétes*]; **grilled -**, salmonetes a la parrilla [*a la parrílja*]; **- pepper** pimiento *m.* [*pimjénto*]

reduction reducción *f.* [*rredukθjón*]; **-s** rebajas *f. pl.* [*rrebáxas*]

reel carrete *m.* [*karréte*] || **2.** rollo *m.* [*róljo*]

referee árbitro *m.* [*árbitro*]

refill recambio *m.* [*rrekámbjo*]

refreshment refresco *m.* [*refrésko*]

refrigerator nevera *f.* [*nebéra*]

refund (to) reembolsar *r.* [*rreembolsár*]

region región *f.* [*rrexjón*]

regulator regulador *m.* [*rreguladór*]

register (to) certificar *r.* [*θertifikár*]: **to - (luggage),** facturar *r.* (el equipaje) [*fakturár el ekipáxe*]; **-ed** *a.* certificado(a) [*θertifikádo*]

registration: - number, matrícula *f.* [*matríkula*]

relax (to) relajar *r.* [*rrelaxár*]

release disparador *m.* [*disparadór*]

remedy remedio *m.* [*rremédjo*]
remove (to) quitar *r.* [*kitár*]; **to - hair,** depilar *r.* [*depilár*]
Renaissance renacimiento *m.* [*rre-naθimjénto*]
rent (to) alquilar *r.* [*alkilár*]
repair (to) reparar *r.* [*rreparár*] || **2.** *n.* reparación *f.* [*rreparaθjón*]; **- garage** taller *m.* de reparaciones [*tallér de rreparaθjónes*]
repeat (to) repetir (i) [*rrepetír*]
reply respuesta *f.* [*rrespwésta*]; **- paid** respuesta pagada [*pagáda*]
reporter reportero *m.* [*rreportéro*]
repose reposo *m.* [*rrepóso*]
representative representante *m.-f.* [*rre-presentánte*]
reproduction reproducción *f.* [*rrepro-dukθjón*]
request ruego *m.* [*rrwégo*], solicitud *f.* [*soliθitúd*]
reservation reserva *f.* [*rresérba*]
reserve (to) reservar *r.* [*rreserbár*] || **2.** hacerse *irr.* reservar [*aθérse*] || **3.** *n.* reserva *f.* [*rresérba*] || **4.** coto *m.* de caza [*kóto de káθa*]; **-d** *a.* reservado(a) [*rreserbádo*]
reservoir depósito *m.* [*depósito*]
residence residencia *f.* [*rresidénθja*]
resort balneario *m.* [*balneárjo*]; **summer -,** lugar *m.* de veraneo [*lugár de beranéo*]
respiration respiración *f.* [*rrespiraθjón*]
rest (to) descansar *r.* [*deskansár*] || **2.** *n.* descanso *m.* [*deskánso*], reposo *m.* [*rrepóso*]
restaurant restaurante *m.* [*rrestau-ránte*]
retina retina *f.* [*rretína*]
return (to) volver (ue) [*bolbér*] (to/a), regresar *r.* [*rregresár*] || **2.** devolver (ue) [*debolbér*] (money, etc.) || **3.** *n.* vuelta *f.* [*bwélta*], regreso *m.* [*rregréso*]; **- journey** ida y vuelta *f.* [*ída i bwélta*]; **- ticket** billete *m.* de ida y vuelta [*biljéte de*]
reverse revés *m.* [*rrebés*]; **-d: - charge,** cobro *m.* revertido [*kóbro rrebertído*]
reversing: - light, faro *m.* de marcha atrás [*fáro de mártcha atrás*]
rewind (to) rebobinar *r.* [*rrebobinár*]; **- handle** manivela *f.* para rebobinado [*manibéla pára rrebobinádo*]; **-er** rebobinado *m.* [*rrebobinádo*]
rheumatism reumatismo *m.* [*rreu-matísmo*]
rib costilla *f.* [*kostíla*]; **-s of mutton,** costillas *pl.* de cordero [*kostíljas de*

kordéro*]; **-s of pork,** costillas de cerdo [*kostíljas de θérdo*]
ribbon cinta *f.* [*θínta*]
rice arroz *m.* [*arróθ*] || **2.** paella *f.* [*paélja*] (Spanish dish): **fried -,** arroz a la cazuela [*arróθ a la kaθwéla*]
rich *a.* rico(a) [*rríko*]
ride (to): to - in a car, ir *irr.* en coche [*ir en kótche*]; **to - a bicycle,** montar *r.* en bicicleta [*montár en biθikléta*]; **to - a horse,** montar a caballo [*a kabáljo*]
riding equitación *f.* [*ekitaθjón*]; **- boots** botas *f. pl.* de montar [*bótas de montár*]; **- school** picadero *m.* [*pika-déro*]
rifle rifle *m.* [*rrífle*]
right *a.* derecho(a) [*derétcho*] || **2.** correcto(a) [*korrékto*] || **3. all -,** de acuerdo [*de akuérdo*]
rigid *a.* rígido(a) [*rríxido*]
ring (to) tocar *r.* [*tokár*]: **to - the bell,** tocar el timbre [*el tímbre*]; **2. to - up,** llamar *r.* por teléfono [*ljamár por telé-fono*] || **3.** *n.* anillo *m.* [*aníljo*] || **4.** ring [*rríng*] (Boxing); **-master** jefe *m.* de pista [*xéfe de písta*]
rinsed aclarado *m.* [*aklarádo*]
ripe *a.* maduro(a) [*madúro*]
river río *m.* [*rrío*]
road calle *f.* [*kálje*] || **2.** carretera *f.* [*karretéra*] || **3.** camino *m.* [*kamíno*] (way); **-house** parador *m.* [*paradór*]
roast *a.* asado(a) [*asádo*]; **- beef** rosbif *m.* [*rrósbif*]; **-ed** asado(a): **spit -,** hecho(a) a l'ast [*étcho a last*]; **- goat** cabritillo *m.* asado [*kabritíljo asádo*]; **- sucking pig** lechón *m.* asado [*letchón asádo*]
rock roca *f.* [*rróka*]; **- cod** mero *m.* [*méro*]; **-ing: - chair,** mecedora *f.* [*meθedóra*]
rod caña *f.* (de pescar) [*kánja de peskár*]; **- case** portacañas *m.* [*portakánjas*]; **- fishing** pesca *f.* con caña [*péska kon*]
roll rollo *m.* [*rróljo*]; **-er** rulo *m.* [*rrúlo*]; **-er skates** patines *m.pl.* de ruedas [*patínes de rrwédas*]
Roman *a.* romano(a) [*rrománo*]
Romanesque *a.* románico(a) [*rromániko*]
roof tejado *m.* [*texádo*]; **- rack** portae-quipajes *m.* [*portaekipáxes*] (of a car)
room habitación *f.* [*abitaθjón*], cuarto *m.* [*kwárto*]: **double -,** habitación doble [*dóble*]; **single -,** habitación individual [*indibidwál*]; **- with balcony,** habi-tación con terraza [*kon terráθa*]; **- with bathroom,** habitación con baño [*kon bánjo*]; **- with double**

bed, habitación de matrimonio [*de matrimónjo*]; - **with shower,** habitación con ducha [*kon dútcha*]; - **with telephone,** habitación con teléfono [*kon teléfono*]

rope cuerda *f.* [*kuérda*]; **-way** pasacabos [*pasakábos*]; - **soled shoes** alpargatas *f. pl.* [*alpargátas*]

rosary rosario *m.* [*rrosárjo*]

rose *a.* rosa [*rrósa*] ‖ **2.** *n.* rosa *f.*; **-wood** palisandro *m.* [*palisándro*]

rosé *a.* rosado(a) [*rrosádo*]; - **wine** vino *m.* rosado [*bíno*]

rotten *a.* podrido(a) [*podrído*]

rouge colorete *m.* [*koloréte*]

rough *a.* agitado(a) [*axitádo*]

round *a.* redondo(a) [*rredóndo*]

route trayecto *m.* [*trajékto*], recorrido *m.* [*rrekorrído*] ‖ **2.** ruta *f.* [*rrúta*]

row (to) remar *r.* [*rremár*] ‖ **2.** *n.* fila *f.* [*fíla*]; **-ing:** - **boat,** bote *m.* [*bóte*]

rubber goma *f.* [*góma*]

rubbish basura *f.* [*basúra*]; - **bag** bolsa *f.* de basura [*bólsa de*]

ruby rubí *m.* [*rrubí*]

rucksack mochila *f.* [*motchíla*]

rugby match partido *m.* de rugby [*partído de rrúghi*]

rule regla *f.* [*rrégla*]

rum ron *m.* [*rron*]: *black -,* ron negro [*négro*]; *white -,* ron blanco [*blánko*]; - **and coffee** carajillo *m.* [*karaxíljo*]; - **and cola** cuba libre *m.* de ron [*kúba líbre de rron*]

run (to) correr *r.* [*korrér*] ‖ **2.** *n.* carrera *f.* [*karréra*] ‖ **3.** recorrido *m.* [*rrekorrído*]; **-ning** marcha *f.* [*mártcha*] ‖ **2.** carrera *f.* [*karréra*]

rupture ruptura *f.* [*rruptúra*], rotura *f.* [*rrotúra*]

Russian: - *salad,* ensaladilla *f.* rusa [*ensaladílja rrúsa*]

rustic *a.* rústico(a) [*rrústiko*]

rut bache *m.* [*bátche*]

S

saccharin sacarina *f.* [*sakarína*]
sack saco *m.* [*sáko*]
saddle silla *f.* de montar [*sílja de montár*]; **- of lamb,** silla de cordero [*de kordéro*]
safe *a.* seguro(a) [*segúro*]; **-conduct** salvoconducto [*salbokondúkto*]; **-deposit** cámara acorazada [*kámara akoraθáda*], caja fuerte [*káxa fuérte*]; **-ty** *n.* seguridad *f.* [*seguridáδ*]; **- belt,** cinturón *m.* de seguridad [*θinturón de*] (car); **- razor,** maquinilla *f.* de afeitar [*makinílja de afejtár*]
saffron azafrán *f.* [*aθafrán*]
sail (to) navegar *r.* [*naβegár*] ‖ **2.** *n.* vela *f.* [*béla*]; **-board,** tabla *f.* de windsurf [*tábla de*]; **-ing** deporte *m.* de vela [*depórte de*]; **- boat,** velero *m.* [*beléro*]; **-or** marinero *m.* [*marinéro*]
salad ensalada *f.* [*ensaláda*]; **asparagus -,** ensalada de espárragos [*de espárragos*]; **cucumber -,** ensalada de pepinos [*de pepínos*]; **- in season,** ensalada de temporada [*de temporáda*]; **lettuce -,** ensalada de lechuga [*de letchúga*]; **lobster -,** ensalada de langosta [*de langósta*]; **mixed -,** ensalada variada [*barjáda*]; **potato -,** ensalada de patatas [*de patátas*]; **tomato -,** ensalada de tomates [*de tomátes*]; **tunny -,** ensalada de atún [*de atún*]; **- bowl** ensaladera *f.* [*ensaladéra*]; **- dressing** aliño *m.* de la ensalada [*alíño de la*]
salami salchichón *m.* [*saltchitchón*] (Spanish type)
sale venta *f.* [*bénta*]; **for (on) -,** en venta [*en*]; **-sgirl** vendedora *f.* [*bendedóra*]; **-sman** vendedor *m.* [*bendedór*]; **-swoman** vendedora *f.* [*bendedóra*]
salmon salmón *m.* [*salmón*]: **smoked -,** salmón ahumado [*aumádo*]
salon salón *m.* [*salón*]
salt sal *f.* [*sal*]; **-ed** *a.* salado(a) [*saláδo*]; **- almonds,** almendras *f. pl.* saladas [*alméndras saládas*]; **- pork,** tocino *m.* [*toθíno*]; **-y** *a.* salado(a) [*saláδo*]
salutation saludo *m.* [*salúdo*]
salute (to) saludar *r.* [*saludár*]
same *a.* mismo(a) [*mísmo*]
sample muestra *f.* [*mwéstra*]: **- of no value,** muestra sin valor [*sin balór*]
sand arena *f.* [*aréna*]

sandal sandalia *f.* [*sandálja*]
sandwich (made with local bread): bocadillo *m.* [*bokadíljo*]: **cheese -,** bocadillo de queso [*de késo*]; **cheese and ham -,** bocadillo de jamón y queso [*de xamón i késo*]; **chicken -,** bocadillo de pollo [*de póljo*]; **Francfurt sausage -,** bocadillo de salchichas [*de saltchítchas*]; **ham -,** bocadillo de jamón [*de xamón*]; **meat -,** bocadillo de carne [*de kárne*]; **omelette -,** bocadillo de tortilla [*de tortílja*]; **pork -,** bocadillo de lomo [*de lómo*]; **sausage (paste) -,** bocadillo de sobrasada [*de sobrasáda*]; **toasted -,** bocadillo caliente [*kaljénte*]
sane *a.* sano(a)
sangría sangría *f.* [*sangría*]; **dry -,** sangría seca [*séka*]; **sweet -,** sangría dulce [*dúlθe*]
sanitary *a.* sanitario(a) [*sanitárjo*]; **- towels** compresas *f. pl.* (higiénicas) [*komprésas (ixjénikas)*]
sapphire zafiro *m.* [*θafíro*]
sardine sardina *f.* [*sardína*]: **fresh -s,** sardinas *pl.* frescas [*sardínas fréskas*]; **fried -s,** sardinas fritas [*frítas*]; **-s in oil,** sardinas en aceite [*en aθéite*]; **pickled -s,** sardinas en escabeche [*en eskabétche*]
satin satén *m.* [*satén*], raso *m.* [*rráso*]
satisfaction satisfacción *f.* [*satisfakθión*]
Saturday sábado *m.* [*sábado*]
sauce salsa *f.* [*sálsa*]: **bechamel -,** salsa bechamel [*betchamél*]; **devil's -,** salsa picante [*pikánte*]; **garlic -,** alioli *m.* [*aliólí*]; **mayonnaise -,** mayonesa *f.* [*majonésa*]; **parsley -,** salsa verde [*bérde*]; **romesco -,** salsa romesco [*rromésko*]; **tomato -,** salsa de tomate [*de tomáte*]; **-boat** salsera *f.* [*salséra*]; **-pan** cacerola *f.* [*kaθeróla*]
saucer platillo *m.* [*platíljo*]
sauna sauna *f.* [*sáuna*]
sausage salchicha *f.* [*saltchítcha*], embutido *m.* [*embutíðo*], butifarra [*butifárra*]; **black pork -,** butifarra negra [*négra*]; **cooked pork -,** butifarra cocida [*koθída*]; **dry spiced -,** fuet *m.* [*fwet*] (catal.); **Frankfurter -,** salchicha *f.* de Frankfurt [*saltchítcha de Fránkfurt*]; **fried pork -,** butifarra frita [*fríta*]; **grilled pork -,** butifarra a la parrilla [*a la parrílja*]; **pork -,** butifarra *f.*; **raw pork -,** butifarra cruda [*krúda*]; **white pork -,** butifarra blanca [*blánka*]

savings ahorros *m. pl.* [aórros]; **- account** cuenta *f.* de ahorros [kwénta de]; **- bank** caja *f.* de ahorros [káxa de]

saw sierra *f.* [sjérra]

say (to) decir *irr.* [deθír]

scale báscula *f.* [báskula]

scallop vieira *f.* [bjéira]; **sea -,** concha *f.* [kóntcha]

scandal escándalo *m.* [eskándalo]

scar cicatriz *f.* [θikatríθ]

scarcely *adv.* apenas [apénas]

scarf bufanda *f.* [bufánda]

schedule programa *f.* [prográma], calendario *m.* [kalendárjo]; **-d** *a.* previsto(a) [prebísto], programado(a) [prográmádo]

school escuela *f.* [eskwéla]; **driving -,** autoescuela [awtoeskwéla]; **language -,** academia de idiomas [akadémja de idjómas]

scissors tijeras *f. pl.* [tixéras]

sconce aplique *m.* [aplíke]

scoop cucharón *m.* [kutcharón]; **-s** cucharillas *f. pl.* [kutcharíljas] (for fishing)

score (to): to - a goal, marcar un tanto [markár un tánto] ‖ **2.** partitura *f.* [partitúra] (musical)

scorpion: - fish, escorpina *f.* [eskorpína]

scrambled *a.* revuelto(a) [rrebwélto]; **- eggs** huevos *m. pl.* revueltos [wébos rrebwéltos]

screen pantalla *f.* [pantálja]

screw tornillo *m.* [torníljo], rosca *f.* [rróska]; **-driver** destornillador *m.* [destorniljadór]; **- top** tapón *m.* de rosca [tapón de rróska]

scuffle riña *f.* [rrínja]

scuba equipo *m.* de submarinismo [ekípo de submarinísmo]; **- diving,** submarinismo [submarinísmo]

sea mar *m.* [mar]; **- bream** besugo *m.* [besúgo]; **red -,** pagel *m.* [paxél]; **-food** mariscos *m. pl.* [marískos]; **- shop (bar),** marisquería *f.* [mariskería]; **-plain** hidroavión *m.* [idroabjón]; **-sick** *a.* mareado(a) [mareádo]; **-sickness** mareos *m. pl.* [maréos]; **-side** costa *f.* kósta; **-snail** bígaro *m.* [bígaro]; **s.-urchin** erizo *m.* de mar [eríθo de mar]

sealing-wax lacre *m.* [lákre]

search (to) buscar *r.* [buskár]

season estación *f.* del año [estaθjón del ánjo]; temporada *f.* [temporáda]; **-al: - fruits,** fruta *f. pl.* del tiempo [frúta del tjémpo]

seat asiento *m.* [asjénto]; **to take a -,** tomar *r.* asiento [tomár]; **stall -,** butaca *f.* [butáka]

second *a.* segundo(a) [segúndo]; **- class** segunda clase *f.* [segúnda kláse]

secur/e seguro *m.* [segúro]; **-ity** seguridad *f.* [seguridád]; **- forces,** fuerzas *f. pl.* de seguridad [fwérθas de]; **- guard,** guardia *m.-f.* jurado [gwárdja xurádo]

sedative calmante *m.* [kalmánte]

see (to) ver *irr.* [ber]

seek (to) buscar *r.* [buskár]

seem (to) parecer (zc) [pareθér]; **it -s to me,** me parece [me paréθe]

self: s.-release, autodisparador *m.* [autodisparadór]; **s.-drive car,** coche sin chófer [kótche sin tchófer]; **s.-service** autoservicio *m.* [autoserbiθjo]

sell (to) vender *r.* [bendér]; **-er** vendedor(a) *m.-f.* [bendedór]

semolina sémola *f.* [sémola]

send (to) enviar *r.* [embjár], remitir *r.* [rremitír]

sender remitente *m.* [rreminénte]

sense sentido *m.* [sentído]

sentiment sentimiento *m.* [sentimjénto]

September septiembre *m.* [setjémbre]

serenade serenata *f.* [serenáta]

serious *a.* serio(a) [sérjo]

sermon sermón *m.* [sermón]

serpent serpiente *f.* [serpjénte]

serum suero *m.* [swéro]

servant criado *m.* [krjádo]

serve (to) servir (i) [serbír]

serviette servilleta *f.* [serbiljéta]; **paper -,** servilleta de papel [de papél]

service servicio *m.* [serbiθjo]; **- station** estación *f.* de servicio [estaθjón de]

set (to) poner *irr.* [ponér], colocar *r.* [kolokár] ‖ **2.** *n.* juego *m.* [xwégo]; conjunto *m.* [konxúnto]; **- of cutlery,** cubierto *m.* [kubjérto]; **-ing** puesta *f.* (de sol) [pwésta de sol] ‖ **3.** engarce *m.* [engárθe]; **- lotion,** fijador *m.* [fixadór]

seven *a.* siete [sjéte]; **-teen** diecisiete [djeθisjéte]; **-ty** setenta [seténta]

sew (to) coser *r.* [kosér]; **-ing** costura *f.* [kostúra]; **- machine,** máquina *f.* de coser [mákina de kosér]

shade contraluz *f.* [kontralúθ]

shake: milk -, batido *m.* [batído]; **banana -,** batido de plátano [de plátano]; **chocolate -,** batido de chocolate [de tchokoláte]; **strawberry -,** batido de fresa [de frésa]; **vanilla -,** batido de vainilla [de bainílja]

shampoo champú *m.* [tchampú]

shape tamaño *m.* [*tamánjo*]

sharp *a.* agudo(a) [*agúdo*], afilado(a) [*afiládo*]

shave (to) afeitar(se) [*afeitárse*]

shaving afeitado *m.* [*afeitádo*]; **- brush** brocha *f.* de afeitar [*brótcba de afeitár*]; **- soap** jabón *m.* de afeitar [*xabón de*]

shawl chal *m.* [*tchal*], mantón *m.* [*mantón*]

she *pron. pers.* ella [*élja*]

sheath funda *f.* [*fúnda*]

sheep cordero *m.* [*kordéro*], oveja *f.* [*obéxa*]; **-'s head** cabeza *f.* de cordero [*cabéθa de*]

sheet sábana *f.* [*sábana*]

shell concha *f.* [*kóntcha*]; **-fish** crustáceos *m. pl.* [*krustáθeos*], mariscos *m. pl.* [*mariskos*]

sherry jerez *m.* [*xeréθ*], vino *m.* de Jerez [*bíno de*]; **dry -,** jerez seco [*séko*]; **sweet -,** jerez dulce [*dúlθe*]

ship barco *m.* [*bárko*], buque *m.* [*búke*]

shirt camisa *f.* [*kamísa*]; **- blouse** blusa *f.* camisera [*blúsa kamiséra*]; **- shop** camisería *f.* [*kamisería*]

shivering escalofríos *m. pl.* [*eskalofríos*]

shock golpe *m.* [*gólpe*], choque *m.* [*tchóke*]; **- absorber** amortiguador *m.* [*amortiguadór*]

shoe zapato *m.* [*θapáto*]; **-s** zapatos *m. pl.* [θapátos], calzado *m.* [*kalθádo*]; *a pair of* **-s,** un par de zapatos [*un par de*]; *leather* **-s,** zapatos de cuero [*de kwéro*]; **-black** limpiabotas *m.* [*limpjabótas*]; **-brush** cepillo *m.* para los zapatos [θepíljo pára los θapátos]; **-cream** crema *f.* para los zapatos [*kréma*]; **-horn** calzador *m.* [*kalθadór*]; **-laces** cordones *m. pl.* para los zapatos [*kordónes*]; **- shop** zapatería *f.* [*θapatería*]; **-tree** contrafuerte *m.* [*kontrafwérte*]

shoot (to) disparar *r.* [*disparár*] (gun) ‖ **2.** chutar *r.* [*tchutár*] (football)

shooting tiro *m.* [*tíro*] ‖ **2.** caza *f.* [*káθa*]; **- gallery** tiro *m.* al blanco [*tíro al blánko*]; **- jacket** cazadora *f.* [*kaθadóra*]; **- licence** permiso *m.* de caza [*permíso de káθa*]

shop tienda *f.* [*tjénda*]; **- assistant** dependiente *m.* [*dependjénte*] , dependienta *f.* [*dependjénta*]; **-ping: to go -,** ir *irr.* de compras [*ir de kómpras*], ir *irr.* a comprar [*a komprár*]

shore orilla *f.* [*orílja*], costa *f.* [*kósta*]

short *a.* corto(a) [*kórto*] ‖ **2.** breve [*brébe*]; **-en (to)** acortar *r.* [*akortár*]

shot tiro *m.* [*tíro*], disparo *m.* [*dispáro*]; **-gun** escopeta *f.* [*eskopéta*]

shoulder hombro *m.* [*ómbro*] ‖ **2.** espaldilla *f.* [*espaldílja*] (lamb)

shovel pala *f.* [*pála*]

show (to) mostrar (ue) [*mostrár*], indicar *r.* [*indikár*] ‖ **2.** *n.* espectáculo *m.* [*espektákulo*]

shower chubasco *m.* [*tchubásko*]; **- bath** ducha *f.* [*dútcha*]

showing proyección *f.* [*projekθjón*] (film)

showy *a.* extremado(a) [*ekstremádo*]; vistoso(a) [*bistóso*]

shrimp camarón *m.* [*kamarón*]

shrink (to) encoger(se) *r.* [*enkoxérse*]

shut (to) cerrar (ie) [*θerrár*] ‖ **2.** *a.* cerrado(a) [*θerrádo*]; **-ter** obturador *m.* [*obturadór*]

sick *a.* enfermo(a) [*enférmo*]; **-ness** enfermedad *f.* [*enfermedád*]

side lado *m.* [*ládo*]; **- comb** peineta *f.* [*peinéta*]; **- shows** atracciones *f. pl.* [*atrakθjónes*]

sight vista *f.* [*bista*]; **-seeing** recorrido *m.* (por la ciudad) [*rrekorrído por la θjudád*]

sign (to) firmar *r.* [*firmár*]

signal señal *f.* [*senjál*]

signature firma *f.* [*fírma*]

silent *a.* silencioso(a) [*silenθjóso*]

silk seda *f.* (natural) [*séda (naturál)*]

silly *a.* tonto(a) [*tónto*], necio(a) [*néθjo*]

silver plata *f.* [*pláta*]; *of* **-,** de plata [*de*]; **s.-plated** plata chapada [*tchapáda*]; **- gilt** plata dorada [*doráda*]; **-ware** objetos *m. pl.* de plata [*obxétos de*]

simple *a.* simple [*símple*]

simultaneous *a.* simultáneo [*simultáneo*]

since *prep.* desde [*désde*] ‖ **2.** *conj.* ya que [*ja ke*]

sing (to) cantar *r.* [*kantár*]; **-er** cantante *m.-f.,* [*kantánte*]; **-ing** canto *m.* [*kánto*]

sink (to) hundir(se) *r.* [*undírse*]

Sir señor *m.* [*senjór*]

sirloin solomillo *m.* [*solomíljo*]; **- steak** entrecot *m.* [*entrekót*]

sit (to) estar *irr.* sentado(a) [*estár sentádo*] ‖ **2.** *to* **- down,** sentarse [*sentárse*]; **-ting- room,** salón *m.* [*salón*]

six *a.* seis [*séis*]; **-teen** dieciséis [*djeθiséis*]; **-ty** sesenta [*sesénta*]

size medida *f.* [*medída*], tamaño *m.* [*tamánjo*] ‖ **2.** talla *f.* [*tálja*]

skate (to) patinar *r.* [*patinár*] ‖ **2.** *n.* patín *m.* [*patín*]; *ice* **-,** patín *m.* de hielo [*de jélo*] ‖ **3.** raya *f.* [*rrája*]

ski (to) esquiar *r.* [*eskjár*] ‖ **2.** *n.* esquí *m.* [*eskí*]; **- chair** telesilla *f.* [*telesílja*]; **-er** esquiador(a) *m.-f.* [*eskjadór*]; **-ing**: **- boots,** botas *f. pl.* de esquiar [*bótas de*]; **- lift** telesquí *m.* [*teleskí*]; **- sticks** bastones *m. pl.* de esquiar [*bastónes de eskjár*]

skin piel *f.* [*pjel*]; **- cleansing** limpieza *f.* de cutis [*limpjéθa de kútis*]

skirt falda *f.* [*fálda*]

sky cielo *m.* [*θjélo*]

slacks pantalones *m. pl.* [*pantalónes*]

sleep (to) dormir (ue) [*dormír*]; **-iness** somnolencia *f.* [*somnolénθja*]; **-ing**: **- bag,** saco *m.* de dormir [*sáko de dormír*]; **- car,** coche-cama *m.* [*kótche káma*]; **-lessness** insomnio *m.* [*insómnjo*]

sleeve manga *f.* [*mánga*]; **-less** sin mangas [*sin mángas*]

sleigh trineo *m.* [*trinéo*]; **- bell,** cascabel [*kaskaβél*]

slice rebanada *f.* [*rrebanáda*] (of bread/de pan)

slide diapositiva *f.* [*djapositíba*]

slipper zapatilla *f.* [*θapatílja*], chancleta *f.* [*tchankléta*]; **woolen -,** escarpín *m.* [*eskarpín*]

slope cuesta *f.* [*kwésta*], pendiente *f.* [*pendjénte*]

sloop balandro *m.* [*balándro*]

slow *a.* lento(a) [*lénto*]; **-ly** *adv.* despacio [*despáβjo*]

small *a.* pequeño(a) [*pekénjo*]

smart *a.* elegante [*elegánte*]

smell (to) oler (ue) [*olér*]

smile (to) sonreír(se) (i) [*sonrreírse*] ‖ **2.** *n.* sonrisa *f.* [*sonrrísa*]

smoke (to) fumar *r.* [*fumár*] ‖ **2.** *n.* humo *m.* [*úmo*]; **-d** *a.* ahumado(a) [*aumádo*]; **-r** fumador *m.* [*fumadór*]: **-'s requisites,** artículos *m. pl.* para fumadores [*artíkulos pára*]

smoking: - car, vagón *m.* para fumadores [*bagón pára fumadóres*]; **- room,** cuarto *m.* de fumar [*kwárto de fumár*]

snack comida *f.* ligera [*komída lixéra*], bocado *m.* [*bokádo*]

snail caracol *m.* [*karakól*]

snap: - fastener, cierre *m.* [*θjérre*]

snare trampa *f.* [*trámpa*]

sneeze (to) estornudar *r.* [*estornudár*]

snorkel respirador *m.* [*rrespiradór*]

snow (to) nevar (ie) [*nebár*] ‖ **2.** *n.* nieve *f.* [*njébe*]; **-fall** nevada *f.* [*nebáda*]

so *adv.* así [*así*]; **- long,** hasta la vista [*ásta la bísta*]

soap jabón *m.* [*xabón*]; **- powder** detergente *m.* en polvo [*deterxénte en pólbo*]

sock calcetín *m.* [*kalθetín*]: **pair of -s,** par *m.* de calcetines [*par de kalθetínes*]

soda: - water, soda *f.* [*sóda*], sifón *m.* [*sifón*]

sofa sofá *m.* [*sofá*]

soft *a.* blando(a) [*blándo*], suave [*swábe*]; **-ener** suavizante *m.* [*swabiθánte*]; **-ening**: **- cream,** crema *f.* suavizante [*kréma*]

sole planta *f.* [*plánta*] (foot) ‖ **2.** suela *f.* [*swéla*] (shoe) ‖ **3.** lenguado *m.* [*lenguádo*] (fish)

some/body *pron.* alguien [*álgjen*]; **-thing** algo [*álgo*]; **-times** *adv.* a veces [*a béθes*]

somniferous somnífero *m.* [*somnífero*]

sonata sonata *f.* [*sonáta*]

son hijo *m.* [*íxo*]; **s.-in-law,** hijo político [*íxo polítiko*]; yerno *m.* [*jérno*] (fam.)

sore *a.* inflamado(a) [*inflamádo*]: **to have a - throat,** tener *irr.* anginas [*tenér anxínas*]

sorry *a.* triste [*tríste*] ‖ **2. I am -,** lo siento [*lo sjénto*]

sort *f.* clase [*kláse*]

soup sopa *f.* [*sópa*]: **asparagus -,** sopa de espárragos [*de espárragos*]; **bean -,** sopa de judías [*de xudías*]; **chicken -,** sopa de gallina [*de galjína*]; **clear -,** sopa clara [*klára*]; **cold -,** gazpacho *m.* [*gaθpátcho*] (of bread, water, tomato and garlic); **fish -,** sopa de pescado [*de peskádo*]; **garlic -,** sopa de ajo [*de áxo*]; **lentil -,** sopa de lentejas [*de lentéxas*]; **mushroom -,** sopa de champiñones [*de tchampinjónes*]; **noodle -,** sopa de pasta [*de pásta*]; **onion -,** sopa de cebolla [*de θebólja*]; **oxtail -,** sopa de rabo de buey [*de rrábo de bwei*]; **pea -,** sopa de guisantes [*de gisántes*]; **shellfish -,** sopa de mariscos [*de marískos*]; **- of the day,** sopa del día [*del día*]; **thick -,** sopa espesa [*espésa*]; **tomato -,** sopa de tomate [*de tomáte*]; **turtle -,** sopa de tortuga [*de tortúga*]; **vegetable -,** sopa de verdura [*de berdúra*]; **vermicelli -,** sopa de fideos [*de fidéos*]

sour *a.* ácido(a) [*aθido*], agrio(a) [*ágrjo*]; **-ness** acidez *f.* [*aθidéθ*]

south sur *m.* [*sur*]

souvenir recuerdo *m.* [*rrekwérdo*]; **- shop** tienda *f.* de recuerdos [*tjénda de rrekwérdos*]

spade pala *f.* [*pála*]

spaghetti espaguetis *m. pl.* [*espagétis*], fideos *m. pl.* [*fidéos*]

Spanish *a.* español(a) [*espanjól*]; **- style** a la española [*a la espanjóla*]

spare de recambio [*de rrekámbjo*]; **- part** pieza *f.* de recambio [*pjéθa de*]; **- wheel** rueda *f.* de recambio [*rruéda de*]

sparkling *a.* espumoso(a) [*espumóso*]; **- mineral water** agua *f.* mineral con gas [*ágwa minerál kon gas*]; **- wine** vino *m.* espumoso [*bíno espumóso*]

spats botines *m. pl.* [*botínes*]

speak (to) hablar *r.* [*ablár*] (with/con)

special *a.* especial [*espeθjál*], particular [*partikulár*]

spectacle espectáculo *m.* [*espektákulo*]

spectator espectador(a) *m.-f.* [*espektadór*]

speed velocidad *f.* [*beloθidád*]; **- trial** carrera *f.* de velocidad [*karréra de*]

spend (to) gastar *r.* [*gastár*] (money) ‖ **2.** pasar *r.* [*pasár*]: **to - holidays,** pasar las vacaciones [*las bakaθjónes*]

spic/e especia *f.* [*espéθja*], **-y** *a.* picante [*pikánte*]

spider: - crab, centollo *m.* [*θentóljo*], noca *f.* [*nóka*]

spike pincho *m.* [*píntcho*], púa *f.* [*púa*]; **-nard** nardo *m.* [*nárdo*]

spin: - dried *a.* centrifugado(a) [*θentrifugádo*]

spinach espinacas *f. pl.* [*espinákas*]

spindle eje *m.* [*éxe*]

spiny: - lobster, langosta *f.* [*langósta*]

spirits bebida *f.* alcohólica [*bebída alkoólika*], aguardiente *m.* [*agwardjénte*]

spit asador *m.* [*asadór*]

spleen bazo *m.* [*báθo*]

spoilt *a.* estropeado(a) [*estropeádo*]

sponge esponja *f.* [*espónxa*]; **- de luffa,** esponja vegetal [*bexetál*]; **- cake** bizcocho *m.* [*biθkótcho*]: **light -,** madalena *f.* [*madaléna*]

spoon cuchara *f.* [*kutchára*]: **tea -,** cucharilla *f.* [*kutcharílja*], **-ful** cucharada *f.* [*kutcharáda*]

sport deporte *m.* [*depórte*]; **-s club** club *m.* deportivo [*klub deportíbo*]; **-s field** campo *m.* de juego [*kámpo de xwégo*]; **-s goods** artículos *m. pl.* de deporte [*artíkulos de depórte*]; **-sman** deportista *m.* [*deportísta*]; **-s shop** tienda *f.* de artículos de deporte [*tjénda de artíkulos de depórte*]; **-'s wear** prendas *f. pl.* deportivas [*préndas deportíbas*]

sporting: - gun, escopeta *f.* [*eskopéta*]

spot mancha *f.* [*mántcha*], **-ted** *a.* de lunares [*de lunáres*]

spray aerosol *m.* [*aerosól*]

spring primavera *f.* [*primabéra*] ‖ **2.** fuente *f.* [*fuénte*]; **- onion** cebolla *f.* tierna [*θebólja tjérna*]

sprout brote *m.* [*bróte*]: **Brussels -s,** coles *f. pl.* de Bruselas [*kóles de brusélas*]

square *a.* cuadrado(a) [*kwadrádo*] ‖ **2.** *n.* plaza *f.* [*pláθa*]; **- kilometre** kilómetro *m.* cuadrado [*kilómetro kwadrádo*]; **- metre** metro *m.* cuadrado [*métro*]

squeak (to) chirriar *r.* [*tchirrjár*]

squid calamar *m.* [*kalamár*]: **- fried in batter,** calamares *pl.* a la romana [*kalamáres a la rromána*]; **grilled -s,** calamares a la plancha [*a la plántcha*]; **stuffed -s,** calamares rellenos [*rreljénos*]; **-s with a black sauce,** calamares en su tinta [*en su tínta*]

stadium estadio *m.* [*estádjo*]

stage escenario *m.* [*esθenárjo*]

staircase escalera *f.* [*eskaléra*]

stamp (to) franquear *r.* ‖ **2.** *n.* sello *m.* [*séljo*]

stand tribuna *f.* [*tribúna*]; **-ing** gradas *f. pl.* [*grádas*]

star estrella *f.* [*estrélja*]

start (to) comenzar (ie) [*komenθár*] ‖ **2.** poner *irr.* en marcha [*ponér en mártcha*]: **to - off,** arrancar *r.* [*arrankár*] ‖ **3.** ponerse *irr.* en marcha [*ponérse en mártcha*] ‖ **4.** *n.* origen *m.* [*oríxen*] (bus line), inicio *m.* [*iníθjo*]; **-er: - motor,** motor *m.* de arranque [*motór de arránke*]; **-ing** arranque *m.* [*arránke*]

state estado *m.* [*estádo*]

station estación *f.* [*estaθjón*]; **- master** jefe *m.* de estación [*xéfe de*]

stationer's papelería *f.* [*papelería*]

statue estatua *f.* [*estátwa*] ‖ **2.** figura *f.* [*figúra*]

stay (to) quedarse *r.* [*kedárse*]

steak bistec *m.* [*bisték*]: **barbecued -,** churrasco *m.* [*tchurrásko*]; **fried -,** bistec frito [*fríto*]; **grilled -,** bistec a la brasa [*a la brása*]

steal (to) robar *r.* [*rrobár*]

steering dirección *f.* [*direkθjón*]; **- rod** barra *f.* de dirección [*bárra de*]; **- wheel** volante *m.* [*bolánte*]

stew estofado *m.* [*estofádo*], guisado *m.* [*gisádo*]; **- of white beans,** fabada *f.* asturiana [*fabáda asturjána*] (with pork, ham, sausage, black pudding, etc.); **- with potatoes,** estofado *m.* [*estofádo*], cocido *m.* [*koθído*], **-ed** *a.* estofado(a) [*estofádo*], guisado(a) [*gisádo*]; **- fish (assorted)** zarzuela *f.* de pescado [*θarθwéla de peskádo*];

- **meat (assorted)** zarzuela de carne [de kárne]
steward camarero m. [kamaréro] (ship); **-ess** azafata f. [aθafáta] (plane) ‖ **2.** camarera f. [kamaréra] (ship)
stew-pan olla f. [ólja], cacerola f. [kaθeróla]
stick stik m. [stik]; **-s of bread,** bastones m. pl. [bastónes], palitos m. pl. [palítos] (bread)
sticker adhesivo m. [adesíbo]
stiff a. tieso(a) [tjéso]
still a. quieto(a) [kjéto], tranquilo(a) [trankílo] ‖ **2.** adv. todavía [todabía]
sting picadura f. [pikadúra]
stocking media f. [médja]
stomach estómago m. [estómago]; **-ache** dolor m. de estómago [dolór de]
stone piedra f. [pjédra] ‖ **2.** hueso m. [wéso]; **with -s,** con hueso [con]; **without -s (pips),** sin hueso [sin]
stool taburete m. [taburéte]
stop (to) parar(se) r. [parárse], detener(se) irr. [detenérse] ‖ **2.** n. alto m. [álto] ‖ **3.** parada f. [paráda]
store almacén m. [almaθén]: **department -,** grandes almacenes pl. [grándes almaθénes]
storm tormenta f. [torménta], **-y** a. tempestuoso(a) [tempestwóso]
story historia f. [istórja], cuento m. [kwénto]
stove estufa f. [estúfa]
straight a. recto(a) [rrékto], derecho(a) [derétcho]
strange a. raro(a) [rráro], extraño(a) [ekstránjo]
strap correa f. [korréa]
strawberr/ies fresas f. pl. [frésas]: **- and cream,** fresas con nata [frésas kon náta]; **-y** fresa f. [frésa], fresón m. [fresón]: **compote of -,** compota de fresa [kompóta de]; **- jam** mermelada f. de fresa [mermeláda de]; **- shake** batido m. de fresa [batído de]; **- tart** tarta f. de fresa [tárta de]
street calle f. [kálje], **- lamp** farola f. [faróla]; **one-way -,** calle de dirección única [de direkθjón únika]
strenghener reforzador m. [rreforθadór]
stretcher tensor m. [tensór]
strong a. fuerte [fwérte]
structure estructura f. [estruktúra]
student estudiante m.-f. [estudjánte]
studio estudio m. [estúdjo]
stuffed a. relleno(a) [rrelléno], **- olives** aceitunas f. pl. rellenas [aθeitúnas rrelljénas]

subcutaneous a. subcutáneo(a) [subkutáneo]
submerge (to) sumergirse r. [sumerxírse]
subway paso m. subterráneo [páso subterráneo]
success éxito m. [éksito]
succulent a. suculento(a) [sukulénto]
such pron. tal [tal], tales pl. [táles]
sufficient a. suficiente [sufiθjénte], bastante [bastánte]
suffocation ahogo m. [aógo]
sugar azúcar m. [aθúkar]: **lump of -,** terrón m. de azúcar [terrón de aθúkar]; **-ed: - almonds,** peladillas f. pl. [peladíljas]; **- plum** confite m. [konfíte]
suit traje m. [tráxe], **wet -,** traje isotérmico [isotérmiko]; **-case** maleta f. [maléta]
suite suite f. [swíte]
sulphamides sulfamidas f. pl. [sulfamídas]
sultry a. bochornoso(a) [botchornóso]
sum suma f. [súma]
summer (to) veranear r. [beraneár] ‖ **2.** n. verano m. [beráno]
sump cárter m. [kárter]
sun sol m. [sol]; **-bathing** baños m.pl. de sol [bánjos de]; **-bathe (to)** tomar r. el sol [tomár el sol]; **-burn** quemadura f. de sol [kemadúra de]; **-day** domingo m. [domíngo]; **-glasses** gafas f. pl. de sol [gáfas de]; **-shade** parasol m. [parasól], sombrilla f. [sombrílja]; **-stroke** insolación f. [insolaθjón]; **-tan (oil)** bronceador m. [bronθeadór], aceite m. bronceador [aθéite]; **-ny: to be -,** hacer irr. sol [aθér sol]
supermarket supermercado m. [supermerkádo]
supper cena f. [θéna]: **to have -,** cenar r. [θenár]
supplier surtidor m. [surtidór]
support soporte m. [sopórte]
suppository supositorio m. [supositórjo]
sure a. seguro(a) [segúro]
surface superficie f. [superfíθje]
surgeon cirujano m. [θiruxáno]
surname apellido m. [apeljído]
suspension suspensión f. [suspensjón]
sweater suéter m. [swéter]
sweating sudoración f. [sudoraθjón]
sweep (to) barrer r. [barrér]
sweet a. dulce [dúlθe] ‖ **2.** n. -s dulces m. pl. [dúlθes], **-breads** mollejas [molléxas], lechecillas f. pl. [letcheθíljas]; **- bun** ensaimada f. [ensaimáda]; **- marmalade** mermelada f. de naranja dulce [mermeláda de naránxa]

swelling hinchazón *f.* [*íntchaθón*]
swim (to) nadar *r.* [*nadár*] ‖ **2.** *n.* **-suit,** traje *m.* de baño [*tráxe de bánjo*], bañador *m.* [*banjadór*]; **-mer** nadador(a) *m.-f.* [*nadadór*]; **-ming** natación *f.* [*nataθjón*]; **-pool,** piscina *f.* [*piθína*]

swing columpio *m.* [*kolúmpjo*]
switch interruptor *m.* [*interruptór*]; **-board** centralita *f.* [*θentralíta*] (telephone)
sword espada *f.* [*espáda*]
syrup jarabe *m.* [*xarábe*]

T

table mesa *f.* [*mésa*]; **- clock** reloj *m.* de sobremesa [*rrelóx de sobremésa*]; **-cloth** mantel *m.* [*mantél*]; **- d'hote** a la carta [*a la kárta*]; **- linen** ropa *f.* de mesa [*rrópa de mésa*]; **- tennis** tenis *m.* de mesa [*ténis de*]; **-ware** vajilla *f.* [*baxílja*]; **- wine** vino *m.* de mesa [*bíno de*]

tableau tablao *m.* [*tabláo*]

tablet comprimido *m.* [*komprimído*], tableta *f.* [*tabléta*] ‖ **2.** pastilla *f.* [*pastílja*]; **- of soap,** pastilla de jabón [*de xabón*]

tackle aparejos *m. pl.* [*aparéxos*]

tailor sastre *m.* [*sástre*]; **t.-made** hecho(a) a medida [*étcho a medída*]

take (to) tomar *r.* [*tomár*], coger *r.* [*koxér*]: **to - a medicine,** tomar un medicamento [*tomár un medikaménto*] ‖ **2. to - effect,** hacer *irr.* efecto [*aθér efékto*] ‖ **3. to - part,** participar *r.* [*partiθipár*] (in/en) ‖ **4.** llevar *r.* [*ljebár*] (to/a) ‖ **5. to - off,** quitarse *r.* (una cosa) [*kitárse úna kósa*] (shoe, etc.)

talcum: - powder, polvos *m. pl.* de talco [*pólbos de tálko*]

talk (to) hablar *r.* [*ablár*]

tall *a.* alto(a) [*álto*]

tambourine pandereta *f.* [*pandaréta*]

tan *a.* tostado(a) [*tostádo*]

tangerine mandarina *f.* [*mandarína*]

tap grifo *m.* [*grífo*]

tape cinta *f.* [*θínta*]

tapioca tapioca *f.* [*tapjóka*]

tariff tarifa *f.* [*tarífa*]

tart tarta *f.* [*tárta*], pastel *m.* [*pastél*]: **orange -,** tarta de naranja [*de naránxa*]; **pineapple -,** tarta de piña [*de pínja*]; **strawberry -,** tarta de fresa [*de frésa*]

tassel borla *f.* [*bórla*];

taste gusto *m.* [*gústo*], sabor *m.* [*sabór*]; **-less** *a.* soso(a) [*sóso*]

tavern taberna *f.* [*tabérna*]

tax impuesto *m.* [*impwésto*]

taxi taxi *m.* [*táksi*]; **- driver** taxista *m.* [*taksísta*]; **- rank** parada *f.* de taxis [*paráda de táksis*]

tea té *m.* [*te*]; **- and rum,** té con ron [*te kon rron*]; **lemon -,** té con limón [*kon limón*]; **- with milk,** té con leche [*kon létche*]; **- bags** bolsitas *f. pl.* de té [*bolsítas de te*]; **-spoon** cucharilla *f.* [*kutcharílja*]

team equipo *m.* [*ekípo*]

teat tetilla *f.* [*tetílja*]

telegram telegrama *m.* [*telegráma*]; **- letter** carta *f.* telegrama [*kárta*]

telegraph telégrafo *m.* [*telégrafo*], **-ic** *a.* telegráfico(a) [*telegráfiko*]: **- postal order,** giro (postal) telegráfico [*xíro postál telegráfiko*]; **- office** oficina *f.* de telégrafos [*ofiθína de telégrafos*]

telephone teléfono *m.* [*teléfono*]; **- box** cabina *f.* telefónica [*kabína telefónika*]; **public -es,** locutorio *m.* telefónico [*lokutórjo telefóniko*]; **- call** llamada *f.* de teléfono [*ljamáda de*]; **-exchange** central *f.* de teléfonos [*θentrál de teléfonos*]; **- list** guía *f.* de teléfonos [*gía de teléfonos*]; **- number** número *m.* de teléfono [*número de*] ‖ **2.** *vb.* llamar *r.* por teléfono [*ljamár por teléfono*], telefonear *r.* [*telefoneár*]

television televisión *f.* [*telebisjón*]; **- set** televisor *m.* [*telebisór*]

tell (to) contar (ue) [*kontár*], decir *irr.* [*deθír*]

temperature temperatura *f.* [*temperatúra*]

temple templo *m.* [*témplo*]

tender *a.* tierno(a) [*tjérno*]; **-loin** solomillo *m.* [*solomíljo*]

tennis tenis *m.* [*ténis*]; **- equipment** equipo *m.* de tenis [*ekípo de*]; **- player** tenista *m.-f.* [*tenísta*]; **- shoes** botas *f. pl.* de tenis [*bótas de*]

tent tienda *f.* de campaña [*tjénda de kampánja*]

terminal terminal *f.* [*terminál*]

terrace terraza *f.* [*terráθa*]

terrible *a.* terrible [*terríble*]

test (to) (com)probar (ue) [*komprobár*], ensayar *r.* [*ensayár*] ‖ **2.** *n.* prueba *f.* [*prwéba*], ensayo *m.* [*ensájo*]

than que [*ke*]

thank (to) dar *irr.* las gracias [*dar las gráθjas*]; **- you!,** ¡gracias! [*gráθjas*]

the *art. def.* el [*el*], la [*la*] ‖ **2.** los [*los*], las [*las*] *pl.*

theatre teatro *m.* [*teátro*]

theft robo *m.* [*rróbo*]

their *a. pos.* su(s) [*su(s)*]

then *adv.* entonces [*entónθes*]

there *adv.* allí [*aljí*] ‖ **2. - is (are) ...,** hay ... [*aí*]

thermometer termómetro *m.* [*termómetro*]

thermos: - flask, termo *m.* [*térmo*]

these *a. dem.* estos(as) [*éstos*]

thigh muslo *m.* [*múslo*]
thin (to) adelgazarse *r.* [*adelgaθárse*] ‖ **2. to - out,** vaciar *r.* [*baθjár*] ‖ **3.** *a.* delgado(a) [*delgádo*]
thing cosa *f.* [*kósa*]
thimble dedal *m.* [*dedál*]
think (to) pensar (ie) [*pensár*] ‖ **2.** creer *r.* [*kreér*] (to believe)
thirsty *a.* sediento(a) [*sedjénto*]: **to be -,** tener *irr.* sed [*tenér sed*]
thirt/een *a.* trece [*tréθe*], **-y** treinta [*tréinta*]
this *a. dem.* este [*éste*], esta [*ésta*]
thousand *a.* mil [*mil*]
thread hilo *m.* [*ílo*]: **reel of -,** carrete *m.* de hilo [*karréte de*]
three *a.* tres [*tres*]
threaten (to) amenazar *r.* [*amenaθár*]
throat garganta *f.* [*gargánta*]
throw (to) tirar *r.* [*tirár*], lanzar *r.* [*lanθár*]; **-ing** lanzamiento *m.* [*lanθamjénto*]
thunder (to) tronar (ue) [*tronár*] ‖ **2.** *n.* trueno *m.* [*trwéno*]
Thursday jueves *m.* [*xwébes*]
ticket billete *m.* [*biljéte*], pasaje *m.* [*pasáxe*] (plane) ‖ **2.** entrada *f.* [*entráda*] (concert, etc.)
tide marea *f.* [*maréa*]
tie lazo *m.* [*láθo*], nudo *m.* [*núdo*] ‖ **2.** corbata *f.* [*korbáta*]: **-pin** alfiler *m.* de corbata [*alfilér de*]
tight (fitting) *a.* ceñido(a) [*θeñído*]; **-en (to)** estrechar *r.* [*estretchár*]
time tiempo *m.* [*tjémpo*]: **what - is it?,** ¿qué hora es? [*ke óra es*]; **-table** horario *m.* [*orárjo*] (flights, trains, etc.)
tin lata *f.* [*láta*]
tincture tintura *f.* [*tintúra*]
tint (to) teñir (i) [*teñír*]
tip propina *f.* [*propína*]
tired *a.* cansado(a) [*kansádo*]; **-ness** cansancio *m.* [*kansánθjo*]
toast (slices) pan *m.* tostado [*pan tostádo*]: **- slices,** tostadas *f. pl.* [*tostádas*]; **-ed** *a.* tostado(a) [*tostádo*]
tobacco tabaco *m.* [*tabáko*]: **black -,** tabaco negro [*négro*]; **mild -,** tabaco rubio [*rrúbjo*]; **cut -,** picadura *f.* [*pikadúra*]; **pipe -,** tabaco *m.* de pipa [*tabáko de pípa*]; **-nist's** estanco *m.* [*estánko*]
today *adv.* hoy [*oi*]
toe: - cap, puntera *f.* [*puntéra*]
together *adv.* juntos(as) [*xúntos*]
toilet lavabo *m.* [*labábo*], servicios *m. pl.* [*serbíθjos*]; **- paper** papel *m.* higiénico [*papél ixjéniko*]; **- soap** jabón *m.* de tocador [*xabón de tokadór*]

tomato tomate *m.* [*tomáte*]: **dressed -es,** tomates *pl.* aliñados [*tomátes aliñádos*]; **green -es,** tomates verdes [*bérdes*]; **stuffed -es,** tomates rellenos [*rreljénos*]; **- sauce** salsa *f.* de tomate [*sálsa de*]; **- soup** sopa *f.* de tomate [*sópa de*]
tomorrow *adv.* mañana [*mañána*]
tongs pinzas *f. pl.* [*pínθas*]
tongue lengua *f.* [*léngwa*]: **baked -,** lengua al horno [*al órno*]; **ox -,** lengua de buey [*de bwei*]; **steamed -,** lengua a la marinera [*a la marinéra*]
tonic tónico *m.* [*tóniko*]; **- water** tónica *f.* [*tónika*]
tonight *adv.* esta noche [*ésta nótche*]
tonsil amígdala *f.* [*amígdala*]
too *adv.* demasiado [*demasjádo*] ‖ **2. - much (many),** demasiado(a), (demasiados(as)): **- much money,** demasiado dinero [*demasjádo dinéro*]; **- many persons,** demasiadas personas [*demasjádas persónas*] ‖ **3.** *adv.* también [*tambjén*] (also)
tool herramienta *f.* [*erramjénta*]; **- box** caja *f.* de herramientas [*káxa de*]
tooth diente *m.* [*djénte*], muela *f.* [*mwéla*]: **- brush** cepillo *m.* de dientes [*θepíljo de djéntes*]; **-pick** palillo *m.* [*palíljo*]
topaz topacio *m.* [*topáθjo*]
touch (to) tocar *r.* [*tokár*]; **-ing: - up,** retoque *m.* [*rretóke*]
tough *a.* duro(a) [*dúro*]
tour viaje *m.* [*bjáxe*], excursión *f.* [*ekskursjón*]
tourist turista *m.-f.* [*turísta*]; **- guide** guía *m.-f.* turístico(a) [*gía turístiko*]; **- office** oficina *f.* de turismo [*ofiθína de turismo*]
towel toalla *f.* [*toálja*]: **sanitary -,** compresa *f.* higiénica [*komprésa ixjénika*]
tower torre *f.* [*tórre*]
town ciudad *f.* [*θjudád*]; **- hall** ayuntamiento *m.* [*ajuntamjénto*]
toy juguete *m.* [*xugéte*]
track pista *f.* [*písta*] ‖ **2.** vía *f.* [*bía*]
tractor tractor *m.* [*traktór*]
traffic tráfico *m.* [*tráfiko*]; **- policeman** guardia *m.* de tráfico [*gwárdja de tráfiko*]
train tren *m.* [*tren*]
tram tranvía *m.* [*trambía*]
trampoline trampolín *m.* [*trampolín*]
tranquilizer tranquilizante *m.* [*trankiliθánte*]
transfer (to) hacer *irr.* trasbordo [*aθér trasbórdo*] ‖ **2.** *n.* trasbordo *m.* [*trasbórdo*] ‖ **3.** trasferencia *f.* [*trasferénθja*] (money)

transmission transmisión *f.* [*transmisjón*]

transmit (to) expedir (i) [*ekspedír*], enviar *r.* [*embjár*]

travel (to) viajar *r.* [*bjaxár*] ‖ **2.** *n.* viaje *m.* [*bjáxe*]; **- agency** agencia *f.* de viajes [*axénθja de bjáxes*]; **- goods** artículos *m. pl.* de viaje [*artíkulos de*]; **-ler** viajero(a) *m.-f.* [*bjaxéro*]: **-'s cheque,** cheque *m.* de viaje [*tchéke de bjáxe*]

tray bandeja *f.* [*bandéxa*]

trim (to) cortar *r.* (el pelo) [*kortár*], arreglar *r.* [*arreglár*]; **-med** *a.* arreglado(a) [*arregládo*] (hair)

trinket dije *m.* [*díxe*]

trip viaje *m.* [*bjáxe*], excursión *f.* [*ekskursjón*]

tripe callos *m. pl.* [*káljos*]: **- fried and casseroled** *(with paprika sauce and tomatoes)*, callos a la madrileña [*a la madrilénja*]

tripod trípode *m.* [*trípode*]

trotters pies *m. pl.* de cerdo [*pjes de θérdo*]

trousers pantalones *m. pl.* [*pantalónes*]

trout trucha *f.* [*trútcha*]

trunk: - call, llamada *f.* interurbana [*ljamáda interurbána*], conferencia *f.* [*konferénθja*]

try (to) probar (ue) [*probár*], intentar *r.* [*intentár*]: **to - on a suit,** probar(se) (ue) un traje [*probárse un tráxe*]

tube tubo *m.* [*túbo*]

Tuesday martes *m.* [*mártes*]

tulip tulipán *m.* [*tulipán*]

tulle tul *m.* [*tul*]

tuning reglaje *m.* [*regláxe*]

tunny atún *m.* [*atún*]: **- in olive oil,** atún en aceite [*en aθéite*]; **pickled -,** atún en escabeche [*en eskabétche*]; **fresh -,** atún fresco [*frésko*]; **stripper -,** bonito *m.* [*boníto*]

turbine turbina *f.* [*turbína*]

turbot rodaballo *m.* [*rrodabáljo*]

turkey pavo *m.* [*pábo*]: **stuffed -,** pavo relleno [*rreljéno*]

turnip nabo *m.* [*nábo*]

turn (to) torcer (ue) [*torθér*], girar *r.* [*xirár*]; **-stile** taquilla *f.* [*takílja*]

turquoise turquesa *f.* [*turkésa*]

tweed paño *m.* de lana [*pánjo de lána*]

twelve *a.* doce [*dóθe*]

twenty *a.* veinte [*béinte*]

twisted: - bread, trenzas *f. pl.* [*trénθas*]

two *a.* dos [*dos*]

typewriter máquina *f.* de escribir [*mákina de eskribír*]; **- ribbon** cinta *f.* para máquina (de escribir) [*θínta pára*]

typical *a.* típico(a) [*típiko*]

tyre cubierta *f.* [*kubjérta*], neumático *m.* [*neumátiko*]; **- burst** reventón *m.* [*rrebentón*]

U

ulcer úlcera *f.* [*úlθera*]: **gastric -,** úlcera de estómago [*de estómago*]; **duodenal -,** úlcera de duodeno [*de dwodéno*]

umbrella paraguas *m.* [*parágwas*]

uncle tío *m.* [*tío*]

uncomfortable *a.* incómodo(a) [*inkómodo*]

uncooked *a.* crudo(a) [*krúdo*]

under *prep.* bajo [*báxo*], debajo de [*debáxo de*]; **-done** poco hecho(a) [*póko étcho*]; **-ground** metro *m.* [*métro*]; **-pants** calzoncillos *m. pl.* [*kalθonθíljos*]; **-stand (to)** comprender *r.* [*komprendér*], entender (ie) [*entendér*]; **-water: - fishing,** pesca *f.* submarina [*péska submarína*]; **-fishing equipment,** equipo *m.* de pesca submarina [*ekípo de*]; **-wear** ropa *f.* interior [*rrópa interjór*]; **-write (to)** firmar *r.* [*firmár*]

undress (to) desnudarse *r.* [*desnudárse*], quitarse *r.* la ropa [*kitárse la rrópa*]

university universidad *f.* [*unibersidád*]; **- choral group** tuna *f.* universitaria [*túna unibersitárja*]

unmarried *a.* soltero(a) [*soltéro*]

unpleasant *a.* desagradable [*desagradáble*]

unwell *a.* indispuesto(a) [*indispwésto*]

up *adv.* hacia arriba [*áθja arríba*]; **-holstery** tapicería *f.* [*tapiθería*]; **-per** *a.* superior [*superjór*]: **- lip,** labio *m.* superior [*lábjo*]; **-stairs** *adv.* (escalera) arriba [*(eskaléra) arríba*]; **-wards** *adv.* hacia arriba [*áθja arríba*]

urgent *a.* urgente [*urxénte*]; **-ly** *adv.* urgentemente [*urxenteménte*]

us *pron. pers.* nos [*nos*]

utensil utensilio *m.* [*utensíljo*]

V

vacation vacaciones *f. pl.* [*bakaθjónes*]
vaccinate (to) vacunar *r.* [*bakunár*]; **-d** *a.* vacunado(a) [*bakunádo*]
vaccination vacuna *f.* [*bakúna*] ‖ **2.** vacunación *f.* [*bakunaθjón*]; **- certificate** certificado *m.* de vacunación [*θertifikádo de*]
value valor *m.* [*balór*], precio *m.* [*préθjo*]: **declared -,** valor declarado [*balór deklarádo*] ‖ **2.** importe *m.* [*impórte*]
valve válvula *f.* [*bálbula*]
vanilla vainilla *f.* [*bainílja*]
variety: - show, variedades *f. pl.* [*barjedádes*]
vase jarrón *m.* [*xarrón*]
veal ternera *f.* [*ternéra*], carne *f.* de ternera [*kárne de*]: **roast -,** ternera asada [*asáda*]; **stewed -,** ternera *f.* a la cazuela [*a la kaθwéla*]; **- chop** chuleta *f.* de ternera [*tchuléta de*]
vegetables verduras *f. pl.* [*berdúras*] ‖ **2.** legumbres *f. pl.* [*legúmbres*]: **boiled (cooked) -,** legumbres cocidas [*koθídas*]

vehicle vehículo *m.* [*beíkulo*]
vein vena *f.* [*béna*]
velvet terciopelo *m.* [*terθjopélo*]
ventilat/ed *a.* ventilado(a) [*bentiládo*]; **-ion** ventilación *f.* [*bentilaθjón*]; **-or** ventilador *m.* [*bentiladór*]
vermicelli fideos *m. pl.* [*fidéos*]: **fried -,** fideos a la cazuela [*a la kaθwéla*]
vermouth vermut *m.* [*bermút*]
very *adv.* muy [*muí*]
vest camiseta *f.* [*kamiséta*]: **half-sleeved -,** camiseta *f.* de media manga [*de médja mánga*]; **sleeveless -,** camiseta sin manga [*sin mánga*]
vestibule vestíbulo *m.* [*bestíbulo*]
vibrate (to) vibrar *r.* [*bibrár*]
victory victoria *f.* [*biktórja*]
view vista *f.* [*bísta*]; **-finder** visor *m.* [*bisór*]
vinegar vinagre *m.* [*binágre*]
violet violeta *f.* [*bjoléta*]
violin violín *m.* [*bjolín*]
visit (to) visitar *r.* [*bisitár*] ‖ **2.** *n.* visita *f.* [*bisíta*]
vitamin vitamina *f.* [*bitamína*]
vocalist cantor *m.* [*kantór*]
vodka vodca *f.* [*bódka*]
vomiting vómitos *m. pl.* [*bómitos*]
voucher bono *m.* [*bóno*], vale *m.* [*bále*]

waistcoat chaleco *m.* [*tchaléko*]

wait (to) esperar *r.* [*esperár*] ‖ **2.** servir (i) [*serbír*] (at table); **-er** camarero *m.* [*kamaréro*]; **-ing** espera *f.* [*espéra*]: **- room** sala *f.* de espera [*sála de*]; **-ress** camarera *f.* [*kamaréra*]

wake (to) despertar(se) (ie) [*despertárse*]

walk (to) pasear *r.* [*paseár*], andar *irr.* [*andár*] ‖ **2.** *n.* paseo *m.* [*paséo*]

wall pared *f.* [*paréd*], muro *m.* [*múro*]: **- clock** reloj *m.* de pared [*rrelóx de paréd*]; **-et** cartera *f.* [*kartéra*]; **- paper** papel *m.* pintado [*papél pintádo*]

walnut nuez *f.* [*nweθ*]

want (to) desear *r.* [*deseár*], querer *irr.* [*kerér*]

wardrobe armario *m.* [*armárjo*], guardarropa *m.* [*gwardarrópa*]

warm *a.* caliente [*kaljénte*]: **- drink,** bebida *f.* caliente [*bebída*]

warn (to) avisar *r.* [*abisár*], advertir (ie) [*adbertír*]

wash (to) lavar *r.* [*labár*]

watch reloj *m.* [*relóx*]: **pocket -,** reloj de bolsillo [*de bolsíljo*]; **-maker's** relojería *f.* [*rreloxería*]

water agua *f.* [*ágwa*]: **mineral -,** agua mineral [*minerál*]; **sparkling mineral -,** agua mineral con gas [*kon gas*]; **still mineral -,** agua mineral sin gas [*sin gas*]; **tonic -,** tónica *f.* [*tónika*]; **- bottle** cantimplora *f.* [*kantimplóra*]; **- bicycle** bicicleta *f.* acuática [*biθikléta akwátika*]; **- closet** water [*wáter*]; **- colour** pintura *f.* a la acuarela [*pintúra a la akwaréla*]; **-cress** berro *m.* [*bérro*]; **-melon** sandía *f.* [*sandía*]; **- polo** water-polo *m.* [*wáter pólo*]; **- proof** *a.* impermeable [*impermeáble*]; **- pump** bomba *f.* de agua [*bómba de água*]; **w.-skiing** esquí acuático [*eskí akwátiko*]; **w.-skis** esquís *m. pl.* acuáticos [*eskís akwátikos*]; **- scooter** patín *m.* (de pedales) [*patín (de pedáles)*]

wave ola *f.* [*óla*] (sea) ‖ **2.** onda *f.* [*ónda*]

wax cera *f.* [*θéra*]: **depilatory -,** cera de depilación [*de depilaθjón*]

way camino *m.* [*kamíno*]

weak *a.* flojo(a) [*flóxo*]

weather tiempo *m.* [*tjémpo*]

wear ropa *f.* [*rrópa*]

week semana *f.* [*semána*]; **-ly** semanario *m.* [*semanárjo*]

weight (to) pesar *r.* [*pesár*] ‖ **2.** *n.* peso *m.* [*péso*]; **- belt** cinturón *m.* de lastre [*θinturón de lástre*]

well *adv.* bien [*bjén*]; **w.-done** muy hecho(a) [*mui étcho*]

wheel rueda *f.* [*rrwéda*]: **spinning -,** rueca *f.* [*rrwéka*]

whipped: - cream, nata *f.* [*náta*]

whisker: side -, patilla *f.* [*patílja*]

whisky whisky *m.* [*wíski*]: **Bourbon -,** whisky americano [*amerikáno*]; **Canadian -,** whisky canadiense [*kanadjénse*]; **Scotch -,** whisky escocés [*eskoθés*]; **Irish -,** whisky irlandés [*irlandés*]; **Spanish -,** whisky español [*espanjól*]; **- with ice,** whisky con hielo [*kon jélo*]

whit/e *a.* blanco(a) [*blánko*]: **- fish** pescado *m.* blanco [*peskádo*]; **-ing** pescadilla *f.* [*peskadílja*]

wholemeal: - bread, pan *m.* integral [*pan integrál*]

wide *a.* ancho(a) [*ántcho*], extenso(a) [*eksténso*]: **- angle** gran angular *m.* [*gran angulár*]; **-n (to)** ensanchar *r.* [*ensantchár*]

width anchura *f.* [*antchúra*] ‖ **2.** de ancho [*de ántcho*]

wig peluca *f.* [*pelúka*]

wild *a.* salvaje [*salbáxe*]: **- boar** jabalí *m.* [*xabalí*]

win (to) ganar *r.* [*ganár*]

wind viento *m.* [*bjénto*]

window ventana *f.* [*bentána*] ‖ **2.** ventanilla *f.* [*bentanílja*]

winder bobina *f.* [*bobína*]

windscreen parabrisas *m.* [*parabrísas*]; **- wipers** limpiaparabrisas *m. pl.* [*limpjaparabrísas*]

wine vino *m.* [*bíno*]: **after dinner -,** vino de postre [*de póstre*]; **bottled -,** vino embotellado [*emboteljádo*]; **bottle of -,** botella *f.* de vino [*botélja de*]; **claret -,** vino clarete [*klaréte*]; **clear -,** vino claro [*kláro*]; **dark -,** vino negro [*négro*]; **dry -,** vino seco [*séko*]; **glass of -,** vaso *m.* de vino [*báso de*]; **- of the house,** vino de la casa [*de la kása*]; **ordinary -,** vino corriente [*korrjénte*]; **red -,** vino tinto [*tínto*]; **rosé -,** vino rosado [*rrosádo*]; **sparkling -,** vino espumoso [*espumóso*]; **sweet -,** vino dulce [*dúlθe*]; **table -,** vino de mesa [*de mésa*]; **white -,** vino blanco [*blánko*]; **- glass** copa *f.* [*kópa*], vaso *m.* [*báso*]; **- jug** porrón *m.* [*porrón*]; **- shop** bodega *f.* [*bodéga*], tienda *f.*

de vinos (y licores) [*tjénda de bínos (i likóres)*]

wing ala *f.* [*ála*]

winner vencedor(a) *m.-f.* [*benθedór*], ganador(a) *m.-f.* [*ganadór*] (of a prize, etc.)

winter invierno *m.* [*imbjérno*]; - **sports** deportes *m. pl.* de nieve [*depórtes de njébe*]

withdraw (to) retirar *r.* [*rretirár*], cobrar *r.* [*kobrár*] (money); -**al** cobro *m.* [*kóbro*], reintegro *m.* [*rreintégro*]

witness testigo *m.-f.* [*testígo*]

wood madera *f.* [*madéra*]: **of** -, de madera [*de*]

wool lana *f.* [*lána*]

work (to) trabajar *r.* [*trabaxár*], funcionar *r.* [*funθjonár*] ‖ **2.** *n.* trabajo *m.* [*trabáxo*] ‖ **3.** obra *f.* [*óbra*]: - **of art,** obra de arte [*de árte*]; -**manship** hechura *f.* [*etchúra*]

worsted estambre *m.* [*estámbre*]

worth: to be -, valer *irr* [*balér*]

wrap (to): **to** - **up,** envolver (ue) [*embolbér*]

write (to) escribir *r.* [*eskribír*]

writing: - materials, artículos *m. pl.* de papelería [*artíkulos de papelería*]; - **paper** papel *m.* de carta [*papél de kárta*]

wrought: - iron lamp, lámpara *f.* de hierro forjado [*lámpara de jérro forxádo*]

yacht yate *m.* [*játe*]
year año *m.* [*ánjo*]
yellow *a.* amarillo(a) [*amaríljo*]

zip: - *fastener,* cremallera *f.* [*krema-ljéra*]

VI.

SPANISH-ENGLISH

GASTRONOMY

DICTIONARY

aceitunas *n. f. pl.* olives ‖ - *negras* black olives ‖ - *rellenas* stuffed olives ‖ - *verdes* green olives

aceite *n. m.* oil ‖ - *de girasol* subflower oil ‖ - *de oliva* olive oil

acelgas *n. f. pl.* chards

achicoria *n. f.* chicory

agua *n. f.* water ‖ - *mineral* mineral water ‖ - *mineral con gas* sparkling mineral water ‖ - *mineral sin gas* still mineral water

ahumado, da *a.* smoked

ajo *n. m.* garlic

ajillo, al *expr.* with garlic

albaricoque *n. m.* apricot

albóndigas *n. f. pl.* meat balls ‖ - *a la bilbaína* meat balls Bilbao style *(in a casserole, with sauce of onions, carrots, flour, broth, tomato purée and white wine)* ‖ - *con salsa* meat balls with sauce *(of oil, onions, flour, dry sherry and broth of meat; cooked in a casserole)* ‖ - *montañesas* meat balls Santander style *(of beef, egg, onions, parsley; fried)*

alcachofas *n. f. pl.* artichokes ‖ - *a la vinagreta* artichokes in vinegar ‖ - *fritas* fried artichokes

alioli *n. m.* garlic sauce *(a kind of mayonnaise sauce but without eggs; made of garlic, oil and water)*

almejas *n. f. pl.* clams ‖ - *a la canaria* clams Canarian style *(in a casserole with sauce of parsley, garlic, tomato sauce, pepper, white wine, salt and oil)* ‖ - *a la marinera* steamed clams *(in a casserole, with sauce of oil or butter, onions, parsley, pepper and salt)* ‖ - *a la sanluqueña* clams Sanlúcar style *(stemed in a casserole with sauce of water, paprika, white wine and salt)* ‖ - *a la valenciana* clams Valencia style *(steamed in a casserole with tomatoes, black pepper, garlic, parsley, oil and salt)* ‖ - *al natural* natural clams *(uncooked with lemon)* ‖ - *con finas hierbas* clams with herbs *(baked in the oven with onions, mushrooms, butter, breadcrumbs, parsley and salt)* ‖ - *de Fuenterrabía a la marinera* steamed clams Fuenterrabia style *(in a casserole with sauce of oil, onions, paprika, white wine, garlic, white pepper and salt)*

almendras *n. f. pl.* almonds ‖ - *saladas* salted almonds ‖ - *tostadas* toasted almonds

almuerzo *n. m.* lunch

alubias *n. f. pl.* broad beans

anguila *n. f.* eel ‖ - *ahumada* fumed eel

angulas *n. f. pl.* baby eels ‖ - *a la cazuela* baby eels in casserole *(with olive oil, garlic, pepper and salt)*

aperitivo *n. m.* aperitive

apio *n. m.* celery

arenque *n. m.* herring || - ***salado*** pickled herring

arroz *n. m.* rice || - ***a la aragonesa*** rice Aragón style *(in a casserole, with rabbit, pork, squids, crabs, garlic, peas, pepper and other spices)* || - ***a la catalana*** rice Catalan style *(in a casserole or paella pan with ham, sausages, onions, lard, parsley, pepper, broth, garlic and salt)* || - ***a la cazuela*** rice in casserole *(with potatoes, onions and meat)* || - ***a la cubana*** rice Cuban style *(with fried egg, fried banana and tomato sauce)* || - ***a la leonesa*** rice León style *(in a casserole with chicken, prawns, clams, eel, bacon, pepper, garlic, bay leaf, tomato, crabs, white wine, parsley, onions, paprika, oil, peas, sausages, water and salt)* || - ***a la mallorquina*** rice Mallorca style *(in a casserole and baked in the oven; with red mullets, angler fish, pieces of sausage, onions, oil, tomatoes, clams or mussels, garlic, green or red peppers, peas, French beans, saffron, pepper and salt)* || - ***a la marinera*** steamed rice *(in a casserole or paella pan; with red peppers, paprika, oil, fish (angler fish, rock cod, eel, etc.), garlic, saffron, water or broth and salt)* || - ***a la milanesa*** rice Milan style *(boiled, with ham, tomatoes, peas and cheese)* || - ***a la sevillana*** rice Sevilla style *(in a casserole and baked in the oven, with squids, crabs, ham, red peppers, onions, saffron, oil, angler fish, clams, hard boiled eggs, peas, garlic and parsley)* || - ***a la paella*** (see: paella) || - ***a la valenciana*** (see: paella Valencia style) || - ***al estilo barcelonés*** rice Barcelona style *(in a casserole or paella pan; with chicken, onions, peppers, squids, white pork sausage (boiled), clams, tomatoes, garlic, pepper, parsley, oil, water and salt)* || - ***blanco*** boiled rice || - ***canario*** rice Canarian style *(in a casserole, with pork, banana, eggs, tomatoes, onions, oil, water and salt)* || - ***con bacalao*** rice with cod *(in a casserole, of cod, peppers, onions, paprika, fried tomato, garlic, peas, mussels, boiled artichokes, parsley, water, pepper, salt and saffron)* || - ***Costa Brava*** rice Costa Brava style *(in a paella pan, with mussels, squid, large prawns, garlic, purée of tomatoes, water and salt)*

asado, a *a.* **1.** roasted || *n. m.* **2.** roasted meat

atún *n. m.* tunny || - ***a la plancha*** grilled tunny || - ***en aceite*** tunny en olive oil || - ***en escabeche*** pickled tunny || - ***fresco*** fresh tunny

avellanas *n. f. pl.* hazel nuts

azafrán *n. m.* saffron

B

bacalao *n. m.* **1.** (fresh) cod **2.** salted and dried cod || - ***a la bilbaína*** cod Bilbao style *(boiled, served with sauce in a casserole; with peppers, oil, lard, onions, ham, water, hard boiled yolk, sugar, nut meg and salt)* || - ***a la catalana*** cod Catalan style *(in a casserole and baked in the oven; with fried tomato, pepper, toasted almonds, garlic, saffron, oil, paprika, onions and salt)* || - ***a la "llauna"*** cod in casserole *(prepared in an earthenware casserole and baked in the oven (with garlic, parsley, tomato and toasted bread)* || - ***a la madrileña*** cod Madrid style *(in a frying pan, afterwards cooked in a casserole; with sauce of onions, lemon, pepper, flour, clove, nut meg and oil)* || - ***a la mallorquina*** cod Mallorca style *(boiled; with water, white wine, flour, onions, garlic, parsley, lemon, oil; served with toasted bread)* || - ***a la riojana*** cod Rioja style *(in a casserole, with sauce, spiced sausage (paprika), onions, oil, tomatoes, peppers and water)* || - ***a la valenciana*** cod

Valencia style *(in a casserole with boiled rice baked in the oven; onions, oil, eggs, tomatoes, bay leaf, parsley, garlic, breadcrumbs, flour, pepper, salt and water)* ‖ - *a la vizcaína* cod Vizcaya style *(in a casserole with sauce; lard or bacon, red peppers, onions, garlic, hard boiled yolk, bread slices, oil and salt)* ‖ - *al ajo* cod with garlic *(fried in a pan, with white pepper, paprika, oil, garlic, vinegar and water)* ‖ - *al "pil-pil"* cod "pil-pil" *(in a casserole with sauce of oil and garlic)* ‖ - *en salsa verde al estilo navarro* cod Navarra style with green sauce *(in a casserole, with fresh peas, onions, parsley, pepper, garlic, water, salt and oil)* ‖ - *con tomate* cod with tomato sauce

batido *n. m.* shake ‖ - *de chocolate* chocolate shake ‖ - *de fresa* strawberry shake ‖ - *de plátano* banana shake ‖ - *de vainilla* vanilla shake

beicon *n. m.* bacon

berberechos *n. m. pl.* cockles

berenjenas *n. f. pl.* aubergines ‖ - *asadas* roasted aubergines ‖ - *fritas* fried aubergines ‖ - *rellenas* stuffed aubergines ‖ - *rellenas al estilo balear* stuffed aubergines Balear style *(fried in a pan and baked in the oven; stuffed with minced meat, ham, onions, tomato, flour, eggs, breadcrumbs, garlic, milk and salt)*

besugo *n. m.* bream ‖ - *a la guipuzcoana* bream Guipúzcoa style *(barbecued, with sauce of lemon, oil, garlic and salt)* ‖ - *al ajo arriero* bream country style with garlic *(boiled, with onions, parsley, vinegar, sauce of garlic, flour and paprika)* ‖ - *al horno* bream baked in the oven ‖ - *al natural* bream natural style *(boiled in a casserole and baked in the oven; with white pepper, lemon, water or fish broth, paprika, onions, oil and salt)* ‖ - *con almendras* bream with almonds *(in a casserole baked in the oven; with sauce of toasted almonds, lemon, onions, flour, broth of meat or fish, oil, parsley, pepper and salt)* ‖ - *en salsa* bream with sauce *(in a casserole; with flour, oil, garlic, parsley, peppers, tomato sauce and salt)* ‖ - *mechado* larded bream *(in a casserole and baked in the oven; with lard, garlic, lemon, oil, broth of meat, vinegar, pepper and salt)*

bicarbonato *n. m.* bicarbonate

bistec *n. m.* steak ‖ - *a la brasa* barbecued steak ‖ - *a la plancha* grilled steak ‖ - *frito* fried steak

bizcocho *n. m.* sponge cake

bocadillo *n. m.* sandwich (made with local bread) ‖ - *caliente* warm sandwich (on the grill) ‖ - *de carne* meat sandwich ‖ - *de salchichas de Frankfurt* Francfort sausage sandwich ‖ - *de jamón* ham sandwich ‖ - *de jamón y queso* cheese and ham sandwich ‖ - *de lomo* pork sandwich ‖ - *de queso* cheese sandwich ‖ - *de sobrasada* sausage (paste) sandwich ‖ - *de tortilla* omelette sandwich

bonito *n. m.* tunny ‖ - *a la riojana* tunny Rioja style *(in a casserole, with garlic, tomato purée, red peppers, oil, pepper, water and salt)* ‖ - *fresco con aceitunas* fresh tunny with olives *(pickled and fried; with sauce of garlic, vinegar, white wine, bay leaf, oil, green olives, water, pepper and salt)*

boquerones *n. m. pl.* fresh anchovies ‖ - *a la vinagreta* anchovies in vinegar ‖ - *fritos* fried anchovies

brandada de bacalao *n. f.* cod soufflé *(in a casserole, with onions, butter, parsley, paprika, pepper, hard boiled yolk, milk, water, oil and salt)*

brasa *n. f.* barbecue ‖ *a la* - barbecued

brócoli *n. m.* broccoli

brécol *n. m.* broccoli

budín *n. m.* pudding

bullabesa *n. f.* bouillabaisse (Frensh fish soup)

buñuelos *n. m. pl.* deep fried batter mixture ‖ - *de bacalao* deep fried batter mixture of cod *(with chopped cod, flour, milk, eggs, oil and water; fried in very hot oil)*

butifarra *n. f.* pork sausage ‖ - *a la parrilla* barbecued pork sausage ‖ - *con alubias* grilled pork sausage with white beans ‖ - *frita* fried pork sausage ‖ - *negra* black pork sausage

C

cabeza *n. f.* head ‖ - *de jabalí* boar's head ‖ - *de ternera* veal's head

cabritillo *n. m.* goat ‖ - *asado* roast goat

cacahuetes *n. m. pl.* peanuts ‖ - *salados* salted peanuts ‖ - *tostados* toasted peanuts

cacao *n. m.* cocoa

café *n. m.* coffee ‖ - *con hielo* black coffee on ice cubes ‖ - *con leche* white coffee ‖ - *helado* iced coffee ‖ - *solo* black coffee ‖ - *cortado* coffee with a dash of milk

calabacines *n. m. pl.* baby marrows ‖ - *asados* grilled baby marrows (with salt)

calamares *n. m. pl.* squids ‖ - *a la mallorquina* squids Mallorca style *(stuffed and stewed in a casserole; with onions, raisins, pine nuts, breadcrumbs, eggs, white pepper, oil, water, white wine and salt)* ‖ - *a la plancha* grilled squids ‖ - *a la romana* squids Roman style *(fried in batter)* ‖ - *a la santanderina* squids Santander style *(stuffed and stewed in a casserole; with onions, garlic, tomatoes, ham, parsley, sugar, bread, nut meg, broth of meat or fish, paprika, salt, oil and pepper)* ‖ - *a lo nina* squids Canarian style *(stewed in a casserole; with onions, tomatoes, garlic, parsley, bay leaf, pepper, vinegar, oil and breadcrumbs)* ‖ - *en su tinta* squids with a black sauce made from its own "ink" *(lightly fried in a pan and stewed in a casserole; with sauce onions, tomatoes, oil, bread, garlic, parsley, brandy, breadcrumbs, water and salt)* ‖ - *fritos a la andaluza* fried squids Andalusian style *(fried in a pan with oil, flour and salt)* ‖ - *rellenos* stuffed squids

caldeirada gallega *n. f.* fish stew Galicia style *(in an earthenware casserole; with eel, angler fish, rock cod or hake, white wine, flour, onions, garlic, bay leaf, parsley, toasted bread slices, oil, water and salt; the broth and the fish are separately served)*

caldereta de pescado de Gijón *n. f.* fish stew Gijón style *(in a casserole; different kinds of little fish, bass, gilthead bream, red mullets, large prawns, mussels, etc., oil, onion, paprika, water, pepper, parsley, sherry, nut meg, peppers and salt)*

caldereta extremeña *n. f.* fish stew Extremadura style *(in an earthenware casserole; with sauce, meat and liver of lamb, garlic, wine, peppers, bay leaf, black pepper, paprika, oil, water and salt)*

calderete *n. m.* meat stew Navarra style *(of veal (rabbit or lamb), with potatoes, garlic, onion, parsley, bay leaf, spiced sausage, bacon, tomato and brandy. All ingredients* *are stewed together with the meat in an earthenware casserole; served with boiled asparagus, artichokes and French beans)*

caldo *n. m.* broth ‖ - *de carne* meat broth ‖ - *de gallina* chicken broth ‖ - *de pescado* fish broth ‖ - *de pescado a la murciana* fish broth Murcia style *(in a casserole; different kinds of fish, potatoes, oil, onions, tomatoes, saffron, pepper, paprika, water and salt)* ‖ *caldo gallego* meat broth Galicia style *(in an earthenware casserole, of cabbage, potatoes, white beans, ham, lard, spicy sausage (paprika), garlic, veal, chicken, bacon, water, bay leaf, salt, etc.)* ‖ - *vegetal* vegetable broth

callos *n. m. pl.* tripe ‖ - *a la extremeña* tripe Extremadura style *(with lam's trotters, oil, onions, water, flour, paprika, black pork sausage, garlic, parsley and salt; stewed in a casserole)* ‖ - *a la gallega* tripe Galicia style *(in a casserole, with lemon, vinegar, water, veal's trotters, onion, garlic, lard, bread, spicy pork sausage, boiled chick peas, pepper, nut meg, clove, paprika and salt)* ‖ - *a la madrileña* tripe Madrid style *(in a casserole; tripe, veal's trotters, ham, spicy pork sausage (paprika), red peppers, parsley, tomato purée, water, vinegar, onion, garlic, leek, carrots, parsley, flour, black pepper, paprika and salt)* ‖ - *a la montañesa* tripe Cantabria style *(in a casserole; tripe of veal or lamb, onions, garlic, pepper, paprika, clove, water, bay leaf and salt)* ‖ - *a la murciana* tripe Murcia style *(tripe, lamb's trotters, chick peas, lard, ham, spicy pork sausage (paprika), water, herbs, saffron and salt)* ‖ - *picantes* spicy tripe *(in a casserole; tripe, trotters, ears, pork, etc.; flour, breadcrumbs, water, onions, oil, garlic, bay leaf, clove, black pepper, tomatoes, spicy sauce and salt)* ‖ - *de ternera San Carlos* veal tripe San Carlos style *(fried and baked in the oven; with sauce; veal tripe, fresh breadcrumbs, oil, white wine, eggs, tomatoes, flour, onions, garlic, lemon, potatoes, pepper and salt)*

camarones *n. m. pl.* shrimps ‖ - *a la andaluza* shrimps Andalusian style *(fried in oil; with tomatoes, flour, oil, garlic and salt)*

canelones *n. m. pl.* cannelloni *(finely minced meat served inside a hot pastry like casing with white sauce)* ‖ - *al estilo catalán* cannelloni Catalan style *(with white sauce, roasted in the oven; minced pork meat, chicken liver, tomato purée, grated cheese, oil, onions, sherry, breast of chicken, milk, butter, ham, truffles, water and salt)*

canapés *n. m. pl.* canapes

cangrejos *n. m. pl.* crabs ‖ - *a la pamplonesa* crabs Pamplona style *(stewed in a casserole; with parsley, pepper, clove, onions, carrots, white wine and salt)* ‖ - *de mar* sea crabs ‖ - *de río* river crabs

caña *n. f.* glass of beer

caracoles *n. m. pl.* snails ‖ - *a la alcoyana* snails Alcoy style *(in an earthenware casserole; with onions, garlic, bacon, tomato sauce, bay leaf, parsley, pepper, slat, herbs and oil)* ‖ - *a la andaluza* snails Andalusian style *(in a casserole with water, oil, garlic, toasted almonds, paprika, tomatoes, onions, saffron, pepper, lemon and salt)* ‖ - *a la extremeña* snails Extremadura style *(in an earthenware casserole, with water, butter, parsley, garlic, clove, bay leaf, flour, hard boiled yolk, lemon and salt)* ‖ - *a la madrileña* snails Madrid style *(in a casserole, with bay leaf, paprika, pepper, black pork sausage, garlic sausage, flour, salt, water and oil)* ‖ - *a la maña* snails Aragon style *(with onions, garlic, parsley, tomato sauce, paprika, flour, oil, bay leaf, salt and water)* ‖ - *a la marinera* steamed snails *(in a casserole, with vinegar, water, red wine, flour, garlic, bay leaf, onions, oil, salted pork, bread and* salt) ‖ - *a la murciana* snails Murcia style *(in a casserole with sauce; ham, onions, tomatoes, garlic, oil, white wine, paprika, flour, fresh peppermint, herbs and salt)* ‖ - *a la riojana* snails Rioja style *(in an earthenware casserole; with bay leaf, oil, onions, garlic, parsley, tomato sauce, flour, peppers, broth, ham and salt)* ‖ - *al borno* snails baked in the oven *(in a heat-resistent dish, with water, onions, carrots, bay leaf, garlic, pepper, parsley and salt)*

carajillo *n. m.* coffee with liqueur ‖ - *de anís* coffee with aniseed ‖ - *de coñac* coffee with brandy ‖ - *de ron* coffee with rum

carne *n. f.* meat ‖ - *a la brasa* barbecued meat ‖ - *almendrada* loin of pork with almonds *(fried and baked in the oven; with almonds, hard boiled egg, white pepper, milk, flour, lard, red wine, water and salt)* ‖ - *asada* roast beef ‖ - *de buey* beef ‖ - *de buey asado* roast beef ‖ - *de carnero* mutton ‖ - *de cerdo* pork ‖ - *de cerdo asado* roast pork ‖ - *de cordero* lamb ‖ - *de cordero asado* roast lamb ‖ - *de ternera* veal ‖ - *de ternera asada* roast veal ‖ - *estofada* stewed meat ‖ - *guisada* braised meat ‖ - *montañesa* stewed meat Cantabrian style *(in a casserole, with sauce, onions, white wine, rice, water, broth of meat, pepper, flour, butter and salt)* ‖ - *picada* minced meat

carnero *n. m.* mutton ‖ - *asado* roast mutton ‖ - *guisado* stewed mutton

carpa *n. f.* carp

carta *n. f.* carte, menu ‖ *a la* - á la carte ‖ - *de bebidas* carte of drinks ‖ - *de vinos* carte of wines

castañas *n. f. pl.* chestnuts

cava *n. m.* sparkling wine (made in Spain) ‖ - *brut* brut sparkling wine ‖ - *brut natural* natural brut sparkling wine ‖ - *seco* dry sparkling wine ‖ - *semiseco* half dry sparkling wine

caviar *n. m.* caviar ‖ - *iraní* Iranian caviar ‖ - *ruso* Russian caviar

caza *n. f.* game

cazuela *n. f.* heat resistant dish, casserole ‖ *a la* - made in a casserole ‖ - *a lo Cho María* fish stew Cho María style *(lightly fried and cooked in a casserole; with potatoes, peppers, saffron, onions, tomatoes, garlic, toasted almonds, oil, flour, broth of meat and salt)* ‖ - *a lo nina* fish stew Nina style *(in a casserole, with potatoes, peppers, tomatoes, saffron, onions, garlic, parsley, paprika, pepper, oil, water and salt)*

cebolla *n. f.* onion ‖ - *tierna* spring onion

cena *n. f.* supper

cenar *vb.* to have supper

centollo *n. m.* spider crab ‖ - *relleno* stuffed spider crab *(boiled in slated water and emptied; stuffing of the meat, onion, garlic, and parsley; it is fried and covered with breadcrumbles and grated cheese; baked in the oven)*

cerveza *n. f.* beer ‖ - *de barril* draught beer ‖ - *embotellada* bottled beer ‖ - *negra* black beer

champán *n. m.* champagne

chocolate *n. m.* chocolate ‖ - *a la española* chocolate Spanish style (with milk) ‖ - *a la francesa* chocolate French style ‖ - *a la suiza* chocolate Swiss style (with whipped cream)

chorizo *n. m.* spicy sausage (with paprika)

chuletas *n. f. pl.* chops ‖ - *con alioli* barbecued chops (with garlic sauce) ‖ - *de cerdo* pork chops ‖ - *de cerdo a la madrileña* pork chops Madrid style *(in a casserole, with oil, garlic, parsley, paprika, bay leaf, pepper and salt; served with roasted potatoes or tomato sauce)* ‖ - *de cerdo a la naranja* pork chops with oranges *(lightly grilled and cooked in a casserole; with sauce of oranges, water, dry sherry, oil, black pepper and salt)* ‖ - *de cerdo a la riojana* pork chops Rioja style *(barbecued and served with red peppers)* ‖ - *de cordero* lamb chops ‖ - *de cordero a la navarra* lamb chops Navarra style *(fried and cooked in a casserole, with ham, onion, tomatoes, sugar, spicy sausage (paprika), lard oil and salt)* ‖ - *de ternera a la castellana* veal chops Castilian style *(in a casserole, with sauce of lard, dry sherry, meat broth, oil, garlic, pepper, water and salt; served with asparagus or French beans)* ‖ - *de ternera a la riojana* veal Rioja style *(larded and fried; with eggs, peppers, tomato purée, white wine, meat broth and salt)* ‖ - *de ternera de Langreo* veal chops Langreo style *(baked in the oven, stuffed with minced meat, flour, egg, garlic, parsley, oil, pepper and salt)* ‖ - *de ternera en salsa de vino* veal in wine sauce *(fried, with sauce of garlic, parsley, breadcrumbs, meat broth, red wine, lard and salt)*

churrasco *n. m.* steak Argentine style

churros *n. m. pl.* light, dough nut-type fritter *(sprinkled with sugar and served hot)*

ciervo *n. m.* deer

ciruela *n. f.* plum

civet *n. m.* ragout ‖ - *de ciervo* jugged deer ‖ - *de liebre* jugged hare

clarete *n. m.* claret wine

cocido *n. m.* stew *(of boiled beef and chick peas, etc.)* ‖ - *andaluz* stew Andalusian style *(chick peas, beef, lard, ham bone, tomatoes, French beans, baby marrows, sausage, potatoes, paprika, water and salt)* ‖ - *castellano* stew Castilian style *(of beef, veal bone, ham bone, spicy sausage (paprika), bacon, potatoes, chick peas, carrots, cabbage, garlic, vegetables in season; noodle soup of the broth; soup, meat and vegetables are separately served)* ‖ - *euskalduna* stew Basque style *(meat, ham, chicken, lard, oil, salted pork bones, chick peas, brown beans, cabbage, onion, spicy sausage (paprika) and tomato; the meat and vegetables are separately served; noodle soup of the broth)* ‖ - *extremeño* stew Extremadura style *(meat, chicken, lard, spicy sausage (paprika), black pork sausage, onion, herbs, chick peas, potatoes, cabbage, clove; served with boiled rice; noodle soup of the broth)* ‖ - *guipuzcoano* stew Guipúzcoa style *(of white beans, potatoes, lard, cabbage, carrots, garlic, leek, paprika, bay leaf and oil; soup of the broth and bread)* ‖ - *madrileño* stew Madrid style *(oil, water, chick peas, cabbage, potatoes, onion, garlic, carrots, lard, breast of beef, spicy sausage (paprika), black pork sausage and chicken; soup of the broth and bread, noodles or rice. The meat and vegetables are separately served)* ‖ - *manchego* stew La Mancha style *(chick peas, lard, ears, head, and ribs of pork, spicy sausage (paprika), carrots; soup of the broth with potatoes or bread)*

cóctel *n. m.* cocktail ‖ - *de gambas* prawn cocktail ‖ - *de mariscos* seafood cocktail

cochinillo *n. m.* sucking pig ‖ - *a la zamorana* sucking pig Zamora style *(baked in the oven, with lard, garlic, bay leaf and water)* ‖ - *asado* roasted sucking pig

codornices *n. f. pl.* quails ‖ - *a la riojana* quails Rioja style *(lightly fried and used as stuffing for peppers; stewed with ham, onions, tomatoes, garlic, oil, white wine, lard and salt)* ‖ - *con pochas* quails with beans *(cooked with the beans, ham bone, oil, onions, garlic, tomatoes and salt)*

codorniz *n. f.* quail

col *n. f.* cabbage || - *de Bruselas* Brussels sprouts || - *valenciana* cabbage

coliflor *n. f.* cauliflower || - *a la gallega* cauliflower Galicia style *(boiled in a casserole; with water, oil, paprika, vinegar, nut meg, parsley and salt)* || - *al ajo arriero* cauliflower country style with garlic *(boiled, with garlic, oil, paprika, salt and vinegar)*

compota *n. f.* compote || - *de manzana* apple compote

conchas de mariscos *n. f. pl.* sea scallops

conejo *n. m.* rabbit || - *al ajillo* rabbit with garlic *(olive oil, garlic, water, salt and brandy)* || - *a la alicantina* rabbit Alicante style *(in a casserole, with oil, lard, garlic, black pepper.bay leaf, dry sherry, water or meat broth, vinegar and salt)* || - *conejo a la brasa* barbecued rabbit || - *a la navarra* rabbit Navarra style *(in an earthenware casserole, with tomatoes, lemon, dry white wine, spring onions, parsley, garlic, salt and white pepper, bay leaf, lard and meat broth)* || - *asado* roasted rabbit || - *al vino del Campo de Borja* rabbit Campo de Borja style with wine *(in vinegar and fried, with carrots, leek, onions, celery, pepper, red wine, brandy, oil and salt)* || - *guisado* braised rabbit *(with bacon, lard, milk, white wine, onion, bread, clove, parsley, pepper, water and salt)*

confitura *n. f.* preserved fruit

congrio *n. m.* conger eel || - *al ajo arriero* conger eel country style *(fried, with garlic, flour, paprika, vinegar and yolk)* || - *a la costera* conger eel seaside style *(boiled, with potatoes, white wine, onions, parsley, bay leaf, oil and salt)* || - *con guisantes* conger eel with peas *(in an earthenware casserole, with onion, boiled peas, parsley, flour, salt, dry white wine and water)* || - *al estilo de Tarragona* conger eel Tarragona style *(in a casserole; with hard boiled eggs, lemon, garlic, garlic sauce, onions, tomatoes, bay leaf, parsley and oil)*

consomé *n. m.* consome

coñac *n. m.* brandy

corderito *n. m.* sucking lamb || - *a la levantina* sucking lamb Levante style *(in a casserole, with lard, pepper, onion, tomato, garlic, herbs, bay leaf, lemon, yolk and salt)*

cordero *n. m.* lamb || - *a la menorquina* lamb Menorca style *(roasted, with spicy sausage (paprika), lard, pepper, potatoes, lettuce and salt)* || - *al estilo de Sahagún* lamb Sahagún style *(in a casserole; with oil, pepper, onions, parsley, tomato, garlic, bay leaf, broth, potatoes and salt)* || - *asado* roasted lamb || - *asado a la riojana* roasted lamb Rioja style *(in an earthenware casserole, with lard, garlic, onions, parsley, peppercorns, vinegar, white wine, bay leaf, water, or meat broth; served with lettuce or potatoes)* || - *asado de Tierra de Campos* roasted lamb Tierra de Campos style *(in a casserole, with cabbage, oil, liqueur, lard, carrots, white wine, garlic, bay leaf, parsley, onions, potatoes, green peppers and salt)* || - *en chilindrón* roasted lamb Navarra style *(in an earthenware casserole; with lard, oil, tomatoes, onions, garlic, red peppers and salt)* || - *lechal a la Murciana* sucking lamb Murcia style *(baked in the oven; with lard, pine nuts, hard boiled eggs, lemon, potatoes and salt)* || - *guisado* stewed lamb (with sauce)

costillas *n. f. pl.* ribs || - *de cerdo* ribs of pork || - *de cordero* ribs of lamb

crema *n. f.* cream, custard || - *catalana* Catalan cream || - *de esparragos* asparagus cream || - *de espinacas* spinach cream || - *de guisantes* cream of peas || - *de champiñones* cream of mushrooms || - *de tomate* tomato cream

croquetas *n. f. pl.* croquettes ‖ **- de bacalao** cod croquettes ‖ **- de cangrejo** crab croquettes ‖ **- de carne** meat croquettes ‖ **- de jamón** ham croquettes ‖ **- de patata** potato croquettes ‖ **- de pescado** fish croquettes ‖ **- de pollo** chicken croquettes

crustáceos *n. m. pl.* shellfish

cuba libre *n. m.* cola with rum, lemon and ice cubes

cubierto *n. m.* cover, set of cutlery

D

dátil *n. m.* date

desayuno *n. m.* breakfast

dorada *n. f.* guit head bream

E

embutido *n. m.* sausages

empanada *n. f.* pie *(stuffed with meat, tunny, etc.)* ‖ **- de atún** tunny pie ‖ **- de carne** meat pie

empanadilla *n. f.* small pie *(stuffed with meat, tunny, etc.)* ‖ **- de atún** small tunny pie ‖ **- de carne** small meat pie ‖ **- de queso** small cheese pie

endibia *n. f.* endive

ensaimada *n. f.* large flat soft bun (with spongy interior) ‖ **- rellena** large flat soft bun *(filled with sweet made of yourd and syrup)*

ensalada *n. f.* salad ‖ **- catalana** Catalan salad *(of lettuce, tomatoes, onions and different kinds of sausage)* ‖ **- a la madrileña** salad Madrid style *(lettuce, leek, onions, olives, tunny in vinegar, hard, boiled eggs, tomatoes, oil, vinegar and salt)* ‖ **- de lechuga** lettuce salad ‖ **- de espárragos** asparagus salad ‖ **- de langosta** spiny lobster salad ‖ **- de pepinos** cucumber salad ‖ **- de tomate** tomato salad ‖ **- mixta** mixed salad ‖ **- variada** mixed salad ‖ **- verde** green salad ‖ **- de temporada** salad in season ‖ **- de atún** tunny salad

ensaladilla rusa *n. f.* Russian salad

entrecot *n. m.* entrecot ‖ **- de ternera** veal entrecot ‖ **- de buey** beef entrecot ‖ **- a la parrilla** barbecued entrecot

entremeses *n. m. pl.* hors d'oeuvres ‖ **- variados** mixed hors d'oeuvres

escalope *n. m.* escalope ‖ **- a la milanesa** Milanese escalope ‖ **- a la vienesa** Vienese escalope ‖ **- de cerdo** pork escalope ‖ **- de ternera** veal escalope

escarola *n. f.* batavian endive

escudella catalana *n. f.* Catalan stew *(of chick peas, lard, onions, tomatoes, pork sausage, water, pepper, hard boiled eggs and salt)*

escudella y carn d'olla Catalan stew with meat *(veal, lard, chick peas, black sausage, potatoes, bones, chicken, water, pork tail, carrots, celery, cabbage, meat balls (of minced veal, egg, breadcrumbs, milk, pork, flour and salt; noodle or rice soup of the broth)*

espárragos *n. m. pl.* asparagus ‖ **- a la madrileña** asparagus Madrid style *(boiled with sauce of yolk, vinegar, pepper, butter, salt and water)* ‖ **- de lata** tinned asparagus ‖ **- frescos** fresh asparagus ‖ **puntas de -** asparagus tips

espalda *n. f.* shoulder ‖ **- de cordero** lamb shoulder

espinacas *n. f. pl.* spinach ‖ **- a la catalana** spinach Catalan style *(sautéed; with olive oil, raisins, pine nuts, anchovies, garlic, water, pepper and salt)*

esqueixada *n. f.* Catalan cod salad *(with cod, tunny, tomatoes, red peppers, onions, black olives, oil, vinegar and salt)*

estofado *n. m.* stewed meat with potatoes ‖ **- de buey** stewed beef *(in a casserole; with lard, onions, veal trotters, carrots, red wine, vinegar, parsley, herbs, pepper and salt)* ‖ **- de carnero** stewed mutton *(with onions, carrots, parsley, bay leaf, pepper, red wine, water and salt)* ‖ **- de ternera** stewed veal *(in a casserole; with bacon, pig's trotters, olives, white wine, lard, salt and tomato purée)* ‖ **- de toro** stewed bull *(in an earthenware casserole; with white wine, olive oil, red wine, vinegar, onion, garlic, dried peppers and salt)*

fabada asturiana stewed beans Asturian style *(in an earthenware casserole; with ham, bacon, pig's trotters, salted pig's ear, black sausage, spicy sausage (paprika), white beans, onions, garlic, bay leaf, peppercorns, water and salt)*

faisán *n. m.* pheasant

falda de ternera *n. f.* breast of veal

fideos *n. m. pl.* vermicelli ‖ **- a la cazuela** vermicelli in casserole *(with lard, pork ribs, garlic, parsley, tomatoes, paprika, water or meat broth, grated cheese and salt)*

filete *n. m.* fillet ‖ **- a la aragonesa** fillet Aragon style *(lightly fried and then stewed in a casserole; with flour, lard, white wine, water or meat broth, parsley, garlic, pepper, cinnamon, potatoes and salt)* ‖ **- de buey** beef fillet ‖ **- de cerdo** pork fillet ‖ **- de lenguado** fillet sole ‖ **- de lenguado a la romana** fillet sole Roman style *(fried in batter)* ‖ **- de lenguado al vino blanco** fillet sole with white wine *(sauce of white wine)* ‖ **- de merluza** fillet of hake ‖ **- de rape** fillet of angler fish ‖ **- de ternera** veal fillet

flan *n. m.* caramel custard

foie-gras *n. m.* paté

frambuesas *n. f. pl.* raspberries ‖ **mermelada de -** raspberry jam

fresas *n. f. pl.* strawberries ‖ **compota de -** compote of strawberries ‖ **batido de -** strawberry mix ‖ **mermelada de -** strawberry jam ‖ **tarta de -** strawberry tart ‖ **- con nata** strawberries with whipped cream ‖ **- con vino de moscatel** strawberries with muscatel ‖ **- con zumo de naranja** strawberries with orange juice

fresones *n. m. pl.* strawberries (garden)

fricandó *n. m.* ragout ‖ - *de ternera* veal ragout

fritada de carne *n. f.* fried meat assortment *(different kinds of meat fried in a pan)*

fritada de pescado *n. f.* fried fish assortment *(different kinds of meat and seafood fried in a pan)*

fritura *n. f.* see fritada

fruta *n. f.* fruit ‖ - *de temporada* fruit in season

fuet *n. m.* kind of dry, spiced Catalan sausage

G

galletas *n. f. pl.* biscuits

gallina *n. f.* chicken

gambas *n. f. pl.* prawns ‖ - *al ajillo* prawns with garlic *(fried in a small earthenware casserole)* ‖ - *a la plancha* grilled prawns ‖ - *fritas* fried prawns ‖ *cóctel de* - prawn cocktail

garbanzos *n. m. pl* chick peas ‖ - *a la catalana* chick peas Catalan style *(in an earthenware casserole; with lard, onions, tomatoes, pork sausage, pine nuts, pepper, water, salt and hard boiled eggs)*

gaseosa *n. f.* white lemonade

gazpacho *n. m.* cold soup Andalusian style *(of water, olive oil, bread, tomatoes, garlic, cucumbers, vinegar, pepper, green peppers and salt)*

gelatina *n. f.* jelly

ginebra *n. m.* gin

granada *n. f.* pomegranate

granizado *n. m.* : - *de café* coffee served with ground ice ‖ - *de limón* lemonade served with ground ice ‖ - *de menta* peppermint drink served with ground ice

grelos *n. m. pl.* turnip green

grosellas *n. f. pl.* red currants

guisado, da *a.* **1.** stewed, braised **2.** *n. m.* stew

guisantes *n. m. pl.* peas

H

habas *n. f. pl.* broad beans ‖ - *a la catalana* stewed beans Catalan style *(in an earthenware casserole; with bacon, onions, black sausage, tomato, garlic, ham, oil, lard, herbs, clove, pepper, cinnamon, meat broth, muscatel, parsley, celery and salt)*

hamburguesa *n. f.* hamburger ‖ - *con queso* cheeseburger

helado *n. m.* ice cream ‖ - *de biscuit* egg and cream ice cram ‖ - *de chocolate* chocolate ice cream ‖ - *de crocante* almond ice cream ‖ - *de fresa* strawberry ice cream ‖ - *de ron y pasas* ice cream with rum and raisins ‖ - *de vainilla* vanilla ice cream ‖ - *variado* mixed ice cream

hielo *n. m.* ice ‖ *cubitos de* - ice cubes

hígado *n. m.* liver ‖ - *al ajillo* liver fried with garlic ‖ - *de buey* beef liver ‖ - *de cerdo* pork liver ‖ - *de pollo* chicken liver ‖ - *de ternera* veal liver ‖ - *frito* fried liver ‖ - *guisado* braised liver

higos *n. m. pl.* figs ‖ - *secos* dried figs

horchata *n. f.:* - *de almendras* cold milk drink (of crushed almonds, etc.) ‖ - *de chufa* milk drink of ground almonds

horno *n. m.* oven ‖ *al* - baked in the oven

hueso *n. m.* bone ‖ - *de jamón* ham bone ‖ *con -s* with bones ‖ *sin -s* without bones

huevos *n. m. pl.* eggs ‖ - *a la catalana* eggs Catalan style *(in a small earthenware casseroles; with butter, pork sausage, tomatoes, oil, and salt)* ‖ - *a la flamenca* eggs Flamenca style *(in a casserole; with ham, spicy sausage (paprika), peas, peppers, tomatoes, onions, garlic, paprika, oil, asparagus, salt and some sugar)* ‖ - *a la madrileña* eggs Madrid style *(in an earthenware casserole; with water, vinegar, tomato sauce, pepper, grated cheese and salt)* ‖ - *al horno* eggs baked in the oven *(in an earthenware casserole; tomatoes, eggs, ham, oil, spicy sausage (paprika), red peppers and salt)* ‖ - *al nido* eggs in the "nest" *(yolk on potato purée baked in the oven)* ‖ - *al plato a la navarra* eggs Navarra style *(in small earthenware casseroles, baked in the oven, with spicy sausage (paprika), tomatoes, grated cheese, butter or oil, pepper, parsley and salt)* ‖ - *con jamón* fried eggs with ham *(bread, oil and salt)* ‖ - *duros* hard boiled eggs ‖ - *escalfados* poached eggs ‖ - *fritos* fried eggs ‖ - *pasados por agua* boiled eggs ‖ - *revueltos* scambled eggs ‖ - *rellenos* stuffed eggs

J

jabalí *n. m.* wild boar

jamón *n. m.* ham ‖ - *cocido* cooked ham ‖ *codillo de* - knuckle of ham ‖ - *con melón* cured ham with melon ‖ - *de Jabugo* cured ham of Jabugo ‖ - *de York* cooked ham ‖ - *del país* country ham ‖ - *en dulce* ham boiled in white wine ‖ - *serrano* cured ham

jerez *n. m.* sherry ‖ - *seco* dry sherry ‖ - *dulce* sweet sherry

judías *n. f. pl.* beans ‖ - *blancas* white beans ‖ - *blancas a la castellana* white beans Castilian style *(with oil, onions, garlic, tomatoes, salt, pepper, parsley and water)* ‖ - *a la catalana* brown beans Catalan style *(with lard, onions, garlic, bay leaf, oil, flour and salt)* ‖ - *cocidas* boiled beans ‖ - *verdes* French beans ‖ - *verdes a la castellana* French beans Castilian style *(with red peppers, garlic, oil, parsley, water and salt)* ‖ - *verdes a la riojana* French beans Rioja style *(with lard, pork ribs, spicy sausage (paprika), onions, garlic, flour, pepper, water, salt and oil)* ‖ - *verdes salteadas* sautéed French beans *(with butter, lemon juice, parsley, water and salt)*

L

langosta *n. f.* spiny lobster ‖ - *a la catalana* spiny lobster Catalan style *(in a casserole; different coatings of the lobster, bake fillets; with parsley, chocolate, oil, white wine, pepper, nutmeg, paprika and salt)* ‖ - *a la guipuzcoana* spiny lobster Guipúzcoa style *(with sauce of pepper, lard, fish, broth and salt)* ‖ - *a la mallorquina* spiny lobster Mallorca style *(with sauce of vinegar, oil, white pepper and mayonnaise; served with lettuce or celery salad)* ‖ - *spiny lobster* Basque style *(with sauce of onions, red peppers, oil, flour, white wine, tomatoes, saffron, garlic, parsley; baked in the oven)*

langostinos *n. m. pl.* crayfish

laurel *n. m.* bay leaf

leche *n. f.* milk ‖ - *condensada* condensed milk ‖ - *descremada* milk without cream ‖ - *desnatada* milk without cream

lechón *n. m.* sucking pig ‖ - *asado* roast sucking pig ‖ - *al horno* sucking pig baked in the oven

lechuga *n. f.* lettuce

legumbres *n. f. pl.* vegetables, legumes ‖ - *cocidas* boiled legumes

lengua *n. f.* tongue ‖ - *al horno* tongue baked in the oven ‖ - *a la marinera* steamed tongue ‖ - *de buey* beef tongue ‖ - *de ternera* veal tongue

lenguado *n. m.* sole ‖ - *a la madrileña* sole Madrid style *(fried; with stuffed clams)* ‖ - *a la riojana* sole Rioja style *(fried; with garlic, red peppers, oil, fish broth, etc.)*

lentejas *n. f. pl.* lentils ‖ - *cocidas* boiled lentils

licor *n. m.* liqueur ‖ - *de anís* aniseed ‖ - *de menta* peppermint liqueur ‖ - *de naranja* orange liqueur ‖ - *estomacal* digestive liqueur

liebre *n. f.* hare ‖ - *al estilo de Cáceres* hare Cáceres style *(soaked in white wine and fried; with white wine, garlic, onions, lard, black pepper, bay leaf, clove and salt)* ‖ - *asada* roast hare ‖ - *en su salsa* hare with sauce *(soaked in white wine, lightly fried and baked in the oven; with white wine, garlic, water, flour, lard, onions, carrots, nutmeg, meat broth and salt)* ‖ - *estofada* stewed hare *(in a casserole; with lard, parsley, bay leaf, pepper and salt)*

limón *n. m.* lemon

limonada *n. f.* lemonade

lombarda *n. f.* red cabbage

lomo *n. m.* pork loin ‖ - *a la mallorquina* pork loin Mallorca style *(coated with breadcrumbs and fried; with spicy sausage (paprika), oil and salt)* ‖ - *de cerdo a la gallega* pork loin Galicia style *(soaked and lightly fried, then baked in the oven; with white wine, water, paprika, onion, oil, garlic, lemon and salt)* ‖ - *de cerdo al estilo vasco* pork loin Basque style *(in a casserole; with lard, milk, garlic, white pepper and salt)*

lubina *n. f.* bass ‖ - *a la asturiana* bass Asturian style *(in a casserole baked in the oven, with onions, white wine, clams, paprika, oil, parsley, toasted bread, water and salt)* ‖ - *a la leonesa* bass Leon style *(in an earthenware casserole baked in the* oven; with flour, clams, white wine, oil, toasted bread, paprika, parsley and salt) ‖ **- al horno** bass baked in the oven (with lard, butter, lemon and salt) ‖ **- Albufera** bass Albufera style (lightly roasted in an earthenware casserole, then baked in the oven; with onions, garlic, water, sauce, parsley and salt)

lucio n. m. pike

M

macarrones n. m. pl. macaroni

macedonia de fruta n. f. fruit salad

magras n. f. pl. pork fillets

maíz n. m. maize

manos de cerdo n. f. pl. pig's trotters

mantecadas n. f. pl. short cake

mantequilla n. f. butter

manzana n. f. apple ‖ **compota de** - apple compote ‖ **tarta de** - apple tart

manzanilla n. f. **1.** manzanilla wine (sherry) ‖ **2.** camomile ‖ **infusión de** - camomile tea

mariscos n. m. pl. seafood (prawns, crabs, lobsters, prawns, mussels, clams, oysters, etc.)

marrones n. m. pl. marron

mayonesa n. f. mayonnaise

mazapán n. m. marsipan

medallones de ternera n. m. pl. sirloin

mejillones n. m. pl. mussels ‖ **- a la cazuela** mussels in casserole (with tomatoes, garlic, oil, peppers, sugar, salt and parsley; cooked in a casserole) ‖ **- a la marinera** steamed mussels (in a sauce of white wine, cooked in an earthenware casserole) ‖ **- en salsa a la santanderina** mussels Santander style with sauce (in an earthenware casserole; with onions, tomato, parsley, garlic, breadcrumbs, dry sherry, oil, water and salt)

mel y mató n. m. fresh cheese Catalan style (with honey)

melocotones n. m. pl. peaches ‖ **- en almíbar** peaches in syrup

melón n. m. melon

menestra n. f. vegetable stew ‖ **- a la murciana** vegetable stew Murcia style (of peas, potatoes, French beans, ham, onions, asparagus, tomatoes, artichokes, lemon, hard boiled eggs, meat broth, oil and salt) ‖ **- de Tudela** vegetable stew Tudela style (in a casserole; with peas, artichokes, peppers, ham, asparagus, parsley, garlic, cinnamon, hard boiled eggs, water or broth, lard and salt) ‖ **- riojana** vegetable stew Rioja style (of beans, peas, artichokes, lard, ham, hard boiled eggs, onions, garlic, tomatoes, bay leaf, white Rioja wine, toasted bread, saffron, oil, pepper, water and salt)

menú *n. m.* menu ‖ **- del día** menu of the day ‖ **- turístico** tourist menu

menudillos de gallina *n. m. pl.* chicken giblets

merengue *n. m.* meringue

merluza *n. f.* hake ‖ **- a la baturra** hake Aragon style *(in an earthenware casserole baked in the oven; with onions, meat broth, tomato sauce, flour, pepper, oil and salt)* ‖ **- a la catalana** hake Catalan style *(in a casserole, with sauce; onions, parsley, flour, oil, water, broth, bay leaf, nutmeg, garlic sauce, saffron, boiled peas, boiled mussels and salt)* ‖ **- a la gallega** hake Galicia style *(boiled, with herbs, aby leaf, parsley, oil, vinegar, onions, garlic and potatoes; with sauce of oil, vinegar and paprika)* ‖ **- a la romana** hake Roman style *(fried in batter)* ‖ **- a la vasca** hake Basque style *(in an earthenware casserole; with asparagus, boiled peas, clams, garlic, parsley, oil, flour, fish broth, water and salt)* ‖ **- al horno** hake baked in the oven ‖ **- asada** roasted hake *(with sauce of prawns, oil, dry sherry, breadcrumbs, red peppers, parsley and salt)* ‖ **- canaria** hake Canarian style *(coated with breadcrumbs and fried; with potatoes, butter, hard boiled eggs, lemon, toasted bread and salt)* ‖ **- frita** fried hake

mero *n. m.* rock cod ‖ **- a la asturiana** rock cod Asturian style *(baked in the oven; with olives, onions, flour, mussels, white wine, tomato purée, parsley, paprika, water and salt)* ‖ **- a la valenciana** rock cod Valencia style *(fried with sauce of oil, flour, garlic, water, saffron, parsley and salt)* ‖ **sopa de -** rock cod soup

miel *n. f.* honey

migas *n. f. pl.* breadcrumbs *(fried in oil with several ingredients)*

minuta *n. f.* menu

moluscos *n. m. pl.* molluscs

morcilla *n. f.* black pudding

mortadela *n. f.* mortadella

moscatel *n. m.* muscatel

mostaza *n. f.* mustard

muslo *n. m.* leg ‖ **- de pavo** leg of turkey ‖ **- de pollo** leg of chicken

naranja *n.f* orange

naranjada *n. f.* orangeade

nata *n. f.* whipped cream ‖ **- azucarada** sugared whipped cream ‖ **- sin azúcar** whipped cream without sugar

orejas *n. f. pl.* ears ‖ **- de cerdo** pork ears

P

paella *n. f.* paella *(a typical Spanish rice dish; with peas, peppers, fish, meat, rabbit, seafood; cooked in an "paella pan")* ‖ - **alicantina** paella Alicante style *(rice, peppers, oil, garlic, tomatoes, artichokes, peas, saffron, paprika, eel, angler fish, mussels, water and salt)* ‖ - **a la valenciana** paella Valencia style *(rice, oil, chicken, pork, ham, small sausages, onions, red peppers, boiled white beans, artichokes, snails, garlic, parsley, bay leaf, tomatoes, paprika, meat broth, boiled peas, saffron and salt)* ‖ - **de carne** paella with meat *(rice, meat, chicken, rabbit, etc.)* ‖ - **de pescado** paella with fish *(fish, seafood, etc.)* ‖ - **marinera** paella seaman style *(rice with fish, seafood, etc.)*

paletilla *n. f.* breast ‖ - **de carnero** breast of mutton

pan *n. m.* bread ‖ - **blanco** white bread ‖ - **con tomate** bread with tomato, oil and salt ‖ - **de molde** English bread ‖ - **integral** wholemeal bread ‖ - **tostado** toasted bread ‖ **barra de** - baguette

panecillo *n. m.* bread roll

parrilla *n. f.* barbecue ‖ **a la** - barbecued

parrillada de carne *n. f.* barbecued meat assortment *(different kinds of meat, game, poultry, etc.)*

parrillada de pescado *n. f.* barbecued fish assortment *(different kinds of fish and seafood)* ‖ - **a la cántabra** barbecued fish assortment Cantabria style *(of hake, rock cod, bass, angler fish, oil, garlic, prawns and salt)*

pasta *n. f.* paste ‖ - **de sopa** noodles ‖ **-s** small cakes

pata *n. f.* foot ‖ - **de cerdo** pig's trotter ‖ - **de ternera** veal's trotter ‖ - **de cordero** lamb's trotter

patatas *n. f. pl.* potatoes ‖ - **asadas** roasted potatoes ‖ - **bravas** chillied potatoes ‖ - **fritas** fried potatoes ‖ - **hervidas** boiled potatoes

pato *n. m.* duck ‖ - **a la naranja** duck à l'orange ‖ - **a la tolosana** duck Tolosa style *(in a casserole, with herbs, onions, flour, meat broth, white wine, salt, clove and oil)* ‖ - **asado** roast duck

pavo *n. m.* turkey ‖ - **a la andaluza** turkey Andalusian style *(in a casserole, with onions, tomatoes, garlic, white wine, bay leaf, clove, paprika, green peppers, oil, water and salt)* ‖ - **relleno** stuffed turkey *(filling of roasted sausages, pork loin, white beans, old wine, dried plums, lard, onions, carrots, cinnamon, pepper and salt)*

pechuga *n. f.* breast *(of poultry)* ‖ - **de pollo** breast of chicken

pepino *n. m.* cucumber

pera *n. f.* pear

perca *n. f.* perch

perdices *n. f. pl.* partridges ‖ - **a la asturiana** partridges Asturian style *(in an earthenware casserole, with lard, onions, carrots, flour, apple cider, herbs, nutmeg, oil, broth, pepper and salt)* ‖ - **al estilo murciano** partridges Murcia style *(in an earthenware casserole baked in the oven; with stuffing of liver, anchovies, egg, breadcrumbs, parsley, garlic and pepper; prepared in the casserole with white wine,* tomatoes, lard, green peppers, broth, oil and salt) ‖ - **estofadas** stewed partidges *(in an earthenwarre casserole, with sauce of onions, garlic, clove, bay leaf, oil, white wine, vinegar, chocolate and salt; served with potatoes or mushrooms)*; - **extremeñas** partridges Extremadura style *(fried; with oil, toasted almonds, onions, breadcrumbs, paprika, black pepper, water, garlic, parsley, dry sherry, toasted bread and salt)*

perdiz *n. f.* partridge ‖ - **a la catalana** partridge Catalan style *(in a casserole; with lard, flour, meat broth, pepper, herbs, garlic, lemon and salt)* ‖ - **a la manchega** partridge La Mancha style *(fried; with oil, lard, ham, garlic, bay leaf, cloves, cinnamon, black pepper, roasted bread and salt)*

perejil *n. m.* parsley

pescadilla *n. f.* whiting

pescado *n. m.* fish ‖ - **a la brasa** barbecued fish ‖ - **a la plancha** grilled fish ‖ - **al horno** fish baked in the oven ‖ - **frito** fried fish ‖ - **guisado** stewed fish ‖ - **hervido** boiled fish

pichones *n. m.* pigeons ‖ - **a la montañesa** pigeons Santander style *(in a casserole, fried in batter of flour, milk, slat and one raw egg; lard dry sherry, bay leaf and parsley. Served on roasted bread slices)*

pierna *n. f.* leg ‖ - **de cabrito** leg of goat ‖ - **de cabrito** al estilo de Badajoz *(larded and cooked in a casserole; with lard, white wine, garlic and potatoes. Served with vegetables or lettuce)* ‖ - **de carnero** leg of mutton ‖ - **de cordero** leg of lamb ‖ - **de ternera** leg of veal

pies *n. m. pl.* trotters ‖ - **de cerdo** pig's trotters ‖ - **de ternera** veal's trotters

pimentón *n. m.* paprika ‖ - **dulce** sweet paprika ‖ - **picante** hot paprika

pimienta *n. f.* pepper ‖ - **blanca** white pepper ‖ - **en grano** peppercorn ‖ - **negra** black pepper

pimientos *n. m. pl.* peppers ‖ - **rojos** red peppers ‖ - **verdes** green peppers ‖ - **rellenos** stuffed peppers ‖ - **rellenos a la riojana** stuffed peppers Rioja style *(lightly fried and stewed in an earthenware casserole; stuffing of minced meat, eggs, nutmeg, pepper, garlic, parsley, onions paprika; some water or brothand salt)* ‖ - **rellenos al estilo de Avilés** stuffed peppers Avilés style *(in a casserole baked in tne oven; stuffed with minced meat of trotters (without bone), onion, garlic, tomato and old wine)*

pinchito *n. m.* meat snack served hot on a metal skewer ‖ - **moruno** highly spiced meat snack served on a metal skewer

piña *n. f.* pineapple ‖ - **natural** natural pineapple ‖ - **en almíbar** pinned pineapple in syrup

piñones *n. m. pl.* pine nuts

pisto *n. m.* scrambled eggs *(with vegetables)* ‖ - **a la bilbaína** scrambled eggs Bilbao style *(with baby marrows, green peppers, onions, garlic, tomato, oil, pepper and salt)* ‖ - **asturiano** scrambled eggs Asturian style *(with onions, peppers, ham, parsley, oil and salt)* ‖ - **castellano** scrambled eggs Castilian style *(with baby marrows, potatoes, lard, onions, bacon, red peppers, tomatoes, meat broth, oil, pepper and salt)* ‖ - **gallego** scrambled eggs Galicia style *(with ham, pork, oil, potatoes, green peppers, baby marrows, onions, tomatoes and salt)*

plancha *n. f.* grill ‖ **a la** - grilled

plátano *n. m.* banana

platito *n. m.* small plate

plato *n. m.* plate, dish ‖ - *caliente* warm dish ‖ - *combinado* combined dish ‖ - *frío* cold dish ‖ *primer* - first course ‖ *segundo* - second course ‖ - *de sopa* soup plate ‖ - *llano* dinner plate

pochas *n. f. pl.* white beans

pollo *n. m.* chicken ‖ - *a la española* chicken Spanish style *(stuffed with veal stomachs and lard; cooked in sauce of white wine and broth)* ‖ - *a la extremeña* chicken Extremadura style *(in a casserole baked in the oven, with ham, onions, tomatoes, brandy, oil and salt)* ‖ - *a la manchega* chicken La Mancha style *(fried and then baked in an earthenware casserole; with oil, lard, ham, garlic, bay leaf, cinnamon and salt)* ‖ - *a la vizcaína* chicken Vizcaya style *(fried, with lard, onions, green peppers, white wine, tomatoes, garlic, pepper and salt)* ‖ - *a l'ast* spit roasted chicken ‖ - *al estilo murciano* chicken Murcia style *(in a casserole, with tomatoes, peppers, oil and salt)* ‖ - *asado* roast chicken ‖ - *frito* fried chicken ‖ - *guisado* braised chicken *(in a casserole, with sauce)* ‖ - *relleno* stuffed chicken

postre *n. m.* dessert ‖ *de* - as dessert

potaje *n. m.* vegetable stew ‖ - *a la murciana* vegetable stew Murcia style *(of white beans, chick peas, spinach, tomatoes, onions, flour, cod, vinegar, peppers, hard boiled eggs, toasted bread and salt)* ‖ - *canario* vegetable stew Canarian style *(with white beans, lard, baby marrows, fresh maize, onions, garlic, potatoes, tomatoes, water and salt)* ‖ - *castellano* vegetable stew Castilian style *(with chick peas, cod, water, clove, onions, herbs, carrots, spinach, oil, toasted bread slices, garlic and salt)* ‖ - *de judías a la catalana* stewed beans Catalan style *(in a casserole; white beans, lard, black pudding, old wine, herbs, ham, onions, water and salt)* ‖ - *madrileño* vegetable stew Madrid style *(with black pudding, chicken, tomatoes, leek, egg (white), carrots, sherry, oil, water and salt)* ‖ - *navarro* vegetable stew Navarra style *(with carrots, onions, spicy sausage (paprika), bread, eggs, onions, oil, broth and salt)* ‖ - *valenciano* vegetable stew Valencia style *(with chick peas, garlic, parsley, onions, peppercorns, spinach, oil, sweet paprika, bread, yolk, lemon, water and salt)*

pote *n. m.* **1.** pot ‖ **2.** vegetable stew ‖ - *asturiano* vegetable stew Asturian style *(in a casserole; with white beans, black pudding, spicy sausage (paprika), ham bone, lard, cabbage, potatoes, garlic, paprika, oil and salt)* ‖ - *gallego* vegetable stew Galicia style *(with white beans, lard, cabbage, garlic, potatoes, water and salt)*

propina *n. f.* tip

puchero *n. m.* **1.** cooking pot ‖ **2.** stew of meat and vegetables

pulpito *n. m.* baby octopus ‖ -*s a la plancha* grilled baby octopus

pulpo *n. m.* octopus ‖ - *a la gallega* octopus Galician style *(boiled and served with a spicy sauce)* ‖ -*s a la riojana* octopus Rioja style *(boiled and cooked in a casserole; with red peppers, tomato purée, old wine, onions, oil, water and salt)* ‖ -*s al estilo vasco* octopus Basque style *(in an earthenware casserole; with onions, tomatoes, oil, white wine, garlic, bay leaf, parsley, white pepper and salt)*

puré *n. m.* purée ‖ - *de espinacas* purée of spinach ‖ - *de guisantes* purée of peas ‖ - *de habas* purée of broad beans ‖ - *de patatas* purée of potatoes ‖ - *de tomate* purée of tomatoes

Q

queso *n. m.* cheese ‖ - *de bola* Edam cheese ‖ - *de Emental* Emental cheese ‖ - *fresco* fresh cheese ‖ - *gruyère* Gruyère cheese ‖ - *manchego* Manchego cheese *(of the Spanish region La Mancha)* ‖ - *parmesano* Parmesan cheese ‖ - *rallado* grated cheese ‖ - *seco* dry cheese ‖ - *semiseco* half dry cheese ‖ - *tierno* cream cheese ‖ -*s variados* assorted cheeses

R

rábano *n. m.* radish

rabo de buey *n. m.* oxtail

ración *n. f.* portion ‖ *una - de queso* a portion of cheese

ragú *n. m.* ragout

rana *n. f.* frog ‖ *anca de* - frog's leg

rape *n. m.* angler fish ‖ - *a la Costa Brava* angler fish Costa Brava style *(baked in the oven, with peas, onion, oil, red peppers, mussels, saffron, white wine, garlic, parsley, oil and salt)* ‖ - *a la levantina* angler fish Levante style *(in a casserole; with sauce of milk, onion, garlic, flour, saffron, parsley, oil and salt)* ‖ - *a la malagueña* angler fish Málaga style *(in an earthenware casserole baked in the oven; with sauce of tomatoes, bread, onions, saffron, garlic, toasted almonds, oil, black pepper, parsley and salt)* ‖ - *a la marinera* steamed angler fish *(in an earthenware casserole, with sauce)* ‖ - *a la parrilla* barbecued angler fish ‖ - *a la romana* angler fish Roman style *(fried in batter)* ‖ - *frito* fried angler fish

raviolis *n. m. pl.* ravioli

rebanada de pan *n. f.* slice of bread

rebozado, da *a.* coated with breadcrumbs

refresco *n. m.* soft drink

relleno, na *a.* **1.** stuffed ‖ **2.** *n. m.* stuffing, filling

remolacha *n. f.* beetroot

repollo *n. m.* cabbage

repostería *n. f.* confectionery

revoltillo *n. m.* scrambled eggs

revuelto *n. m.* scrambled eggs ‖ - *de champiñones* scrambled eggs with mushrooms ‖ - *de espárragos* scrambled eggs with asparagus ‖ - *de gambas* scrambled eggs with prawns ‖ - *de jamón* scrambled eggs with ham ‖ - *de setas* scrambled eggs with mushrooms ‖ - *de tomate* scrambled eggs with tomatoes

riñones *n. m. pl.* kidneys ‖ - *a la montañesa* kidneys Santander style *(spit roasted kidneys of lamb, with lard, mushrooms, tomatoes, roasted sausages, pepper, salt and oil; served on roasted bread slices)* ‖ - *al Jerez* kidneys Jerez style *(veal kidneys in a* casserole; with sherry, oil, parsley, garlic, salt and water; served with rice) ‖ - **salteados** sautéed veal kidneys *(with pepper, oil, vinegar, lard, parsley, garlic, dry white wine and salt)*

rodaballo *n. m.* turbot

romesco *n. m.* Romesco sauce *(sauce from Tarragona, specially for fish and seafood)*

ron *n. m.* rum ‖ - **blanco** white rum ‖ - **negro** black rum

rosado *n. m.* rosé wine

rosbif *n. m.* roast beef

rosquilla *n.f.* ring-shaped pastry *(fried in oil)*

S

sal *n. f.* salt

salado, da *a.* salty

salchichas *n. f. pl.* sausages ‖ - **de cóctel** cocktail sausages ‖ - **de Frankfurt** Francfurt sausages ‖ - **del país** roasted pork sausages

salchichón *n. m.* type of Spanish salami

salmón *n. m.* salmon ‖ - **ahumado** smoked salmon ‖ - **a la asturiana** salmon Asturian style *(barbecued, with oil, breadcrumbs, parsley, lemon and salt)* ‖ - **a la bearnesa** salmon Bearnesa style *(in a casserole; with salt, water, white wine, parsley and Bearnesa sauce)* ‖ - **al horno** salmon baked in the oven ‖ - **a la plancha** grilled salmon ‖ - **fresco** fresh salmon

salmonete *n. m.* red mullet ‖ -**s a la parrilla** barbecued red mullets

salpicón de marisco *n. m.* seafood cocktail (salad)

salsa *n. f.* sauce ‖ - **alioli** garlic sauce *(of garlic, oil and salt)* ‖ - **andaluza** Andalusian sauce *(of pumpkin, tomato, peppercorns, garlic, vinegar, water and salt)* ‖ - **aragonesa** sauce Aragón style *(of yolk, lemon juice, white pepper, oil, water and salt)* ‖ - **bechamel** bechamel sauce *(white sauce of flour, milk, etc.)* ‖ - **catalana** Catalan sauce *(of white wine, onions, parsley, garlic, clove, bay leaf, oil, pepper and salt)* ‖ - **de menta** peppermint sauce *(of fresh peppermint leaves, vinegar, sugar, white pepper, butter and salt)* ‖ - **de piñones** sauce of pine nuts *(pinenuts, meat broth, garlic, hard boiled yolk and salt)* ‖ - **de tomate** tomato sauce ‖ - **española** Spanish sauce *(of onions, carrots, flour, pieces of meat, tomato, oil, sherry and broth)* ‖ - **holandesa** Dutch sauce ‖ - **mayonesa** mayonnaise sauce ‖ - **picante** spicy sauce *(of tomato purée, vinegar, white wine, onions, cucumbers, butter, capers and parsley)* ‖ - **riojana** Rioja sauce *(of onions, oil, red wine, Spanish sauce)* ‖ - **romesco** romesco sauce *(from Tarragona; of dried peppers, one slice of bread, garlic, vinegar, toasted almonds, tomatoes, white pepper, oil and salt; specially for fish and seafood)* ‖ - **verde** parsley sauce

sandía *n. f.* watermelon

sangría *n. f.* sangría *(cold drink of red wine and fruits)* ‖ - **dulce** sweet sangría *(cold drink of sweet red wine)* ‖ - **seca** dry sangría *(cold drink of dry red wine)* ‖ - **semiseca** half dry sangría *(cold drink of half dry red wine)*

sardinas *n. f. pl.* sardines ‖ - *a la asturiana* sardines Asturian style *(baked in the oven; with lard, onions, tomatoes, bay leaf, dry white wine, pepper, garlic and salt)* ‖ - *a la brasa* barbecued sardines ‖ - *a la madrileña* sardines Madrid style *(in a casserole; with onions, tomato sauce, fresh tomatoes, pepper, oil, salt, white wine, parsley and bay leaf)* ‖ - *a la navarra* sardines Navarra style *(baked in the oven; with garlic, parsley, breadcrumbs, oil, onions, paprika and salt)* ‖ - *a la parrilla* barbecued sardines ‖ - *a la plancha* grilled sardines ‖ - *de lata* tinned sardines ‖ - *en aceite* sardines in oil ‖ - *en escabeche* pickled sardines ‖ - *frescas* fresh sardines ‖ - *fritas* fried sardines

sesos *n. m. pl.* brains ‖ - *a la romana* brains Roman style *(fried in batter)*

setas *n. f. pl.* mushrooms ‖ - *al ajillo* mushrooms with garlic ‖ - *a la brasa* barbecued mushrooms ‖ - *a la plancha* grilled mushrooms

sifón *n. m.* soda water

silla de cordero *n. f.* saddle of lamb

sobrasada *n. f.* type of Majorcan sausage

sofrito *n. m.* tomatoes, onions, etc. lightly fried in oil (it forms the basic flavouring of many dishes)

solomillo *n. m.* sirloin ‖ - *de buey* sirloin of beef ‖ - *de ternera* sirloin of veal

sopa *n. f.* soup ‖ - *a la montañesa* soup Santander style *(with vermicelli, cabbage, leek, onions, tomato purée, potatoes, oil, water and salt)* ‖ - *a la riojana* soup Rioja style *(with pieces of meat, chick peas, carrots, onions, small spicy sausages (paprika), celery, water and salt)* ‖ - *valenciana* soup Valencia style *(with peas, potatoes, oil, tomatoes, rice, bone of ham, French beans, cabbage, onions, parsley, pepper, water, salt and sugar)* ‖ - *de ajo* garlic soup ‖ - *de arroz* rice soup ‖ - *de cangrejos* crab soup ‖ - *de champiñones* mushroom soup ‖ - *de cebolla* onion soup ‖ - *de espárragos* asparagus soup ‖ - *de fideos* vermicelli soup ‖ - *de gallina* chicken soup ‖ - *de guisantes* pea soup ‖ - *de judías* bean soup ‖ - *del día* soup of the day ‖ - *de lentejas* lentil soup ‖ - *de mariscos* shellfish soup ‖ - *de mero* grouper soup ‖ - *de pan* bread soup ‖ - *de pasta* noodle soup ‖ - *de patatas* potato soup ‖ - *de pescado* fish soup ‖ - *de rabo de buey* oxtail soup ‖ - *de rape* angler fish soup ‖ - *de tortuga* mock turtle soup ‖ - *de verdura* vegetable soup ‖ - *marinera* soup of fish and shellfish

suquet de pescado *n. m.* fish stew Catalan style *(different kinds of fish and seafood)*

T

tallarines *n. m. pl.* type of small clams

tapa *n. f.* small aperitive snack

tarta *n. f.* tart ‖ - *al whisky* whisky tart ‖ - *de chocolate* chocolate tart ‖ - *de fresas* strawberry tart ‖ - *de manzana* apple tart ‖ - *de nueces* walnut tart ‖ - *de queso* cheese tart ‖ - *helada* ice cream tart

taza *n. f.* cup ‖ - *de café* cup of coffee ‖ - *de chocolate* cup of chocolate ‖ - *de té* cup of tea

tenca *n. f.* tench

ternasco *n. m.* lamb baked in the oven *(with white wine, lard, lemon and salt)*

ternera *n. f.* veal ‖ - *a la asturiana* veal Asturian style *(fried; with lard, flour, salt, meat broth, tomatoes, onions and oil)* ‖ - *a la cazuela* veal in casserole ‖ - *a la manchega* veal La Mancha style *(baked in the oven; with lemon, onions, tomatoes, peppers, oil and salt)* ‖ - *asada* roast veal ‖ - *estofada* stewed veal

tocino *n. m.* lard

tomate *n. m.* tomato ‖ - *frito* fried concentrated tomato ‖ - *natural triturado* tomato purée ‖ -*s asados* roasted tomatoes ‖ -*s aliñados* tomatoes prepared with vinegar, oil and salt ‖ -*s enteros (en lata)* tinned tomatoes ‖ -*s rellenos* stuffed tomatoes ‖ -*s verdes* green tomatoes

torta *n. f.* tart

tortilla *n. f.* omelette ‖ - *a la española* Spanish omelette ‖ - *a la francesa* French omelette ‖ - *a la paisana* omelette country style ‖ - *de alcachofas* artichoke omelette ‖ - *de atún* tunny omelette ‖ - *de berenjenas* aubergine omelette ‖ - *de calabacines* omelette of baby marrows ‖ - *de champiñones* mushroom omelette ‖ - *de espárragos* asparagus omelette ‖ - *de espinacas* spinach omelette ‖ - *de gambas* prawn omelette ‖ - *de habas* of broad beans ‖ - *de jamón* ham omelette ‖ - *de judías* bean omelette ‖ - *de mariscos* seafood omelette ‖ - *de patatas* potato omelette ‖ - *de patatas y cebolla* potato omelette with onions ‖ - *de queso* cheese omelette

tripas *n. f. pl.* tripe

trucha *n. f.* trout ‖ -*s a la española* trouts Spanish style *(barbecued; stuffed with lard, parsley, onions, pepper and salt)* ‖ -*s a la montañesa* trouts Santander style *(in a casserole, with onions, white wine, water, bay leaf, pepper, flour and salt)* ‖ -*s a la navarra* trouts Navarra style *(in a casserole; with yolk, red wine, onions, potatoes, pepper, herbs, bay leaf and salt)* ‖ -*s con jamón* trouts with ham *(fried, with bacon, ham, oil and salt)*

trufa *n. f.* truffles ‖ -*s heladas* chocolate truffles (iced)

turrón *n. m.* a type of nougat made of almonds and honey.

uvas *n. f. pl.* grapes

vaso *n. m.* (drinking) glass

verdura *n. f.* (green) vegetables ‖ - *hervida* boiled vegetables ‖ - *salteada* sautéed vegetables ‖ -*s variadas* assorted vegetables

vermut *n. m.* vermouth

vieiras *n. f. pl.* scallops

vinagre *n. m.* vinegar

vino *n. m.* wine || - *a granel* wine in bulk || - *blanco* white wine || - *clarete* claret wine || - *de la casa* wine of the house || - *de Jerez* sherry || - *de Málaga* Málaga wine || - *de mesa* table wine || - *de postre* after dinner wine || - *de Ribeiro* Ribeiro wine || - *de Rioja* Rioja wine || - *dulce* sweet wine || - *espumoso* sparkling wine || - *generoso* table wine || - *negro* red wine || - *rancio* old wine || - *rosado* rosé coloured wine || - *seco* dry wine || - *tinto* red wine

vodka *n. m.* vodka.

whisky *n. m.* whisky || - *escocés* Scoth whisky || - *español* Spanish whisky || - *irlandés* Irish whisky

yema *n. f.* yolk

zanahoria *n. f.* carrot

zarzuela de carne *n. f.* meat cooked in casserole *(different types of meat with a lightly spicy sauce)*

zarzuela de mariscos *n. f.* fish and seafood cooked in casserole *(squids, angler fish, eel, prawns, rock cod or hake, Dublin bay lobsters, clams, oil, onions, garlic, tomato sauce, white wine, saffron, parsley, pepper and salt, with a lightly spicy sauce)*

zumo *n. m.* juice || - *de albaricoque* apricot juice || - *de fruta* fruit juice || - *de limón* lemon juice || - *de manzana* apple juice || - *de melocotón* peach juice || - *de naranja* orange juice || - *de pera* pear juice || - *de tomate* tomato juice || - *de uva* grape juice || - *de zanahoria* carrot juice

VII.

SIGNS,

NOTICES AND

LABELS

A. (ático)	Attic
Abanicos	Fans
Acueducto	Aqueduct
Aduana	Customs
Aeropuerto	Airport
Agencia de viajes	Travel Agency
Agua	Water
(no) potable	Not drinking-water
Aire	Air
Al acueducto	To the Aqueduct
Al aeropuerto	To the Airport
A la playa	To the Beach
Alfombras	Carpets
Almacenes	Warehouse
Alquiler de...	Hire of...
bicicletas	Bycicle Hire
caballos	Horses for Hire
coches	Cars for Hire
motos	Motor-cycles for Hire
patines	Hire of skates
Andén	Platform
Andén dirección...	Platform to ...
Antes de entrar dejen salir	Let others out before coming in
Antigüedades	Antiques
Alarma	Alarm
Aparcamiento	Parking
	Parking Space
	Car Park
vigilado	- guarded
Apartamentos	Apartments
en alquiler	to let
en venta	for Sale
Aparthotel	Apartment-Hotel
Armas	Weapons
Armería	Armoury
Artículos	Goods
a declarar	Goods to declare
de deporte	Sporting Goods
de limpieza	Cleaning Materials
de regalo	Gifts
de viaje	Travel Goods
para el fumador	Smokers' Requisites
para el hogar	Articles for the Home
Ascensor	Lift
Aseos públicos	Public Lavatories
Asientos	Seats
Asistencia Médica	Medical Assistance
Atención	Attention
Atención al tren	Watch for the Train
Ático	Attic
Atraques	Mooring berths
Autobanco	Car-Bank
Autobús	Bus

Autobuses, parada de	Bus stop
Autopista	Motorway
Avenida	Avenue
Avión	Aircraft, airplane
Ayuntamiento	Town Council
	Town Hall

B

Banca	Bank
Banco	Bank
Bañadores	Bathing Costumes
Baños	Baths
Bar	Bar
Barbería	Barber's
Batería de cocina	Metal kitchen utensils
Bebidas	Drinks
Biblioteca	Library
Billetes	Tickets
Bisutería	Imitation Jewellery
Bodega	Wine Shop (or Bar) / Cellar
Boite	Club (open to the public)
Bolera	Bowling Center
Bolsos	Handbags
Bombonería	Sweets and Chocolates Shop
Bote	Kitty
de propinas	Box for tips
Boutique	Boutique
para caballeros	for Gentlemen
para jóvenes	for Teenagers
para novias	for Brides
para señoras	for Ladies

C

C (caliente)	Hot (taps)
Caballeros	Gentlemen
Cabaré	Cabaret
Café	Cafe
cantante	Live music café
teatro	Theatre-Cafe
Cafetería	Coffee Shop
Caja	Cash
de ahorros	Savings Bank
Caliente	Warm
Calle	Street
Callejón sin salida	Blind Alley
Calle Mayor	High Street
Calzados	Footwear
Cambio	Change
de divisas	Exchange
Camino cortado por obras	Way blocked for works

particular	Private Road
privado	Private Road
Camisería	Shirt Shop
Camping	Camping Site
Campo de fútbol	Football Stadium
Carnicería	Butcher's
Carretera nº ... cortada	Road Nº ... blocked
Carrocería	Bodywork
Carta (menú)	Menu
Cartelera de espectáculos	Shows' list
Casa Consistorial	Town Hall
Casa Cuartel de la Guardia Civil	Local Headquarters
	of Guardia Civil
Casetas	Bathing Huts
Catedral	Cathedral
Caza	Hunting
Ceda el paso	Give Way
Cementerio	Cemetery
Centro ciudad	City Centre / Downtown
Centro médico / de salud	Medical Aid Centre
Cerrado	Closed
en domingo	on Sundays
Cervecería	Public House (Beer)
Chacinería	Pork Butcher's
Charcutería	Pork Butcher's
Cheque	Cheques
de viajero	Travellers' Cheques
de regalos	Gift Voucher
Cierren la Puerta	Please Close the Door
Cigarrillos	Cigarettes
Cine	Cinema
Cinturones	Belts
Circo	Circus
Claustro	Cloister
Clínica	Hospital
Coches	Cars
de alquiler	for Hire
de choque	Dodgem's
de segunda mano	Secondhand cars
para bebés	Prams
Colchonería	Store selling mattresses
Colmado	Grocer's
Comidas	Meals
Comisaría de Policía	Police Station
Compañía	Company
Compra-venta	Buying and Selling
Confección	
para caballero	Mens' Wear
para niña	Girls' Wear
para niño	Boys' Wear
para señora	Ladies' Wear
Confecciones	Ready made Clothes
para caballeros	for Men
para niñas y niños	for children
para señoras	for ladies
Confesiones	Confessions
Confitería	Cake shop
Conserjería	Reception

Consigna	Luggage Office
Correos	Post Office
Correspondencia	Connection (station, airport)
Corsetería	Lingerie Shop
Coto	Enclosed Land
Cristal	Glass
Cristalería	Glassware
Cruz Roja	The Red Cross
Cuartel	Headquarters
Cubertería	Cutlery
Cuentas Corrientes	Current Accounts
Cuidado con el perro	Beware of the Dog
Cuidado con el tren	Watch for the Train
Cunas y muebles para bebés	Cots and Nursery Furniture

D

Dejen salir	Let people out first
Deportes	Sports
Descanso	Interval
Destino	Destination
Desvío obligatorio	Obligatory Diversion
Devoluciones	Returns
Dirección	Direction (towards...)
Discos	Records
Discoteca	Disco
Dispensario	Medical Aid Centre
Diputación Provincial	Provincial Government Offices
Diversiones	Entertainments
Droguería	Drugstore

E

Electrodomésticos	Household Electrical Appliances
Embarque	Boarding
Empujar	Push
Encajes y bordados	Laces and Trimmings
Enlace	Connecting Passage
Entrada	Way in
a la autopista	Entrance in Motorway
libre	Free Admision
nacional	Domestic Entry
Entradas	Tickets
Entrar sin llamar	Enter without knocking
Entresuelo	Mezzanine Floor
Equipaje	Luggage
Bodega de equipaje	Luggage Hold
Es peligroso bañarse	It is dangerous to bathe here
Estacionamiento con horario limitado	Limited Time Parking
Estación de servicio	Service Station
Estadio	Stadium
Estanco	Tobacconist's

Excepto carga y descarga	Exept for Loading and Unloading
Excursiones	Excursions, trips
Exhiba billete, abono o pase	Show your ticket, voucher or pass
Extensión	Area
telefónica	Extension
Extintor de incendios	Fire Extinguisher
Extranjero	Overseas

F

F	Cold (taps)
Facturación de equipajes	Check-in
Farmacia	Chemist´s
Farmacias abiertas durante todo el día	Chemist's open all day from ... in
de ...mañana a ... noche	the morning to ... at night
Farmacias abiertas en servicio de	24 hours Chemist's
urgencia durante todo el día	
y toda la noche	
Farmacias de Guardia más próximas	Nearest Chemist's on duty
(Las) Farmacias más próximas...	The nearest Chemist's are the following
Feria	Fair
FFCC	Railways
Ferretería	Ironmongery
Fiesta Mayor	Local Festivity
Final del Estacionamiento de horario	End of limited time parking
limitado	
Flamenco	Flamenco
Floristería	Florist's Shop
Fósforos	Matches
Fotocopias al instante	Instant Photocopies
Fotografía	Photography
Fotografías en ... minutos	Photographs in ... minutes
Frágil	Fragile
Frío, a	Cold
Frutas	Fruit
Frutería	Fruit Shop
Funicular	Cable car
Futura mamá	Mother-to-be

G

Gasolina	Petrol
Gasolinera	Petrol Station
Géneros de Punto	Knitwear
Giro	
bancario	Credit Transfer
postal	Money Order
Golf	Golf
Golosinas	Sweets
Guantes	Gloves
Guardarropa	Cloakroom
Guardería infantil	Nursery School

H

Helados	Ice Cream
Hielo	Ice
Hipódromo	Horse Racing Stadium
Horario	Timetable
de atención al público	Opening Time
de misas	Times of Masses
de trenes	Train Timetable
de vuelos	Flights Timetable
Hospital	Hospital
Hostal	Hotel (Boarding House)
Hotel	Hotel

I

Iglesia	Church
Imposiciones	Deposits (of money)
Información	Information
Turística	Tourists Information
Instrumentos	Instruments
de música	Musical Instruments
de precisión	Precision Instruments
Interflora	International Flower Service
Intermedio	Intermediate (Interlude)
Introduzca ... monedas de ...	Insert ... coins of ...

J

Jardín zoológico	Zoo
Joyería	Jewellery
Juguetería	Toy store
Juguetes	Toys

L

Labores	Knitting
Lámparas	Lamps
Lanas para labores	Knitting Wools
Lanchas	Yachts
Lavabos	Toilets
Lavado de coches	Car Washing Service
Lavado y engrase	Washing and Greasing
Lavandería	Laundry
Lencería	Lingerie Department
Libre	Free

Librería	Bookshop
Libretas de ahorro	Bankbooks
Libros de ocasión	Second Hand Books
Limosnas	Alms
Limpiabotas	Shoe-black
Líneas Aéreas	Airlines
Líneas Marítimas	Shipping Lines
Liquidación total	Clearance Sales
Lista de bodas	Wedding List
Llegada	Arrival
Lotería	Lottery

M

Marisquería	Seafood Restaurant
Marroquinería	Leather Goods
Material escolar	School materials
Material Fotográfico	Photographic Material
Medias	Stockings
Médico	Doctor
Menaje	Household Goods
Menú	Menu
de la casa	Set Menu
del día	Menu of the Day
Mercado	Market
Mercería	Habersdashery
Mesón	Old-style bar
Metro	Underground, tube
Minigolf	Miniature Golf
Ministerio	Ministry
Mingitorios	Public toilets
Misas	Masses
Monasterio	Monastery
Motel	Motel
Muebles	Furniture
de cocina	Kitchen Fittings
de jardín	Garden Furniture
Museo	Museum
Música	Music

N

Nada que declarar	Nothing to declare
Niebla	Fog
No conversar con el conductor	Do not talk to the driver
No doblar	Do not fold
No fumar	No Smoking
No funciona	Out of order
No pasar	No Way
No sujetar las puertas	Do not restrain the doors
No tocar	Do not touch
No tocar el género	Please do not touch

Normal   Normal
Nº de vuelo   Flight Nº

O

Objetos de regalo	Gifts
Obras	Works (Road)
Ocupado	Busy
Oferta especial	Special Offer
Oficina de información turística	Tourist Information Office
Oficinas	Offices
Optica	Optician's
Ortopedia	Orthopaedic's

P

Panadería	Bakery
Paños cocina	Dishcloths
Pañuelos	Handkerchiefs
Papelera	Wastepaper Basket
Papelería	Stationery
Paraguas	Umbrella
Parque	Park
de atracciones	Amusement Park
de bomberos	Fire Station
infantil	Nursery room
Pasaje de ...	Passage of...
Paseo de	... Alley
Paso subterráneo	Subway
Pastelería	Cake Shop
Peaje	Toll
P.B. (planta baja)	Ground Floor
Peatones	Pedestrians
Peces	Fishes
Peligro	Danger
de desprendimiento	Beware Falling Rocks
de incendio	Fire Hazard
de muerte	Life Danger
Peluquería	Hairdresser's
canina	Dog Trimming Shop
Perfumería	Perfume Shop
(4) Personas	(4) People
Pesca	Fishing
Pescadería	Fishmonger's
Pesca salada	Sea Fish
Picadero	Riding School
Pidan parada con la suficiente antelación	Ask for the Stop in advance
Pinacoteca	Picture Gallery
Piscina	Swimming Pool
Piso por alquilar	Flat to Let
Planta baja	Ground Floor
Platos combinados	Combined Dishes

Platos del día	Today's Specialities
Playa	Beach
particular	Private Beach
Plaza de...	... Square
Plaza de Toros	Bull Ring
Plaza mayor	Main Square
(4) plazas	(4) Places
Policía	Police
Pollos a l'ast	Spit Roasted Chicken
Por alquilar	For Hire
Por avión	By Air
Portería	Porter's Office
Pral.	Principal
Precaución	Watch!
obras	Works in progress
Precio	Price
Prendas deportivas	Sports Wear
Prohibida la entrada	No entry
- a los perros	Dogs are not allowed
Prohibido	Not allowed
asomarse al exterior	Do not lean out
bañarse	Bathing forbidden
el paso	No entry
escupir	No spitting
fijar carteles	No signs
fumar	No smoking
pasar	No entry
pescar	Fishing forbidden
pisar el césped	Do not walk on the grass
Primera clase	First Class
Principal	Principal
Provincias	Provinces
Ptas.	Pesetas
Pub	Pub
Puerta	Door
Puerto	Port
Puerto cerrado	Mountain Pass Closed
Punto	Point, Place

Q

Quiniela	Football Pool
Quirófano	Surgery Room

R

Raciones	Assorted dishes available
Razón	Information
Rebajas	Sales
Recambios	Spare parts
Recepción	Reception

Recién pintado	Wet Paint
Recuerdos	Souvenirs
Reembolso	Repayment
Regalos	Presents, gifts
Reintegros	Reimbursements
Relojería	Watchmaker's
RENFE	Spanish National Railways
Reparación	Repair
de automóviles	Car Repair
de calzado	Shoe Repair
Reservado	Reserved
el derecho de admisión	Right of Admission Reserved
Todos los derechos reservados	All rights reserved
Reservas	Reservations
Restaurantes	Restaurants
Retretes	Lavatories
Ropa de cama	Bed Linen
Ropa de mesa	Table Linen

S

S.A.	Limited Company
Sacristía	Sacristy
Sala	Room, Hall
de curas	Ward (hospital)
de espera	Waiting Room
de fiestas	Dance Hall
de proyecciones	Projection Room
Saldos	Sales
Salida	Way Out
de camiones	Lorries Exit
de emergencia	Emergency Exit
internacional	International Departures
nacional	Domestic Departures
Salón	Hall, Salon
de baile	Dance Hall
de belleza	Beauty Salon
de fiestas	Dance Hall (with Show)
Saneamiento	Bathroom and Lavatory Fittings
Sanitarios	Toilets
Se admiten,cheques de viajero	Travellers' Cheques Accepted
Se alquila	For Hire / To Let
Segunda Clase	Second Class
Señoras	Ladies
Se prohibe el uso de cámaras fotográficas	Photography Prohibited
Se prohibe fumar	No Smoking
Se ruega no fumar	Please do not to smoke
Se vende	For sale
Servicio	Service
diurno	Day Service
nocturno	Night Service
oficial	On Official Service
Servicios	Toilets
Servicio(s) médico(s)	Medical Service(s)

Silencio	Silence
Sírvase frío	Serve chilled
Sobreático	Flat over Attic Flat
Sombrerería	Hat Shop
Sombreros	Hats
Souvenirs	Souvenirs
Subida	Way Up
Supermercado	Supermarket

T

Tabacalera S.A.	State Tobacco Monopoly
Tabaco	Tobacco
Taberna	Tavern
Tablao flamenco	Flamenco Dancing Show
Taller de reparaciones	Repair Garage
Tapicería	Upholstery
Taquilla	Pay Box
Taxi	Taxi
Teatro	Theatre
Tejidos	Textile Materials
Telecabina	Overhead Cable Transport
Teleférico	Overhead Cable Way
Teléfono	Telephone
Teléfonos	Public Telephones
Telegramas	Telegrams
Telesilla	Ski Lift Chair
Telesquí	Ski Lift
Templo	Temple
Tercera clase	Third Class
Terminal	Terminal
Terraza	Terrace, balcony
Tintorería	Dry Cleaner's
Tirar	Pull
Tiro al blanco	Target Shooting
Toallas	Towels
Transferencias telegráficas	Transfers (of money) Telegraphic Transfers
Tranvía	Tramway
Túnel de lavado	Automatic Car Wash
Turismos	Cars

U

Ultramarinos	Grocer's
Uniformes de servicio militares	Uniforms Maids (Servants) Uniforms Military Uniforms
Urgencias	Emergency ward
Urgente	Urgent
Uso obligatorio de cadenas	Wheel Chains Obligatory
Utensilios de cocina	Cooking utensils

V

Vado permanente	Permanent Exit (hence no parking here)
Vajilla	Glassware
Variedades	Varieties
Vedado	Enclosure (Game, Birds, etc.)
Vendido	Sold
Venta anticipada	Advance Booking
Venta de localidades	Booking Office (Seats)
Verdulería	Green Grocery
Verduras	Vegetables
Vía	Track
Viento	Wind
Vinos	Wines
Vinos y licores	Wines and Spirits
Vuelos	Flights
chárter	Charter Flights

W.C.	W.C.
Whisky bar	Whisky Bar

Z

Zapatería	Shoe Shop
Zapatero	Shoe Repairer